THE DAY OF THE LORD IS AT HAND

SEVENTH EDITION | ISAIAH 13:6

Behold, he cometh with clouds: and every eye shall see him, and they also which pierced him: and all kindreds of the earth shall wail because of him. Even so, Amen. Revelation 1:7

BENJAMIN BARUCH

The Day of the LORD is at Hand

Benjamin Baruch

SEVENTH EDITION

2000 YEARS AGO, MESSIAH CAME, yet the religious leaders of that day missed their hour of visitation, having misunderstood bible prophecy. Today in these last days, the men of this world are making the same mistake. Once again, the LORD has lifted up voices in the wilderness to speak the truth. This is their account!

First Edition	September, 1998
Second Edition	March, 2004
Third Edition	April, 2005
Fourth Edition	November, 2006
Fifth Edition	September, 2007
Sixth Edition	April, 2012
Seventh Edition	December, 2014
Second Printing	January, 2019
Third Printing	March, 2021

ISBN-13: 978-0692359044   ISBN-10: 0692359044

Look for Benjamin's other books including *Search the Scriptures, Vol. One: Out of the Darkness* on Amazon.com. You may also find other teaching materials at BenjaminBaruch.net.

Dedication

This book is dedicated to my LORD JESUS CHRIST, for He alone is Holy, Righteous and True, and He alone is worthy of all of our Praise, for all of the Glory and all of the Honor is His and His alone.

He is the KING of Kings and the LORD of Lords and He is the only begotten Son of the Father, who in His great love and His everlasting mercy has saved us from the wrath which is soon to come.

By His faithfulness He causes His chosen ones to stand in Robes of Righteousness, for by His grace, we have been appointed to walk in good works which He has prepared before the foundation of the world. And having so blessed us with His love and mercy, He bestows upon us the greatest of honors; He calls us His friends.

The Day of the LORD is at Hand

TABLE OF CONTENTS

Other books by Benjamin Baruch include the Search the Scriptures Series:

Volume I   Out of the Darkness

Volume II   You Shall Know the Truth

Volume III   The Remnant Shall Return

Volume IV   I AM the Door

Benjamin Baruch and JR Nyquist collaborated together to publish: The New Tactics of Global War

Reflections on the Changing Balance of Power in the Final Days of Peace

Preface

I wish to thank my dear friends who have stood by my side and held up my hands in their prayers; for without your help, this Seventh Edition would never have been possible. Your prayers and encouragement were instrumental in allowing me to share this word which I have received from the Lord Jesus Christ with His elect in this final hour.

I also wish to thank the many men of wisdom who have been raised up to speak the truth to America, including David Wilkerson, Dumitru Duduman, and Henry Gruver, among countless others who have had the courage to speak the truth to the American people. They shall stand in white among the saints of the ages, who have been faithful in proclaiming the true word of God. I have been blessed to meet these men, save brother Duduman, who went to be with the Lord in early 1996. His suffering at the hands of our enemies is an inspiration to us all. The contents of this book are a summary of the revelation that the servants of Jesus Christ are speaking to America and her church in this final hour.

The word of the Lord is always hard for the natural man to bear. It exposes our sin and demands we change. The word of God is always the truth. Even if no man receives it, it remains true and if a word be from God, then the day shall declare it. And this is such a word.

Psalm 12:6 declares "The words of the LORD are pure words: as silver tried in a furnace of earth, they are purified seven times." And thus this Seventh Edition is presented to the Lord for the edification of the saints as a true word which has now been purified seven times.

I pray, dear reader, you will take the time to carefully read the words of this book, and to prayerfully test them, both in the Spirit and in the word of God, to see if they be of God.

May the Lord Jesus Christ bless you,

Benjamin Baruch

Foreword

My name is Benjamin. I am neither an author nor a prophet. My educational background is in Business and Finance. I spent over 20 years preparing for a career as a professional money manager, first acquiring a license as a Certified Public Accountant and then as a Chartered Financial Analyst. In 1995 I was called into the office of the Chairman of my company, and informed that he was placing me in charge of several Wall Street accounts. Suddenly, I was responsible for directing investment policy for millions of dollars in America's stock market. I was honored and elated and I was scared. Wall Street is a dangerous place, full of deception and error where mistakes can be costly, very costly. I walked back to my office wondering what do I do now. Where do I start? I had all of the advanced training, thousands of hours of exhaustive research, and years upon years of work experience with intensity you cannot even imagine. What I did next began to change my career and my entire life. I knelt down in my office and prayed.

The Lord honored my prayers, and He blessed the work of my hands; my first year's results were outstanding, yet by early 1996 I knew the market was at risk, and that one day large, spectacular losses would occur. So in early 1996 I began to pray in earnest. I usually arrive at the office around 5 a.m., and the first thing I did every day, was to pray and ask the Lord "show me the end of this matter". Almost a year passed and I hadn't received an answer; then one day shortly after my 40th birthday, I heard from the Lord, and when he answered me, he did so literally, for he showed me the end of the matter, and I saw with my eyes what is to come.

This book is a summary of everything the Lord revealed unto me. It is also a warning to the people of America and Israel. I stand as one small voice among the many men of wisdom whom the Lord is raising up in this final hour to declare what the Spirit is saying to His chosen ones:

THE LORD GOD ALMIGHTY

IS STANDING NOW

READY TO JUDGE

THE ENTIRE EARTH

CHAPTER

1

TAKE HEED THAT
NO MAN DECEIVE YOU
Matthew 24:4

Jesus Christ began to answer the question His disciples posed regarding the signs of His Second Coming and the end of the age in the Gospel of Matthew chapter 24. The Lord's first response was a warning, for the last days would be a time of great deception with false prophets, false teachers and false doctrines abounding such that even the elect would find themselves deceived if they did not take heed. Jesus continued His answer saying *"For many shall come in my name, saying, I am anointed; and shall deceive many".* [1]

There would be many who come in the name of Jesus Christ proclaiming the truth that Jesus of Nazareth is the Messiah of Israel, yet they would be false teachers and false prophets, who would teach and deceive many. The word for *"deceive"* is *plan-ah'-o* [2] which means to go astray from the truth, to err, seduce, wander, and be out of the way. *"But evil men and seducers shall wax worse and worse, deceiving, and being deceived."* [3]

The word used of seducers is *go'-ace* [4] which means a wizard, as muttering spells, an imposter, a seducer! These false teachers are actually speaking spells and evil enchantments with the words of their false doctrines. This is the terrible time Jesus warned us would come at the end of the age *"Little children, let no man deceive you: he that doeth righteousness is righteous, even as he is righteous. He that committed sin is of the devil; for the devil sinneth from the beginning."* 1 John 3:7

THE PARABLE OF THE FIG TREE

In the twentieth century, the world witnessed the budding of the Fig Tree, which is the restoration of the nation of Israel back to their land. This is the sign spoken of by the prophets signaling we are in the last days, and that the Lord is coming back soon. Jesus spoke of this sign in a parable. The Lord taught many parables, but this was the only parable He instructed us to learn the meaning of, for this is the sign that He is standing at the door. *"Now learn a parable of the fig tree; When his branch is yet tender, and puts forth leaves, know that summer is nigh: So likewise ye, when ye shall see all these things, know that it is near, even at the doors."* Matthew 24:32-33

THE DAY OF THE LORD IS AT HAND

Israel is the fig tree, and her leaves came forth in the early part of the 20th century. We are living in the last days spoken of by the prophets, and the Lord is now standing at the door. We are presently entering into the midnight hour, and the darkest part of the night lies just ahead.

The purpose of this book is to reveal the mystery of the Revelation of Jesus Christ, the true Messiah of Israel, which has been hidden by God from those wise in their own eyes, and revealed unto babes. I shall give insight and understanding to the writings of the prophets, and reveal the true order of the events which will precede the Second coming of our Lord.

Two thousand years ago the religious leaders of Israel were looking for the coming of the Messiah, yet having misunderstood Bible prophecy, they missed their hour of visitation. Today, the religious leaders of the Christian Church are making the same mistake, having misunderstood Bible prophecy regarding the Second Coming of the Lord. Their hour of visitation is at hand, and the Lord is coming as a thief in the night, in ways of which they are unaware.

Once again, the Lord has raised up men of wisdom in the wilderness to speak the truth, and to warn the church of the impending judgment, which must begin in the household of God.

JUDGMENT BEGINS IN THE HOUSE OF GOD

For the time is come that judgment must begin at the house of God: and if it first begins with us, what shall the end be of them that obey not the gospel of God? And if the righteous scarcely be saved, where shall the ungodly and the sinner appear? 1 Peter 4:17-18

The Judgment of God always begins within His house. The prophet Ezekiel was shown the judgment by God of ancient Israel.

"The Lord said to him, `Go through the midst of the city, through the midst of Jerusalem, and put a mark on the foreheads of the men who sigh and groan over all the abominations which are being committed in its midst.' But to the others He said in my hearing, `Go through the city after him and strike; do not let your eye have pity, and do not spare. Utterly slay old men, young men, maidens, little children, and women, but do not touch any man on whom is the mark; and you shall start from my sanctuary.' So they started with the elders who were before the temple." [6]

Before addressing the issues of what is about to come, I wish to summarize the consensus view of end time prophecy held today by many within the church in America, and by the power of God's spirit, I will correct the many errors contained therein.

2

THE CHURCH IN AMERICA HAS BEEN DECEIVED

The believers in America are looking for the Second Coming of the Messiah with the following assumptions and expectations:

1. The signs of Matthew 24 evidence we are in the last days.
2. A revived Roman Empire representing a union of ten nations will rise to power at the time of the end.
3. The antichrist will then sign a seven-year peace treaty with the nation of Israel marking the beginning of the seven-year Great Tribulation.
4. America is strangely absent from the prophetic writings.
5. The Church will be raptured out of the earth before the beginning of the seven-year tribulation.
6. The Church is looking forward to a great end time revival before the hour of judgment begins.

Each of these commonly held views are wrong and are based upon vain thinking with no scriptural basis whatsoever. These errors will be addressed and corrected through the course of this text. Some will dismiss this message, refusing to believe the leadership of the Church could be deceived. Yet the Lord warned us specifically to *"take heed that no man deceives you."*

The Lord does not give idle warnings, for the warnings and admonitions of the Lord are themselves prophecy of what would come. The Lord is actually saying: "In the last days, the majority will be deceived, take heed that it doesn't happen to you!" Not only is deception of the church possible, it was prophesied to come.

> *For the time will come when they will not endure sound doctrine; but after their own lusts shall they heap to themselves teachers, having itching ears; And they shall turn away their ears from the truth, and shall be turned unto fables. 2 Timothy 4:3-4*

I have not written this book seeking to enter into a debate with theologians nor to introduce controversy or dissension, but the truth of God will always divide. My mission is to publish the word of truth for the remnant, which my God shall call, and to provide a true witness to the word of prophecy. I shall do both through the grace of my Lord. I will show the biblical basis for this message, while revealing the true meaning of the prophecies including the order and the detail of events, which will shortly come to pass.

THE DAY OF THE LORD IS AT HAND

THE EARLY BIRTH PAINS OF THE KINGDOM

What then are the signs of the end of the age and the second coming of the Lord? Prophecy teachers point to the statements made by Jesus in Matthew 24:6-8 as the answer: "And ye shall hear of wars and rumors of wars: see that ye be not troubled: for all these things must come to pass, but the end is not yet. For nation shall rise against nation, and kingdom against kingdom: and there shall be famines, and pestilences, and earthquakes, in diverse places. All these are just the beginning of sorrows."

These signs have been cited as evidence that we are in the last days. Jesus said these signs are only the beginning of the sorrows that the earth must first endure, before the great tribulation, but they are not the signs of the end of the age. Scripture warns us: "Knowing this first, that there shall come in the last days scoffers, walking after their own lusts, and saying, where is the promise of his coming? For since the fathers fell asleep, all things continue as they were from the beginning of the creation." [8]

The time of the end would witness scoffers who would deride the message of truth regarding the return of the Lord. The word used for scoffers is *emp-aheek-tace'* [9] which means a derider, and a false teacher, a mocker or a scoffer. At the time of the end, these scoffers will even be found as false teachers within the Church itself.

THE PERSECUTION OF THE TRUE BELIEVERS

Prophecy teachers completely miss the next point the Lord makes in His discourse regarding the events of the end of the age in Matthew 24:9-14: "Then shall they deliver you up to be afflicted, and shall kill you: and ye shall be hated of all nations for my name's sake. And then shall many be offended, and shall betray one another, and shall hate one another. And many false prophets shall rise, and shall deceive many. And because iniquity shall abound, the love of many shall wax cold. But he that shall endure unto the end, the same shall be saved. And this gospel of the kingdom shall be preached in all the world for a witness unto all nations; and then shall the end come."

Following the signs which are the *"beginning of sorrows"*, the Lord tells us "then" the true believers will be delivered up to be afflicted *"and they shall kill you and you shall be hated of all nations."* This time of persecution precedes the tribulation and will come suddenly as a snare! One day soon, the majority of the people in the Church will awaken and realize they have been lied to, and deceived by their leaders, who did not warn them this persecution was coming. The *"many"* who considered themselves Christians, will then become *"offended"* and *"betray"* one another.

4

Take Heed That No Man Deceive You

American believers are neither emotionally nor spiritually prepared for the sudden and intense persecution which is about to fall upon them, and when it comes, and it will surely come; the majority will be utterly devastated.

The word for *"many"* in the original Greek is *pol-oos'*; which means most, plenteous or the majority. Jesus is warning us, in the midst of intense worldwide persecution, the majority of professing Christians will become offended, and betray one another. Only a faithful few will continue to hold the true profession of the faith that Jesus Christ is Lord and he is the only way, the only truth and the only life.

> *If the world hates you, you know that it has hated me before it hated you. If you were of the world, the world would love its own; but because you are not of the world, but I chose you out of the world, therefore the world hates you. Remember the word that I said to you, `A slave is not greater than his master.' If they persecuted me, they will also persecute you; if they kept my word, they will keep yours also. But all these things they will do to you for my name's sake, because they do not know the One who sent me.* [10]

The word in Greek for *"offended"* is *skan-dal-id'-zo* which means to entrap, and to trip up, to stumble or entice to sin, to fall into apostasy. Nominal professing Christians will stumble and fall under the persecution, and will deny the faith. These apostate believers will then turn on and betray the true brethren of the Lord. The word for *"betray"* in the Greek is *par-ad-id'-o-mee* which means to surrender, to yield up, or to deliver. The Greek for *"hate"* is *mis-eh'-o*; which means to detest and to persecute. Jesus has warned us that a worldwide persecution is coming *"before"* the tribulation.

This persecution will be so intense that the majority of those claiming to be Christian will become offended and stumble into apostasy, and they shall then deliver up the chosen ones to persecution unto death! Only those who endure unto the end will be saved. The Greek word for endure is *hoop-om-en'-o* [11] which means to remain; to bear trials, to persevere. Only those who remain faithful to the Lord, and patiently endure the trial of this persecution will be saved.

The Lord warned of a worldwide persecution of true believers. All nations will hate the chosen ones. Dear reader, this includes the United States of America, where up to the hour of this writing, believers have enjoyed unprecedented freedom. Yet in the Lord's own words, we know this will change and a time of violent persecution is coming very soon in America. The cup of iniquity is now full, arrogant pride, the spirit of greed, and the perversion of America's many abominations have now defiled the land.

THE DAY OF THE LORD IS AT HAND

A generation of American Christians has been watching the early birth pains convinced by their teachers that the next event would be the rapture of the church, yet what must follow next is persecution, a most intense persecution. The twentieth century has witnessed more martyrs for the name of Jesus Christ than any other. Today in many nations thousands of believers are dying every day. America will witness such sorrows before the *"sign of the end."*

THE SIGN OF THE END OF THE AGE

Jesus tells us after the worldwide persecution of the church, we will then see the sign which marks the beginning of the end of the age: the abomination of desolation spoken of by Daniel the prophet standing in the holy place.

> *When ye therefore shall see the abomination of desolation spoken of by Daniel the prophet, stand in the holy place, whoso readeth, let him understand: Then let them which be in Judaea flee into the mountains: Let him which is on the housetop not come down to take anything out of his house: Neither let him which is in the field return back to take his clothes. And woe unto them that are with child, and to them that give suck in those days! But pray ye that your flight be not in the winter, neither on a Sabbath day: For then shall be great tribulation such as was not since the beginning of the world to this time, no, nor ever shall be. Matthew 24:15-21*

This sign which marks the end of the age, and the beginning of the Great Tribulation, is the stopping of the daily altar sacrifice on the Temple Mount and the setting up of the abomination of desolation in the holy place. The Lord tells those in Judea to flee immediately, for this event marks the beginning of the Great Tribulation.

Jesus also warns us to pray that our flight won't come at the end of winter or on a Sabbath day. This warning is also prophetic. The Lord is actually telling us the Great tribulation will begin at the end of winter and on a Sabbath day and the warning is to his remnant. They are to pray that their flight would not come during this time. The remnant is to be in position early, before the world is snared on that day! We are also warned that those with child, still needing milk will experience woe on that day. This is also a spiritual prophecy, for those who are babes in the faith and still needing the milk of the word will have great trouble standing on that day.

What exactly does Daniel the prophet tell us about the abomination of desolation? In chapter 12, we learn that from the stopping of the daily sacrifice, which is the morning and evening oblation offering of the temple worship, to the setting up of the abomination that brings desolation, there

6

shall be 1,290 days. *"And from the time that the daily sacrifice shall be taken away, and the abomination that maketh desolate set up, there shall be a thousand two hundred and ninety days."* [12]

Daniel prophesies about the abomination in chapter 11 writing that the antichrist *"shall pollute the sanctuary"* and *"shall take away the daily sacrifice."* [13] He shall then set up the abomination of desolation upon the holy place. We are also told that the antichrist is *"vile person to whom they shall not give the honor of the kingdom"*.[14] This man will be considered vile and will have been passed over for the title of king.

He is a prince who has been rejected and considered unworthy to rule. Daniel continues telling us *"but he shall come in peaceably, and obtain the kingdom by flatteries"*.[15] The false Messiah will come in under the disguise of peace, and will conquer the earth with flattering words. We are also told *"and after the league made with him, he shall work deceitfully: for he shall come up, and shall become strong with a small people"* [16] He will work deceitfully following a league or an alliance of a small group of people who have seized the kingdom by deception. Daniel continues *"he shall do that which his fathers have not done, nor his father's fathers"*. [17] He shall accomplish the goal which his ancestors were incapable of, uniting a worldwide empire under a single crown once again.

> And in his estate shall stand up a vile person, to whom they shall not give the honour of the kingdom: but he shall come in peaceably, and obtain the kingdom by flatteries. And after the league made with him he shall work deceitfully: for he shall come up, and shall become strong with a small people. He shall enter peaceably ... and he shall do that which his fathers have not done, nor his fathers' fathers. Daniel 11:21-24

After he seizes power, the false messiah will exalt himself above every god, and will speak blasphemy against the true God of heaven. *"He shall prosper until the time of the indignation be accomplished, for that which is determined shall be done."*[18] The events of the Great Tribulation and the coming false Messiah have been determined, for they are predestined to occur and they shall be accomplished.

The Scripture refers to this time as *"the indignation."* In Hebrew, this word is זַעַם *zah'-am*[19] and it means great fury, anger, indignation and rage, especially of God's displeasure with sin. The last days of planet earth is the time for the outpouring of God's wrath and judgment for the sins of mankind, and the outpouring will continue until the indignation of the Lord is accomplished in full!

And arms shall stand on his part, and they shall pollute the sanctuary of strength, and shall take away the daily sacrifice, and they shall place the abomination that maketh desolate. And such as do wickedly against the covenant shall he corrupt by flatteries: but the people that do know their God shall be strong and do exploits. And they that understand among the people shall instruct many: And the king shall do according to his will; and he shall exalt himself, and magnify himself above every God, and shall speak against the God of gods, and shall prosper till the indignation be accomplished: for that that is determined shall be done. Daniel 11:31-36

Some scholars teach that Antiochus Epiphanes fulfilled these prophecies when he desecrated the temple and stopped the daily sacrifice around 164 B.C. This is only partially correct. Antiochus Epiphanes foreshadowed these events, but their final fulfillment would await the time appointed at the end of the age.

In Daniel 11:27 we are told this king will do mischief and speak lies, but he shall not prosper *"for yet the end shall be at the time appointed."* [20] He will not succeed, for the end has been appointed to occur within the days of his rule. This tells us these events occur at the time of the end. In Daniel 12:1 we are also told *"and at that time"* which refers to the preceding events of chapter 11, *"there shall be a time of trouble, such as never was"*. This is the time which is known as the *"time of Jacob's trouble"*[21] prophesied by Jeremiah. This is the Great Tribulation at the end of the age, and Israel shall be delivered out of it! God will yet preserve and deliver a chosen remnant in the midst of the most terrible time the world has ever known.

This is also the time when *"the wise shall shine as the brightness of the firmament; and they that turn many to righteousness as the stars for ever and ever. But thou, O Daniel, shut up the words, and seal the book, even to the time of the end: many shall run to and fro, and knowledge shall be increased."*[22]

The prophecy in Daniel 12 tells us *"knowledge shall be increased"* at the time of the end. In the secular world, the knowledge of mankind has greatly increased in these last days. In the spiritual world, the knowledge of prophetic truth has also increased now that we are at the time of the end. Read this entire book dear reader, and witness for yourself the amazing knowledge the Lord is now revealing to his people. *"And at that time shall Michael stand up. The great prince which stands for the children of thy people: and there shall be a time of trouble, such as never was since there was a nation even to that same time: and at that time thy people shall be delivered, every one that shall be found written in the book. And they that be wise shall shine as the brightness of the firmament; and they that turn many to righteousness as the stars for ever and ever. But thou, Daniel, shut up the words, and seal the book, even to the time of the end."* Daniel 12:1-4.

THE IMAGE OF THE BEAST

The *"abomination which makes desolate"* is the *"image of the beast"* which will be set upon the Temple Mount in Jerusalem. The apostle John was also given insight into these days in the book of Revelation. In John's vision of chapter 13, he saw a beast with seven heads and ten horns rising up from the sea. One of the heads was wounded unto death, and then healed, and the whole world wondered after the beast.

The horn, which was wounded, is the antichrist. He will be given a mouth to utter blasphemy, and power to rule for 42 months, which is 3 ½ years. John saw another beast coming out of the earth, with two horns as a lamb, appearing to be innocent and harmless, but possessing the mouth of the dragon. This beast will speak for the red dragon. This is the false prophet, who will stand before the antichrist, and cause all the people of the earth to worship the beast, and to make an image of the beast which is the abomination of desolation, and it will be set upon the Temple Mount.

The setting up of the image of the beast is the abomination of desolation for it profanes the Holy place in Jerusalem. It also violates the law of the Lord our God, where men are commanded to worship only the Lord, and are prohibited from making and worshipping graven images. The false prophet leads mankind to worship the image of the beast, and to worship the dragon, who gave his power to the beast.

> *And he opened his mouth in blasphemy against God. And it was given unto him to make war with the saints, and to overcome them And I beheld another beast coming up out of the earth: and he had two horns like a lamb, and he spoke as a dragon and causes the earth and them which dwell therein to worship the first beast, whose deadly wound was healed. And that they should make an image to the beast. And he causes all to receive a mark in their right hand, or in their foreheads: And that no man might buy or sell, save he that had the mark, Here is wisdom. Let him that hath understanding count the number of the beast: for it is the number of a man; and his number is Six hundred threescore and six (666). Revelation 13:6-18*

Satan has attempted from the beginning to counterfeit the work of the true Messiah. In his efforts to deceive mankind, the antichrist will appear to the nations as having received a *"deadly wound"* which is healed, presenting a counterfeit resurrection. He will then require that no one may buy or sell without his mark, which is the number of his name, 666. I will discuss the number of the beast in the chapter - *Here is the Mind which has Wisdom.*

THE DAY OF THE LORD IS AT HAND

DANIEL'S SEVENTY WEEKS PROPHECY

The stopping of the sacrifices is also mentioned in Daniel's prophecy of the seventy weeks. This prophecy is one of the most important prophecies in the Scripture, for in it, we are given insight into the timing of the first and the second coming of the Messiah.

> *Seventy weeks are determined upon thy people and upon thy holy city, to finish the transgression, and to make an end of sins, and to make reconciliation for iniquity, and to bring in everlasting righteousness, and to seal up the vision and prophecy, and to anoint the most Holy. Know therefore and understand, that from the going forth of the commandment to restore and to build Jerusalem unto the Messiah the Prince shall be seven weeks, and threescore and two weeks: the street shall be built again, and the wall, even in troublous times. And after threescore and two weeks shall Messiah be cut off: but not for himself: and the people of the prince that shall come shall destroy the city and the sanctuary; and the end thereof shall be with a flood, and unto the end of the war desolations are determined. And he shall confirm the covenant with many for one week: and in the midst of the week he shall cause the sacrifice and the oblation to cease, and for the overspreading of abominations he shall make it desolate, even until the consummation, and that determined shall be poured upon the desolate. Daniel 9:24-27*

Daniel's seventy weeks prophecy has fascinated scholars over the centuries. The seventy weeks represents weeks of years, which have been determined, or predestined to come upon the nation of Israel and the Holy City of Jerusalem. Daniel writes that *"from the going forth of the commandment to restore and build Jerusalem until Messiah the Prince shall be seven weeks and sixty two weeks and after sixty two weeks shall Messiah be cut off, but not for himself".*[23]

Daniel's prophecy reveals the timing of the coming of the Messiah. He first refers to him as Messiah the Prince, speaking of Him in His second coming, as a ruler of the earth, but not as a King, only as a prince. He also refers to him as the Messiah who would be *"cut off, but not for himself"* speaking of the first coming, when the Messiah would come not as a Prince, but as the suffering servant who would die for the nation.

In perfect literal fulfillment of Daniel's prophecy, Jesus Christ was born *"sixty-two weeks"* from the first decree to rebuild Jerusalem, after which he shed his precious blood on the Feast of Passover as the Holy Lamb of God. Jesus fulfilled the prophecy of His first coming exactly as Daniel prophesied almost 500 years earlier!

WHO HAS BELIEVED OUR REPORT

Isaiah prophesied of the suffering of the Messiah declaring that He would be cut off, not for His own sins, but for the sins of the people. *"He was wounded for our transgressions and bruised for our iniquities... and by His stripes we are healed."*[24] This is Yeshua, who is the Son of the Most High God. He was beaten and bruised for our sins, and wounded for our transgressions, and by the stripes which were cut into His back, we are healed. He was taken on the Feast day of Pesach, which the Gentiles call Passover, and was brought as a lamb to the slaughter. On that day they massacred my Lord. And it was for me that He died. Yes, for all of us who are the little flock of the Father, who Isaiah calls *"the remnant"*.[25] He did not even open His mouth in protest, and without a word of complaint, He laid His life down and was "cut off' from the land of the living.

"For God so loved the world that he gave his only begotten Son, that whosoever believeth in him should not perish, but have everlasting life." [26] It pleased our Father in Heaven, to bruise His son that we His children might not perish but obtain life everlasting; for this reason, Jesus made His soul *"an offering for sin"* and the Father God declares *"My righteous servant shall justify many!"*

> *Who hath believed our report? And to whom is the arm of the Lord revealed? For he shall grow up before him as a tender plant, and as a root out of a dry ground: he hath no form nor comeliness; and when we shall see him, there is no beauty that we should desire him. He is despised and rejected of men: a man of sorrows, and acquainted with grief: and we hid as it were our faces from him; he was despised, and we esteemed him not. Surely he hath borne our griefs, and carried our sorrows: yet we did esteem him stricken, smitten of God, and afflicted. But he was wounded for our transgressions; he was bruised for our iniquities: the chastisement of our peace was upon him; and with his stripes we are healed. All we like sheep have gone astray; we have turned everyone to his own way; and the Lord hath laid on him the iniquity of us all. He was oppressed, and he was afflicted, yet he opened not his mouth: he is brought as a lamb to the slaughter. As a sheep before her shearers is dumb, so he opened not his mouth, for he was cut off out of the land of the living: for the transgression of my people was he stricken. And he made his grave with the wicked, and with the rich in his death; because he had done no violence, neither was any deceit in his mouth. Yet it pleased the Lord to bruise him; ... He shall see of the travail of his soul, and shall be satisfied: by his knowledge shall my righteous servant justify many.' for he shall bear their iniquities.*
> *Isaiah 53:1-12*

THEY SHALL SMITE THE JUDGE OF ISRAEL WITH A ROD

The prophet Micah declares *"they shall smite the judge of Israel with a rod upon the cheek."* [27] This is Jesus for He is both King and Judge of Israel. Throughout the Scripture the prophets testify that the Lord himself would come to save His people. And He did come, just as Daniel prophesied, and He was then *"cut off, but not for himself"*.

> *For unto us a child is born, unto us a son is given: and the government shall be upon his shoulder: and his name shall be called Wonderful, Counselor, The mighty God, The everlasting Father, The Prince of Peace. Of the increase of his government and peace there shall be no end, upon the throne of David, and upon his kingdom, to order it, and to establish it with judgment and with justice from henceforth even forever. The zeal of the Lord of hosts will perform this.* [28]

THE LORD SHALL PROVIDE HIMSELF A LAMB

Many of the prophets of Israel have spoken of the Lord coming Himself, to save His people, and to die in their place. Abraham's heart was torn when the Lord commanded him to offer up Isaac as a sacrifice and a burnt offering. In Genesis we read how the great Patriarch of the faith obeyed, and prepared to kill his only son. This commandment by the Lord foreshadowed the Lord sending His son to die for the people. Abraham and Isaac departed alone, leaving with only the fire and the wood. Isaac questioned his father, *"My father, behold the fire and the wood: but where is the lamb for a burnt offering? And Abraham said, my son, God will provide himself a lamb for a burnt offering."*[29]

Abraham's answer was prophetic, for the Lord had determined to provide Himself, as the Lamb of God, to be the burnt offering for the sins of the world. His words in the Hebrew read *"Elohiym yir'eh low aseh la' olaah baniy."* Truly the Scripture declares *"God will provide himself a lamb."*

THEY HAVE PIERCED MY HANDS AND FEET

David prophesied of the crucifixion of the Lord in Psalm 22. This prophecy includes the words spoken by the Lord as He hung upon the cross. *"My God, my God, why hast thou forsaken me"* [30] cried the Lord. The bulls of Bashan are the evil spirits which attacked the Lord while on the cross.

> *Strong bulls of Bashan have beset me... they gaped upon me with their mouths, as a ravening and a roaring lion. My heart is like wax, it is melted... and my tongue cleaves to my jaws.* [31]

Take Heed That No Man Deceive You

The prophecy even describes the mocking of the crowd: *"all they that see me laugh at me... He trusted in the Lord ... let Him deliver him."* [32] These very words of scorn were spoken against our Lord on that day. *"Though hast brought me into the dust of death, for dogs have compassed about me... they have pierced my hands and my feet"* [33] cries the Messiah of Israel. Who has believed our report? To whom is the arm of the Lord revealed? Who hears from God? Let him reveal it! *The Lord has spoken! Hear Him!*

> *God, my God, why hast thou forsaken me? why art thou so far from helping me, and from the words of my roaring? I am a worm, and no man; a reproach of men, and despised of the people. All they that see me laugh me to scorn: they shoot out the lip, they shake the head, saying, He trusted on the LORD that he would deliver him: let him deliver him, seeing he delighted in him. Be not far from me; for trouble is near; for there is none to help. Many bulls have compassed me: strong bulls of Bashan have beset me round. They gaped upon me with their mouths, as a ravening and a roaring lion. I am poured out like water, and all my bones are out of joint: my heart is like wax; it is melted in the midst of my bowels. My strength is dried up like a potsherd; and my tongue cleaves to my jaws; and thou hast brought me into the dust of death. For dogs have compassed me: the assembly of the wicked have enclosed me: they pierced my hands and my feet .They part my garments among them, and cast lots upon my vesture. Save me from the lion's mouth: for thou hast heard me from the horns of the unicorns. I will declare thy name unto my brethren: in the midst of the congregation will I praise thee. For the kingdom is the LORD'S: and he is the governor among the nations. Psalm 22:1-31*

HEAR O ISRAEL - THE LORD IS OUR GOD AND THE LORD IS ONE!

Yeshua יֵשׁוּעַ is the true Messiah of Israel. He is the Good Shepherd, who laid down His life for his sheep, and having loved his own who were in the world, he loved them until the end. Even while the Lord hung on the cross, he continued to think about each one of his chosen ones. He endured all of this suffering so we could escape the wrath which is soon to come. This is his agape love. This is the death to self which his gospel demands. He is the way, the truth and the life, and no one comes to the Father by any other name. Yeshua, whom the gentiles call Jesus, is the Lord God Almighty come in the flesh, and let all the earth be silent before Him! Every one of the prophets of Israel testified of Him! Hear O Israel, The Lord is our God, and the Lord is One, and Blessed be His glorious Name whose Kingdom is forever and ever.

HIS NAME IS WRITTEN KING OF KINGS AND LORD OF LORDS

In exact fulfillment of the prophecies, Jesus Christ rose on the third day, as the first fruits of the resurrection from the dead. Jesus is about to return to this earth, and now He will be called *"Faithful and True"* for He will soon judge the entire earth. Each of us will stand before Him very soon. His eyes are as flames of fire, and His clothes have been dipped in blood. He is the lamb who was slain, and having endured the suffering of the cross and its shame, He now comes to smite the nations!

He will tread them in the winepress of His fierce wrath! Jesus spoke of this judgment of the earth when He said *"I am come to send fire on the earth; and what will I, if it be already kindled? But I have a baptism to be baptized with; and how am I straitened till it be accomplished! Suppose ye that I am come to give peace on earth? I tell you, Nay; but rather division."*[34] Yeshua was straightened until His baptism on the cross was accomplished. His words *"I am coming to send fire on the earth"* will now be fulfilled. *"Alas! For that day is great, so that none is like it: it is even the time of Jacob's trouble; but he shall be saved out of it."* [35]

> And I saw heaven opened, and behold a white horse; and he that sat upon him was called Faithful and True, and in righteousness he doth judge and make war. His eyes were as a flame of fire, and on his head were many crowns; and he had a name written, that no man knew, but he himself and he was clothed with a vesture dipped in blood: and his name is called The Word of God. And the armies which were in heaven followed him upon white horses, clothed in fine linen, white and clean. And out of his mouth goes a sharp sword, that with it he should smite the nations: and he shall rule them with a rod of iron: and he treads the winepress of the fierceness and wrath of Almighty God. And he hath on his vesture and on his thigh a name written, KING OF KINGS, AND LORD OF LORDS. *Revelation 19:11-16*

THE SIXTY-TWO WEEKS AND THE FIRST COMING

The birth and death of the Messiah were prophesied in Daniel's seventy weeks prophecy of Daniel chapter nine. Present day theologians assume the seven weeks must be added to the sixty-two weeks, and that sixty-nine weeks occurred between the 1st Decree to rebuild Jerusalem, issued by Artaxerxes in the time of Nehemiah, until the first coming of Jesus Christ. They also assume the sixty-nine weeks was fulfilled at the time of the crucifixion. Both of these assumptions are incorrect, and inconsistent with the words of Daniel's prophecy and the true historical record.

Take Heed That No Man Deceive You

Sir Isaac Newton, one of the greatest minds the world has ever known, and a devoted student of the book of Daniel, wrote _Observations upon the prophecies of Daniel and the Apocalypse of St. John,_ which was published six years after his death in London, in 1733. Newton was an expert in both ancient history and ancient languages. He also studied the prophecies of Daniel in depth throughout his lifetime. Newton reasoned the weeks of years must represent Sabbath years, which occur every seven years on the Biblical calendar. Therefore, Daniel's prophecy of the seventy weeks must be understood from the sacred calendar of Israel, which is lunar based, and not based on the solar calendar of the pagan nations.

"Daniel's prophecy was grounded on Jeremiah's concerning the 70 years of captivity, and therefore must be understood from the same type of years as the seventy, and those are Jewish as the prophecy was given in Judea before the captivity. And lastly, because Daniel reckoned by weeks of years, which is a way of reckoning peculiar to Jewish years. For their days run by seven, and the last day of every seven is a Sabbath, so their years also run by sevens and the last year is also a Sabbath year, and seven such weeks of years made a Jubilee." [37] Newton reasoned the sixty-two weeks were fulfilled at time of the birth of Jesus Christ. Historians recount the commandment of Artaxerxes in the days of Nehemiah as being issued in the year 444 BC. Sixty-two weeks totals 434 years, but within each seven weeks of years, a Jubilee would occur, so eight Jubilee years must be added to the sixty-two years, thus the prophecy points to the birth of the Lord 442 years later, in the year 2 BC.

Newton understood the seven weeks prophecy of Daniel 9:25 would be fulfilled at the end of the age; as the prophet declared "from the going forth of the commandment to restore Jerusalem until the coming of Messiah the Prince shall be seven weeks." Newton wrote "This part of the prophecy, being therefore not yet fulfilled, I shall not attempt a particular interpretation of it, but content myself with observing, that as the seventy and sixty two weeks were Jewish weeks, ending with sabbatical years, so the seven weeks are the compass of a Jubilee, and begin and end with actions proper for a Jubilee, and of the highest nature for which a Jubilee can be kept: and that since the commandment to return and to build Jerusalem, precedes the Messiah appearing as the Prince some forty-nine years; it may perhaps come forth not from the Jews themselves, but from some other... The manner I know not. Let time be the interpreter."[38]

Forty-nine years is the cycle of time between the years of Jubilee, which occur every 50th year. The Jubilee is the year of redemption, and is also known as the favorable year of the Lord. The fulfillment of the sixty-two weeks prophecy at the birth of the Lord required adding the missing eight Jubilees. So too, the seven weeks prophecy requires us to add a Jubilee.

THE DAY OF THE LORD IS AT HAND

THE YEAR OF JUBILEE - SEVEN WEEKS OF YEARS

Newton wrote: "This prophecy of the Messiah ... relates to both comings, and assigns the times thereof. We avoid also the doing violence to the language of Daniel, by taking the seven weeks and sixty-two weeks for one number. Had that been Daniel's meaning, he would have said sixty-nine weeks, and not seven weeks and sixty-two weeks, a way of numbering used by no nation. In our way the years are Jewish years ending with sabbatical years, which is very remarkable. Others either count by lunar years, or by weeks not Judaic: and, which is worst, they ground their interpretations on erroneous chronology"[39] The year of Jubilee was the year of redemption of all property, freedom for all slaves and a year of rest and restoration for both the land and the people of Israel. The Jubilee is the 50th year, even as the feast of Pentecost follows the feast of seven weeks on the 50th day. Daniel's prophecy of the seven weeks which precede the second coming of the Lord uses the exact same words in the Hebrew as the law of Jubilee contained in Leviticus.

> And thou shalt number seven Sabbaths of years unto thee, seven times seven years; and the space of the seven Sabbaths of years shall be unto thee forty and nine years. Then shalt thou cause the trumpet of the jubilee to sound on the tenth day of the seventh month, in the Day of Atonement. And ye shall hallow the fiftieth year, and proclaim liberty throughout all the land unto all the inhabitants thereof it shall be a jubilee unto you, and ye shall return every man unto his possession, and ye shall return every man unto his family. A jubilee shall that fiftieth year be unto you.
> Leviticus 25:8-11

The trumpet to announce the Jubilee is blown on Yom Kippur to prepare the people for the coming of the Jubilee of the Lord. The apostle John also heard a trumpet when he was caught up in the spirit to witness the Revelation of the Day of the Lord. It too began with the blowing of a trumpet to announce the final 70th Jubilee of Israel. *"I was in the Spirit on the Lord's Day, and heard behind me a great voice, as of a trumpet"* [40] John is speaking of more than just a Sabbath day, for the Revelation is fulfilled during the 7th day of creation, which is the Final Sabbath Day of the Lord. The Messiah proclaimed: *"the day of vengeance is in mine heart, and the year of my redeemed is come."* [41] The Jubilee is the favorable year of the Lord, and the year of our redemption by our God. In Isaiah 61, the Scripture prophesies the second coming of the Messiah, this time in judgment: *"To proclaim the acceptable (Jubilee) year of the Lord, and the day of vengeance of our God."*[42] The birth of Jesus in 2 BC occurred during a Jubilee year, and brought us the acceptable or favorable year of the Lord. The 50th year following the commandment to restore Jerusalem, will bring both the birth of the man-child and beginning of the day of vengeance of our God.

16

Take Heed That No Man Deceive You

The birth of the man-child of the book of Revelation is the revealing of the Messiah, as a Prince and this will occur seven weeks following the command to restore the Holy City of Jerusalem. Seven weeks is the span of time of the counting of the Omer, and the compass of time from the feast of First Fruit to Pentecost; these 49 days have only one purpose, they point to the 50th day of Shavuot or Pentecost. Daniel's prophecy of the seven sevens, translated as weeks, speaks of 49 years, which as the counting of the Omer, also points to the 50th year. The 49 days following the Passover point to the Feast of Weeks which is the day of Pentecost, the 50th day. This is the very day the Lord came down to give Moses the Torah and, on that day, the mountains burned and melted like wax.

The ministry of Jesus Christ at the end of the age begins in a way few understand, for the mystery of the Revelation of Jesus Christ has been hidden by God from the beginning of time, and only revealed to a few until this final hour. The Messiah of Israel is both a conquering King and a humble servant. In His first coming, Jesus Christ came as a suffering servant, and as the True Passover Lamb to die for the sins of His people. In the second coming, our Lord will come among us as the Lion from the tribe of Judah and reveal himself as our Mighty Deliverer.

His first coming began through a supernatural birth in which the Son of God became a man and walked among us. His second coming will also begin with a supernatural birth, only this time through the spirit. A company of men will become born again totally, and filled with the Holy Spirit without measure. These are the 144,000 who will stand with the Lamb in the time of the book of Revelation. These men are the first fruits of the Lord, and they will walk out in their lives, the second half of the seven-year ministry of Jesus Christ during the Great Tribulation.

This is the mystery of the revelation of the word of God fulfilled literally; Christ in us, the hope of glory. It may be hard to comprehend, but hold your objections for a moment and open your heart and mind and understand the Second Coming, where the Lord comes with the clouds, is preceded by the revelation of Jesus Christ in His people during the Great Tribulation. This is what Jesus meant in Luke 17:30 when he said: *"In the day when the Son of man is revealed"*. The context of this verse is the beginning of the Great Tribulation, and we are told in Luke's account that on this day the Son of man will be revealed! This is the same day that the abomination of desolation will be seen on the Temple Mount, as declared in Matthew 24. On the same day, the Son of man is revealed within a remnant of His people as declared by Luke. Then the Lord will begin the second half of his seven-year ministry upon the earth.

Newton understood this, and reasoned that sometime during the twentieth century, Israel would be restored as a nation during a Jubilee year, and thereafter, a commandment to restore the Holy City of Jerusalem would be issued, which would begin the final seven weeks prophecy to be followed by a 50th year, after which the Messiah would be revealed among us as a Prince.

Israel was reborn as a nation in 1948 but the Holy City was not under Israeli control until 1967. The Knesset established The Company for the Reconstruction and Development of the Jewish Quarter in the Old City of Jerusalem, Ltd. in April of 1969. Assuming this act begins the 50-year count and that the prophecy requires using complete years based upon the spiritual calendar, the countdown would begin in the spring of 1970 and the 50th year would begin in March of 2020 and end in March of 2021.

The sign of Revelation 12 first appeared in the heavens in the fall of 2017 in which the Virgin was pregnant for nine months, while crowned with 12 stars. She was clothed with the sun when she gave birth on the feast of trumpets 2017 foreshadowing the soon birth of the man-child company. The coming of the 144,000 anointed ones as princes of Israel was prophesied in Isaiah 32:1: *"Behold, a king shall reign in righteousness, and his princes shall rule in the judgment."* Daniel's 70 weeks prophecy also reveals the Messiah would come sixty-two weeks following the decree issued by Artaxerxes to restore Jerusalem in the time of Ezra the High Priest, and he did come within this window of time, when he was born in a manger in the year 2 B.C. Newton confirmed the fulfillment of this Scripture occurred at the birth of Christ, and not at the time of his death on the cross. The prophecy foretold His first coming as the time of his birth and then *"after [sixty-two weeks] shall Messiah be cut off."* [44] The Messiah is not cut off at the sixty-two weeks but *"after"*. He was born following the fulfillment of the sixty-two weeks, and then later was cut off. Daniel also writes *"he shall confirm the covenant with many for one week."* [45]

Consider this: if the religious leaders in the years following the birth of Jesus had been told the Messiah had come as prophesied by Daniel, they would have protested in unbelief. Yet, he had come; only now he was among them as a small child and his ministry would wait some thirty years. So too the birth of the man-child may not be an event which is noticed by the world, or the religious leaders in this hour, and neither does the Great Tribulation necessarily begin at the same time, for the prophecy tells us in *"in the day when the Son of Man is revealed"* then we are to flee. The revealing of the Son of man within the man-child company, marks the beginning of the tribulation. As in the case of his first coming, the birth of the Messiah preceded his ministry by thirty years. Similarly, the birth of the man-child may precede their ministry during the Great Tribulation by a period of time.

THE SEVENTIETH WEEK OF DANIEL

Seventy weeks are determined upon thy people and upon thy holy city, to finish the transgression, and to make an end of sins, and to make reconciliation for iniquity, and to bring in everlasting righteousness, and to seal up the vision and prophecy, and to anoint the most Holy. Daniel 9:24

Jesus began his ministry walking out of the wilderness of Jordan, after being first baptized by John, and filled with the Holy Spirit. After he had fasted for forty days, he then came among his people as the Good Shepherd, and as the Humble Servant of God, who sought his lost sheep for 3 ½ years. Jesus then died for their sins, giving his life as the Holy Lamb of God. Modern scholars have made many errors regarding bible prophecy. Jesus has a seven-year ministry upon the earth, and his seven-year ministry is the 70th week of Daniel, and it is already half over.

He is the true Messiah who confirms the true covenant which his Father God made with his people, for one week, or seven years. He has already confirmed the covenant by Grace and Truth. In His first 3 ½ year ministry as a humble servant sent to be the Holy Lamb of God, he walked in perfect obedience to the Law of the Lord.

During the second half of the 70th week of Daniel, which is known as the *"time of Jacob's trouble"*, [46] he will again confirm his covenant with his people, only this time, he will first be born again within his anointed remnant, coming within his people as a Prince, for before he comes with the clouds as the Lord of Lords and the King of Kings, he must first fulfill the second half of his seven year ministry on the earth. He doesn't come among us as a lamb this time. No! This time, he will first be revealed within the remnant of his people as the Lion from the tribe of Judah!

"Behold, the people shall rise up as a great lion, and lift up himself as a young lion: he shall not lie down until he eat of the prey, and drink the blood of the slain." [47]

AND TO ANOINT THE MOST HOLY

The Lord will accomplish the complete fulfillment of all prophecy during the 70th week. *"Seventy weeks are determined ... to finish the transgression, and to make an end of sins, and to make reconciliation for iniquity, and to bring in everlasting righteousness and to seal up the vision and prophecy, and to anoint the most Holy."*[48]

THE DAY OF THE LORD IS AT HAND

By the end of the seventy weeks, transgression will be finished and sin will end. The Lord shall also *"make reconciliation for iniquity"* and the word for *"reconciliation"* is כפר *kaw-far*[49] which means to cover, to be merciful, and to forgive. The Lord will bring a complete cancellation of the charges against His elect during the seventieth week. The vision of the prophets will also be sealed up by the end of the seventieth week. The word *"to seal up"* is חתם *khaw-tham'* [50] which means to close up and to seal and the word for *"vision"* is חזון *khaw-zone'* [51] which means a dream, or a revelation. The word for *"prophecy"* is נביא *nav-vee* [52] which speaks literally of a prophet or an inspired man. The verse literally means, during the seventieth week, the Lord will give final pardon for sins, and seal up the revelation of the prophets of God. Prophecy and revelation continue unto the last days, and are only sealed up at the end of the seventieth week.

The final act of the seventieth week is *"to anoint the most Holy."* The word for *"to anoint"* is משח *maw-shakh* [53] which means to cover with oil, to anoint and to consecrate unto God. *Maw-shakh* is the root word for the title of Messiah, the Anointed One. After the sixty-two weeks, Jesus was anointed with the Holy Spirit in fulfillment of this prophecy. The word for *"holy"* in Hebrew is קדש *ko'-desh* [54] which means a sacred or consecrated place, or that which is most holy. The Hebrew word for *"Holies"* in this text is קדשים, *kadashiym*. The text in Hebrew reads קדש קדשים, *kodesh kadashiym*, the Holy of Holies.

Scholars assume this prophecy was fulfilled with the anointing of Jesus Christ in His first 3 ½ year ministry as a man. All prophecy is dual, and must be fulfilled twice, and this prophecy must also be fulfilled again for the Holiest place, that which has been consecrated unto the Lord will be anointed once again, during the second half of the seventieth week. Jesus told us that anointed ones would come in his name in the last days; they are his forerunners, and they will not only come in his name, they will also come with his authority and with the very character of the Lord himself fully formed within their hearts, for it is the Lord who both comes in them, and through them as God. *"Behold, your house is left unto you desolate: and verily I say unto you, Ye shall not see me, until the time come when ye shall say, Blessed is he that cometh in the name of the Lord."* Luke 13:35

The Greek word for *"in the name of"* in this text is ὄνομα, *on'-om-ah*, and it means to come in the name of another and also to come in their authority and with the character of the one represented. When our Beloved Lord comes in the clouds along with the armies of Heaven, his robe will read KING of Kings, and LORD of Lords. He doesn't come in the name of the

20

Take Heed That No Man Deceive You

Lord, for he is the Lord; the ones who come in his name are merely his anointed servants. And they have been chosen by the Father, and set apart as the First Fruits offering presented to His Son; and they too must be completely sanctified in the fire, separated unto God and thoroughly purged of the flesh, so that their vessels may also become Most Holy unto the Lord.

The scripture defines that which is most holy unto the Lord as *"anything which a man sets apart to the Lord out of all that he has is most holy to the Lord."* [55] That which is the Lord's portion, and which has been set apart unto Him, is the most holy of the Lord. *"And thou shall put the mercy seat upon the ark of the testimony in the most holy place."* [56] That which has been set apart unto the Lord, shall have the mercy seat of God placed there in the spirit. Remember that the New Covenant fulfills in the spirit all of the substance of the Old Covenant, which was given to Israel in the natural. Jesus was born in the natural, under the laws of the Old Covenant, and was anointed as the Most Holy place of God, and not a temple made with hands of men, but by the Lord. In the second coming, the Lord is preparing another temple to dwell in, and this temple will also be made *"most holy"* for it too, has been consecrated, and set apart unto God.

"And they shall call them the holy people, the redeemed of the Lord." [51] The redeemed of the Lord are the most holy, and they shall endure until the end of the tribulation, and they will see the sign of the Son of Man in the heavens! This holy remnant is also called the *"holy seed"* in Scripture: *"Then said I, Lord, how long? And he answered, Until the cities be wasted without inhabitant, and the houses without man, and the land be utterly desolate, And the Lord have removed men far away, and there be a great forsaking in the midst of the land. But yet in it shall be a tenth, and it shall return, and shall be eaten: as a teil tree, and as an oak, whose substance is in them, when they cast their leaves: so the holy seed shall be the substance thereof."* [58]

The holy seed is the portion set apart unto the Lord. They are His special treasure, and during the second half of the seventieth week of Daniel, the seed which is most holy, shall be anointed without measure. *"And that which is left ... it is a thing most holy of the offerings of the Lord made by fire."*[59] In the harvest of the earth which is coming, the most holy shall endure the fire and remain for the most holy gifts are the Lord's portion and they are those who are *"reserved from the fire, for every offering of theirs... which they shall render to Me, shall be most holy"* [60]

The most holy are reserved from the fire, for they are the Lord's portion. The fire which is coming will purify the people of God, but the remnant is already pure. They are the First Fruits of the Lord and need not be burned.

21

THE DAY OF THE LORD IS AT HAND

"And it shall come to pass, that in all the land, saith the Lord, two parts therein shall be cut off and die; but the third shall be left therein. And I will bring the third part through the fire, and will refine them as silver is refined, and will try them as gold is tried: they shall call on my name, and I will hear them: I will say, It is my people: and they shall say, The Lord is my God." [61]

The most holy place is the temple of the Lord, which he has built in the heart of the sanctified believer. The Song of Solomon presents a picture of the remnant, having been hidden in the wilderness, now coming forth leaning on Him; *"Who is this that cometh up from the wilderness, leaning upon her beloved?"* [62]

The Lord is their beloved, and they lean upon Him. They have no strength of their own, for their strength is in the Lord. The prophecy for the tribe of Benjamin is also a picture of the blessings upon the remnant: *"Of Benjamin he said, the beloved of the Lord shall dwell in safety by Him; and the Lord shall cover him all the day long, and he shall dwell between his shoulders."* [63]

And, behold, the glory of the God of Israel came from the way of the east: and his voice was like a noise of many waters: and the earth shined with his glory and I fell upon my face. The spirit took me up, and brought me into the inner court; and, behold, the glory of the Lord filled the house. And I heard him speaking unto me out of the house; and the man stood by me. And he said unto me, Son of man, the place of my throne, and the place of the soles of my feet, where I will dwell in the midst of the children of Israel forever, and my holy name, shall the house of Israel no more defile by their abominations that they have committed: wherefore I have consumed them in mine anger. Thou son of man, show the house to the house of Israel, that they may be ashamed of their iniquities: and let them measure the pattern. And if they be ashamed of all that they have done, show them the form of the house, and all the ordinances thereof ... and all the laws thereof and write it in their sight, that they may keep the whole form thereof, and all the ordinances thereof, and do them. This is the law of the house; upon the top of the mountain the whole limit thereof round about shall be most holy. Ezekiel 43:2-12

The Lord admonishes all believers to *"Watch ye therefore, and pray always, that ye may be accounted worthy to escape all these things that shall come to pass, and to stand before the Son of man."* [64]

The ones who are accounted worthy to stand and endure the hour of testing are the Most Holy of the Lord. They have sanctified their lives to the Lord, and they stand separated unto God.

HE SHALL CAUSE THE SACRIFICE TO CEASE

Jesus, as the Servant Messiah, confirmed His Father's covenant by keeping the law perfectly, and then dying as the Passover lamb for the sins of the world. Jesus came forth from the Father to confirm His covenant for one week. *"He shall confirm the covenant with many for one week: and in the midst of the week he shall cause the sacrifice and the oblation to cease."* [65] In the midst of the week, at the end of his first 3½ years of ministry, the Lord Jesus Christ gave His own life as the perfect sacrifice, and thereby did away with the need for the sacrificial system of the Old Covenant. *"Sacrifice and offering and burnt offerings and offering for sin thou wouldest not, neither hadst pleasure therein; which are offered by the law; Then said he, Lo, I come to do thy will, O God. He taketh away the first that he may establish the second. By which we are sanctified through the offering of the body of Jesus Christ once for all."* [66]

The prophecy also says because of *"the overspreading of abomination, he shall make it desolate... even until the consummation"*. [67] At the coming of Jesus Christ, the land was filled or *"overspread"* with abominations, and therefore it was made desolate until the *"consummation"* which means until the time of the end. After the death of our Lord the Romans came and stopped the temple sacrifice, destroying the temple and the nation, leaving the land desolate. The Romans also enacted a property tax shortly after the death of our Lord based on the number of trees on each property. The Jews, being shrewd tax planners, promptly cut down most of the trees, and thus the land became a desolate wilderness, and so the prophecy was fulfilled literally.

The phrase *"until the consummation"* also means that the land will remain desolate until the time of the end. Only after the return to the land, which began in the late 19th century, did the Jews began to replant the trees and restore the land. Israel will soon begin to rebuild the physical Temple of the Lord, and their first step will be to restart the daily sacrifice. While Israel begins to build the 3rd Temple, the Lord will also begin to build His 3rd temple, and to bring in the fullness of the 3rd day prophesied by Amos, for this Temple is built in the hearts of His people.

Today in Israel, the Orthodox Jews are preparing to rebuild the temple. The altar has been prepared, and the priesthood trained in the Levitical laws of sacrifice. All that remains is for the Jews to be given access to the Temple Mount.

Following World War III, Israel will take back the Temple Mount and the Orthodox will be given permission to cleanse the ground and restart the altar as the first step in rebuilding the Temple. Once the sacrifice is started, it will soon be stopped, and then the second half of the 70th week of Daniel will begin. The stopping of the altar on the Temple Mount and the subsequent setting up of the abomination of desolation will mark the beginning of the Great Tribulation. I will discuss the ministry of the Lord Jesus Christ during the second half of the 70th week in greater detail in the chapter entitled: *The Lord shall be the Hope of His people.*

THE OTHER PRINCE WHO IS COMING

In addition to revealing the timing of the first and second coming of Messiah, Daniel also reveals another prince shall come; *"and the people of the prince that shall come, shall destroy the city and the sanctuary"* [68] speaking of the Roman destruction of Jerusalem in 70 AD.

This is the antichrist, who I shall refer to as the little prince; he comes in his own name, rising out of the land which was at one time was part of the Roman Empire, and he makes his appearance to the world, taking his seat of authority as a *"prince"*. It is of this prince Jesus spoke saying, *"I am come in my Father's name, and ye receive me not: if another shall come in his own name, him ye will receive."*[69] Jesus Christ had come in his Father's name, and him the nation had rejected; another messiah would one day come in his own name, and him, the nation would receive.

CONFIRMATION OF THE OTHER COVENANT

The little prince will also confirm a *'covenant with the many'* for one week and in the midst of this seven-year confirmation, he too will stop the daily sacrifice on the Temple Mount and cause the oblation to cease. What is this covenant with the many? This covenant was made by Israel without the counsel of the Lord. It was made in the flesh, and the scripture calls it the *"covenant with death"* [70] because it was made with the sons of darkness, and will be confirmed by the antichrist. This covenant was also made with the *"many"*. Israel has already entered into this covenant. It is known as the Oslo Peace Accord and it was signed on the White House lawn in 1993. It too is a peace treaty with 'the many' and in the aftermath of World War III, the anti-Christ will be revealed before the nations by confirming the covenant of death; and then shall the final seven years of human history begin.

The Hebrew word for confirm is גבר, *gabar* which means to strengthen, or make stronger. Satan is still attempting to counterfeit all the works of true Messiah; thus, he creates his own covenant with Israel, and his false messiah also confirms this false covenant for seven years. The prophecy clearly states the little prince shall one day confirm a peace treaty, which Israel signed with her enemies. Some of the new Bible versions mistranslate this verse implying the little prince will make the covenant. That is not correct. He only confirms it; he makes it stronger, giving his seal of approval to it and his strength in supporting and enforcing it. Thus, the stage will be set, and the perfect counterfeit will be in place; as the true messiah begins to confirm again the true covenant of God, the little prince will also confirm the false covenant created by his father, the Devil. The second half of the 70th week will begin when the sacrifice is stopped by the little prince, and then the Great Tribulation will come as a snare upon all mankind. Both princes will then fulfill their covenants with Israel; the true Messiah, Jesus Christ, comes as the "*Lion of Judah*" to deliver His remnant and to judge the entire earth, while the little prince comes as the "*son of perdition*" [71] to cast the final deception upon the nations.

THE COVENANT WITH RABIN

On September 13, 1993, on the eve of Rosh Hashanah which begins the Civil New Year of Israel, for the first time in history, 3,000 witnesses gathered on the White House lawn to watch Yitzhak Rabin and Yasser Arafat sign what would be called the Peace and Security agreement. The western news media would announce to the world, "Today, on the White House lawn, 3,000 witnesses gathered to observe the signing of the most historic peace treaty in the history of mankind, for today, after nearly 4,000 years of conflict, the descendants of Isaac and Ishmael have made peace." [72]

Notice the name of the man who signed the treaty – Rabin; and the word for "*many*" in the Hebrew is רבים, *rabim*. Rabin's name is inferred within the prophecy itself! 3,000 is also the covenant number of God. When Moses received the law and came down from the mountain, and saw the children of Israel had made the golden calf, three thousand died in the ensuing judgment. "*And the children of Levi did to the word of Moses: and there fell of the people that day about three thousand men.*" [73] When the Holy Spirit fell on Pentecost, three thousand were saved as a sign the New Covenant had been accepted by the Lord. "*Then they that gladly received his word were baptized: and the same day there were added unto them about three thousand souls.*" [74]

The Lord uses the same covenant number of 3,000 to alert us that this is the final covenant spoken of by the Prophet Daniel. The covenant with the many, the covenant Israel initiates with hell itself, is the covenant with Rabin. The Lord also has given us other signs to witness we are at the door. The year 1997 was the 3,000th anniversary of Jerusalem. 3,000 years ago, David built an altar, on the threshing floor of Ornan, and thus Jerusalem became the capital of Israel. Today, the descendants of David are preparing another altar, which will usher in the time of the threshing floor for the nation, after Israel takes back the Temple Mount. Isaiah speaks of this covenant and the apostate leaders who would rule Israel in the last days: "*Wherefore hear the word of the Lord, ye scornful men that rule this people in Jerusalem. Because ye have said, We have made a covenant with death, and with hell are we at agreement; when the overflowing scourge shall pass through, it shall not come unto us: for we have made lies our refuge, and under falsehood have we hid ourselves."* [75]

Isaiah calls the leaders of modern apostate Israel *"scornful men"* for they reject the Word of God, and the promise God made to Abraham through which the Jewish people inherited the right to possess the land of Israel. God never gave actual ownership of the land to Israel, they are merely allowed to live there and they have no legal right to surrender the land of Israel to their enemies. *"The land shall not be sold forever: for the land is mine."* [76]

The Lord has never authorized signing a peace treaty with His enemies, or surrendering any part of the land. Isaiah calls the leaders of this apostate people who enter into such a treaty as *"scoffers"*, for they mock the word of the Lord promising the land of Israel to Abraham and his descendants forever. Rabbi Charlop wrote, "It is clear and simple that the Jewish People must never, Heaven forbid, cede any part of the Land. Any concession of a piece of land, whether large or small, that is blessed with the holiness of Eretz Yisrael, is considered a form of `denying a connection to the Land.' Anyone upon whom rests the name of Israel is forbidden to deny his Judaism or his connection to the Land of Israel. We learn from our forefathers, that for as long as Abraham thought to share the Land with Lot, God did not speak with him. We see clearly that it is forbidden to agree to cede even part of the Land and God is angered by this as if the entire Land was given over. I would like to point out that the ruling handed down by the Rabbis of Israel during the previous government that there is a clear prohibition to withdraw from any part of Eretz Yisrael is still true and valid today. In fact, this government is obligated even more to preserve the Land of Israel, and is forbidden to sign any document that means the handing over of parts of the Land. Furthermore, if such a document is signed, it has no validity. May Hashem preserve us and our Holy Land." [77] Amen!

Isaiah called the leaders of apostate Israel who entered into this agreement, scoffers. Prime Minister of Israel Yitzchak Rabin mocked the promises of God and was quoted as saying the Bible is not a grant deed for the land of Israel. These apostate leaders of Israel who signed the covenant of death all claimed they did not believe in Greater Israel, or God's promise to Abraham to give the land to the children of Israel in Genesis 12:7: *"And the Lord appeared unto Abram, and said, Unto thy seed will I give this land: and there built he an altar unto the Lord, who appeared unto him."*

On the day of Rabin's assassination, the Torah teaching for the Sabbath which began that evening was this very passage of Scripture establishing God's promise of the Abrahamic Covenant. This promise to Abraham and his seed is the foundation of the faith of the elect and the Lord does not tolerate those who mock His Holy Word.

This same promise is repeated in the law of the Lord, which was given to Israel before they entered into the land. We do well to heed this command!

> *You shall utterly destroy all the places where the nations whom you shall dispossess serve their gods, on the high mountains and on the hills and under every green tree. And you shall tear down their altars and smash their sacred pillars and burn their Asherim with fire, and you shall cut down the engraved images of their gods, and you shall obliterate their name from that place. You shall not act like this toward the Lord your God. But you shall seek the Lord at the place which the Lord your God shall choose from all your tribes, to establish His name there for His dwelling, and there you shall come. And there you shall bring your burnt offerings, your sacrifices, your tithes, the contribution of your hand ...and rejoice in all your undertakings in which the Lord your God has blessed you. You shall not do at all, what we are doing here today, every man doing whatever is right in his own eyes; for you have not as yet come to the resting place and the inheritance which the Lord your God is giving you. And you shall rejoice before the Lord your God, you and your sons, and daughters, be careful that you do not offer your burnt offerings in every cultic place you see, but in the place which the Lord chooses in one of your tribes, there you shall offer your burnt offerings, and there you shall do all that I command you.* [78]*

The Lord does not tolerate mixing paganism with the worship of the true God of Israel, and we shall see in this text, that the modern Christian church has embraced many pagan rituals in the worship of God. The Lord does not change. Paganism remains an abomination before our God, and the tribulation which is immediately ahead will cleanse the land of this wickedness! Both the idolaters and their idols shall be consumed in the fire which is coming!

THE COVENANT WITH DEATH

Shimon Peres in his book, *The New Middle East,* states the reason Israel entered into the Peace and Security Agreement is that they are tired of war. He continues saying we have signed this agreement "so that the overflowing scourge of war will pass us by." [79] His statements are almost an exact quote of the prophecy regarding the Covenant with death of Isaiah 28.

After the treaty was signed, terrorist bombs began to explode in Jerusalem; Shimon Peres went to the scene of the bombing of bus number 18, which was targeted twice. The crowds greeted him by shouting "You have signed a covenant with death" again quoting the very words the prophet Isaiah spoke concerning this false peace covenant.

27

It turns out that the name *"Peres"* פרס is also in the Bible. It was written by the hand of God upon the walls of Babylon 2,500 years earlier as the final word of judgment pronounced against the king of Babylon.[80] The name Peres means to split up or to divide, and is translated by the prophet Daniel as *"Thy kingdom is divided."* Shimon Peres was the architect of the peace plan through which Israel agreed to surrender her land for a mere promise of peace, thus dividing its kingdom. The name of the man responsible for this plan is Peres. The verdict: your kingdom is divided!

THE COVENANT WITH DEATH SHALL BE DISANNULLED

Isaiah continues saying *"your covenant with death will be disannulled, and your agreement with hell shall not stand"*. Isaiah reveals this treaty, which was signed with the forces of hell in the spiritual world, shall not stand. No, this covenant will not bring peace at all, for the other side of this covenant is war. A great war is coming and it will be called World War III before it is over! This is the war spoken of in Ezekiel 38. Isaiah goes on to say that the critics of this agreement would complain *"The bed is too short on which to stretch out, and the blanket is too small to wrap oneself in."*[81] The treaty would be deemed inadequate; it wouldn't solve the conflict or bring peace, for it was signed with the father of lies. After Rabin was assassinated in 1995, the leaders of the world gathered in Jerusalem at his funeral service. "Each speaker called for the confirming of the Middle East peace accord so that the life of Rabin would not be in vain. They literally called for an agreement with his grave to continue the peace process. We watched as the world leaders came and confirmed the Middle East peace process. Standing in the front row of Rabin's funeral among the world leaders was a prince of the Roman empire." [82]

Jerusalem and the Middle East peace process had now been moved onto the center stage of world politics. The death of Rabin gave new meaning to the prophecy regarding the covenant with death. The covenant with the many, the covenant with Rabin, now truly had become a 'covenant with the grave.'

The Lord gives a final warning admonishing you: do not mock this prophecy, unless you want the bands which bind you to be made stronger! The prophet also tells us the timing of this prophecy, for it refers to events at the end of the age, for at that time the Lord will bring His judgment upon the entire earth!

> *Your covenant with death shall be annulled, and your agreement with hell shall not stand. For the Lord shall rise up as in mount Perazim, he shall be wroth as in the valley of Gibeon, that he may do his work, his strange work; and bring to pass his act, his strange act. Now therefore be ye not mockers, lest your bands be made strong: for I have heard from the Lord God of hosts a consumption, even determined upon the whole earth.* [83]

The Lord describes His judgment as a *"consumption"* כָּלָה, *kaw-law* [84] which means a complete destruction, to be utterly consumed, a determined full and utter end! The Lord has determined a complete *"consumption"* shall come in the whole land! And will you not fear Him? Indeed, in the days ahead all flesh shall learn the fear of my Lord!

> *For though thy people Israel, be as the sand of the sea, yet a remnant of them shall return: the consumption decreed shall overflow with righteousness. For the Lord God of hosts shall make a consumption, even determined, in the midst of all the land.* [85]

THE WAR OF EZEKIEL 38

The covenant with death will be cancelled by war; the war of Ezekiel 38. In chapter 37, the prophet is shown a valley full of dry bones. This is a picture of the whole house of Israel, having been destroyed as a nation; they lay scattered among the gentile peoples as dry bones. *"Then he said unto me, Son of man, these bones are the whole house of Israel: behold, they say, our bones are dried, and our hope is lost... Thus saith the Lord God; Behold, O my people, I will open your graves, and cause you to come up out of your graves, and bring you into the land of Israel and shall put my spirit in you, and ye shall live, and I shall place you in your own land: then shall ye know that I the Lord have spoken it, and performed it."* [86]

Following the destruction of Jerusalem in 70 AD, the people were cast out of the land, and the Israelites wandered among the nations as outcasts for two thousand years, until the end of times came, and then we were brought to the place of total desolation, in the death camps of the Nazis; it was there, in the midst of the Shoah, that the children of Israel cried out from the bottom of their hearts and from the depths of total despair saying "our hope is lost".

Most Americans cannot comprehend what it means to have lost all hope. We Israelis have known this all too well. God then begins speaking to these bones for they are yet His people, and though the Lord judged the nation Israel for rejecting His truth, He has never forsaken us, and we remain his people. In the last days, God promised to restore His chosen nation to their own land a second time. As Newton declared - let time be the interpreter.

> *Thus saith the Lord God; Behold, I will take the children of Israel from among the heathen, whether they be God, and will gather them on every side, and bring them into their own land: And I will make them one nation in the land upon the mountains of Israel ...I will save them out of all their dwelling places, wherein they have sinned, and will cleanse them: so shall they be my people, and I will be their God. I will make a covenant of peace with them; it shall be an everlasting covenant with them: and I*

will set my sanctuary in the midst of them for evermore. My tabernacle also shall be with them: yea, I will be their God, and they shall be my people. Ezekiel 37:21-28

Ezekiel continues prophesying that after Israel is restored to the land, then the Lord will call forth from the north a great nation from the land of Magog with many allies. This prophecy speaks to the ancient peoples who lived in the land that is now Russia, and at the time of the end, they shall come along with Persia, Ethiopia and Libya, and many nations against the mountains of Israel, *"which have always been waste."* This desolation lasted two thousand years until the land began to be restored. The prophet speaks of the Great War, in which the land of Israel is overrun like a storm, saying *"thou shalt come into the land that is brought back from the sword."* The land of Israel first fell under the sword of the Romans, now in the last days, another great army will attack Israel; it is described as a *"storm"* and it *"shall be like a cloud to cover the land."*

In the next war Israel will be overrun, her enemies will cover the land like a cloud, and then the Lord will arise to defend his people and redeem his land.

And the word of the Lord came unto me, saying, Son of man, set thy face against Gog, the land of Magog, and prophesy against him. Thus saith the Lord God; Behold, I am against thee, O Gog, And I will turn thee back, and put hooks into thy jaws, and I will bring thee forth, and all thine army, horses and horsemen, all of them clothed with all sorts of armor, Persia, Ethiopia, and Libya with them and many people with thee... in the latter years thou shalt come into the land that is brought back from the sword, and is gathered out of many people, against the mountains of Israel, which have been always waste: but it is brought forth out of the nations, and they shall dwell safely all of them. Thou shalt ascend and come like a storm, thou shalt be like a cloud to cover the land, thou, and all thy bands, and many people with thee. Ezekiel 38:1-9

Do not fear Israel, though these great armies shall come against you, the Lord himself shall defend you! The God of Israel says at that time, *"My fury shall come up in my face!"* and *"in my jealousy and in the fire of my wrath"* the Almighty God will respond and fight Israel's enemies Himself! Then there shall be a great shaking in the land of Israel! The Almighty One is going to literally shake the entire nation when He strikes His enemies with the rod of His wrath. The Lord describes the sword, which He will call forth against the enemies of Israel.

This sword will rain upon them with an overflowing rain of fire and brimstone! And great hailstones shall fall to the earth and the ground itself shall shake for the wrath of the Lord, which is poured out. This prophecy describes the thermonuclear weapons, which Israel will use as its last line of defense. This is a literal prophecy. The *"great hailstones"* which shall fall are the byproduct of an atmospheric detonation. The intense heat of a nuclear weapon causes huge hailstones to form, and then fall from the sky. The ground will shake as well, when the enemies of Israel fall upon the mountains, under the fire of the wrath of God!

> *And it shall come to pass at the same time when Gog shall come against the land of Israel, saith the Lord God that my fury shall come up in my face. For in my jealousy and in the fire of my wrath have I spoken, surely in that day there shall be a great shaking in the land of Israel; and I will call for a sword against him throughout all my mountains, saith the Lord God: every man's sword shall be against his brother. And I will plead against him with pestilence and with blood; and I will rain upon him, and upon his bands, and upon the many people that are with him, an overflowing rain, and great hailstones, fire, and brimstone. Thus will I magnify myself, and sanctify myself; and I will be known in the eyes of many nations, and they shall know that I am the Lord. Ezekiel 38:18-23*

THE NEXT MIDDLE EAST WAR

The following quotes are from Jeffrey Nyquist's writings: "Dr. Hugh Cort, author of *The American Hiroshima: Iran's Plan for an Attack on the United States* stated 'Deterrence will not work with the fanatical Islamic radicals that rule Iran. These rulers are like suicide bombers, who do not care if they die, as long as their victims get blown up as well. Radical Islam is not afraid to use nuclear weapons against America', explains Dr. Cort: The top newspaper in Iran, Kayhan, supervised by Supreme Leader Khamenei, said 'If Iran is attacked, there are elements in America who will detonate nuclear bombs in American cities.'"

"Cort says the Islamic Republic has created the 'Jerusalem Force'; one of Iran's most secret paramilitary organizations tasked with intelligence operations related to targeting the United States for nuclear and biological weapons. Some of the Jerusalem Force agents have been working undercover in the United States for more than a decade. 'There is a strong possibility,' says Dr. Cort, 'that Iran's American Hiroshima will not only be a nuclear attack, but a chemical, biological, and involve assault troops.... In addition, there may also be an EMP attack. Iran has chemical weapons, and there is evidence Iran has biological weapons as well, including anthrax.' The smuggling of WMDs into the United States is not original to Iran. During the Cold War, the Soviet KGB and GRU invented the whole idea."

"During the 1970's and 80's the Soviets prepared ways of smuggling nuclear and biological weapons into the United States. In 1998 Russian Colonel

THE DAY OF THE LORD IS AT HAND

Stanislav Lunev, himself a defector to the west, explained that the chosen routes for smuggling WMDs into the U.S. would be those used by narcotics traffickers. Curiously, GRU defector Viktor Suvorov says (in his book *Spetsnaz*) that the Soviets conceived of organizing something they called 'Gray Terror' in which the United States would be attacked by terrorists with no traceable connection to Moscow. These terrorists would be 'mercenaries recruited by intermediaries' wrote Suvorov, explaining that this terrorism would divert the intelligence and military resources of the West away from Russia, paving the way for successful Russian moves."

"There is a great difference, however, between Iranian nuclear strategy and Russian nuclear strategy. Unlike the Iranians, the Russians thoroughly understand the principle of winning a nuclear war. Their idea is simple, and elegant. It is unwise to openly engage in a nuclear war with a nuclear power. Only a covert nuclear attack promises safety for the attacker. If nuclear bombs are detonated against American cities, it's best if the Americans cannot identify the attacking country. Better yet, if the Americans misidentify the attacking country."

Following the events of September 11th, the first phase of the next world war began as the President of the United States formally declared war on an ideology which he called 'terrorism'. For the first time in history, a nation declared war on an idea. Shortly thereafter, the U.S. invaded Afghanistan and then Iraq. Both of these military occupations continue (albeit the Iraq occupation is now through corporate mercenary forces) and the press is now filled with rumors of war, ISIS, Ukraine, Syria, Iraq, Iran, even the possibility of war with Russia or China is now being discussed in the main stream news.

The entire Middle East has been destabilized, and the nations of the world are now mobilizing for the next world war. The Arab Spring has brought radicalization across the region. Russian forces are now engaged in the Syrian civil war, while Iran moves ever closer to acquiring nuclear weapons. Hezbollah terrorists are amassing weapons on Israel's northern border from Iran while Hamas has seized control of the Gaza strip on Israel's southern border. American military assets are positioned throughout the region in preparation for an expanded war with Iran which has already begun with the proxy war now being fought in Syria, a key ally of Iran. Russia has invaded the Ukraine and the fuse to world war is now lit on the shores of the Black Sea. While the nations all prepare for war, the world also stands on the edge of a financial abyss. These wars now being waged in the Middle-East are the early chapters, or the precursor of World War III. U.S. aggression in the wars of Iraq and Afghanistan was called by the Lord "the Beast Wars", for the forces of antichrist have been manipulating American foreign policy from behind the scenes and using the U.S. to set the stage for World War III.

Take Heed That No Man Deceive You

The first events to occur in the book of Revelation, before the rise of the antichrist, are pictured in the breaking of the first four seals of the scroll. When the first seal is broken, a rider on a White Horse goes forth conquering and to conquer. This first horseman is pictured in 'white' wearing a crown, for he is perceived by the world as a force for good, and as fighting for peace and democracy.

Thus, he wears a crown, for the world views him as having legitimate authority to lead the nations. The rider on the white horse was viewed as the only 'good' superpower during much of its 70-year reign over the nations. But now, in truth, he brings only war, for he has become a mere puppet for the powers of darkness which have overrun and taken control of this once proud land. And the nation, which has now become an empire of lies, pictured by a white horse, is very easy to identify, for it is led by a president who also lives in a White House.

In the coming world war, both Israel and the United States will be attacked by an alliance of nations, and US foreign policy is leading America down this road to ruin. Amazingly the American public, and much of the American church, actually supports this madness. Under the guise of promoting democracy in these countries, the actions of the United States are hardening the resolve of the enemies of the West while depleting the military resources of the US. This fact is obvious when you examine the military balance of power, yet the American people scarcely seem to notice, and for the most part couldn't care less.

In late 2004, an expert on American foreign policy from one of the Ivy League think tanks spoke to a large group of intelligent Americans. He spoke at great length how the U.S. policy of creating a democratic government in Iraq was doomed to failure, concluding that the leadership that promoted such madness must be either mentally impaired or insane. The majority of the listening audience concurred and offered their opinion of how foolish and ignorant the Bush administration must be to pursue such an obviously doomed agenda.

No one in the room even stopped to consider that the true purpose has been carefully hidden from the public eye, veiled within lies and deceptions, while the wars in Iraq and Afghanistan were actually pursuing another agenda. This agenda was designed in hell, and is built upon lies and deceit, for the purpose of bringing the world to the brink of destruction, and ordering the events of history in order to allow the coming judgment upon America and to open the door for the antichrist to rise to power and to seize the throne of a one world government. As of this writing, American forces have formally evacuated Iraq while the internal civil war continues to deteriorate. The early hopes for an American victory and the successful creation of a pro-western democracy in Iraq faded into the realization that U.S. forces were trapped in the middle of a Shite-Sunni civil war. Iran, Syria, Al Qaeda and other Arab nations have all entered into the conflict either directly or by proxy. U.S. hopes of bringing democracy the Middle East are gone. American military forces in Iraq have been replaced by corporate mercenaries while the American government continues to spin the defeat of American foreign policy as a victory. At the same time, the war in Afghanistan is a stalemate with the withdrawal of American forces looming in the near future. This too was one more defeat for the U.S. Unfortunately; the enemies of the United States consider an American defeat a certainty.

The Arabs and particularly the leaders themselves, who once dreaded American military might, and its outreach and ability to punish them on the eve of the invasion of Iraq, fear the United States no more. The inability to cope with the insurrection has been eye-opening for the Islamists and pro-American rulers alike. The former are now encouraged and emboldened to take on the United States and its allies, and the latter are fearful that the U.S. would not be able to save them in their hour of need. Therefore, erstwhile U.S. allies now seek compromise with the Islamists and Jihadists threatening them, thus assisting the anti-American forces. [92]

The news continues to reveal evidence of the gathering storm, which as dark clouds now cover the horizon but only those with an ear to hear can hear the thunder of God's prophetic word as he speaks audibly to his remnant warning them: *"Summer is coming soon: tell the people to clean their houses."* Summer represents the time of God's judgment, and is referenced in many places relative to the prophecy of the coming of the judgment of God and the harvest of the wheat; the word in Hebrew means the reaping, or cutting or the time of the reaper.

> *And he said, Amos, what seest thou? And I said, a basket of summer fruit. Then said the Lord unto me, the end is come upon my people of Israel; I will not again pass by them anymore."*[93] *"Now learn a parable of the fig tree; when her branch is yet tender, and puts forth leaves, ye know that summer is near."*[94] *"Then was the iron, the clay, the brass, the silver, and the gold, broken to pieces together, and became like the chaff of the summer threshing floors; and the wind carried them away.* [95]

After this Great War, the Lord will no longer hide His face from Israel. From that point forward, God says they shall know that He is the Lord.

JERUSALEM THE STUMBLING BLOCK OF THE NATIONS

The Peace and Security Agreement is silent on the subject of the city of Jerusalem. The architects did not even attempt to negotiate the Holy city. They knew they would never get an agreement on Jerusalem; their strategy was to leave Jerusalem out of the peace process in hope that the parties would be so committed, that Jerusalem could be negotiated at the end. This strategy is doomed to fail. The Lord tells us, after the covenant with death is cancelled by the war, He will then rise up as in mount Perazim and He will be "wroth." [96]

> *For the Lord shall rise up as in mount Perazim, he shall be wroth as in the valley of Gibeon, that he may do his work, his strange work; and bring to pass his act, his strange act.* [97]

The Lord will then begin to *"do his work"*, which He calls *"His strange work"*, and *"to bring to pass His act, His strange act."* The strange work of the Lord is the judgment of God, which begins with the next war. God refers to His judgment, as *"His strange act"* for the Lord takes no joy in the judgment of the wicked.

It also appears as *"a strange act"* to the people of God, who in spite of the many warnings, will be taken completely off guard, and surprised when the judgment falls. The prophet Zechariah speaks of the city of Jerusalem, which in the last days will become a stumbling block to all the nations. Jerusalem is to become a burden for all peoples, and all who attempt to come against Jerusalem shall be destroyed. This prophecy is already being fulfilled, as the nations of the world are all focused on the question of Jerusalem. The UN itself has spent the majority of its energies attempting to deal with the problem of Jerusalem as over a third of the UN Security Council actions deal with Israel.

The Lord proclaims *"though all the people of the earth be gathered together against Jerusalem"* [98] in that day the Lord himself will fight for His people. He will then open the eyes of Judah, while smiting all of Israel's enemies with blindness.

> *Behold, I will make Jerusalem a cup of trembling... and in that day will make Jerusalem a burdensome stone for all people: all that burden themselves with it shall be cut in pieces, though all the people of the earth be gathered together against it. In that day, saith the Lord, I will smite every horse with astonishment, and his rider with madness: and I will open mine eyes upon the house of Judah, and will smite every horse of the people with blindness. Zechariah 12:2-4*

The Lord declares in that day, He will defend Jerusalem Himself. And those that are feeble among His people shall be as valiant as David, and the house of David shall be as God, and as the angel of the Lord before them. The Lord himself will destroy these nations which have gathered together to come against Israel and to capture Jerusalem.

THE DAY OF THE LORD IS AT HAND

In that day shall the Lord defend the inhabitants of Jerusalem; and he that is feeble among them at that day shall be as David; and the house of David shall be as God, as the angel of the Lord before them. And it shall come to pass in that day, that I will seek to destroy all the nations that come against Jerusalem. Zechariah 12:8-9

The Lord then will pour out His spirit upon my brethren in Israel, and they shall see the light of the Lord. Their eyes will be opened and they will recognize Yeshua whom we call Jesus is Messiah, and they will know it was Him who they pierced. And everyone will mourn for their sin, and for the Lord whom they rejected. But the Lord, who is so rich in His great mercy, will pour out His spirit of healing. A fountain of the Holy Spirit will open for my brethren in Israel, and they will weep, and cast down on their faces before the Lord. And He will have compassion on them, as a Father who has found His lost son whom He feared was dead. Oh there shall be such mourning, followed by such great rejoicing, when the remnant of Israel is turned again unto the Lord.

And I will pour upon the house of David, and upon the inhabitants of Jerusalem, the spirit of grace and of supplications: and they shall look upon me whom they have pierced, and they shall mourn for him, as one mourns for his only son, and shall be in bitterness for him, as one that is in bitterness for his firstborn." [99] `In that day there shall be a fountain opened to the house of David and to the inhabitants of Jerusalem for sin and for uncleanness and one shall say unto him, What are these wounds in thine hands? Then he shall answer those with which I was wounded in the house of my friends. [100]

Following the next war, Israel will take back the Temple Mount, and the Orthodox Jews will set up an altar and begin again the daily sacrifice. Thus the stage will be set for the Great Tribulation to begin. The true Messiah, the Lord Jesus Christ, who is the KING of Kings and the LORD of Lords, will then begin to fulfill the second half of His seven-year ministry upon the earth. He will once again confirm the covenant which His Father made with Israel, only now He will come as the LION OF JUDAH and as THE JUDGE OF THE ENTIRE EARTH. To those whose robes are white, and who walk before Him in holiness and truth, having repented of their sin and having been washed in His blood which He shed as the Lamb of God, He comes now as the MIGHTY DELIVERER!

To those who have rejected His truth and despised His grace, He comes with the full fury of the wrath of God! And to the backsliders within the corrupt church of Laodicea, He comes with a fire to purify and to cleanse, for the wedding feast is about to begin, and each of the guests must put on a robe of white. If we refuse to repent, and to cleanse our hearts by the washing of His word, if we are truly His, then He will do this work in us Himself by FIRE! And the little prince, he is just a small bit player, who is only reading his lines, and he has only a small part in the story of the Revelation of JESUS CHRIST, THE SON OF THE MOST HIGH GOD, THE HOLY ONE OF ISRAEL. BARUCH HASHEM! AMEN!

Fear GOD, and give glory unto him; for the hour of his judgment is come: and worship him that made heaven, and earth, and the sea, and the fountains of waters. Revelation 14:7

THE DAY OF THE LORD IS AT HAND

CHAPTER

2

THEY THAT UNDERSTAND AMONG THE PEOPLE SHALL INSTRUCT MANY

Daniel 11:33

The book of Daniel contains many prophecies in the form of visions and dreams revealing the events of the end of the age, and the kingdoms which would come to power preceding the second coming of the Lord. Much of the book is in symbolic form and requires interpretation. Daniel himself inquired of the angel what would be the fulfillment of the visions that he saw. *"I heard, but I understood not, then said I, O my Lord, what shall be the end of these things? And he said go thy way, Daniel: for the words are closed up and sealed till the time of the end."*[1]

THE BOOK IS SEALED UNTIL THE TIME OF THE END

The angel responds to Daniel, telling him the prophecies contained in his visions are to be sealed until the time of the end, and that no further explanation would be given. It is little wonder that men of God who labored to read this sealed book over the many centuries of the church age failed to discern the true meaning for the book of Daniel had been sealed, and its true meaning has been kept secret until the time of the end. Only now has the book been opened by the Lord, and its true meaning finally revealed. The prophet Isaiah speaks of the Lord sealing up prophecy saying:

And the vision of all is become unto you as the words of a book that is sealed, which men deliver to one that is learned, saying, Read this, I pray thee: and he saith, I cannot; for it is sealed: And the book is delivered to him that is not learned, saying, Read this, I pray thee: and he saith, I am not learned. Wherefore the Lord said, For as much as this people draw near me with their mouth, and with their lips do honor me, but have removed their heart far from me, and their fear toward me is taught by the precept of men: Therefore, behold, I will proceed to do a marvelous work among this people, even a marvelous work and a wonder: for the wisdom of their wise men shall perish, and the understanding of their prudent men shall be hid. [2]

THE DAY OF THE LORD IS AT HAND

The Lord declares in the word that He turns His face away from His people because of their sins.

> *The vision is become as a book that is sealed... for this people draw near me with their mouth ... but have removed their heart far from me, and their fear toward me is taught by men. Isaiah 29:11-13*

Such was also the case in the time of Samuel the prophet *"And the child Samuel ministered unto the Lord before Eli. And the word of the Lord was precious in those days; there was no open vision."*[3] The Lord had sealed up vision, and closed the meaning of the prophetic writings because of the great sin of the people. Today, our nation and people are under the same curse, for the land is full of wickedness, and there is no open vision, and most Christians can no longer even bear to hear the word of the Lord. The people also cannot see their signs, either in the heavens or the earth, in which the fulfillment of theses prophecies is occurring right before their eyes, yet they cannot see, for their eyes are blinded. *"We do not see our signs; there is no longer any prophet, nor is there any among us who knows how long."* [4] Yet God always preserves a remnant, and this handful of remnant saints can still hear and receive the word of the Lord! How awesome is our God!

MEN OF WISDOM SHALL COME

This is the hour which has been appointed for the books to be unsealed, and for the men of wisdom to be revealed who shall raise their voices in the wilderness declaring to the whole world: "Make straight the way of the Lord, for the Day of the Lord is at hand!" When the prophecy teachers speak about the end times, they all miss one sign: the scripture reveals that in the last days, men of insight will come and give understanding to the many and they will be known as the Men of Wisdom.

These chosen ones have been prepared by God himself. Until now they have been hidden away, like David and his mighty men in the cave at Adullam. *"And he hath made my mouth like a sharp sword; in the shadow of his hand hath he hid me."*[5] These anointed messengers have walked the same path as Joseph, who waited in prison until the day that his word came to pass. The life of Joseph was filled with suffering and sorrow until the appointed time for his rising among the people. Joseph first had to be purged with fire before the Lord would use him. Rejection and repudiation, hatred and jealousy, false accusation and abandonment – these were all used by the Lord to purify Joseph for the hour of his ministry to the people.

The men of wisdom, whom the Lord is now raising up, have walked the same path. This must be, for whenever God chooses to use a man, He first must empty him. The fires endured by these broken ones have been intense for the Lord has prepared them *"by the spirit of judgment, and by the spirit of burning."*[6] Out of these flames, the Lord has forged a people for Himself with a faith made of steel. In their mouths, He has placed a sharpened swift sword. They shall teach the people the truth, and shall cast down the altars of Ba'al!

The secret things belong to the Lord, and therefore only God can reveal them. They have been hidden as a parable, or as a grain of corn buried in the ground. The word for parable in Hebrew is משל, *mashal*, which means a superior mental ability or deep insight, or a proverb, but the word also means to have dominion as a governor, to reign or to cause to rule. Joseph had superior knowledge into all dreams and visions, and through his insights, he was promoted as ruler over all of Egypt.

The men of wisdom, whom the Lord is now raising up, have insight and deep understanding into the hidden things of God. They also shall be given the power to rule by the Lord, for these men of wisdom are the Joseph company of this hour, and after they unveil the hidden and secret things of the Lord, from among them shall come forth those who have been appointed as rulers over the household of God in the final days ahead.

> *And they that understand among the people shall instruct many: yet they shall fall by the sword, and by flame, by captivity, and by spoil, many days. Now when they shall fall, they shall be helped with a little help: but many shall cleave to them with flatteries. And some of them of understanding shall fall, to try them, and to purge, and to make them white, even to the time of the end: because it is yet for a time appointed. Daniel 11:33-35*

Why haven't the prophecy teachers told us to look for the men of wisdom? And where would you expect them to be found? The anointed messengers of the Lord will be found in the wilderness, even as John the Baptist came before the first coming of the Lord. Isaiah speaks of these messengers and where they will be found:

THE VOICES IN THE WILDERNESS CRY OUT

> *The voice of him that cries in the wilderness, prepare ye the way of the Lord, make straight in the desert a highway for our God. Every valley shall be exalted, and every mountain and hill shall be made low: and the crooked shall be made straight and the rough places plain: And the glory of the Lord shall be revealed, and all flesh shall see it together: for the mouth of the Lord hath spoken it. Isaiah 40:3-5*

THE DAY OF THE LORD IS AT HAND

On the eve of the first coming of the Messiah, His messenger was found in the wilderness before his showing to the common people. His father, Zacharias prophesied of John:

> *And thou, child, shall be called the prophet of the Highest: for thou shall go before the face of the Lord to prepare His ways; To give knowledge of salvation unto His people by the remission of their sins, through the tender mercy of our God; whereby the dayspring from on high has visited us, to give light to them that sit in darkness and in the shadow of death, to guide our feet into the way of peace. And the child grew, and waxed strong in spirit, and was in the deserts till the day of his showing unto Israel. Luke 1:76-80*

John was not sent to speak to the religious leaders who ruled the people in their own wisdom, and who had rejected the truth of God. John was sent instead to the poor, the sinners and the outcasts. Jesus spoke of John and revealed that he fulfilled the prophecy of Isaiah 40: *"Jesus began to say unto the multitudes concerning John, what went ye out into the wilderness to see? A reed shaken with the wind? But what went ye out for to see? A prophet? yea, I say unto you, and more than a prophet. For this is he, of whom it is written, Behold, I send my messenger before thy face, which shall prepare thy way before thee. Verily I say unto you, among them that are born of women there hath not risen a greater than John the Baptist: ... For all the prophets and the law prophesied until John. And if ye will receive it, this is Elias, which was to come."*

IF YOU WILL RECEIVE IT - THIS IS ELIJAH WHO IS TO COME

The Lord reveals a mystery - John the Baptist fulfilled the prophecy of the coming of Elijah in the Spirit. Elijah was the greatest prophet in the history of Israel, and he appeared suddenly, in one of the nation's darkest hours. Israel had fallen into terrible apostasy, and a great evil had assumed the throne. King Ahab ruled under the dominance of the wicked Queen Jezebel and their iniquity covered the land like a cloud. While false prophets proclaimed the doctrines of Ba'al, the people had forgotten the Lord Jehovah ruled Israel. It was in this, the darkest hour in the history of the nation that Elijah suddenly appeared out of the wilderness. In Malachi, the Lord promises to send Elijah again before the Great and Awesome Day of the Lord.

> *For, behold, the day cometh, that shall burn as an oven; and all the proud, yea, and all that do wickedly, shall be stubble: and the day that cometh shall burn them up, saith the Lord of hosts, that it shall leave them neither root nor branch. But unto you that fear my name shall the Sun of righteousness arise with healing in his wings; and ye shall go forth, and grow up as calves of the stall. And ye shall tread down the wicked; for they shall be ashes under the soles of your feet in the day that I shall do*

42

this, saith the Lord of hosts. Remember the Law of Moses my servant, which I commanded unto him in Horeb for all Israel, with the statutes and judgments. Behold, I will send you Elijah the prophet before the coming of the great and dreadful day of the Lord: And he shall turn the heart of the fathers to the children, and the heart of the children to their fathers, lest I come and smite the earth with a curse. Malachi 4:1-6

ELIJAH MUST COME AGAIN

This prophecy in Malachi will be fulfilled again, before the Second Coming of the Lord, when he comes to judge the earth with fire! We are instructed in this prophecy to "remember the Law of Moses." Why does the Lord remind the people to remember the law? Because in the last days, a great apostasy would come, and the people will have forsaken the word of God, turning the grace of God given to them through Jesus, into a license for willful sin. God promises that he will send Elijah the prophet once again, before in the Great and Dreadful Day of the Lord. Jesus referred to this prophecy, and told us that John fulfilled this word in his first coming. Yet this prophecy reveals Elijah will yet appear again, a second time, before the Second Coming at the beginning of the Great and Dreadful Day of the LORD.

Dear reader, know and understand, the events of the First Coming parallel the Second Coming. Elijah, or the one who comes in his office and anointing, shall also suddenly appear before the Great and Awesome Day of the Lord. The land will again be found covered in deep darkness while the people of God will have again turned from the truth. The false prophets of Ba'al will again spin their webs of deception, and the throne will be ruled by a weak king like Ahab under the dominance of a wicked woman like Jezebel. Such is the present hour, and Elijah is about to come forth suddenly, as if out of the wilderness. He will burst forth from outside of the organized religious institutions of our day, for many of them have fallen under the influence of Ba'al. We are told of only one interaction that John had with the religious leaders, when they came out to see him. His response was direct and to the point:

> *But when he saw many of the Pharisees and Sadducees come to his baptism, he said unto them, O generation of vipers, who hath warned you to flee from the wrath to come? Bring forth therefore fruits meet for repentance: And think not to say within yourselves, We have Abraham to our father: for I say unto you, that God is able of these stones to raise up children unto Abraham. And now also the axe is laid unto the root of the trees: therefore every tree, which brings not forth good fruit, is hewn down, and cast into the fire. Matthew 3:7-10*

THE DAY OF THE LORD IS AT HAND

The messengers of the Second Coming are the Men of Wisdom and they are about to suddenly appear coming out from the wilderness. They will be rejected by the religious leaders and sent instead to the poor, and the outcasts, who will hear the true words of God. It will not be just one voice this time. No, before the Second Coming, many men will come forth and raise their voices proclaiming the Day of the Lord is at hand!

These men of understanding among the people *"shall instruct many."* They will share their revelation knowledge which they have received from the Lord with many others. It will be their passion, for the word of God will burn within these men. Yet we are also told that the men of understanding will be tested, and that they will fall and when they fall, they will be helped with a little help, and many will join them with flatteries or hypocrisy.

HERE IS THE MIND WHICH HAS WISDOM

What signs do we have that we can use to identify the men of wisdom, who have the true understanding of the Scripture? How will we discern their voice and message from all the other voices, which will be speaking at the time of the end?

It has been the practice of kings to test their wise men with riddles, for this was the proof that they were indeed men of wisdom. Our Lord uses the same test, providing riddles in Scripture as prophetic mysteries, by which we may know and discern that those who can answer the riddle truthfully have the mind of wisdom. This wisdom is not of human knowledge, or higher learning, though the men of understanding whom God calls may possess both. The mind of wisdom spoken of in the Scripture is one to whom the secret mysteries of God have been revealed by the Spirit of God. These mysteries are not discovered, nor are they reasoned with the mind of man, but they are revealed by God to whomever he chooses to reveal them. As Daniel exclaims:

> *"Blessed be the name of God for ever and ever; for wisdom and might are his, and he changes the times and the seasons ... he removes kings, and sets up kings; he gives wisdom to the wise, he reveals the secret things, for he alone knows what is in the darkness."* [8]

Scripture gives us specific tests we can use to identify the men of understanding who have the mind of wisdom. First, everything they speak and teach will confirm and be consistent with both the whole counsel of the Word of God, which is Holy Scripture and the testimony of His prophets. *"To the law and to the testimony: if they speak not according to this word, it is because there is no light in them."* [9]

Second, they are able to count the number of the beast, and identify the antichrist before he is revealed to the world. *"And I stood upon the sand of the sea, and saw a beast rise up out of the sea ... the beast which I saw was like unto a leopard, and his feet were as the feet of a bear, and his mouth as the mouth of a lion: and the dragon gave him his power, and his seat, and great authority... Here is wisdom. Let him that has understanding count the number of the beast. - for it is the number of a man and his number is Six hundred threescore and six." Revelation 13*

Third, the men of wisdom are also able to solve the riddle of the woman Mystery Babylon and the beast on which she rides as spoken in Revelation: *"I saw a woman sit upon a scarlet colored beast, full of names of blasphemy, having seven heads and ten horns. And the woman was arrayed in purple and scarlet color, and decked with gold and precious stones and pearls, having a golden cup in her hand full of abominations and filthiness of her fornication. And upon her forehead was a name written, MYSTERY, BABYLON THE GREAT, THE MOTHER OF HARLOTS AND ABOMINATIONS OF THE EARTH... here is the mind which has wisdom."* [11]

Each of the above tests will be answered in the chapter entitled *"Here is the Mind which has Wisdom"* to prove to you, dear reader, this message is indeed from men of God.

THE DREAM OF THE KING OF BABYLON

The center piece of Bible prophecy are the writings of Daniel. They provide us our first glimpse into the events at the end of the age. The first of these is the dream given to King Nebuchadnezzar which greatly troubles him. He then asks the wise men of his kingdom to tell him both the dream and its interpretation. None of the magicians could answer the king in this matter so the king became enraged, and ordered all the wise men of the kingdom to be killed. Daniel, whose life was now at risk, sought the Lord for the revelation of the king's dream and God answered him in a night vision. In thanksgiving, Daniel declares the sovereignty of the Lord, for the Lord alone changes times and seasons, removes and establishes kings, gives wisdom unto the wise, and He alone reveals the deep and secret things.

> *When the secret was revealed unto Daniel in a night vision, then Daniel blessed the God of heaven. Daniel answered and said, Blessed be the name of God for ever and ever: for wisdom and might are his: And he changes the times and the seasons: he removes kings, and sets up kings: he gives wisdom unto the wise, and knowledge to them that know understanding: He reveals the deep and secret things: he knows what is in the darkness, and the light dwells with him. Daniel 2:19-22*

THE DAY OF THE LORD IS AT HAND

Daniel then answers the king giving the glory in this matter to the Lord, and declaring that the God in heaven alone revealed this secret. The king's dream reveals that which will come in the latter days. Daniel wasn't given the meaning and the interpretation of the dream for any wisdom that was in him, for it was the Lord who revealed the matter. Even as the Lord showed Daniel the king's dream, it is the Lord who unsealed the prophetic writings in this last hour.

> *Daniel answered in the presence of the king, and said, The secret which the king hath demanded cannot the wise men, the astrologers, the magicians, the soothsayers, shew unto the king; But there is a God in heaven that reveals secrets, and makes known to the king what shall be in the latter days... But as for me, this secret is not revealed to me for any wisdom that I have more than any living, but for their sakes that shall make known the interpretation to the king, and that thou might know the thoughts of thy heart. Daniel 2:27-30*

Daniel then makes known the king's dream declaring it before all:

> *Thou, O king, saw and behold a great image. This great image, whose brightness was excellent, stood before thee; and the form thereof was terrible. This image's head was of fine gold, his breast and his arms of silver, his belly and his thighs of brass, His legs of iron, his feet part of iron and part of clay. Thou saw till that a stone was cut out without hands, which smote the image upon his feet ... and the image became like the chaff of the summer threshing floors; and the wind carried them away... and the stone that smote the image became a great mountain, and filled the whole earth. Daniel 2:30-35*

After making known the king's dream, Daniel then gives the interpretation:

> *Thou, O king... Thou art this head of gold. And after thee shall arise another kingdom inferior to thee, and another third kingdom of brass, And the fourth kingdom shall be strong as iron: forasmuch as iron breaks in pieces and subdues all things: and as iron that breaks all these, shall it break in pieces and bruise. And whereas thou saw the feet and toes, part of potters' clay, and part of iron, the kingdom shall be divided; And so the kingdom shall be partly strong, and partly broken. And whereas thou saw iron mixed with miry clay, they shall mingle themselves with the seed of men: but they shall not cleave one to another, and in the days of these kings shall the God of heaven set up a kingdom, which shall never be destroyed ... Then king Nebuchadnezzar fell upon his face... The king answered unto Daniel, and said, of a truth it is, that your God is a God of gods, and a Lord of kings, and a revealer of secrets, seeing thou could reveal this secret. Daniel 2:36-4.*

46

THE IMAGE OF MYSTERY BABYLON THE GREAT

The image of the king's dream represents the ruling kingdoms of the earth from that time until the First Coming of the Messiah. Nebuchadnezzar, the king of Babylon, is the head of Gold and ancient Babylon is the first kingdom. Next, Media Persia would come to power represented by the silver arms. Third, Greece under Alexander the Great would conquer and rule the earth represented by the thighs of brass. Finally, Rome would come pictured as the legs of Iron. These four empires preceded the first coming of the Lord. Lastly, we are shown that Rome, after its collapse, would be divided into ten kingdoms, portrayed by the ten toes mixed with iron and clay. Thus, the vision of this great statue is our first clue to the prophetic revelation of the end of the age, and the identification of Mystery Babylon.

When we look at a statue, we discern its identity from its face. We don't think to ask whose toes are those. Once you identify a statue by its face, you know the name for the whole body. The statue of the king's dream is the image of Mystery Babylon the Great, the ruling kingdoms of the earth. Each of the successive kingdoms, which would rule after ancient Babylon are part of Mystery Babylon. The image of the king's dream represents the kingdom of Satan, which would rule over the earth in diverse times and places.

This is why the identity of Mystery Babylon has confused so many. Her true identity has been hidden, while her name and place of authority change throughout time. Only through the revelation of the Spirit, can those with the mind of wisdom discern her true identity. I will speak much more on the dimensions of Mystery Babylon in subsequent chapters, but for the moment let me summarize by stating Babylon was both a kingdom, or a political power, and a religion in its first manifestation. Nebuchadnezzar was both king and god to the citizens of ancient Babylon. In its future forms, we will see that Mystery Babylon divides itself into a separation of church and state depicted by the two legs of iron. The false religion of Babylon has continued from that time until the present with its identity hidden from the people, for the great deceiver comes as an angel of light.

One of the principles of Bible prophecy is dualism, where prophecy is fulfilled twice. This principle is revealed in Job 33:14 "For God speaks once, yes twice, *yet man* perceives it not." This principle was revealed by Joseph interpreting the Pharaoh's dream, *"The dream was doubled unto Pharaoh twice; it is because the thing is established by God, and God will shortly bring it to pass."*[12]

The coming of the Messiah is an example. God promised to send a messiah, while the Israelites looked for the Lord to fulfill all of the prophecies in his first coming, not realizing He would come twice, first as the Lamb of God, while His ministry as the mighty deliverer would await his second coming.

THE DAY OF THE LORD IS AT HAND

The fact that the modern church is making the same mistakes as the nation of Israel 2,000 years ago is another such dualism. The Lord sending His messengers speaking in the wilderness to the poor is a third. The fact that only a remnant recognized His first coming is also being repeated. Joseph, Mary, Simeon, Anna and a handful of others recognized the time of the first coming of the Lord.

> *There was a man in Jerusalem whose name was Simeon ...and it was revealed unto him by the Holy Ghost, that he should not see death, before he had seen the Lord's Christ... There was one Anna, a prophetess,... she served God with fasting and prayers night and day...And she coming in that instant gave thanks likewise unto the Lord, and spoke of him to all them. Luke 2:25-39*

Today, on the eve of the Second Coming, a small remnant has also been shown the day of the Lord is at hand. In Daniel's prophecies we find further examples of this dualism.

THE FOUR KINGDOMS WHICH PRECEDE
THE RETURN OF THE LORD

In chapter seven, Daniel receives a vision of four kingdoms, which would rise to power on the earth prior to the Second Coming of the Lord. These will parallel the first four kingdoms of the king's dream in amazing ways.

> *Daniel spoke and said, I saw in my vision by night, and, behold, the four winds of the heaven strove upon the great sea. And four great beasts came up from the sea, diverse one from another. The first was like a lion, and had eagle's wings: I beheld till the wings thereof were plucked, and it was lifted up from the earth, and made stand upon the feet as a man, and a man's heart was given to it. And behold another beast, a second, like to a bear. and it raised up itself on one side, and it had three ribs in the mouth of it between the teeth of it: and they said thus unto it, Arise, devour much flesh. After this I beheld, and lo another, like a leopard, which had upon the back of it four wings of a fowl; the beast had also four heads: and dominion was given to it. After this I saw in the night visions, and behold a fourth beast, dreadful and terrible, and strong exceedingly; and it had great iron teeth: it devoured and brake in pieces, and stamped the residue with the feet of it: and it was diverse from all the beasts that were before it; and it had ten horns. I considered the horns, and, behold, there came up among them another little horn, before whom there were three of the first horns plucked up by the roots: and, behold, in this horn were eyes like the eyes of man, and a mouth speaking great things. Daniel 7:2-8*

THE LION WITH WINGS OF AN EAGLE
BRITAIN AND AMERICA

The first kingdom is presented as a Lion with Eagles wings. This is England and her colonies in America. England is pictured as a Lion and the House of Windsor, the Royal family of England, presents the Heraldic Beast as its symbol; it has the head of a lion, the body of a leopard, and the feet of a bear. This is the exact picture of the beast as revealed in Revelation 13 and America, the eagle, came forth out of the Lion, which is England. Thus, in perfect prophetic parallel to the statue of Mystery Babylon in the king's dream, England and her daughter, America are in the position of modern Babylon, the head of gold. Both England and Ancient Babylon were known for the splendor and majesty of their Royalty and both empires also had kings who went insane while in power. Historians recorded the insanity of members of the British Monarchy including the well-known madness of King George III. [18] The story of the madness of Nebuchadnezzar is contained in Daniel.

> *The same hour was the thing fulfilled upon Nebuchadnezzar: and he was driven from men, and did eat grass as oxen, and his body was wet with the dew of heaven, till his hairs were grown like eagles' feathers, and his nails like birds' claws. And at the end of the days I Nebuchadnezzar lifted up mine eyes unto heaven, and mine understanding returned unto me, and I blessed the most High, and I praised and honored him that lives forever, whose dominion is an everlasting dominion, and his kingdom is from generation to generation: And all the inhabitants of the earth are reputed as nothing: and he doeth according to his will in the army of heaven, and among the inhabitants of the earth: and none can stay his hand, or say unto him, What doest thou? Daniel 4:33-35*

THE BEAR DEVOURING MUCH FLESH - COMMUNIST RUSSIA

The second kingdom is likened unto a Bear and represents Russia with its counterpart Media Persia. This beast is told to arise and devour much flesh, and so the Communist Empire has been the bloodiest in terms of murder. It is interesting that Media Persia came to power in an alliance of two peoples, while the Soviet revolution was led by two men Trotsky and Lenin, representing Russian and Ukraine. Adding to the parallel, the communists killed the royal family during the revolution. According to historians, when the Medes and Persians seized power, they executed the royal family of Belshazzar. The Media Persia Empire endured the rule of seven kings, and then fell to Alexander's armies. Michael Gorbachev was the seventh Premier of the Soviet Union at the time of its collapse. [14]

THE LEOPARD WITH FOUR HEADS - NAZI GERMANY

Next, we see the Leopard, Nazi Germany, and its parallel of Ancient Greece under Alexander. Historians recount how Alexander conquered the world in record time and ruled for twelve years. In the modern era, the Nazi Blitzkrieg or lightening war is a similar fulfillment. Another striking parallel, Hitler came to power in 1933 and also ruled for twelve years.[15] We are told in the prophecy that the leopard had four heads, and when the horn of Greece was broken, four heads came to power for when Greece fell, four kings divided the kingdom.

> *Therefore the he goat waxed very great: and when he was strong, the great horn was broken; and from it came up four notable ones toward the four winds of heaven and the rough goat is the king of Greece: and the great horn that is between his eyes is the first king. Now that being broken, whereas four stood up for it, four kingdoms shall stand up out of the nation, but not in his power. Daniel 8:10, 21-22*

In perfect parallel fulfillment, when Nazi Germany fell, the allies divided Germany into four districts, ruled by four kings, the Americans, British, French and Russians. After a time, the four kingdoms, which succeeded Greece, organized into two - one in the east and the other in the west. The kingdom in the west ultimately dominated and subdued the Eastern Empire in the rise to power of ancient Rome. This foreshadows the birth of the final antichrist kingdom in the west. In the modern era, the four-part division of Germany was also organized into two kingdoms - of east and west. The US led NATO alliance rose to power in the west, while Russia and its Warsaw Pact subdued the eastern half. In exact parallel fulfillment, the eastern half collapsed with the fall of the Berlin wall in 1989.

Now the empires of the world will be subdued by the fourth beast, which is the New World Order of the United Nations. This final empire has been given birth in, and modeled after, the United States of America.

THE FALL OF ROME AND THE DESTRUCTION OF AMERICA

The parallels between ancient Rome and modern America are also very real. Both empires were symbolized by an Eagle and both were republics with an elected body of representatives called the Senate. When Rome conquered its subject states, it allowed them to maintain regional autonomy under the dominion of Rome. The United States, in its leadership of the western democracies, dominates its allies in similar fashion. The United Nations, modeled after the US, when brought to full power, will continue the same format. The nations of the world will have rights and autonomy similar to the states of America, while the central government of the United Nations will retain absolute sovereignty in whatever area it chooses. The evolution of the Roman government from a democratic republic to a fascist state of despotic tyranny will also repeat itself as the New World Order comes to power. Rome fell from within; its demise the result of the hedonism and the immorality of its people. America too is crumbling from within; and the moral decline of the leaders of our nation is now the subject of the tabloid papers. Rome lost her freedoms and the Emperor became a despot in its final days.

America too, is about to lose her freedom under the weight of Executive Orders, and the tyranny of UN domination. After her collapse, Rome divided into ten regional powers, signified by the ten toes. The emergency plans under Federal Emergency Management Agency (FEMA) call for the division of government in time of national crisis into ten FEMA regions. The collapse of the Roman Empire resulted in the division of power described as ten toes and in the last days; these toes will give birth literally to the ten kings of the Beast Empire. The parallel fulfillment is that out of the destruction of America, the UN will assume full global power and bring about the rule of the antichrist. The United Nations has already divided the earth into ten regional power blocs with North America as number one. The United States is also a type of Israel. Israel was created by God under the Old Covenant to bring the Messiah into the world. America was raised up by the Lord under the New Covenant, to share the truth of the Messiah with the world. Israel was destroyed as a nation during the reign of her 42nd king. [16] President George W. Bush was the 42nd individual to serve as President of the United States of America. One can argue that the America we all knew and loved, along with any semblance of truth in the public discourse was destroyed during his term, and the usurper who followed Bush was not even a lawful occupant of the office wherein he sat.

The ten toes of the collapsed Roman Empire are described as a mixture of clay and iron. We are told *"they shall mingle themselves with the seed of men"*. [17] This reference foretells the strategy of the ten kings to use intermarriage to consolidate their power. The reference to the toes as a mixture of clay and iron also speaks of the demonic nature of this group. Clay is used to describe mankind in scripture, while the iron speaks of the dark spiritual powers. Many historians recount the arranged marriages among the ruling class of Europe, where the wealthiest families of the earth have been engaging in intermarriage for hundreds of years. The LA Times writes of one such family "The Hapsburgs are keeping up the age-old family tradition of strategic marriage." [18] These are the descendants of the rulers of the collapsed Roman Empire. These rulers will give birth to the ten kings of the beast who will be literally born into this group of families. This small group, who call themselves the Elite, formed an alliance, which they call The Order of the

Illuminati through which they will create the final One World Government of Lucifer.

THE SECRET ORDER OF THE ILLUMINATI

The Order of the Illuminati has remained unseen for centuries, only recently beginning to allow press about itself. The Economist magazine published one of the few articles ever written about the Order entitled "The Good Network Guide" in December 1992. It discussed the various secret societies of the world, ranking them in terms of power, secrecy and exclusivity. The article covered The Skull and Bones fraternity, The Communist Party, The Trilateral Commission, and Freemasonry among others. Each of these groups was formed by, and is controlled by the Order of the Illuminati. The last organization discussed was the Order of the Illuminati itself, which was given the highest ranking in all categories:

"Beyond all these networks lies the mother of all networks, the Order of the Illuminati, known to some as the True Rulers of the World Though this secret body has hovered unseen over all history, its most public flowering was in the Enlightenment. Adam Wieshaupt, a former Jesuit revealed its purpose and system of mutual surveillance to the world on May 1st, 1776. Since then the order has taken a keen interest in another newborn of that year. It is significant that many American presidents have been Illuminati; some have been killed by the Illuminati; and the Illuminati symbol of the eye in the pyramid still graces the dollar bill. The conspiracy is immense and terrifying. It is the network of those who run networks. Given its power, you should assume that anyone writing about the order must be lying or part of a conspiracy to confound you. In wondering about the Illuminati, merely remember this. You have never arrived." [19]

This Order is the league made with the antichrist. These are the Luciferians, who serve the prince of the air of the present age. The seal of the Great Pyramid on the dollar bill is their symbol, which reads "Annui Coeptis" and "Novus Ordo Seclorum". The translation from Latin means "Announcing the Birth of the New World Order." This is the New World Order of the beast, and the government of the US is the model for this Order, a union of independent states under a supreme central government. The model has now been extended to the world with the formation of the United Nations, and after the next world crisis, engineered by the Order; the UN will be brought to full global power.

Press stories on the Illuminati are rare. One of the few stories to be published in recent years states: "Many of the world's power brokers and power seekers will wind their way up a narrow, avalanche prone Alpine valley in the remote eastern resort of Davos this week for six days of deal-making, deep thinking and fun. Headliners at this year's World Economic Forum, which opens Thursday, include Microsoft billionaire Bill Gates, U.S. House Speaker Newt Gingrich, top Russians and, as usual, key players from the Middle East. The group of Illuminati, including top scientists and experts in a range of fields will have their pick of a bewildering array of meetings." [20]

And after the league made with him, he shall work deceitfully: for he shall come up, and shall become strong with a small people. He shall enter peaceably even upon the fattest places of the province; and he shall do that which his fathers have not done, nor his fathers' fathers. Daniel 11:23-24

The ten horns of the beast are the rulers who consolidate the power of the UN, and then give it unto the beast. I will discuss what the Order plans to do to the daughter of Babylon, America, as they bring their New World Order to full power in the chapter entitled *"Babylon the Great is Fallen, Fallen."* The motto of this group is "Ordo Ab Chao" which means "Order out of Chaos". The beast will soon create a world crisis, to compel the nations of the earth to surrender their sovereignty to the UN in order to preserve the "Peace and Security" of the planet.

This is how the prince enters *"peaceably"* and takes the throne by *"intrigue"* and *"deception."* He is doing the work of his father, the father of lies, and there is no truth in him. *"And the ten horns which thou sawest are ten kings, which have received no kingdom as yet; but receive power as kings one hour with the beast. These have one mind, and shall give their power and strength unto the beast." Revelation 17:12-13*

THE NEW WORLD ORDER OF THE LION, THE BEAR AND THE LEOPARD

In Revelation chapter 13 the apostle John sees the same Beast Empire in a vision: *"And I stood upon the sand of the sea, and saw a beast rise up out of the sea, having seven heads and ten horns, and upon his horns ten crowns, and upon his heads the name of blasphemy. And the beast which I saw was like unto a leopard, and his feet were as the feet of a bear, and his mouth as the mouth of a lion: and the dragon gave him his power, and his seat, and great authority." Revelation 13:1-2*

The beast John witnesses rising up from the sea is comprised of the Lion, the Leopard and the Bear and it also has ten horns, but now seven heads are apparent and the Eagles wings are missing. It is also one beast, now united in power, which it receives from the dragon. This is the fourth beast witnessed by Daniel, which evolves out of the ten toes of the ruined Roman Empire and comes to power out of an alliance of the English, German and Russian nations. America is no longer in the prophetic picture, for she has been judged and destroyed immediately before the beast empire comes to power.

> *"The first was like a lion, and had eagle's wings: I beheld till the wings thereof were plucked, and it was lifted up from the earth, and made stand upon the feet as a man, and a man's heart was given to it."* [21]

After the eagle's wings are plucked from the Lion, which is symbolic of the destruction of America in WW3, the Lion will be lifted up above the earth. This symbolizes the rising of the antichrist kingdom, as the Lion will be the head of the final beast empire. The dominion and seat of authority of the final antichrist empire will reside in England. The antichrist is pictured as a Lion, for he will come out of the Royal Family of England. The Lion also is symbolic of the false Messiah who comes to conquer the earth as a counterfeit of the true Messiah, who is the Lion from the tribe of Judah.

The Lion is then made to stand upon its feet as a man, and a man's heart is given to it. The antichrist is the heart of a man given to the Lion. He is the *"king of fierce countenance"* who *"understanding dark sentences, shall stand up."*[22] We are told *"his power shall be mighty, but not by his own power"*[23] for the antichrist will rule in the power of the dragon *"and his mouth as the mouth of a lion... the dragon gave him his power, and his seat, and great authority."* [24]

The prophecy that the Lion will be mighty, but not of his own power is also fulfilled by the Lions use of the Eagles wings. Over the years when using its wings, it appeared as an Eagle, as it used the power of America to be mighty. Now endued with the power of the dragon, the Lion destroys the Eagle, and then is lifted up rising to power over the entire earth!

> *And in the latter time of their kingdom, when the transgressors are come to the full, a king of fierce countenance, and understanding dark sentences, shall stand up. And his power shall be mighty, but not by his own power: and he shall destroy wonderfully, and shall prosper, and practice, and shall destroy the mighty and the holy people ... and by peace shall destroy many: he shall also stand up against the Prince of princes; but he shall be broken. Daniel 8:23-25*

AND BY PEACE HE SHALL DESTROY MANY

We are told that *"by peace shall he destroy many."* [25] This is the mission of the United Nations, to preserve peace and security, and it is by peace that the final beast empire comes to power and *"he shall destroy wonderfully"* [26] The destruction that he brings will be incredible, fantastic. Note also he destroys two people groups, *"and he shall destroy the mighty and the holy people."* [27]

The term *"people"* refers to nations. First, he destroys the mighty nation, the one remaining super power at the time of his ascension to the throne. Then he turns to destroy the holy people. This speaks of the final judgment on

America, the mighty people, and then the persecution of the saints of the Most High. Daniel is then shown that during the reign of the last World Empire, the King of Kings will come and establish His kingdom upon the earth, which shall be an everlasting kingdom.

> *I beheld till the thrones were cast down, and the Ancient of hair of his head like the pure wool: his throne was like the fiery flame, and his wheels as burning fire. A fiery stream issued and came forth from before him: thousand thousands ministered unto him, and ten thousand times ten thousand stood before him: the judgment was set, and the books were opened I saw in the night visions, and, behold, one like the Son of man came with the clouds of heaven and came to the Ancient of days, and they brought him near before him. And there was given him dominion, and glory, and a kingdom, that all people, nations, and languages, should serve him: his dominion is an everlasting dominion which shall not pass away, and his kingdom that which shall not be destroyed. Daniel 7:9-15*

Daniel then is told the meaning of the vision of the fourth beast.

> *These great beasts, which are four, are four kings, which shall arise out of the earth... The fourth beast shall be the fourth kingdom upon earth, which shall be diverse from all kingdoms, and shall devour the whole earth, and shall tread it down, and break it in pieces. And the ten horns out of this kingdom are ten kings that shall arise: and another shall rise after them; and he shall be diverse from the first, and he shall subdue three kings. And he shall speak great words against the most High, and shall wear out the saints of the most High, and think to change times and laws: and they shall be given into his hand until a time and times and the dividing of time Daniel 7:17-25*

THE ONE WORLD GOVERNMENT
OF THE UNITED NATIONS

The fourth beast will be diverse, and different from all the others. The final world government comes to power by an alliance of nations through treaties. The United Nations is the fourth beast. The UN is unlike any other world empire, for it comes to power by deception, promising peace and security. The ten horns are ten kings who will rule this beast system in its short time upon the earth, and the antichrist, the little horn, subdues or overthrows three of them in his rise to power. He then makes war with the saints of the Most High, and prevails against them.

"And he shall speak great words against the Most High, and shall wear out the saints of the Most High." [28] He wears them out in slave labor camps in which the believers will be persecuted. His changes of times and laws speaks of his

55

violation of the covenant of God and the stopping of the altar sacrifice on the Temple Mount.

We are told the saints of the Most High are given into his hand *"they shall be given into his hand until a time and times and the dividing of time"*.[29] The time and times and a dividing of a time is the 3 ½ years that the prince rules the beast empire. The apostle John also speaks of this period of rule:

> *And there was given unto him a mouth speaking great things and blasphemies; and power was given unto him to continue forty and two months. And he opened his mouth in blasphemy against God, to blaspheme his name, and his tabernacle, and them that dwell in heaven. And it was given unto him to make war with the saints, and to overcome them: and power was given him over all kindreds, and tongues, and nations. And all that dwell upon the earth shall worship him, whose names are not written in the book of life of the Lamb slain from the foundation of the world. If any man have an ear, let him hear. He that leadeth into captivity shall go into captivity: he that kills with the sword must be killed with the sword. Here is the patience and the faith of the saints." Revelation 13:5-10*

THE ANTICHRIST - THE OTHER LION WHO IS COMING

The Lion is given a mouth, the mouth of the man of sin, and power for 42 months, which is 3 ½ years. It is given to him to make war with the saints, and to overcome them. We are also told, whoever leads others into captivity, must also go into captivity. This is the reason why saints are chosen to go into captivity under the beast. They have led others into captivity by their lifestyle of idolatry and by the dark counsel of their words without knowledge. Dear reader, if your lifestyle includes idolatry in any form, or if your counsel is formed within the darkness of this present evil age, you are leading others into captivity by your example. If you do not repent of this sin now, you will go into captivity with the many.

Daniel is given a further vision of these kingdoms in chapter eight. The goat refers to Greece, and the four notable ones speak of the division of Alexander's empire into four parts. Then the vision takes us to the time of the end, when the little horn, the antichrist comes to power. We are told that he, the prince, will magnify himself, and lift himself up after he takes away the daily sacrifice. The stopping of the daily sacrifice marks the beginning of the second half of the 70th week of Daniel's prophecy.

Thus, begins his reign of terror upon the earth for a time, times and half a time. We are then given a clue to the timing of the events during the Great

They That Understand Among The People Shall Instruct Many

Tribulation, for from the day that the sacrifice stops, which marks the beginning of the final 3½ years, there shall be 2,300 evenings and mornings. The original text reads ערב *erev* and בקר *boqer*, which literally means evenings and mornings. Thus, from the day that the daily sacrifice is taken away, there shall be 2,300 evenings and mornings, or 1,150 days. These count the number of missed sacrifices, which were required at both evening and morning.

> *And I saw in a vision; and it came to pass, when I saw, that I was at Shushan in the palace, which is in the province of Elam; and I saw in a vision, and I was by the river of Ulai. Daniel 8:2*

> *Therefore the he goat waxed very great: and when he was strong, the great horn was broken; and from it came up four notable ones toward the four winds of heaven. And out of one of them came forth a little horn... And it waxed great, even to the host of heaven; and it cast down some of the host and of the stars to the ground, and stamped upon them. Yea, he magnified himself even to the prince of the host, and by him the daily sacrifice was taken away, and it cast down the truth to the ground: and it practised, and prospered. Then I heard one saint speaking, and another saint said unto that certain saint which spake, How long shall be the vision concerning the daily sacrifice, and the transgression of desolation, to give both the sanctuary and the host to be trodden under foot? And he said unto me, Unto two thousand and three hundred days (evenings and mornings); then shall the sanctuary be cleansed. Daniel 8:8-14*

Daniel is then given the explanation of the vision. He is told that the vision is of the time of the end of the world. The angel then explains that the ram is the kingdom of Media and Persia and that the goat is the king of Greece. At the time of the end, out of one of the four kingdoms, which rose out of the empire of Greece, another king will come. This king will arise when the transgressors have come to full power. This king, who is the prince who shall come, will have a fierce countenance, and he will understand dark sentences. These dark sentences speak of the occult nature of the prince's power and these dark words are of evil.

> *And I heard a man's voice... Gabriel, make this man to understand the vision ... he said unto me, Understand, O son of man: for at the time of the end shall be the vision... Behold, I will make thee know what shall be in the last end of the indignation: for at the time appointed the end shall be. The ram which thou sawest having two horns are the kings of Media and Persia. And the rough goat is the king of Greece: and the great horn that is between his eyes is the first king. Now that being broken, whereas four stood up for it, four kingdoms shall stand up out of the nation, but not in his power. And in the latter time of their kingdom, when the transgressors are come to the full, a king of fierce countenance, and understanding dark*

sentences, shall stand up. And his power shall be mighty, but not by his own power: and he shall destroy wonderfully, and shall prosper, and practice, and shall destroy the mighty and the holy people and by peace shall destroy many.   Daniel 8:16-25

At the end of the prophecy, Daniel is told to go his way, for the book shall be sealed until the time of the end. The wicked shall continue in wickedness, and none of the wicked shall understand these things, but the wise shall understand and from the abomination of desolation, which is the image of the beast in the holy place, there shall be 1,290 days and blessed are they who wait for and see the 1,335th day.

And he said go thy way, Daniel: for the words are closed up and sealed till the time of the end. Many shall be purified, and made white, and tried; but the wicked shall do wickedly: and none of the wicked shall understand; but the wise shall understand. And from the time that the daily sacrifice shall be taken away, and the abomination that makes desolate set up, there shall be a thousand two hundred and ninety days. Daniel 12:9-11

THE TIMING OF THE GREAT TRIBULATION

The Great Tribulation shall last for 3 ½ years, and it shall be a time of trouble such as never was. The Scripture provides numerous timelines for the events of the tribulation. The following table illustrates how these days fit together.

From the stopping of the altar there are 2,300 evenings and mornings or 1,150 days. From the abomination being set up there shall be 1,290 days. In Revelation we are told there is period of five months when the earth is covered in darkness. Here is the meaning of this matter. From the day the altar stops there are 1,150 days of sunlight, then 150 days of darkness for a total of 1,300 days. The image of the beast is erected 10 days after the altar stops, which gives us the total of 1,290 days from when the abomination is erected on the holy place.

And the fifth angel sounded, and I saw a star fall from heaven unto the earth: and to him was given the key of the bottomless pit. And he opened the bottomless pit; and there arose a smoke out of the pit, as the smoke of a great furnace; and the sun and the air were darkened by reason of the smoke of the pit. And there came out of the smoke locusts upon the earth: and unto them was given power, as the scorpions of the earth have power. And it was commanded them that they should not hurt the grass of the earth, neither any green thing, neither any tree; but only those men which have not the seal of God in their heads. Revelation 9:1-4.

They That Understand Among The People Shall Instruct Many

The rising of the one world government of the antichrist shall occur by the spring of 2018, after which the final 3 ½ years which is known as the time of the Great Tribulation shall begin. The time of the Great Tribulation period can be presented as follows:

Total time from beginning of the sign of the altar stopping:

[------------------------- 1,300 days --]

Stopping of the Altar for 2,300 evening and mornings:

[--------------- 1,150 days ---------------]

Days of Darkness at the end:

[-----5 months or 150 days---]

Time from setting up the abomination of desolation:

[------------------------ 1,290 days -------------------------------]

Time between the altar stopping and the abomination being set up:

[10 days]

He that hath an ear let him hear what the Spirit saith unto the churches; He that overcomes shall not be hurt of the second death. Revelation 2:11

THE DAY OF THE LORD IS AT HAND

CHAPTER
3
THEN THE WORD OF THE LORD CAME UNTO ME
Jeremiah 1:4

The Lord declares in his word that he will do nothing without first revealing the matter to his servants the prophets. God always reveals what he is about to do, through those individuals who can hear his voice. He calls them his servants, the prophets.

> *Surely the Lord God will do nothing, but he revealeth his secret unto his servants the prophets. The lion hath roared, who will not fear? the Lord God hath spoken, who can but prophesy?* [1]

The Lord always choses prophets from among the people to bring the final warning before the sword of judgment falls in the land. The prophets of God were ordinary men, whom the Lord called from among the common people. The Lord does not call great men, nor does he call the wealthy, or those who are wise in their own eyes. The Lord says he looks unto the humble and those with a broken and contrite heart.

The appointment of a prophet is of the Lord alone. Many men have appointed themselves leaders in the Church, but no man can appoint himself a prophet before God. The modern Church tends to revere the prophets of old, yet they were simple men whom the Lord called and gifted with an ear to hear his voice. Their ministry was to simply tell the people, those things which God had said.

I AM NEITHER A PROPHET NOR A PROPHET'S SON

Amos was such a prophet; he speaks of his calling saying: *"I was no prophet, neither was I a prophet's son; but I was a herdsman, and a gatherer of sycamore fruit."* [2] Amos was a simple farm worker. Would we listen today if the Lord called a migrant farm worker as a prophet? What if the man He called was a tax collector? Many within the modern Church believe the Lord no longer calls prophets to declare his word to the people. They assume this must be true because they themselves have never heard the voice of the Lord. How foolish of these men! This is not true, and it is not what the Scriptures teach. They have created this doctrine from their experience. Truly the Scripture declares they *"have walked after the imagination of their own heart."*[3] Paul writing to the Ephesians teaches the five-fold ministry of the church includes *"he gave some, apostles; and some, prophets; and some, evangelists; and some, pastors and teachers."* [4] The Church doesn't believe the Lord has forsaken the ministry of the pastor or teachers? Why then would the Lord forsake the ministry of his prophets?

In many of today's churches the pastor has been exalted to a position of authority and of a teacher, while the other offices are all missing and this is not the Biblical model. In this last hour, the Lord is restoring the five-fold ministry to the true Church. Prophecy has not ended with the writings of the New Testament, and the Lord still speaks to His people. The modern Church has been deceived in so many ways. There are two prophets coming at the time of the end. They are the two witnesses, who shall prophesy against the nations for 1,260 days, and then they will be martyred. The ministry of prophecy obviously continues to the very end of the age. Remember Daniel prophesied that men with wisdom who understood these things would come and give insight to the many. In order to understand these mysteries, you must hear from God.

And when the Lord speaks to you, who can but prophesy? I have been able to hear the audible voice of the Lord from my youth. I was surprised when I learned that the majority of Christians have never heard His voice. From my earliest experience as a believer, hearing the voice of the Lord was a normal part of my daily walk of faith. I will share with you three instances, not to lift myself up, but to confirm to you, dear reader, I am a man who hears from God. These words also contain a prophetic message for you as well.

I ONLY WANTED TO MOVE YOU

In 1977, the Lord spoke to me one morning saying, "I want you to go to the evangelism conference in San Diego but do not seek directions, for I will lead you as you drive your car." I obeyed the Lord and when the day came, I began to drive to San Diego. I said to the Lord, "I am on the freeway now, and all I know is to drive to San Diego and you promised to direct me. Lord, please don't let me get lost." The Lord answered immediately, but He didn't mention the directions, "I have cancelled your hotel reservation..." Then He paused and I said nothing. The Lord continued, "And they have given your room away." Again, He paused as if waiting for me to respond, but I would not answer, "And the hotel is full." That was all. My reservation cancelled, my room gone, and the hotel full. I didn't know what to say, so I looked up to heaven and said, "What do you want me to do, sleep in my car?" He spoke again, "When you get to the hotel, don't get upset, just sit in the lobby and wait for me. I will get you a room. I only wanted to move you." When I got to the hotel, the manager and the desk clerk were very upset. I had a confirmed reservation, and they had a full hotel. I told them, "Don't worry; I am sure you will find me a room. I'll just sit in the lobby and wait."

After forty minutes, they called me up to the desk, and told me they had a cancellation, and they were giving me an executive suite at no additional cost. A man was standing there who overheard this, and said: "I don't want to have a roommate. Can I have the suite and you take the double occupancy room?" In my heart I prayed, "Lord?" "Trade with him." So I took the roommate, and that night after the Friday evening service, I asked him and two other people if they wanted to go upstairs to pray.

We started praying at 10 pm, and after what seemed like only five minutes of prayer, I looked at my watch, and it was 7 am. I told everyone, "its 7 am, does anyone know what just happened to us?" None of us had a clue, but we had to get ready for the new day. That night as the service ended, I asked them, "Does everyone want to go and pray again?" Oh, yes, we all wanted to go and see if we could figure out what had happened to us, so we gathered to pray on the second night. As we prayed, the Lord began to speak audibly to all of us; we all heard him with our ears. He also began to pour out the anointing of the Holy Spirit with such power, and it just kept growing and growing, stronger all through the night. By 4 am, my hands were burning as if on fire. They began to really hurt, and I felt like I was beginning to burn in a real fire. I cried out to the Lord saying "Lord, you're scaring me. My hands are burning and you are hurting me." Jesus answered audibly: "You never thought you would have to pray for that, now did you?" Then the Lord began to laugh! I heard Jesus laugh. Then he reached down from Heaven and grabbed my hands with his hands. I held the hands of the Lord Jesus Christ that day, or more precisely, he held my hands, and then the pain stopped, and the fire didn't burn me anymore.

The next day, in the Sunday morning service, the Lord began to do many miracles. Each time, as God moved in power, I felt the Holy Spirit erupt from within me with fountains of living water. As I went forward for prayer, the elders said to me: "Receive from Jesus Christ, for Jesus has given you everything."

After the service a prophet walked up to me and said: "You will be sent to the Kings of the earth, and to the rich and powerful, to convert them and their wealth to the kingdom of God."

THE DAY OF THE LORD IS AT HAND

A MAN WHO I HAVE BEEN CHASING FOR MANY YEARS

After the conference, I began to drive home with my roommate. His name was Kevin, and I was taking him to a hotel in Anaheim. As we were driving on the freeway, people in other cars slowed down alongside of us, and began to honk, and roll down their windows.

They were weeping and shouting at us. I rolled down my window, to hear them, and they shouted, "Who are you? Who are you?" I turned to Kevin, and said "Kevin, who are we?" "I don't know!" This happened five or six times. We never did answer the people, because we didn't know what to say.

The Lord then began to speak audibly to both of us. "I want you to pray that I remove my anointing from you, for I am sending you back to my church, and they cannot receive you in my presence." I was not really excited about this commandment, but we obeyed the Lord, and then we felt seven waves of the Holy Spirit lift off of us. We knew the anointing had lifted, but we were not aware an afterglow remained. Half way to the hotel, I stopped for gas. As I stepped out of the car, all of the people in the service station began to weep, and repent, and they knelt down on the concrete, and began to cry out to the Lord for mercy. I never uttered a word.

As we continued driving, the Lord began to speak again in an audible voice. "When you get to the hotel in Anaheim, a man who I have been chasing for many years will crash into your car in the parking lot. Get out of the car and speak to him the words that I give you. And don't worry about the car. It will just be a little ding. And besides, it's my car." I responded "Lord, I thought I had the pink slip on this car?" "Everything in the earth is mine, including your car." I turned to Kevin and said, "The Lord is going to crash his car! This is going to be fun. We have to watch when we get to the hotel." I wish I had a video of this; as we drove into the hotel, the two of us were in crash positions! We were looking all around to see who was going to crash into us, but we didn't see a thing. We only felt and heard a big bang! I got out of the car and pointed my finger at the man and said, "I don't know who you are, but the Lord told us we would meet you this way. The Lord says to you, if you don't return to Him and repent of your sin, He is going to kill you. This is your final warning!" He was visibly shaken by my words. I then got into my car and drove off. I never even asked the man his name. And I didn't even look at the damage until the next day; it was only a ding.

When I got home, I walked into the house, and I heard screams coming from my brother's room. I walked in and opened the closet, where he kept his rock and roll albums, and the screams were coming from the albums. I raised my hands and began to pray in the spirit, and the screams got louder.

Then The Word Of The LORD Came Unto Me

The Lord then told me, "I want you to go to the concert tonight at Calvary Chapel, and then go speak to the elders in the prayer room, and then I want you to go talk to Rich and Marty." When I arrived at Calvary Chapel for the Sunday night youth concert, I began to walk across the parking lot, a few hundred people were lined up waiting to get a seat. As I approached the crowd, every person stopped talking and began to stare at me. I walked up towards some friends, and as I got near, they said, "Where have you been? What has happened to you?" "I have been with the Lord." "Well, your face is glowing!"

We sat down for the youth concert, and as the band began to play the new Jesus rock music, I saw thousands of devils fly up out of the stage with my eyes, and they began to fly in a circular pattern over the people. I warred in the spirit, while the church had a good time in the flesh. After the music stopped, the devils left, and the band gave an altar call; I wondered, what are they calling the people to? It would be many years until I would be shown the answer to that question. My second book, *Search the Scriptures, Vol. 1: Out of the Darkness* unveils the depths of this deception in the chapter entitled, *The Ministry of Death*.

After the concert I went to the prayer room, and tried to speak to the elders but they weren't able to hear me. I began to worry a little about when to leave and go to my next assignment. The Lord then began to shout at me "You be about my business! I will tell you when it's time to go." I repented for worrying, and after a few minutes, the Lord told me "Wrap things up, it is time for us to go now." I got in my car, and began to drive to Marty's apartment, which is where they always hung out. As I was driving, the car began to make a perfect left-hand turn; I took my hands off the wheel and shouted "who is driving this car?" After the left turn, I drove about a block and Rich and Marty pulled out in front of me. "How did you find us?" "I have to talk to you." "We are going to shoot pool at a bar, you want to come?" "Lord?" "Go!" "Ok."

As we walked into the bar, the power of God fell and every person in the room jumped out of their seats and into the air. I stood in the middle of the bar, shooting pool and preaching the gospel. I could tell in the spirit that the enemy was trying to hide people in the crowd for fear that I would pray for them. When I left Rich and Marty I was so full of the Holy Spirit I couldn't sleep, I was wide awake and full of the power of God so I drove to the beach in Corona del Mar, and sat on the bluffs overlooking the Pacific Ocean and prayed all night. In the early morning, before the sunrise, I saw Satan fall from heaven. I had been up praying all night for three straight days and wasn't tired at all. In the morning the Lord told me to go to a friend's home, and when they opened the door, they said "Well look who came full of the

Holy Spirit." After a few minutes, the phone rang, and someone called whose son had locked himself in the bathroom with a gun, threatening to kill himself. We prayed and within minutes, the Lord intervened, and then I was caught up in the spirit and saw Satan appear before me. I had a sword in my hand, and I stepped forward striking him in the gut, and he turned into a teddy bear. I pulled the bear off the sword, the stuffing was coming out, and I threw it to the ground and cursed it. Then the Lord spoke to me saying "My people are playing with things they don't understand."

The next incident occurred in 1979 in the land of Israel. I had been asking the Lord for permission to go the Holy Land for years. I would pray often "Lord, I want to go to Israel, can I go?" It was always the same answer, "No, not yet." Then one day, while I was praying and asking Him again, I was surprised when He said, "You can go Friday."

YOU ARE IN THE WRONG PLACE, GET BACK ON THE BUS

I had the most incredible trip to the land. The Lord even provided me a personal tour guide for the entire two weeks. At the end of my trip, I was returning to Jerusalem from a kibbutz outside Tel Aviv. I had to make a bus transfer in a small city. I got out my map, and found the city next to the major freeway from Tel Aviv to Jerusalem. I thought this will be easy to find. The bus passed under the freeway and stopped in the town square and I got off. Sabbath was about to begin, and the city square was deserted. As I stood there, I heard someone behind me: "Benjamin, you are in the wrong place, get back on the bus." I couldn't imagine who would know my name here, so I turned around to see who was speaking to me, and there was no one there! Again, I heard Him: "Benjamin, you are in the wrong place, get back on the bus." At this point, I knew it was the Lord, but rather than getting on the bus, I got out my map. I then held up the map to the sky so the Lord could read it! I told Him, "Lord I have to go to Jerusalem to get my things, remember, and I checked this map, and look Lord." He didn't even mention the map, but now He began shouting at me: "I created this entire country and I know where you are. You are in the wrong place! Get back on the bus. It is leaving. I don't want to have to argue with you again."

YOU ARE IN MY PERFECT WILL RIGHT NOW

At this point the Lord was literally yelling at me. And what did I do? I thought to myself, "I know the Lord wants me on this bus, so I better get on it. But if this is a mistake, He won't hear the end of it, until He gets me out of this mess." I still trusted my little map, and how deep was the rebellion and unbelief in me? Oh how foolish I was to doubt the Lord.

Then The Word Of The LORD Came Unto Me

I got onto the bus and turned to a woman who was seated next to me, and I asked her "Is this Petah Tikva?" No, she said it's the next town. I still had the map in my hand, so I showed it to her and asked, "What's wrong with this map?" "Oh, that's the tourist map. They made a typo, and reversed the cities." She knew of this error! And God had to yell at me to get me to obey him. I began to repent, asking the Lord "please forgive me, I will never doubt you again Lord." I was very embarrassed and I began to wonder why God had said "again." How many times had I argued with the Lord, and not realized it! He began to speak, "You are in my perfect will right now, and I have sent you to the woman you just spoke with to bring to her and her family my truth."

Yaffa and I began to talk, and she invited me to spend the evening with her family and to stay the night at her home. I arrived around 10 PM. The entire family was waiting to have dinner with me. Her father began weeping as he thanked God for the honor of having an American in his home. All of us were weeping as I told him "The honor is mine, for the God of Israel is truly the King of the Universe and I am only His humble servant. I am the one who is honored to be here in His land, with you His people."

At that point, Yaffa's brother came in the room. She told me he was the only survivor from his division in the Sinai tank battle of the Yom Kippur war. His tank had also been hit, and all of the other crew members were killed by the armor piercing round, but it did not touch him. The titanium round also detonated the tank's ammunition, and the crew was completely burned in the ensuing flames, but the fire did not even kindle upon his body. He walked out of that battle the only survivor of Israel. Now I had the honor to share with him and his family, the truth about Yeshua the Messiah. Lest you are tempted to think I am a great man of God, remember He uses foolish things to confound those wise in their own eyes.

These stories are all true. Events such as these one never forgets. I still look back with amazement at the things the Lord did in my life. These words God spoke were also meant for you dear reader: The Lord is about to cancel your reservations and all of the plans you have made in this land. Don't get upset. He is preparing another place for you. He just wants to move you. The Lord is going to create a huge crash in this country. He wants to speak to the people of America who haven't been listening to Him. For the apostates, this is your final warning! And it won't be a little ding this time. He is going to destroy this nation by the time He is through. To His remnant the Lord says: You are in the wrong place. You have been following the map you have made for your life, but your map is wrong! You must get on the bus that is coming. You must find God's plan for your life. Everything is about to change. You will not recognize this nation in the near future.

THE DAY OF THE LORD IS AT HAND

I WISH TO SPEAK TO THIS PEOPLE

When I began praying about the stock market in early 1996, I hadn't heard God's voice for years. I had become backslidden and had fallen away from the Lord. Shortly after God answered me, and showed me what was to come, I was speaking to a group of employees about our retirement plan. As I was finishing my presentation, the Holy Spirit began to fall upon me, and I heard the Lord speak in a loud voice from the back of the room: "I wish to speak to this people." I thought to myself "I don't know what He is going to say, but I have a feeling people are going to get mad at me." I answered the Lord under my breath, "If you wish to speak Lord, go ahead and speak."

I began to share how I had been praying all year, and that God had just answered me. I told them I didn't have time, and this wasn't the proper place to share what He said, but if they were believers, they had better pray. I then began to cry softly. My crying turned into weeping as I remembered what I had seen in the Spirit. The weeping turned into wailing, and I fell face down on the conference room table and began to fulfill the prophecy in the book of Joel, "cry out loud before the great and awesome Day of the Lord." I then heard Him say "Stand on your feet!" As I stood upon my feet, I noticed my right hand was raised to heaven. It seemed to me as if I was watching everything at this point, and I wondered what the Lord would do next. The Spirit of the Lord then spoke in a loud voice: "The Lord God Almighty is standing now, ready to judge the entire earth!" That evening at home, I asked the Lord, "What did you just do to my life?" He answered, "They are going to fire you, but do not fear, you are not being fired, you are being delivered."

Everything the Lord has ever told me has always come to pass. I no longer doubt Him. I can't make Him speak to me, but often times He answers me quickly when I call upon His name. I do not consider myself a prophet, or a great man of faith. I only write this book and testify of these things because He told me, "Warn the people!"

I HAVE CALLED YOU FRIENDS

The Lord always reveals his secrets to those who are close to him. The first example is when God revealed to his friend Abraham his plans to destroy Sodom. *"Shall I hide from Abraham the thing which I do?"* [6] God always warns his friends when he is ready to bring His judgment. Jesus told us:

> *Henceforth I call you not servants; for the servant knows not what his Lord doeth: but I have called you friends; for all things that I have heard of my Father I have made known unto you.* [7]

If we are his friends, then we will hear his voice. The Lord declared this: "*My sheep hear my voice, and I know them, and they follow me.*"[8] There is ample precedent for the Lord revealing his plans to his chosen people in advance. With the greatest event in the history of the world about to occur, the Lord is again warning his friends. Wouldn't you warn your friends? I would. That is why I am writing this book. Dear reader, you are being warned. Listen to His voice!

The Lord uses the example of the lion roaring as a warning of the judgment to come. "*The lion has roared, who will not fear? The Lord God has spoken, who can but prophesy?*" [9] The Lord also refers to the lion as a symbol of this last hour, when the lion has come out of hiding, and the plans of the prince are now being revealed to God's people.

> *The lion is come up from his thicket, and the destroyer of the Gentiles is on his way; he is God forth from his place to make thy land desolate; and thy cities shall be laid waste, without an inhabitant.* [10]

Who will not fear when these things begin to come to pass? The scripture declares only the righteous will stand with no fear: "*The wicked flee when no man pursues: but the righteous are bold as a lion.*" [11] The people who can hear from the Lord are the true prophets. They bear the indignation of the Lord, and their ministry is to warn the people to turn from their sins, lest they be consumed in the judgment. Their voices are always in the minority, and they are usually found in the wilderness, having been rejected by the religious leaders of their day. The true messengers of the Lord are always rejected by the majority of the people, who prefer to listen to the false prophets preach a message of peace and prosperity. Thus, it is today as well.

PROPHETS STILL SPEAK

The people of God are in desperate need of the true prophetic voice of God to be brought forth in this last hour. They are the seers who announce to the people the warnings of Adonai. The true prophets have always had the spiritual discernment to understand their times. It was the function of the prophet to admonish, to warn, to reprove and to denounce existing sin. The prophets are also called as Watchmen. They are set all the night upon the walls of Zion to blow the trumpet and to warn of coming danger. The true prophets receive their prophetic office directly from Hashem; theirs is a life of hardship and suffering, loneliness and rejection. The true word of God has always been hard to bear, and the true messengers of the Lord have always been rejected by the people.

> *And the Lord, the God of their fathers, sent word to them again and again by His messengers, because He had compassion on His people and on His dwelling place; but they continually mocked the messengers of God, despised*

THE DAY OF THE LORD IS AT HAND

His words and scoffed at His prophets, until the wrath of the Lord arose against His people, until there was no remedy. [12]

The message of the true prophets will cause men to shun their company, and to speak all manner of evil against them. They are cast out by friends and family, and rejected by the nation at large, but the LORD JESUS CHRIST is faithful to send His warnings to the people time and time again. The highest prophetic office is held by those who can hear the Lord directly, and those to whom the Lord speaks face to face.

Hear now My words: if there is a prophet among you, I, the Lord, make Myself known to him in a vision; I speak to him in a dream. Not so with My servant Moses; he is faithful in all My house. I speak with him face to face, even plainly, and not in dark sayings; and he sees the form of the Lord. Why then were you not afraid to speak against My servant Moses? [14]

When a man of God speaks the true word of the Lord; their ministry and message will always produce hatred and scorn in the minds of the majority of their listeners for only the remnant can hear and receive the words of the Almighty spoken through his messengers:

Blessed are ye, when men shall hate you, and when they shall separate you from their company, and shall reproach you, and cast out your name as evil, for the Son of man's sake. Rejoice ye in that day, and leap for joy: for, behold, your reward is great in heaven: for in the like manner did their fathers unto the prophets. But woe unto you that are rich! for ye have received your consolation. [15]

The prophets and messengers of God are not trained in the religious schools of man, nor are they raised up from among the religious leadership of the organized Church. None of the prophets of Israel came from the priesthood. They were all called and prepared by God alone. The appearance of Elijah is such an example. *"And Elijah the Tishbite, who was of the inhabitants of Gilead, said unto Ahab, As the Lord God of Israel liveth, before whom I stand."* [16] Elijah's only qualification was that he stood before the Lord God of Israel. Nothing more was said of him. He was an ordinary man who knew his God. John the Baptist was of similar origins, trained on the backside of the desert wilderness. *"And the child grew, and waxed strong in spirit, and was in the deserts till the day of his showing unto Israel."* [17] John had no university or seminary training. He just appeared as the forerunner of the Lord Jesus Christ. God's ways are not man's ways. He still uses the foolish things of this world to confound the wise. People have rebuked me for speaking the word of the Lord saying, "By what authority do you speak these words?" My answer: by the authority of the LORD JESUS CHRIST, the King of Israel.

70

THE JUDGMENT OF ANCIENT ISRAEL

God judged ancient Israel for departing from the truth, and turning to the worship of idols and for following the gods of the pagans. The Lord in His mercy always sent His prophets to warn the people to repent, and return to the Lord, or they would be judged and the nation destroyed. Jeremiah, Isaiah, Ezekiel and many others came and preached the word of the Lord, but the people always refused to listen, turning their ears to the false prophets, while rejecting and in many cases, killing the true prophets of the Most High God.

Each of the prophets of Israel spoke of the specific judgment that would come in their time, but they also spoke of the Day of the Lord, which is the final judgment upon the whole earth. This is another example of the principle of dualism, where the message of the prophets would be fulfilled twice: first, to the specific people to whom the word of the Lord was originally addressed and then again to the people of the last generation at the end of the age.

Jeremiah is one such prophet, who spoke to the children of Israel warning of the destruction of their nation, for the sins of idolatry and immorality, which had filled the land. The prophecies of Jeremiah also speak to the last days Church in America. The Lord never judges a nation without first sending a warning to His people. Before addressing the word of God to our nation, I must first dispel a widely held error in the modern Church. If you fail to discern this error, you will be wide open for deception.

ISRAEL AND THE CHURCH

Many within the modern Christian Church embrace a theology which holds that Israel and the Church are two separate and distinct groups of people, and that God is therefore dealing with them differently. This is one of the great deceptions to descend upon the saints in the last days.

"The concept that God is dealing with Israel in one way and the `Gentile Church' in another is a serious contradiction in Scripture. In God's eyes, there is no such thing as a `Gentile Church'... This is a serious heretical doctrine... This doctrine is often referred to as `replacement theology.' This idea was conceived about 200 years after the cross and then, later, birthed at the same time the Catholic church was birthed, during the Council of Nicaea in AD 325." [18] It was during this Council that "the Gentile Church issued a doctrinal statement that strictly forbade any Jewish Believer to observe the law "[19]

THE DAY OF THE LORD IS AT HAND

The Church has forgotten that Paul tells Gentile believers that they have been *"grafted in among the ever-present Jewish remnant that believe in Christ. He also declares that they are also citizens of the nation of Israel."* [20] The very name of yis-raw-ale [21] means ruled by God. This is the name of the nation of people who are ruled by the Lord. They are his people, and he is their God. Jesus says:

> I am the good shepherd, and know my sheep, and am known of mine. As the Father knoweth me, even so know I the Father: and I lay down my life for the sheep. And other sheep I have, which are not of this fold; them also I must bring, and they shall hear my voice; and there shall be one-fold. [22]

The other sheep Jesus is speaking of are the Gentile believers who would also be gathered into the flock, which is spiritual Israel, the true nation ruled by God. The Lord has only one people, true Israel.

THE CALLED OUT AND CHOSEN ONES

The word "church" is actually not found in the Scripture. The original manuscripts contain the word ekklesia [23] which means the called-out ones, or the chosen ones, and is used to describe a religious congregation (Jewish synagogue, or Christian community of members on earth or saints in heaven or both). The word ekklesia is translated by the scholars as the word "church", but God never intended to create a separate institution apart from spiritual Israel. This false doctrine of "replacement theology" is a part of the last days deception of the church. The Spirit spoke of a great falling away in the last days. The true meaning was the last two days of creation and the great falling away began shortly after the resurrection of our Lord.

Vine's Expository Dictionary of Biblical Words defines "ekklesia" The word is from ek, `out of, and klesis, a 'calling' (kaleo, to call), it is used to designate the gathering of Israel, summoned for any definite purpose, or a gathering regarded as representative of the whole nation. It has two applications to companies of Christians, (a) to the whole company of the redeemed throughout the present era, the company of which Christ said, `I will build My Church,' and which is further described as `the Church which is His Body,' (b) in the singular number to a company consisting of professed believers, and in the plural, with reference to churches in a district. "[24]

Jesus spoke of His own ministry declaring *"But he answered and said, I am not sent but unto the lost sheep of the house of Israel."* [25] The Lord was only sent to save the lost sheep of Israel, and dear reader, if you are not grafted into that company; you have no part in Him. When Jesus was crucified the charge they hung on His cross was that He was the King of Israel. *"He saved others; himself he cannot save. If he be the King of Israel, let him now come down from the* cross, and we will believe him." [26] Nathanael declared this when he first met Jesus - "*Rabbi, thou art the Son of God, thou art the King of Israel.*"[27] Many students of the Scripture fail to understand Paul's writings in Romans where he declares, "*Not as though the word of God hath taken none effect. For they are not all Israel, which are of Israel: Neither, because they are the seed of Abraham, are they all children: but, In Isaac shall thy seed be called.*" [28]

Paul reveals the mystery of God's election of His remnant, for not everyone who is born into natural Israel is saved, but only those who are sons of the promise. He uses the choice by God of Isaac over Ishmael as an example of this. Paul continues to expound upon the mystery that only a remnant was to be saved "*Esaias also crieth concerning Israel, Though the number of the children of Israel be as the sand of the sea, a remnant shall be saved: For he will finish the work, and cut it short in righteousness: because a short work will the Lord make upon the earth.*" [29]

Though the number of the children of Israel would be as the sand of the sea, only a remnant shall be saved. Dear reader, the same is true of modern Christianity, where the number of those professing faith is many millions, yet the true elect of God remain only a remnant. Jesus spoke of them saying: "*Fear not, little flock; for it is your Father's good pleasure to give you the kingdom.*"[30] The true saints of the Most High are indeed only a little flock, while the many who say unto him "Lord, Lord", will all be very surprised when they learn, they only knew his name.

ALL THAT ARE TRUE ISRAEL SHALL BE SAVED

Paul also addresses the issue of whether God has cast away Israel because of the rejection of Messiah by the majority. God has always had a small remnant within the nation of Israel. "*I say then, Hath God cast away his people? God forbid. God hath not cast away his people, which he foreknew. No ye not what the scripture saith of Elias? how he made intercession to God against Israel, saying, Lord, they have killed thy prophets, and tore down thy altars; and I am left alone, and they seek my life. But what saith the answer of God unto him? I have reserved to myself seven thousand men, who have not bowed the knee to the image of Baal. Even so then at this present time also there is a remnant according to the election of grace.*" [31] Paul continues to declare "*blindness in part is happened to Israel, until the fullness of the Gentiles comes in. And so all Israel shall be saved: as it is written, there shall come out of Zion a Deliverer, and he shall turn away ungodliness from Jacob. For this is my covenant unto them, when I shall take away their sins as touching the election, they are beloved for the fathers' sakes. For the gifts and calling of God are without repentance.*" [32]

All that of true spiritual Israel shall be saved. None of them will be lost, nor can any among true Israel be lost, for their salvation is of the Lord.

MY SHEEP HEAR MY VOICE
AND THEY SHALL NEVER PERISH

Jesus declares that His true sheep hear His voice, and they will follow Him. He gives eternal life to them, and they shall never perish. The Father gave the sheep to Jesus as a bride, and no man can pluck them out of the Father's hand. This is true Israel, the people governed by God, and they are a *"little flock"* and a *"remnant saved according to grace."*

> *My sheep hear my voice, and I know them, and they follow me: And I give unto them eternal life; and they shall never perish, neither shall any man pluck them out of my hand. My Father, which gave them me, is greater than all; and no man is able to pluck them out of my Father's hand. John 10:27-29*

> *All that the Father giveth me shall come to me; and him that cometh to me I will in no wise cast out. For I came down from heaven, not to do mine own will, but the will of him that sent me. And this is the Father's will which hath sent me, that of all which he hath given me I should lose nothing, but should raise it up again at the last day. John 6:37-39*

Paul writing to the Ephesians explains that the remnant Gentiles, who are saved, now belong to the commonwealth of Israel, for The Holy One of ISRAEL is the King of this commonwealth. If you are not a citizen of this nation, then your portion is the lake of fire.

> *Wherefore remember, that ye being in time past Gentiles in the flesh ... at that time you were without Christ, being aliens from the commonwealth of Israel, and strangers from the covenants of promise, having no hope, and without God in the world: But now in Christ Jesus you who sometimes were far off are made nigh by the blood of Christ.* [33]

This is the New Covenant, which Jesus, the Messiah of Israel bought with His own blood. This New Covenant was promised to spiritual Israel, and is only made with them: *"Behold, the days come, saith the Lord, when I will make a new covenant with the house of Israel ...For this is the covenant that I will make with the house of Israel after those days, saith the Lord; I will put my laws into their mind, and write them in their hearts: ... and they shall be to me a people"* [34]

The name Israel was first given to Jacob after He wrestled with the Lord and prevailed *"And he said, Thy name shall be called no more Jacob, but Israel: for as a prince hast thou power with God and with men, and hast prevailed."* [35] We know that God let Jacob prevail, much as a father plays with His son, and lets him win. Jacob prevailed because of the mercy of God. When Jesus said, *"I am only sent to the lost sheep of Israel"* He was speaking of spiritual Israel, which includes the Gentiles who have been grafted in to the true vine, which is Jesus. Paul speaks of true Israel saying *"as many as walk according to this rule, peace be on them, and mercy, and upon the Israel of God."* [36]

The Israel of God is true Israel; these are the holy remnant comprising Jews and Gentiles, who have been made one in Christ and who follow the Lord in obedience to Him. The Church in America has been lied to. We marvel at the blindness of the Jews who cannot see that Yeshua, who we call Jesus, is the Messiah of Israel. Yet the Church is also blind to the fact that the Gentiles have been grafted into the true vine which is spiritual Israel. Does God have two peoples, or two nations?

One Christian exclaimed "The church is called the bride of Christ, but Israel was called the wife of God." I answered this man "Yes that is true. If you read Hosea, the Lord shows us the picture of the divorce He sought from natural Israel for their unfaithfulness to Him, but He will marry true Israel again at the wedding feast of the lamb and she is now His bride, betrothed to God and awaiting the blessed day!" The Church is also deceived on the issue of the law of God. Jesus did not come to destroy the law but to fulfill it: *"Think not that I am come to destroy the law or the prophets: I am not come to destroy, but to fulfill. For verily I say unto you, Till heaven and earth pass, one jot or one tittle shall in no wise pass from the law, till all be fulfilled."* [37]

The new Covenant was promised to Israel where God said he would write the Law upon their hearts. The law has not been abolished under the New Covenant. It is still our teacher while we walk in the flesh. Paul in Galatians is speaking to believers who have died to themselves, and are now led by the Spirit. They no longer need the law as a teacher, for they follow the Spirit and obey the law from the heart. Israel and the Church are not separate peoples in the eyes of the Lord. God has chosen one people for himself, and that is spiritual Israel. The mystery of God is that the Lord only saved a remnant according to His grace: *"Even so then at this present time also there is a remnant according to the election of grace."* [38]

Ancient Israel fell into great sin and apostasy, was judged by God, and carried off into captivity to Babylon in the natural. The modern Church has also fallen into apostasy, and has been carried off into captivity to Babylon in the spirit. After the rejection of the Messiah, God destroyed ancient Israel. America and her Church have also rejected the truth of the Messiah, and they too face destruction.

THE DAY OF THE LORD IS AT HAND

I AM THE LORD, I CHANGE NOT

God declares in Malachi that he does not change. He is the same yesterday, today and forever. The Lord is a God of judgment. He will not tolerate the murder of innocent children and the promotion of sexual immorality or sodomy without bringing His judgment. God judged Israel for turning from His truth to darkness. The people worshiped the pagan gods and were engaging in all forms of wickedness. They were worshipping Ashtoreth, the god of sexual immorality. They were also killing their babies, the unwanted fruit of their sinful passions, by burning them alive on the altars of Molech. A fire would be built under the stone hands of the graven image, and when the hands were red hot, they would place the newborn infants upon them. Though they turned a deaf ear to the screams of their own children, the Lord heard, and He turned His ear to the suffering cries of His little ones. His heart was turned with compassion for these poor innocent babies.

And in His nostrils, the fire of His wrath kindled against His now wicked nation. He did not tarry long before bringing His judgment. Today in America, our nation worships the same evil gods, and in our modern clinics we are again murdering His little children. Though America has turned a deaf ear to their cries, the Lord still hears. And His heart breaks for each and every one of these innocent souls. Again, the Lord has become wroth with this his Christian nation. He will not tarry long this time either.

The Word of the Lord came to the prophet Jeremiah to the people of Judah, of the soon and certain judgment for their sins as a nation. This word also speaks in these last days to the believers in America, who consider themselves the people of God, and who are also committing the same sins as ancient Israel. The Lord chose Jeremiah in his sovereignty, and ordained him a prophet unto the nations. This is our first clue that these prophecies extend beyond ancient Israel even unto these last days.

> Then the word of the Lord came unto me, saying, Before I formed thee in the belly I knew thee; and before thou came forth out of the womb I sanctified thee, and I ordained thee a prophet unto the nations. Jeremiah 1:4-5

God has established Jeremiah's word over both the nations and the kingdoms. The word kingdom in this context means a realm, dominion, a reign, or sovereignty. The word nations, refers to the nation states of the Gentiles. Thus, we are told Jeremiah's prophecies would rule over many countries and many empires or dominions which would come. "See, I have this day set thee over the nations and over the kingdoms, to root out, and to pull down, and to destroy, and to throw down, to build, and to plant." Jeremiah 1:10

76

Then The Word Of The LORD Came Unto Me

GOD'S NATION OF THE NEW COVENANT - AMERICA

The prophet Jeremiah spoke for the Lord, telling Israel that in her early years as a nation, she was holy unto the Lord, and God's blessing and protection were upon her. All that fought against her, He destroyed. Now the Lord asks the people, *"What did I do? Why has My nation gone far from Me and walked in vanity and are become vain?"*

> *The word of the Lord came to me, saying, Go and cry in the ears of Jerusalem, saying, Thus saith the Lord; I remember thee, the kindness of thy youth, the love of thine espousals, when thou went after me in the wilderness, ... Israel was holiness unto the Lord, and the first fruits of his increase... Thus saith the Lord, What iniquity have your fathers found in me, that they are gone far from me, and have walked after vanity, and are become vain? Jeremiah 2:1-5*

This is also true of the history of America. When America was a youth, she was holy unto the Lord. Our nation was founded on Biblical principles of justice and truth and religious freedom. Many of our founding fathers were God-fearing souls who loved the Lord. They had come from Europe to the new world in America seeking freedom from the persecution they faced in their own land. Some of them were called separatists; for they believed the disobedient church couldn't be saved. They separated themselves joining together in covenant communities seeking to honor the Lord. One of these groups was pastored by a man named John Robbins who preached his final message before his congregation left for America. Robbins told them he believed the Lord had called them to go into the wilderness to a new land, to build a New Jerusalem, and to restore the temple of the Lord with themselves as the living stones. These were the early pilgrims who sought and honored the Lord. These Godly men and women built our great nation. Our heritage of freedom, peace and prosperity is the fruit of the blessings our forefathers received by their faithful obedience to the God of Israel and His Son Jesus Christ.

THE JUDGMENT OF APOSTATE AMERICA

Today, America is Christian in name only. Sin, lawlessness and wickedness fill our once great land. Dear reader, I trust I need not go on about the sad state of our once great nation, where now the land itself is defiled with the blood of over 50 million murdered innocent babies. Their blood cries out to the Lord. And the HOLY ONE OF ISRAEL watches again as innocent babies are slaughtered. Once again, the Lord's wrath kindles before Him. As he did in ancient Israel, he will again make a quick work of judging this land. They were killing babies at the time of the first coming of Jesus Christ. They are killing babies again! This time the Lord's response will come in one hour.

THE DAY OF THE LORD IS AT HAND

But your iniquities have separated between you and your God, and your sins have hid his face from you, that he will not hear. For your hands are defiled with blood, and your fingers with iniquity; your lips have spoken lies, your tongue hath muttered perverseness. Isaiah 59:2-3

The Lord furthers His complaint against his people that they are divorcing, remarrying and committing sexual sins with many lovers, and thus the land is greatly polluted! Isn't this a picture of America? Indeed, the church in America is full of divorce, abortion, sodomy, and sexual immorality, even as the heathen.

They say, If a man put away his wife, and she go from him, and become another man's, shall he return unto her again? shall not that land be greatly polluted? but thou hast played the harlot with many lovers; yet return again to me, saith the LORD. Jeremiah 3:1

THE LORD OFFERS MERCY TO ALL WHO REPENT

The Lord pleads with his people until the end to repent and return unto him "for I am merciful says the Lord". Dear reader, we need only acknowledge our sin, and return to our first love, and the Lord will deliver us from the judgment that is to come. The Lord also shows us a picture of his remnant, which shall be counted worthy to endure the hour of testing, saying, "I will take one out of a city and two of a family".

Return, thou backsliding Israel, saith the Lord; and I will not cause mine anger to fall upon you: for I am merciful, saith the Lord, and I will not keep anger for ever. Only acknowledge thine iniquity, and that thou hast transgressed against the Lord thy God, and hast scattered thy ways to the strangers under every green tree, and ye have not obeyed my voice, saith the Lord. Turn, 0 backsliding children, saith the Lord; for I am married unto you: and I will take you one of a city, and two of a family, and I will bring you to Zion. Jeremiah 3:12-14

Don't be tempted to trust in anything but God, for He alone is our salvation! Blessed be the name of the Lord. *"Truly in vain is salvation hoped for from the hills, and from the multitude of mountains: truly in the Lord our God is the salvation of Israel."*[39] The hills and the mountains represent the religious institutions of man whose help is only in vain.

These are the mountains, which have raised themselves up against the knowledge of God. There is no hope in religion, or in the teachings of man. Our only hope is in the Lord. He is our salvation, and his chosen ones wait for him and him alone.

THE LORD REPROVES THE MEN AMONG HIS PEOPLE

The Lord then speaks directly to the men of Judah directing us to put away those things which keep us from being tender, the sins which cause us to harden our hearts. Judah represents the remnant, for they were the last tribe to go into captivity. The Lord commands the remnant to break up the fallow ground, representing our hard hearts, and to no longer sow our seeds among the thorns. Jesus spoke in parables about the thorny ground, which represents bad soil, choked by the cares of the world, and which cannot bear fruit for the kingdom of God. Here the Lord tells us to turn away from the things of the world, and no longer sow to them. Sowing represents investing our seed, our time and resources into fruitless activities and sinful relationships, which cannot bear fruit for the kingdom, for they do not represent good soil.

The Lord then commands us to turn to Him with our whole heart, for only then shall we find Him!

> *If thou wilt return, O Israel, saith the Lord, return unto me: and if thou wilt put away thine abominations out of my sight, then shalt thou not remove. And thou shalt swear, The Lord lives, in truth, in judgment, and in righteousness; and the nations shall bless themselves in him, and in him shall they glory. For thus saith the Lord to the men of Judah and Jerusalem, Break up your fallow ground, and sow not among thorns. Jeremiah 4:1-3*

THE JUDGMENT UPON THE CHURCH IN AMERICA

This word is to both the church and to the men and women whom God has appointed as leaders in the community of the faithful. The Lord commands us to cut away the foreskin and circumcise our hearts, speaking of that which is of the flesh, and of this world. The Lord demands that we sanctify ourselves, and walk in holiness and purity. This commandment includes a promise that if we don't obey, and seek true repentance and purify our lives, the Lord will do this work Himself by fire! Here the Lord speaks of the fire of testing that will come upon the entire world to test those who dwell upon the earth. Remember that the Lord promised His judgment would begin in the house of God!

> *Circumcise, yourselves to the Lord, and take away the foreskins of your heart, ye men of Judah and inhabitants of Jerusalem: lest my fury come forth like fire. and burn that none can quench it, because of the evil of your doings. Jeremiah 4:4*

THE DAY OF THE LORD IS AT HAND

For the time is come that judgment must begin at the house of God: and if it first begin at us, what shall the end be of them that obey not the gospel of God? 1 Peter 4:17

The Scripture testifies that we should not consider it strange that we have been appointed to walk through the fiery trial which is to test all believers, for this trial has been appointed by God.

"Beloved, think it not strange concerning the fiery trial which is to try you, as though some strange thing happened unto you." [40]

Jesus himself tells his faithful ones, *"Because thou hast kept the word of my patience, I also will keep thee from the hour of temptation, which shall come upon all the world, to try them that dwell upon the earth. Behold, I come quickly: hold that fast which thou hast, that no man take thy crown."*[41]

Now this keeping is not as some suppose, to remove us from the hour, but rather is to preserve us through the fire even as the ancient Hebrew boys were preserved through the fiery furnace of Babylon.

THE WARNING FROM THE LORD
THE DESTROYER IS COMING

The Lord commands that this word be both declared and published, to blow the trumpet in Zion and to command the people to assemble together, and to go into the safe cities. Judgment is coming upon our nation, and a great destruction shall fall upon our land. The trumpet represents the word of prophecy and is a warning of an approaching enemy, to prepare the people for war. The warning also includes instructions to gather together in groups, and to move to places of refuge, for our nation is about to be destroyed.

We are then told that the lion has come up out of the thicket, which represents hiding. The lion here symbolizes the antichrist, and as the warning trumpets are blowing in the land, the lion has come out of hiding. Today the secret plans of the Illuminati to create a One-World government under the antichrist are now visible, and the destroyer of the gentiles is on his way. He will make your land desolate, and your cities shall be laid waste, without inhabitant. Much has been revealed of the plans to bring the New World Order into existence in the early part of these last days.

The detailed plans of the Illuminati for the judgment upon the Church and America are contained in Chapter Ten, *Babylon the Great is Fallen, Fallen.* America, your hour of judgment is upon you now, and yet, you see it not.

Declare ye in Judah, and publish in Jerusalem; and say, Blow ye the trumpet in the land: cry, gather together, and say, Assemble yourselves, and let us go into the defenced cities. Set up the standard toward Zion: retire, stay not for I will bring evil from the north, and a great destruction. The lion is come up from his thicket, and the destroyer of the Gentiles is on his wax; he is gone forth from his place to make thy land desolate; and thy cities shall be laid waste, without an inhabitant. Jeremiah 4:5-7

The prophecy states the warning of judgment will be first declared in the tribe of Judah, and then published in Jerusalem, which is in the tribe of Benjamin. This has been literally fulfilled, for this word first came forth from the children of Judah, and now has been published by the sons of Benjamin. Oh the wonders of our God, how awesome to observe!

THE LEADERS AMONG GOD'S PEOPLE
SHALL BE ASTONISHED

Once the *"anger of the Lord"* begins to pour out on our nation, it will not turn back, and there will be no release for the people. Further, in the day that the judgment of the Lord is revealed *"the heart of the king shall perish."* There will be nothing the leaders of this nation can do to stop the judgment of God. The freedom of America will be taken from the people, and their authority will fail. Further *"the priests shall be astonished, and the prophets shall wonder."* Your religious leaders will not see this judgment coming. The priests represent the pastors and leaders, who will be utterly astonished and amazed, because they failed to discern the judgment of America. And the false prophets shall all wonder why none of them could see this either.

For this gird you with sackcloth, lament and howl: for the fierce anger of the Lord is not turned back from us. And it shall come to pass at that day saith the Lord, that the heart of the king shall perish, and the heart of the princes and the priests shall be astonished, and the prophets shall wonder. Jeremiah 4:8-9

THE FAMINE OF HEARING THE VOICE OF THE LORD

In the book of Amos, we are told that in the last days there would be a new type of famine in the land, not a famine of bread or water, but of hearing the voice of God. The end of this famine, which is in the spirit, will be death of an even greater kind. *"Where there is no vision, the people perish."* [42] In the days of Samuel the prophet, a similar famine covered the land. *"And the child Samuel ministered unto the Lord before Eli. And the word of the Lord was precious in those days; there was no open vision."* [43]

THE DAY OF THE LORD IS AT HAND

The silence from heaven was the direct result of the wickedness and sin among the people. This is the state of the Church in America today, where so few believers can actually hear the voice of the Lord. No, the people no longer hear from the Lord, but rather, they have turned to the pillow prophets who preach another gospel of peace and prosperity. These prophets cannot see the impending judgment of God upon America, because they are false prophets. Do not listen to them! They are lying to you!

> *Behold, the days come, saith the Lord GOD, that I will send a famine in the land, not a famine of bread, nor a thirst for water, but of hearing the words of the LORD. And they shall wander from sea to sea, and from the north even to the east, they shall run to and fro to seek the word of the LORD, and shall not find it.* Amos 8:11-12

The people will wander from sea to sea, and run to and from seeking to find the word of the Lord, but they shall not find the true bread of life. The masses of people who do not know the Lord, will wander among dry places, and shall find no water for their souls. *"They shall wander from sea to sea... they shall run to and fro to seek the word of the Lord, and shall not find it."* In the midst of this famine, the land is full of a counterfeit word, full of the flesh, but utterly lacking the power of the Spirit. The true prophetic word of God has been hidden in this hour, and reserved only for the remnant. In this final hour, the Lord is uttering His voice like a trumpet, but the famine continues, for many cannot bear to hear the truth.

Jeremiah declares that the people have been greatly deceived, thinking they would have peace, yet the sword that was coming would reach to the very soul. *"For the leaders of this people cause them to err; and they that are led of them are destroyed."* [45] The judgment is referred to as a wind, and it is not to cleanse or to fan, but to destroy.

> *Ah, Lord God! surely thou hast greatly deceived this people saying, Ye shall have peace; whereas the sword reaches unto the soul. At that time shall it be said to this people and to Jerusalem, A dry wind of the high places in the wilderness toward the daughter of my people, not to fan, nor to cleanse, Even a full wind from those places shall come unto me: now also will I give sentence against them. Jeremiah 4:10-12*

THEY HATED KNOWLEDGE
AND DID NOT CHOOSE MY FEAR

The Lord declares that he called but these people refused. They neglected God's counsel, and they spurned the reproof of the Lord. So they shall eat the fruit of their own way and in the day of calamity, they will cry out but the Lord will not answer them!

> *How long, O naive ones, will you love simplicity? And scoffers delight themselves in scoffing, and fools hate knowledge? Turn to my reproof, behold, I will pour out my spirit on you, I will make my words known to you. Because I called, and you refused; I stretched out my hand, and no one paid attention; And you neglected all my counsel, and did not want my reproof; I will even laugh at your calamity; I will mock when your dread comes, When your dread comes like a storm, and your calamity comes on like a whirlwind, when distress {and} anguish come on you. Then they will call on me, but I will not answer; they will seek me diligently, but they shall not find me, because they hated knowledge, and did not choose the fear of the LORD. They would not accept my counsel, they spurned all my reproof. So they shall eat of the fruit of their own way, and be satiated with their own devices. For the waywardness of the naive shall kill them, and the complacency of fools shall destroy them. But he who listens to me shall live securely, and shall be at ease from the dread of evil. Proverbs 1:22-33 NAS*

A GRIEVOUS WHIRLWIND OF THE LORD IS GONE FORTH IN FURY

The Lord again refers to His judgment as a whirlwind: *"Behold, a whirlwind of the Lord is gone forth in fury, even a grievous whirlwind"*.[46] The word *whirlwind* in this text is רעס, *sah'-ar* [47] which means a hurricane, a stormy tempest, and a whirlwind. The people will be caught off guard, thinking they would have peace. Paul tells us of the sudden judgment which shall come in an instant, but admonishes the believers – that the day should not overtake them unaware:

> *For yourselves know perfectly that the day of the Lord so cometh as a thief in the night. For when they shall say, Peace and safety; then sudden destruction cometh upon them, as travail upon a woman with child; and they shall not escape. But ye, brethren, are not in darkness, that that day should overtake you as a thief.* [48]

The judgment of the Lord comes in a time when the people are looking for peace and safety. Then destruction comes suddenly! The present hour fulfills this prophecy perfectly. It appears that the cold war is over, and American democracy has triumphed over Communism. The Russian threat has supposedly ended, and the Middle East has witnessed the signing of the Peace and Security Agreement. Though America sits today as the Queen among the nations, and her citizens dwell at ease, in one hour her judgment shall come. Paul admonishes the believers that this day should not overtake us unaware, as a thief, for we are not in darkness. Paul states clearly, the believers will be present on the day when sudden destruction comes upon the world otherwise it could not overtake them. The true Church is not delivered out before the judgment, but is preserved through the judgment.

The Lord tells us our ways have warranted this judgment, and that it will be bitter, for it will reach to our very soul. Jeremiah laments for the pain in his heart; he can hear the trumpet of war sounding in the land, and he knows that destruction upon destruction is decreed by the Spirit of God. The whole land will be spoiled when sudden judgment comes in a moment in time. The prophet wonders, how long will he hear the trumpet before the day is upon us. Like Jeremiah, I do not know the day or the hour of the judgment to come upon America, but there is not much time left, for the Lord awoke me recently with a very loud voice saying: *"Summer is coming soon, tell the people to clean their houses."* And summer does indeed come soon my friend, very soon indeed. People wake up. Wake from your sleep. This message did not come forth from men but from the King of Israel.

> *Thy way and thy doings have procured these things unto thee; this is thy wickedness, because it is bitter, because it reacheth unto thine heart. My bowels, my bowels! I am pained at my very heart; my heart maketh a noise in me; I cannot hold my peace, because thou hast heard, O my soul, the sound of the trumpet, the alarm of war. Destruction upon destruction is cried; for the whole land is spoiled: suddenly are my tents spoiled, and my curtains in a moment. How long shall I see the standard, and hear the sound of the trumpet? Jeremiah 4:18-21*

The Lord then tells the prophet to go through the city, and see if anyone executes judgment and walks in righteousness. Though all the people speak in the name of the Lord, every one of them in truth speaks falsely.

> *Run ye to and fro through the streets of Jerusalem, and see now, and know, and seek in the broad places thereof, if ye can find a man, if there be any that executeth judgment, that seeketh the truth; and I will pardon it. And though they say, The Lord liveth; surely they swear falsely. Jeremiah 5:1-2*

THE LEADERS OF THE PEOPLE HAVE FORSAKEN THE TRUTH

Jeremiah decides to speak to the leaders of the people, the great men, for they should know the word of the Lord. The prophet expected the religious leaders to hear the word, for they should have known the judgments of the Lord, yet they also were corrupted. Today, in most of the churches of

America, the leaders who claim to know his word cannot recognize the hour of judgment is at hand. The lion and the leopard in the following passage refer to spiritual forces about to be unleashed upon their cities because the people are breaking God's laws and are full of backsliding.

> I will get me unto the great men, and will speak unto them; for they have known the way of the Lord, and the judgment of their God: but these have altogether broken the yoke, and burst the bonds. Wherefore a lion out of the forest shall slay them, and a wolf of the evenings shall spoil them, a leopard shall watch over their cities: every one that goeth out thence shall be torn in pieces: because their transgressions are many, and their backslidings are increased. Jeremiah 5:5-6

THE PEOPLE SPEAK OF PEACE WHEN THERE IS NONE

The people have spoken falsely of the Lord, proclaiming no evil shall come upon them. Jeremiah finds the nation hardened in sin, and embracing a false prophecy of peace. Today's churches fill to overflowing to hear the pillow prophets teach the gospel of prosperity, while the voices declaring the impending judgment of our God are ignored. The great deception of the pre-tribulation rapture has cast a deep sleep over the Church, and they cannot see these events are being fulfilled before their eyes. This great deception will be discussed in detail in the Chapter Eleven, *First there shall come an Apostasy*.

> They have belied the Lord, and said, It is not he; neither shall evil come upon us; neither shall we see sword nor famine: And the prophets shall become wind, and the word is not in them: thus shall it be done unto them. Jeremiah 5:12-13

FEAR YE NOT ME SAITH THE LORD

The Lord confronts the people asking them, *"Will you not fear me?"* Indeed, when the judgment falls, everyone will fear the Lord. The people are full of evil and rebellious hearts, and they have revolted and forsaken the Lord, so that they can no longer even hear his voice, nor do they fear him any longer.

The Lord declares that among *"My people"*, in the household of God, the Church, are wicked men who lay wait and set snares for each other. They are pictured as a cage full of birds, with houses full of deceit. Scripture speaks symbolically of birds as evil spirits. These are demonic powers, which have gained influence over the majority of the men in the Church. What is the result of all their wickedness? They have become rich, and in their wealth, they think themselves blessed of God. Their prophets also speak falsehood and their leaders rule by their own judgment, and not of the Lord. And the people love it this way, but what will you do, when the Lord brings about the end of these things?

> *Fear ye not me? saith the Lord: will ye not tremble at my presence But this people hath a revolting and a rebellious heart; they are revolted and God. Neither say they in their heart, Let us now fear the Lord our God, that giveth rain, both the former and the latter, in his season: he reserveth unto us the appointed weeks of the harvest. Your iniquities have turned away these things, and your sins have withholden good things from you. For among my people are found wicked men: they lay wait, as he that setteth snares; they set a trap, they catch men. As a cage is full of birds, so are their houses full of deceit: therefore they are become great, and waxen rich. They are waxen fat, they shine: yea, they overpass the deeds of the wicked: they judge not the cause, the cause of the fatherless, yet they prosper; and the right of the needy do they not judge. Shall I not visit for these things? saith the Lord: shall not my soul be avenged on such a nation as this? A wonderful and horrible thing is committed in the land; The prophets prophesy falsely, and the priests bear rule by their means; and my people love to have it so: and what will ye do in the end thereof?*
> *Jeremiah 5:22-31*

THE LAODICEAN CHURCH IS BLIND AND NAKED

The Church in America is the Church of Laodicea Jesus spoke of in the book of Revelation. This last days Church thinks itself rich and in need of nothing; Jesus declares it is wretched, miserable, poor, blind and naked. This church is also deaf, unable to hear the word of the Lord. This is the Church in America, full of wealth and in its own mind in need of nothing, yet in reality, oblivious to what the Lord is about to do in this land. Dear reader, do you have ears to hear what the Spirit is saying to the Church?

If you cannot hear the Lord, it is because you are not close to him. It is that simple. His word declares his sheep hear his voice. And if you cannot hear him speak to you through his word and his spirit, then what are you? And what is the chaff to the wheat? I speak to the little ones, who tremble at the word of the Lord. Do not fear if you haven't heard His voice, believe in him and begin praying and fasting. This is the day the Lord spoke of, *"And it shall come to pass, that whosoever shall call on the name of the Lord shall be delivered: for in mount Zion and in Jerusalem shall be deliverance."* [49]

The Lord is standing outside of the Church of Laodicea and knocking at the door. Who will open the door and let Jesus come in as Lord? He shall be saved! Many are called, but few are chosen. Fear not little flock, only repent and return to the Lord.

Then The Word Of The LORD Came Unto Me

And unto the angel of the church of the Laodiceans write I know thy works, that thou art neither cold nor hot: I would thou went cold or hot. So then because thou art lukewarm, and neither cold nor hot, I will spue thee out of my mouth. Because thou sayest, I am rich, and increased with goods, and have need of nothing; and knowest not that thou art wretched, and miserable, and poor, and blind, and naked. Revelation 3:14-17

The prophet wonders, to whom can he speak? Who will listen to the true word of the Lord, that they may give heed to the warnings of the Spirit? Behold, the people hold the true word of God as a reproach, and that which is disgraceful. They will no longer listen to the truth of the Scripture, but rather they follow that which seems right in their own eyes.

To whom shall I speak, and give warning, that they may hear? Behold, their ear is uncircumcised, and they cannot hearken: behold, the word of the Lord is unto them a reproach; they have no delight in it. Jeremiah 6:10

THE PEOPLE REJECT THE TRUE WORDS OF GOD

Because the people will not receive the word of correction, but hold the truth of God as a reproach, the Lord declares he will pour out His judgment on all of them. *"Righteousness exalts a nation: but sin is a reproach to any people."* [50]

Therefore I am full of the fury of the Lord; I am weary with holding in: I will pour it out upon the children abroad and upon the assembly of young men together: for even the husband with the wife shall be taken, the aged with him that is full of days. And their houses shall be turned unto others, with their fields and wives together: for I will stretch out my hand upon the inhabitants of the land, saith the LORD. Jeremiah 6:11-12

The Lord declares all of these people are full of covetousness. Each of them lusts after material gain. All of them love riches, and deal falsely. They lie and speak falsehoods one to another, and they heal the hurts of the people falsely, giving soft words of peace when there is no peace coming.

Is this not the Church of today, with its peace and prosperity teachings, and full of the lust of the eyes and the pride of life? The message of false peace is the pre-tribulation rapture fable, and the Day of Judgment draws nigh.

For from the least of them even unto the greatest of them every one is given to covetousness; and from the prophet even unto the priest every one deals falsely. They have healed also the hurt of the daughter of my people slightly, saying, Peace, peace; when there is no peace. Jeremiah 6:13-14

THE DAY OF THE LORD IS AT HAND

The Lord God of their fathers sent to them by his messengers... because he had compassion on his people... but they mocked the messengers of God, and despised his words and misused his prophets, until the wrath of the Lord arose against his people, till there was no remedy. 2 Chronicles 36:15-16

The days of visitation are come, the days of recompense are come; Israel shall know it: the prophet is (considered) a fool, the spiritual man is (thought to be) mad, for the multitude of thine iniquity, and the great hatred. Hosea 9:7

THE LORD PLEADS WITH HIS PEOPLE TO SEEK THE ANCIENT PATH

The Lord continues to plead with the people to stand in His ways and to see, and to seek the old path which is the good way. This is the path of faith and obedience, and of holiness unto the Lord, but the people refuse to walk in His ways. The Lord also declares, *"Listen to the sound of the trumpet"*, for he has set watchmen, to warn of the impending judgment, but the people refuse to listen to the warnings, being hardened in their self-will and rebellion. Today, this is the state of America, as watchman all over the land, from David Wilkerson, Dumitru Duduman, and others are blowing the trumpet, yet the Church refuses to wake from her sleep.

Thus saith the Lord, Stand ye in the ways, and see, and ask for the old paths, where is the good way, and walk therein, and ye shall find rest for your souls. But they said, We will not walk therein. Also I set watchmen over you, saying, Hearken to the sound of the trumpet. But they said, We will not hearken. Jeremiah 6:16-17

THE PROPHET CONFRONTS THE PEOPLE WITH THE TRUTH

The prophet confronts the people: "Why do you say you are wise, and that you know the ways of God and his law is with you? You claim to have his covenant but you do not keep the law of the Lord nor honor his covenant." Therefore, the wise men shall be ashamed! When the day of his visitation comes upon our nation, they will all be ashamed.

We claim to have his New Covenant, but the majority in the Church no longer obeys the Lord, nor honors His word.

Jesus said *"If ye love me, keep my commandments"*.[51] Our nation is full of professing Christians, who assume they will go to heaven, yet the Lord declares that many on that day will be cast out!

Then The Word Of The LORD Came Unto Me

Not everyone that saith unto me, Lord, Lord, shall enter into the kingdom of heaven; but he that doeth the will of my Father which is in heaven. Many will say to me in that day, Lord, Lord, have we not prophesied in thy name? and in thy name have cast out devils? and in thy name done many wonderful works? And then will I profess unto them, I never knew you: depart from me, ye that work iniquity.[52]

These poor souls were converted, and some had even done miracles in his name, yet they never knew him. Dear reader, ask the Lord to test your heart. Do you know him? Does his word abide in you? Are you abiding in him? Do not trust in the mere confession of faith, but see if you have the love of the Father in your heart and the evidence of salvation, which is the desire to please and obey him as Lord. His sheep hear his voice. Can you hear him speaking through the words in this book?

I asked the Lord, what is different about the many that do not know him, but only know his name. He answered me saying, "These are they who have never received of my character, and were never changed by my words, and have never learned to walk in my ways. To them I will say. Lo Ammi. You are not my people."

How do ye say, we are wise, and the law of the LORD is with us? The wise men are ashamed, they are dismayed and taken: Lo, they have rejected the word of the LORD; and what wisdom is in them? ...everyone from the least even unto the greatest is given to covetousness, from the prophet even unto the priest every one deals falsely. For they have healed the hurt of the daughter of my people slightly, saying, Peace, peace; when there is no peace. Were they ashamed when they had committed abomination? Nay, they were not at all ashamed, neither could they blush: therefore shall they fall among them that fall: in the time of their visitation they shall be cast down, saith the Lord.

...The LORD our God hath put us to silence, and given us water of gall to drink, because we have sinned against the LORD. We looked for peace, but no good came; and for a time of health, and behold trouble! Jeremiah 8:8-15

SUMMER IS ENDED, AND WE ARE NOT SAVED

The Lord asks in the above verse, why do we sit still? He then directs his people who are listening to *"assemble yourselves"* and go into the *"safe cities"* for the time of judgment is at hand. We are then given a prophetic clue of the timing of the judgment: *"The harvest is past, the summer is ended, and we are not saved."* [53]

THE DAY OF THE LORD IS AT HAND

The Feast of Pentecost inaugurated the outpouring of the Holy Spirit, and the beginning of the New Covenant, which gave birth to the church age. Pentecost occurs at the beginning of summer and marks the start of the wheat harvest of Israel. The Feast is celebrated with two loaves of bread which contain leaven. The bread is placed in the fire, until the leaven is purged. The wheat harvest is a picture of the judgment of God. His people are the wheat, and they are judged first.

The judgment of the Church will occur during the time of the wheat harvest, which is the season of summer. And it will be obvious you did not get saved, for by the end of a soon summer, the Church in America will have gone into captivity, to the detention camps, as the nation goes under martial law. This is not the start of the Great Tribulation, or the end of the age. This is just the beginning of the judgment upon the household of God, a judgment that must come first.

THE PROPHET WISHES TO HIDE IN THE WILDERNESS

Jeremiah laments wishing he had a place to hide in the wilderness, so that he might leave his people, for they are an assembly of adulterers and treacherous, deceitful men. The Lord adds the final words stating *"they proceed from evil to evil, and the people do not know me."* These people do not know the Lord. Jesus will say of them *"And then will I profess unto them, I never knew you: depart from me, ye that work iniquity."* [54]

> *Oh that I had in the wilderness a lodging place of wayfaring men; that I might leave my people, and go from them! for they be all adulterers, an assembly of treacherous men. ... They proceed from evil to evil, and they know not me, saith the LORD for every brother will utterly supplant, and every neighbor will walk with slanders. Jeremiah 9:2-4*

The Lord warns us to beware of our neighbor and to not trust our brothers in the Church. The Hebrew for *"supplant"* is עָקַב, *awkab* [55] which means to seize by the heel; to circumvent and to restrain. The Hebrew for *"slanders"* is רָכִיל, *rawkeel* which means a scandal-monger, to carry tales, a talebearer. The Lord is warning His remnant, they are surrounded by brothers who will attempt to trip them, and restrain them. These so-called brothers, also will talk and create scandal regarding the remnant, which appear to those in darkness as if they had lost their minds, for they are building an ark before it rains. Therefore, the Lord says He will melt them by a judgment with fire.

Jesus himself warned us, that before the Great Tribulation, *"Then shall they deliver you up to be afflicted, and shall kill you: and ye shall be hated of all nations for my name's sake. And then shall many be offended, and shall betray one another, and shall hate one another."*[56]

The Lord tells us clearly that persecution of the true church shall first come in all of the nations, and when it comes, the majority will be offended and betray one another. A world-wide persecution precedes the revealing of the antichrist, and the beginning of the Great Tribulation. This persecution is the next event in the United States, and when it comes, it will be sudden and devastating to the sleeping Church in America.

> *Take ye heed every one of his neighbor, and trust ye not in any brother: for every brother will utterly supplant, and every neighbor will walk with slanders. And they will deceive everyone his neighbor, and will not speak the truth: they have taught their tongue to speak lies, and weary themselves to commit iniquity. Thy habitation is in the midst of deceit; through deceit they refuse to know me, saith the Lord. Therefore thus saith the Lord of hosts, Behold, I will melt them.* [57]

THE LORD ASKS - WHO IS WISE THAT UNDERSTANDS

The Lord then asks, *"Who is the wise man that may understand this? And who is he to whom the mouth of the Lord has spoken, that he may declare it?"* Who has wisdom? Who understands what is happening in the land? Who has heard the words of the Lord, that they might declare them? Only the poor in spirit and the brokenhearted can hear the Lord. Only the humble souls will be able to discern this word. *"Many shall be purified, and made white, and tried; but the wicked shall do wickedly: and none of the wicked shall understand; but the wise shall understand."* [58]

> *Who is the wise man that may understand this? And who is he to whom the mouth of the Lord hath spoken, that he may declare it, for what the land perishes and is burned up like a wilderness, that none passes through? Because they have forsaken my law which I set before them, and have not obeyed my voice... But have walked after the imagination of their own heart... I will scatter them and I will send a sword after them... till I have consumed them. Jeremiah 9:12-16*

The Lord declares that after the judgment, the people will forsake the land, and they will be cast out of their homes. Their bodies shall fall as the dung in the open fields, and their dead shall lie littered upon the ground and no one shall even bury them! When the final judgment comes, the dead will greatly outnumber the living. The few souls saved will leave and forsake the land, and no one will even bury the dead in America.

THE DAY OF THE LORD IS AT HAND

For a voice of wailing is heard out of Zion, How are we spoiled! For death is come up into our windows, and is entered into our palaces, to cut off the children from without, and the young men from the streets. Thus saith the LORD, Even the carcasses of men shall fall as dung upon the open field, and as the handful after the harvestman, and none shall gather them. Jeremiah 9:19-22

Then the Lord admonishes those to whom His mysteries are revealed, that they should not glory in their wisdom, but let them glory that they know the Lord. The Lord is a God who loves mercy, justice and righteousness! Let all the earth fear before Him!

Thus saith the Lord, Let not the wise man glory in his wisdom, neither let the mighty man glory in his might, let not the rich man glory in his riches: but let him that glory, glory in this, that he understands and knows me, that I am the Lord which exercise lovingkindness, judgment, and righteousness, in the earth: for in these things I delight, saith the Lord. Behold, the days come, saith the Lord, that I will punish all the house of Israel are uncircumcised in the heart. Jeremiah 9:23-26

LEARN NOT THE CUSTOMS OF THE HEATHEN

The Lord then commands the people not to engage in the customs of the heathen. The Lord specifically points to the pagan festival of Saturnalia, which is the birthday of Tammuz, the son god of ancient Babylon. "The basis of this celebration can be traced back to the kingdom of Nimrod in Ancient Babylon"[59] and the heathen have celebrated this pagan holiday for over 3,000 years. This is the modern holiday of Christmas. The scripture even describes the tradition of cutting down and decorating trees for the feast of Tammuz on December 25th. "There are many features of Christmas that can be traced back to pagan worship such as Christmas trees, yule logs, mistletoe and other things."[60] The early Americans refused to allow the pagan holidays of Christmas and Halloween; both were illegal in America in the first fifty years. These pagan rituals, now absorbed into the apostate Church, are cherished by many people who love the Lord. In their ignorance, they are celebrating the birthday of the antichrist.

God forgives so many sins we commit in ignorance, but when He exposes the sin, He demands that we repent and change. Today, the majority of the people in America couldn't care less what the word of God declares. They esteem it a reproach; they prefer their tradition more than obedience by faith. Thus the judgment will be just upon the disobedient that cry "Lord, Lord" but will not obey him. They refuse to honor him as Lord, seeking rather to please themselves by doing that which is right in their own eyes. Truly these people are following the imaginations of their own heart!

> *Hear ye the word which the Lord speaks unto you, O house of Israel: Thus saith the Lord. Learn not the way of the heathen, and be not dismayed at the signs of heaven; for the heathen are dismayed at them. For the customs of the people are vain: for one cuts a tree out of the forest, the work of the hands of the workman, with the axe. They deck it with silver and with gold; they fasten it with nails and with hammers that it move not. Jeremiah 10:1-4*

The Lord then speaks of the people of the earth, calling them gods who did not create the earth. This speaks of the time that would come, when the people would think themselves gods. The new age movement teaches exactly that. These false teachers, and their deceived followers, shall soon perish from the earth! This section of scripture tells us we are dealing with the end of the world, not an ancient judgment upon Israel, for at this time the heathen who think themselves gods shall perish from the earth. This prophecy is not speaking of the destruction of ancient Israel, but of the heathen nations; this is an end time prophecy of the judgment of the entire world!

> *And the nations shall not be able to abide his indignation. Thus shall ye say unto them, the gods that have not made the heavens and the earth, even they shall perish from the earth, and from under these heavens. He hath made the earth by his power, he hath established the world by his wisdom, and hath stretched out the heavens by his discretion. Jeremiah 10:10-12*

THE LORD DECLARES THE JUDGMENT MUST COME

The Lord tells us why the judgment must come. God rose early and pleaded with His people, demanding them to obey his voice, but they refused. The people committed three sins against the Lord for which the nation will be destroyed:
1. They disobeyed God's laws.
2. They refused to listen to God's voice.
3. Each of them walked after the imagination of their own hearts.

> *For I earnestly protested unto your fathers in the day that I brought them up out of the land of Egypt, even unto this day, rising early and protesting, saying, Obey my voice. Yet they obeyed not, nor inclined their ear, but walked everyone in the imagination of their evil heart: therefore I will bring upon them all the words of this covenant, which I commanded*

them to do; but they did them not. And the Lord said unto me, A conspiracy is found among the men of Judah, and among the inhabitants of Jerusalem. They are turned back to the iniquities of their forefathers, which refused to hear my words; and they went after other gods to serve them: the house of Israel and the house of Judah have broken my covenant, which I made with their fathers. Therefore thus saith the Lord, Behold, I will bring evil upon them, which they shall not be able to escape; and though they shall cry unto me, I will not hearken unto them. Jeremiah 11:7-11

Is this not the condition of the Church and our nation today? How many people, who profess the name of Jesus, truly seek to obey him? How many can hear his voice speaking to them? Almost no one can hear the Lord today. They all claim to follow him, yet the word of God testifies, the people are actually walking in the way that seems right in their own eyes. They are not hearing the Lord at all, but are following the imagination of their own hearts, even as the ancient Israelites did prior to the judgment. Woe unto us, for the summer is coming, and we are not saved!

MANY PASTORS HAVE DESTROYED GOD'S PEOPLE

The Lord then declares that many pastors have destroyed his people. When the Lord uses the word many, he means the vast majority of them. The Lord declares that no man understands or ponders this truth. Only a small remnant, which God is now restoring to his true covenant, can recognize that the pastors in America have deceived and destroyed the people of God. Ancient Israel erred, seeking a king to rule over them, and turned from the Lord. The Church has committed the same act of treason before God, turning to the pastors for guidance, and forsaking the Lord. How have they deceived the people? These blind guides of the blind have been teaching another gospel! This is the gospel of the last days apostasy, and it is built upon four pillars of falsehood:

1. Intellectual conversion without true repentance from the heart
2. Faith without heart felt obedience to the Lord
3. Discipleship without the cross and death to self
4. Religious works of the flesh without the spirit and true holiness

Where are the tears of repentance today? Where is the prayer and fasting among God's people? How many spend quiet time in devotions with God each day? Where is the compassion and the agape love which is the witness of the fruit of the Spirit? Today we find only wealth, and vanities filling the churches which are called by his name.

Many pastors have destroyed my vineyard, they have trodden my portion under foot, they have made my pleasant portion a desolate wilderness. They have made it desolate, and being desolate it mourns unto me; the whole land is made desolate, because no man lays it to heart. Jeremiah 12:10-11

THE PEOPLE WILL BE CARRIED
AWAY INTO CAPTIVITY

The prophet declares he is weeping because the people will be carried away into captivity. Like Jeremiah, we who have heard this message from the Lord have also spent many days weeping for our families and friends. The people we love shall all go into captivity, even as Israel went into slavery under judgment. The Church in America will soon go into captivity, enduring the hardships of slave labor in the death camps of the prince. Yet the people are asleep, having turned away from sound doctrines to falsehoods and fables.

If ye will not hear it, my soul shall weep in secret places for your pride; and mine eye shall weep sore, and run down with tears, because the Lord's flock is carried away captive. Say unto the king and to the queen, humble yourselves, sit down: for your principalities shall come down, even the crown of your glory. The cities of the south shall be shut up, and none shall open them: Judah shall be carried away captive all of it, it shall be wholly carried away captive. Lift up your eyes, and behold them that come from the north ... Wherefore come these things upon me? For the greatness of thine iniquity are thy skirts discovered, and thy heels made bare. Can the Ethiopian change his skin or the leopard his spots? Then may ye also do good, that are accustomed to do evil. This is thy lot, the portion of thy measures from me, saith the Lord; because thou hast forgotten me, and trusted in falsehood. Jeremiah 13:17-25

THE FALSE PROPHETS ARE CRYING "PEACE, PEACE"

Next Jeremiah complains that the false prophets are telling the people they will have peace, and will not see the sword or famine. The Lord replies that these prophets are speaking lies. Dear reader, today's teachers of the pre-tribulation rapture are spreading the same deadly falsehood.

This false teaching has deceived the Church, telling them they will never see the day of evil. These teachers are teaching lies! Notice what the Lord says will happen to these false teachers, and those who listen to them. They shall all be consumed by the sword.

Then said I, Ah, Lord God! Behold, the prophets say unto them. Ye shall not see the sword, neither shall ye have famine; but I will give, you assured peace in this place. Then the Lord said unto me. The prophets prophesy lies in my name: I sent them not, neither have I commanded them, neither spoke unto them: they prophesy unto you a false vision and divination, and a thing of nought, and the deceit of their heart. Therefore thus saith the Lord concerning the prophets that prophesy in my name, and I sent them not, yet they say, Sword and famine shall not be in this land; By sword and famine shall those prophets be consumed. And the people to whom they prophesy shall be cast out in the streets of Jerusalem because of the famine and the sword; and they shall have none to bury them, for I will pour their wickedness upon them. Jeremiah 14:13-16

THE FALSE PROPHETS OF THE LAST DAYS

If you are tempted to think this is not a last days warning, look at Chapter 23 where the Lord declares the same word against these false prophets, telling us that in the last days we would understand perfectly what he is saying. The last days false prophecy of peace, when there will be no peace, is the pre-tribulation rapture. It is a fable, a bedtime story for people who can no longer endure sound doctrine. Paul writes Timothy warning him that in the last days, the Church would no longer want to hear the truth of Scripture, but would turn to stories and fables which had been invented in imaginations of men. *"For the time will come when they will not endure sound doctrine; but after their own lusts shall they heap to themselves teachers, having itching ears; And they shall turn away their ears from the truth, and shall be turned unto fables."*[61]

The Lord declares he will destroy his people, his Christian nation, because they refuse to repent, and will not turn from their own ways to serve God as He commands. Rather they continue in their rebellion, and their disobedience, under the deception of false prophets. Oh my people, why do you perish?

Thou hast forsaken me, saith the LORD, thou art gone backward: therefore will I stretch out my hand against thee, and destroy thee; I am weary with repenting. And I will fan them with a fan in the gates of the land; I will bereave them of children, I will destroy my people, since they return not from their ways. Jeremiah 15:6-7

THE LORD PROMISES DELIVERANCE TO ALL WHO RETURN TO HIM

In the midst of the word of judgment, the Lord continues to promise His people, *"If you will return to me I will deliver you out of the hand of the terrible!"*[62]

Brethren, we must return to the Lord with our whole heart, and to our first love, for the backslider and the hypocrite will be judged!

> *Lord will hear when I call unto him. Stand in awe, and sin not. Commune with your own heart upon your bed, and be still. Selah. Offer the sacrifices of righteousness, and put your trust in the Lord.* [63]

The Lord then declares that he has taken away the peace of this people, and they will not even be buried. After the initial judgment on the Church, the Lord will turn and judge the entire nation. America will suffer both biological and nuclear destruction, and the survivors won't even bury the dead!

> *For thus saith the Lord, Enter not into the house of mourning, neither go to lament or bemoan them: for I have taken away my peace from this people, saith the Lord, even loving kindness and mercies. Both the great and the small shall die in this land: they shall not be buried, neither shall men lament for them, nor cut themselves, nor make themselves bald for them. Jeremiah 16:5-6*

THE LORD PRONOUNCES
JUDGMENT ON THE PASTORS

The Lord then pronounces judgment upon the many pastors who have destroyed his flock with their false teachings. The Lord will replace them with new shepherds, who will teach the truth. When King Balac wished to curse Israel, he hired Balaam the prophet. Balaam was a prophet for profit. He was motivated by money. When he inquired of the Lord, the Lord told him, He would not curse Israel. Balaam, being cunning and knowing the ways of God, told Balac if he could get Israel to break God's laws, only then would the Lord curse His people.

How? They have done two things: They have turned the people to idolatry by bringing paganism within the Church, and with it all forms of idolatry, which includes the lust of this life, and the love of money and pleasure. Second, by this idolatry, they have turned the people to fornication. This speaks of both literal sexual disobedience and spiritual fornication, where the people have left the worship of the true God and are turned to idols, loving their money and their pleasures more than the Lord!

> *Woe unto the pastors that destroy and scatter the sheep of my pasture says the Lord. Therefore thus saith the Lord... Ye have scattered my flock, and driven them away, and have not visited them: behold, I will visit upon you the evil of your doings, saith the Lord. And I will gather the remnant of my flock out of all countries whither I have driven them, and will bring*

them again to their folds; and they shall be fruitful and increase. And I will set up shepherds over them which shall feed them: and they shall fear no more, nor be dismayed, neither shall they be lacking, saith the Lord. Jeremiah 23:1-4

The Lord also promises He will set up new shepherds over his sheep who will feed them the true word of God. But the false shepherds, they will be judged first. The pastors will be the first ones taken into captivity. This is always the case. One day soon, the majority of the pastors in America will be arrested in the middle of the night. This will be the first day the darkness falls in America. The following Sunday, a new pastor will stand among the people declaring, "God has moved your former pastor to a new calling. Today, I am pleased to introduce myself as your new pastor." These new pastors in the government churches will be the servants of the prince! Do you think the elders will object to this? No, they will all be arrested too. This is exactly what happened in Russia, and many other countries, as they fell under tyranny. At this point, the true Church will no longer meet in the government assemblies, but will be found in the homes. In most congregations, they won't even be missed, for only one or two will silently stop attending, after being told by the Lord not to go back to Church. The Lord will appoint His own pastors over His little flock in that day. They will have His heart for the people, and they will feed His sheep the truth.

Again, the Lord declares that the nation is full of adulterers, from the top elected officials in the land to the least of them, and because of swearing, the taking of the Lord's name in vain, the land mourns and is under judgment. The Lord declares both the prophet and the priest are profane, and unclean before him. Yes, in His house, the Church, is all of this wickedness found. Therefore, their way shall become slippery and they shall fall therein. The Lord shall bring evil upon them, even their year of visitation. The Lord tells us these false prophets are actually prophesying under the influence of demons. They have caused the people to err, because they have not uncovered the sin of the people, but have lied to them and promised peace when there is none! Further, these false prophets commit adultery, and being full of deceit, they walk in lies. They also help other evil doers and therefore none of them returns from his wickedness. The Lord says these people remind him of Sodom and Gomorrah, and from these false prophets profanity has filled the entire nation. Therefore, the Lord will judge them.

The land is full of adulterers; for because of swearing the land mourns; the pleasant places of the wilderness are dried up, and their course is evil, For both prophet and priest are profane; yea, in my house have I found their wickedness, saith the Lord. Wherefore their way shall be unto them as slippery ways in the darkness: ... for I will bring evil upon them, even the year of their visitation, saith the Lord. And I have seen folly in the prophets of Samaria; they prophesied in Baal, and caused my people Israel to err they strengthen also the hands of evildoers that none doth return from his wickedness: they are all of them unto me as Sodom, and the inhabitants thereof as Gomorrah. Jeremiah 23:10-14

IN THE LAST DAYS YOU WILL UNDERSTAND PERFECTLY

The Lord tells us, *"Do not listen to the false prophets who bring a message of peace"* by telling the people of God they will not see the day of evil. They are lying! The modern-day false prophets are the mainstream Christian pastors who teach the pre-tribulation rapture doctrine. And the Lord says they speak to a people who despise Him. How do the people despise the Lord? By refusing to obey His word, and continuing in their sins. The Lord then asks, who has stood in His counsel, and heard His word. The ones who are declaring *"a whirlwind is about to fall in America"* and it will not return until *"He has executed!"* What do you think He means by *"executed"*? And when does this message apply? Jeremiah tells us clearly, for *"in the latter days you shall consider (understand) it perfectly."*

> *Thus saith the Lord of hosts, Hearken not unto the words of the prophets that prophesy unto you: they make you vain: they speak a vision of their own heart, and not out of the mouth of the Lord. They say still unto them that despise me, The Lord hath said, Ye shall have peace; and they say unto every one that walks after the imagination of his own heart, No evil shall come upon you. For who hath stood in the counsel of the Lord, and hath perceived and heard his word? who hath marked his word, and heard it? Behold, a whirlwind of the Lord is gone forth in fury, even a grievous whirlwind The anger of the Lord shall not return, until he has executed ...in the latter days ye shall consider it perfectly. Jeremiah 23:16-22*

THE DAY OF THE LORD IS AT HAND

CHAPTER

4

THE DAY OF THE LORD IS AT HAND

For thousands of years, the prophets of God testified that a day would come when the Lord would judge the entire earth. Unlike His judgments in the past, which were upon various nations, at various times, this day would be like none other. This will be the Day of the Lord, and it will come upon the whole earth, as a day of destruction for all the enemies of God. It will also be a day of deliverance for those abiding in Jesus Christ in holiness and purity. The Lord will save His small remnant as He comes in judgment to lay the mountains low, and He will tread the nations in the winepress of His wrath. Having done all He could to save mankind in His death on the cross, the Lord now comes as a Judge, with the full fury of the wrath of God.

IT SHALL COME AS DESTRUCTION
FROM THE ALMIGHTY

What exactly do the prophets say about the Day of the Lord? First, it comes as destruction from the Almighty! This day comes from the Lord, and though He uses men as instruments of His judgment, these things are done by God. The Lord declares, *"Every one of them shall be faint, and all their hearts shall melt, and they shall be afraid!"* I trembled for seven days after I saw the Day of the Lord. One of my friends said to me, "We don't know if you have heard from God, or if you had a breakdown." I told him, it is both. God spoke and I broke, and when you see what I saw, you will break too. I shook like a frightened sinner, found guilty before the Judge of the whole earth. You cannot imagine the emotions that will run through your mind when they take your wife and your children from your side. If you stand there, as I did, you will know what the Lord meant when He said *"They will be amazed when they look at each other, for their faces will appear as if on fire."*

> And they shall be afraid: pangs and sorrows shall take hold of them; they shall be in pain as a woman that travaileth: they shall be amazed one at another: their faces shall be as flames. Isaiah 13:8

Dear reader the present age is drawing to a close. Its end will be with pain and anguish unseen before in the history of man. But the Lord will be a shield to His remnant and to all who return to Him with their whole hearts.

THE DAY OF THE LORD IS AT HAND

To those who will forsake their sins, and who stop serving the gods of the Americans, the promise God made to our father Abraham is to us as well, *"Fear not, I am thy shield, and thy exceeding great reward."* [1] The Lord Jesus Christ delights in mercy and His mercy triumphs over judgment. That is why at this late hour, the Lord has held back His judgment, and He has sent this true word to His people, that whoever would turn with their whole hearts and repent of the apostasy might be delivered. As the Father said of Jesus, *"This is my beloved Son, Hear him."* [2] We must be able to hear from the Lord in this hour!

THE DAY OF THE LORD COMES WITH WRATH

The scripture tells us, the day of the Lord will come with intense stress upon all nations! The Day of the Lord will bring destruction to the kingdom of sin, and to the peoples of this world, who walk only in darkness and follow the prince of the air.

> *Howl ye; for the day of the Lord is at hand: it shall come as a destruction from the Almighty. Therefore shall all hands be faint, and every man's heart shall melt: And they shall be afraid: pangs and sorrows shall take hold of them; they shall be in pain as a woman that travails: they shall be amazed one at another; their faces shall be as flames. Behold, the day of the Lord cometh, cruel both with wrath and fierce anger to lay the land desolate: and he shall destroy the sinners thereof out of it. For the stars of heaven and the constellations thereof shall not give their light: the sun shall be darkened in his going forth, and the moon shall not cause her light to shine. And I will punish the world for their evil, and the wicked for their iniquity; and I will cause the arrogancy of the proud to cease, and will lay low the haughtiness of the terrible. I will make a man more precious than fine gold; even a man than the golden wedge of Ophir. Isaiah 13:6-12*

God says He will make man rarer than the golden wedge of Ophir. The wedge of Ophir was a myth. God is saying in the Day of the Lord, He will make man more precious than a myth! This is a complete destruction which has been determined by the Lord.

> *Enter into the rock, and hide thyself in the dust, for fear of the Lord, and for the glory of his majesty. The lofty looks of man shall be humbled, and the haughtiness of men shall be bowed down, and the Lord alone shall be exalted in that day. For the day of the Lord shall be upon every one that is proud and lofty, and upon every one that is lifted up; and he shall be brought low. Isaiah 2:10-12*

The Day Of The LORD Is At Hand

NOW WILL I RISE, NOW WILL I BE EXALTED

The prophet Isaiah testifies about the day of the Lord: *"Now will I rise, saith the Lord, now will I be exalted, now will I lift myself up."* [3] The Lord will stand to judge the people and, in that day, He will do His "strange work", and bring to pass His "strange act", the work of judgment! God calls this his "strange work", because He does not take pleasure in the destruction of the wicked, nor in the judgment which must come upon the apostate Church. The Lord warns the people, *"do not mock this word of warning, unless you want the bands that bind you to be made stronger."* [4]

Isaiah declares that he has heard from the Lord of a complete destruction, and a total consumption has been determined upon the whole earth. The Day of the Lord is at hand.

> *For the Lord shall rise up as in mount Perazim, he shall be wroth as in the valley of Gibeon, that he may do his work, his strange work; and bring to pass his act, his strange act. Now therefore be ye not mockers, lest your bands be made strong: for I have heard from the Lord God of hosts a consumption, even determined upon the whole earth. Isaiah 28:21-22*

> *And the loftiness of man shall be bowed down, and the haughtiness of men shall be made low: and the Lord alone shall be exalted in that day. And the idols he shall utterly abolish. And they shall go into the holes of the rocks, and into the caves of the earth, for fear of the Lord, and for the glory of his majesty, when he ariseth to shake terribly the earth. Isaiah 2:17-19*

The prophet Joel also spoke about the day of the Lord, declaring that it would be a day of darkness, and of thick darkness. All the inhabitants of the land will tremble. We are commanded to *"blow the trumpet in Zion"* to warn the people, the day of the Lord is at hand. *"Alas the day! For the day of the Lord is at hand, and as destruction from the Almighty shall it come."* [5]

> *Blow ye the trumpet in Zion, and sound an alarm in my holy mountain let all the inhabitants of the land tremble: for the day of the Lord cometh, for it is nigh at hand; A day of darkness and of gloominess, a day of clouds and of thick darkness.* [6]

The Lord shall speak as a roaring lion on that day. His voice will *"thunder from Zion."* God will speak with such power, that *"the heavens and the earth will shake."* Everyone will panic. Fear will strike them all, save His remnant people. Of them, the Lord says, *"the Lord will be the hope of His people and the strength of Israel."* Jesus told us when we see these things coming to pass to look up. In this day, the Lord is the only hope of His people. We have no

103

other. He alone is our Hope. God is my salvation, I will trust and not be afraid, for the Lord even Jehovah, He is my strength and my song. All the songs and verses of Scripture we have learned will take on new meaning in that day.

> *Multitudes, multitudes in the valley of decision: for the day of the Lord is near in the valley of decision. The sun and the moon shall be darkened, and the stars shall withdraw their shining. The Lord also shall roar out of Zion, and utter his voice from Jerusalem; and the heavens and the earth shall shake: but the Lord will be the hope of his people, and the strength of the children of Israel. Joel 3:14-16*

Jesus spoke prophetically of this day, looking forward to the time of judgment, declaring that He will come forth *"to cast fire upon the earth."* This is the second half of His ministry, but first He would have to complete His mission as the Holy Lamb of God. Then, He would come again as a Lion, with fire before Him! Did Jesus come to bring peace and unity? The scripture testifies, *"no, but rather division."* Thereby we know this move to a one world church is a deception. And these supposed Christian leaders, who are now embracing the religions of darkness in unity, and in the so called "doctrine of tolerance", are actually servants of the dragon. *"I have come to cast fire upon the earth; and how I wish it were already kindled! But I have a baptism to undergo, and how distressed I am until it is accomplished! Do you suppose that I came to grant peace on earth? I tell you, no, but rather division"* [7]

THOU ART MY BATTLE AXE AND WEAPON OF WAR

> *The portion of Jacob is not like them; for he is the former of all things: and Israel is the rod of his inheritance: the Lord of hosts is his name. Thou art my battle axe and weapons of war: for with thee will I break in pieces the nations, and with thee will I destroy kingdoms; And with thee will I break in pieces the horse and his rider; and with thee will I break in pieces the chariot and his rider; With thee also will I break in pieces man and woman; and with thee will I break in pieces old and young; I will also break in pieces with thee the shepherd and his flock; and with thee will I break in pieces the husbandman and his yoke of oxen; and with thee will I break in pieces captains and rulers. And I will render unto Babylon and to all the inhabitants of Chaldea all their evil that they have done in Zion in your sight, saith the Lord. Behold, I am against thee, O destroying mountain, saith the Lord, which destroyest all the earth: and I will stretch out mine hand upon thee, and roll thee down from the rocks, and will make thee a burnt mountain. Jeremiah 51:19-25*

The Day Of The LORD Is At Hand

The prophet Amos also declares the Day of the Lord will be a day of judgment where none can escape. *"Woe unto you that desire the day of the Lord! To what end is it for you? The day of the Lord is darkness, and not light. As if a man did flee from a lion, and a bear met him; or went into the house, and leaned his hand on the wall, and a serpent bit him."*[8] The Day of the Lord will be a Day of Judgment, and whatever measure we have used, will be measured back unto us.

Therefore, dear remnant, choose mercy and extend forgiveness to everyone. If we measure others with mercy, we can hope to receive mercy from God, and to escape these things which shall surely come to pass. *"For the day of the Lord is near upon all the heathen: as thou hast done, it shall be done unto thee: thy reward shall return upon thine own head. "*[9]

The Day of the Lord is near; it is even at the door. God declares He will bring distress upon all men, and they will walk like blind men, because they have sinned against the Lord. Let us repent therefore while it is still day, for the night is coming when no man can work. Only the Lord will be able to work in the night which is coming.

> *The great day of the Lord is near, it is near, and hasteth greatly, even the voice of the day of the Lord: the mighty man shall cry there bitterly. That day is a day of wrath, a day of trouble and distress, a day of wasteness and desolation, a day of darkness and gloominess, a day of clouds and thick darkness, A day of the trumpet and alarm against the fenced cities, and against the high towers. And I will bring distress upon men, that they shall walk like blind men, because they have sinned against the Lord: and their blood shall be poured out as dust, and their flesh as the dung. Neither their silver nor their gold shall be able to deliver them in the day of the Lord's wrath; but the whole land shall be devoured by the fire of his jealousy: for he shall make even a speedy riddance of all them that dwell in the land. Zephaniah 1:14-18*

> *For, behold, the Lord cometh forth out of his place, and will come down, and tread upon the high places of the earth. And the mountains shall be molten under him, and the valleys shall be cleft, as wax before the fire, and as the waters that are poured down a steep place. Micah 1:3-4*

THE DAY OF THE LORD IS AT HAND

CHAPTER

5

REMOVE OUT OF
THE MIDST OF BABYLON
Jeremiah 50:8

One of the mysteries of Bible prophecy surrounds the identity of the end time nation called "Mystery Babylon" whose destruction is foretold in the Book of Revelation. As we have seen in chapter two, Daniel revealed the ruling kingdoms of the earth are all part of one empire - the kingdom of Satan, who is the prince of this present world. Each of these ruling empires is part of the same system, Mystery Babylon, which exists both as a political power and as a religious system. In this chapter, we shall review the prophecies surrounding the nation state revealed in Scripture as Mystery Babylon the Great.

> *"And there followed another angel, saying, Babylon is fallen, is fallen, that great city, because she made all nations drink of the wine of the wrath of her fornication."* [1]

In ancient times, cities identified nation states, as well as their capital. Ancient Babylon, in the time of king Nebuchadnezzar, was both a great city, and the capital of the nation state which ruled the earth of that time. The same is true of Rome, which was both a city and a nation state. In the modern era, Bible scholars debate the identity of the end time nation "MYSTERY, BABYLON THE GREAT."

MYSTERY BABYLON THE GREAT

In Revelation 17 we are given several clues to the identity of Babylon:

> *And there came one of the seven angels which had the seven vials, and talked with me, saying unto me, Come hither; I will show unto thee the judgment of the great whore that sits upon many waters: With whom the kings of the earth have committed fornication, and the inhabitants of the earth have been made drunk with the wine of her fornication. And upon her forehead a name was written: MYSTERY, BABYLON THE GREAT, THE MOTHER OF HARLOTS AND ALL ABOMINATIONS OF THE EARTH. And the woman which thou saw is that great city (nation state) which reigns over the kings of the earth.* [2]

These are the clues to the identity of Mystery, Babylon the Great:

1. She is referred to as a great whore, and a prostitute.
2. She is seated upon many waters.
3. The rulers of the have earth engaged in illicit relations with her.
4. She has polluted the inhabitants of the earth with her idolatry, making them drunk.
5. She is the mother of all falsehood and abominations upon the earth at that time.
6. She is the great nation, which rules over the kings of the earth in the last days.
7. She is called Mystery Babylon for her true identity is a secret.

IDENTIFYING THE WOMAN RIDING THE BEAST

First, this nation is identified as a whore and the mother of harlots. "This is a name of great infamy. A whore is one that is married, and has betrayed her husband's bed, has forsaken the guide of her youth, and broken the covenant of God. She had been a prostitute to the kings of the earth, whom she had intoxicated with the wine of her fornication. The appearance she made: it was gay and gaudy, like such sort of creatures: She was arrayed in purple and scarlet color, and decked with gold, and precious stones, and pearls, here were all the allurements of worldly honor and riches, pomp and pride, suited to sensual and worldly minds. Her principal seat and residence upon the beast that had seven heads and ten horns; that is to say, Rome, the city on seven hills, infamous for idolatry, tyranny, and blasphemy. Her name was written upon her forehead. It was the custom of impudent harlots to hang out signs, with their names, that all might know what they were. Now in this observe, she is named from her place of residence - Babylon the great. But that we might not take it for the old Babylon literally so called, we are told there is a mystery in the name; it is some other great city resembling the old Babylon." [3]

From the description of Babylon as a whore, we note that this nation was at one time married to the true God of Heaven but has turned a harlot and has gone whoring after other gods. Thus, we know Mystery Babylon was at one time a Godly nation but has now turned from the true God to the worship of idols and falsehood. She is an apostate!

Second, we are told this nation is seated upon many waters. This reference is both literal and symbolic. The modern nation Babylon physically possesses a land which is seated on many oceans, rivers and great lakes. This also speaks symbolically that she rules many peoples (waters refer to the nations) and has many diverse peoples as citizens or subjects.

Third, we are told this nation has engaged in illicit or immoral acts with the rulers of the other nations of the earth. Modern Babylon has political or economic ties to the rest of the planet through which she has spread her apostasy. Mystery Babylon is also the author of the last day's ecumenical movement through which the one world religion of the beast will subdue the earth.

Fourth, we are told Babylon has polluted the earth with her idolatry and fornication which is the worship of false gods. Babylon has exported her carnal idolatry to all of the other nations, corrupting them with the same idolatry with which she herself is polluted.

Fifth, modern Babylon is the mother of all falsehood and abominations on the earth in the last days, again referring to her export of her lewd and apostate culture and idolatry. She is the leader of all the nations which will be deceived by the little prince.

Finally, her identity is clearly revealed. We are told she is the great nation state which rules the earth in the last days. Can there be any doubt of whom this prophecy speaks?

AMERICA - THE DAUGHTER OF BABYLON

There is only one nation which today fits this prophetic picture and has fulfilled it literally: The United States of America. First, America was founded as a Christian nation under God, the only republic founded for the purposes of God aside from Israel herself. Israel was God's nation under the Old Covenant. The Lord called America for the New Covenant. Modern America has turned into a harlot, having become an apostate from the truth of God. Today, America worships the gods of money, fame and the pleasures of immorality. Thus America fulfills the prophetic type of a whore perfectly.

Second, America is seated upon many waters both literally and symbolically. America physically sits on the Atlantic and Pacific oceans, the Great Lakes and many great rivers, while her influence covers the globe. Symbolically, she sits or rules over many nations through her leadership of the world during the twentieth century. America also has a population from all over the earth. People everywhere dream of the day they too can come to the great land of America. She is the pride of the whole earth.

Third, America is responsible for the United Nations plan for a New World Order, having financed and promoted this plan to conquer the earth for the rich men. Her form of government, a union of independent states, is the model for the One World Government of the prince who is to come, a United

States of the World under the UN. The great seal of the US declares this in Latin, "Announcing the birth of the New World Order."

Fourth, America has polluted the world with her idolatry. The world has gone into debt with American money from American banks, smokes American cigarettes, buys American weapons, has imported America's abortion policies called family planning, and is following the American sponsored UN. The world watches American movies, buys American pornography, listens to American music, and idolizes the American culture of materialism and hedonism. America truly has polluted the earth with her filth.

Fifth, America is the mother of the falsehood of the earth at the time of the end. Her gospel of materialism and secular democracy, have deceived the earth into embracing the one-world system of the anti-Messiah. America is also the mother of the great last day's apostasy of the true faith of Jesus Christ, the one world false religion of the beast, which is the global ecumenical movement being organized under the World Council of Churches. America is also the mother of the final deception of the church, the pre-tribulation rapture fable! All of this falsehood came out of America!

Finally, America is the reigning super power over the earth in these last days. The 20th century has been referred to as the American century. It is America that has led the so-called free world, since the post war era began in 1945. The Scripture is clear; the end time nation called Mystery Babylon is the United States of America! Weep America, for your hour of judgment has come, and no one can deliver you now. "Come out from her My people" says the Lord.

THE VOICES OF MEN OF WISDOM

Many other men of wisdom have given witness that the United States of America is the end time nation Mystery Babylon: David Wilkerson, Dumitru Duduman, among others have all confirmed this word. David Wilkerson writing in his book, *Set The Trumpet to Thy Mouth*, declares: "I believe modern Babylon is present-day America, including its corrupt society and its whorish church system. No other nation fits the description of Revelation. America is going to be destroyed by fire! Sudden destruction is coming and few will escape. Unexpectedly, in one hour, a hydrogen holocaust will engulf America and this nation will be no more. God is going to judge America for its violence, its crimes, its backslidings, it's murdering of millions of babies, it's flaunting of homosexuality ...its corruption, its drunkenness and drug abuse, its form of Godliness without power, its luke warmness toward Christ. Judgment is at the door! Our days are numbered! The church is asleep, the congregations are at ease, and the shepherd's slumber. How they will scoff and laugh at this message. Theologians will reject it... Pillow prophets of peace and prosperity will publicly denounce it... I am blowing the Lord's trumpet with all my might Perhaps only the overcomers will accept and hear the sound of this trumpet blast, but I proceed with these warnings because God called me to be a watchman. "[4]

Dumitru Duduman is another of the men of wisdom, whom the Lord sent to warn the United States. Dumitru is from Romania. He smuggled Bibles into Russia for 15 years, and then was arrested and severely tortured for 5 months. While they were attempting to kill him, the angel of the Lord appeared to him, telling him "plead the Blood of Jesus" and that he would be delivered and sent to America. He was sent to Fullerton in Southern California. There, the angel came to him again to show him what would come in America. Listen to Dumitru in his own words:

"If until now we have lived the way we wanted to, now the time has come when we must stop. It is enough that in the past we did what the world asked us to do. Some lived in wickedness, others in abominations. We must put an end to all these things and return to God so that in the day of trouble, God would save us. I was awake as I am now...I was sitting outside my apartment, and I saw a light coming towards me... the light surrounded me. It was the same angel. He said Dumitru, "I brought you to this country because this country will burn." He showed me all of California. "Do you see what I have shown you? This is as Sodom and Gomorrah. Their sins have reached unto God, and God has decided to punish them by fire. In one day it will burn."

"He then showed me Las Vegas, New York, and Florida. Again, he said 'This is as Sodom and Gomorrah. In one day, it will burn.' I asked how will America burn? 'When America thinks it has peace and quiet, and they rule the world, then from the oceans and from Cuba, Nicaragua, and Central America they will bomb America.' But what will you do with your Church? 'Many churches have left me.' What do you mean? Don't you have people here? 'Tell them this: People glorify people. The honor that Christ deserves men take upon themselves. In the church there is divorce, adultery, sodomy, abortion and all kinds of wickedness. Christ does not live in sin. Christ lives in holiness. Tell them to stop sinning and repent because God never stops forgiving. And all those who stop sinning and repent, God will save them in the day of trouble. As I saved Daniel from the lions, this is how I will save them. As I saved the three young ones from the furnace, this is how I will save them.'"

"The word of God says 1,000 will fall at your side, and 10,000 at your right hand, but you will be protected by the power of God. I told the angel if you are truly the angel of God, everything must be written in the Bible. 'Have you read Jeremiah 51?' I answered, it speaks of old Babylon. 'Read it again.

111

Read it again. It speaks of America not Babylon of old. Have you read Revelation 18? I will open your mind and you will understand.' American brothers, wake up, wake up. Wake from your sleep and repent and return to God. The day of wrath is near." [5]

The Lord has raised up many other voices in this last hour. American brothers and sisters, listen to the word of the Lord. This is your final warning and there is precious little time left.

"In all of man's history on earth there has never been any society, country or people that survived if they allowed either one of two sins to continue- first, the killing of babies, abortion; second, homosexuality! America has both. America cannot stop the bleeding! America will be cut down like a corn field flattened. They won't accept My grace, so now they will have to accept my law! The law demands blood restitution. America will bleed to death. The angel of death is coming. Pride comes before the fall. America says she sits like a queen on a throne prideful. Now comes the fall. It's midnight and mankind doesn't know it! Judgment stalks the land! Warn the people!" [7]

God has given visions to others, calling them also to warn America. One such man was Henry Gruver: "I began to see all of these submarines emerging from under the surface. I was surprised by how close they were to our borders. Then I saw missiles come out of them. They hit eastern coastal cities of the United States. I looked across the country, over in the northwest side and I saw the submarines. I saw missiles coming out and hitting the western coastal cities. I cried out 'Oh God! Oh God! When will this be, and what shall be the sign of its coming?' I heard an audible voice speak to me and say 'when Russia opens her doors and lets the masses go. The free world will occupy themselves with transporting, housing and feeding and caring for the masses, and will let down their weapons and cry peace and safety. Then sudden destruction will come. Then is when it will come.'"[8]

THE JUDGMENT OF AMERICA BABYLON

Scripture refers to America as the daughter of Babylon: *"Behold, a people shall come from the north, and a great nation, and many kings shall be raised up from the coasts of the earth. They shall hold the bow and the lance: they are cruel, and will not shew mercy: their voice shall roar like the sea, and they shall ride upon horses, every one put in array, like a man to the battle, against thee, O daughter of Babylon."* [9]

America is called the daughter of Babylon because she was born a direct descendent of the king of Babylon. We shall see in later chapters; the final king of Babylon will come to power from England. England is the king of the final beast empire, and America is his daughter. She is the Queen among the nations. She is the wings of the lion spoken of in the book of Daniel. Recall the woman standing in the harbor? Is this not the symbol of the great lady, the Queen of the nations? We refer to her as Lady Liberty. And what will become of her promise of freedom? Having turned the harlot, she will now be destroyed and her people will go into slavery. Now let us examine what the Scripture says of the judgments upon the United States.

Our first references come from of Jeremiah, chapters 50 - 51. First, the Lord tells us America will be destroyed by an assembly of nations. Ancient Babylon was only destroyed by the Medes and Persians. This is our first proof that this section of Scripture does not, and cannot, speak of ancient Babylon. These prophecies speak of one of the descendent empires of Babylon. *"For, lo, I will raise and cause to come up against Babylon an assembly of great nations from the north country: and they shall set themselves in array against her; from thence she shall be taken: their arrows shall be as of a mighty expert man; none shall return in vain."*[10]

The Lord tells us a great nation from the north, along with many kings, will make war against the daughter of Babylon. If you go north from the United States, over the pole you will find Russia. Even now the world's intelligence services are all reporting of the formation of an anti-American alliance of many nations being led by Russia. The war which has started in Ukraine, is the fuse which will ignite World War III, and it is already burning.

"Behold, a people shall come from the north, and a great nation and many kings shall be raised up from the coasts of the earth." [11] Many kings are aligning themselves against America Babylon. Ancient Babylon was only attacked by two kings, the Medes and the Persians. The judgment of America will follow soon after the persecution of the Church begins.

The Lord makes His word very clear: He is commanding His people to leave Babylon. They are to flee, and deliver their lives, for this is the time of the Lord's vengeance. *"Flee out of the midst of Babylon, and deliver every man his soul: be not cut off in her iniquity; for this is the time of the Lord's vengeance; he will render unto her a recompense."*[12]

The Day of The Lord is about to begin in the land of America Babylon. All has been made ready, all but the last of the remnant, so the Lord is waiting for the final few, who have been chosen for deliverance. They must first be made white, and then, in the following summer, the fires shall come, and the land of graven images shall begin to burn. And in this land of American Idols, once the fires have ignited, they will not be put out, until they have burned both root and branch from out of this now cursed and wicked nation.

AMERICA WILL BE JUDGED
FOR HER SIN OF COVETING

God says he will judge Babylon by the measure of her covetousness. "O thou that dwells upon many waters, abundant in treasures, thine end is come, and the measure of thy covetousness. [13]

Anyone who has lived outside of the United States will comprehend the level of idolatry and covetousness in America, of which there is no equal in the earth.

How much she hath glorified herself, and lived deliciously, so much torment and sorrow give her. For she saith in her heart, I sit a queen, and am no widow, and shall see no sorrow. Therefore shall her plagues come in one day, death, and mourning, and famine; and she shall be utterly burned with fire: for strong is the Lord God who judges her. [14]

To this degree, she will be judged. The Lord even names the ancient kingdoms, which will attack America including Iraq, Iran and the other Arab nations. *"Set ye up a standard in the land, blow the trumpet among the nations, prepare the nations against her, call together against her the kingdoms of Ararat, Minni, and Ashchenaz."*[15]

The American people sleep securely, unaware of the enemies slipping into their country under the cover of darkness. The prophet Ezekiel speaks of the plot against America,

And thou shalt say, I will go up to the land of unwalled villages; I will go to them that are at rest, that dwell safely, all of them dwelling without walls, and having neither bars nor gates. [16]

This attack on the people who dwell in the land of un-walled cities occurs at the same time as the next Middle East war when Russia and the Arab alliance attack Israel. The people who live in un-walled villages are the Americans! God is speaking of the nuclear destruction of the coastlands of the United States, California, New York, and Miami along with the balance of the east and west coast.

I will send a fire on Magog, and among them that dwell carelessly in the isles: and they shall know that I am the Lord.[17]

The word for "isles" means a habitable spot, dry land, or a coast land. This prophecy speaks of the Americans who dwell carelessly in the distant coastlands. The word *"isles"* in Hebrew is אי, *aleph yod,* which means "anti"[18]

or the negative, and it also represents the flesh, which opposes the spirit. It is a desolate land, a divided land, as in the Hatfield's and the McCoy's. This is a nation of people who are all walking in and under the dominion of the flesh.

Ancient Babylon was conquered in the middle of the night. When the people woke up in the morning, it was over. So too it shall be in America. One Sunday morning, you will awaken and it will be all over for America. Why do I mention Sunday? Remember, the Lord said he would tell us all things in advance. The judgment on the United States occurs on a Sunday. All of the great defeats of America have occurred on the day of her sun god. Pearl Harbor and the Alamo both occurred on a Sunday. America will burn on a Sunday!

AMERICA SHALL BE SURPRISED AND DESOLATE FOREVER

The Lord tells us Babylon, once destroyed, will be desolate forever. Ancient Babylon could not fulfill this prophecy, but once the daughter of Babylon is destroyed, she must remain desolate forever. Ancient Babylon was occupied by the Medes when it fell. The people continued to dwell there under the new rulers. The daughter Babylon in the last days is a different nation! The last days daughter of Babylon will be left totally desolate, following her judgment, and no man shall dwell therein at all.

> *Then shalt thou say, O Lord, thou hast spoken against this place, to cut it off, that none shall remain in it, neither man nor beast, but that it shall be desolate forever.* [19]

The biological and nuclear weapons used on her soil will contaminate the land for 5,000 years. They shall all depart! It is over America. Your hour is at hand. Repent or perish! We are told Babylon, whose power was as a hammer over the earth, will be destroyed with a great destruction, and that she will be taken unaware. The citizens and the leaders of Babylon will be totally surprised by her sudden and complete destruction. *"A sound of battle is in the land, and of great destruction. How is the hammer of the whole earth cut asunder and broken! how is Babylon become a desolation among the nations! I have laid a snare for thee, and thou art also taken, O Babylon, and thou wast not aware: thou art found, and also caught, because thou hast striven against the LORD."* [20] Her fall was symbolized by the sinking of the Titanic. No one believes it is even possible.

God identifies Babylon as the most proud of all of the nations, and that the Lord himself will fight against her on the day of her judgment. *"Behold, I am against thee, O thou most proud, saith the Lord GOD of hosts: for thy day is come, the time that I will visit thee.*"[21]

God tells us He will burn the cities of America. *"And the most proud shall stumble and fall, and none shall raise him up: and I will kindle a fire in his cities, and it shall devour all round about him."*[22] This is consistent with the prophecies of Dumitru Duduman and David Wilkerson among others, which have seen the nuclear destruction of America. Ancient Babylon was not burned, nor devoured. It was overrun in one night while the people slept. In the morning when they awoke it was over. The fall of America will be as sudden, but unlike ancient Babylon, America will burn! And after the nation burns, no man shall dwell there.

We are also told the nation will suffer a drought as a prelude to the destruction of the land. *"A drought is upon her waters; and they shall be dried up: for it is the land of graven images, and they are mad upon their idols."* [23]

The prophecy reveals our nation will be in drought conditions as the hour of destruction draws near. The summer before the final judgment will evidence extreme drought conditions, as a warning of the destruction of America which comes in the fall. This is the final warning to the remnant, that it is time to flee. During a future summer, the Lord will destroy the summer harvest.

The Lord is so rich in His mercy; He provides us a clear warning of when these things will come to pass. Watch the weather reports across the country, and don't expect the media to draw a lot of attention to the truth. And with the seventh edition of the book, the drought across much of the southwestern US is reaching epic proportions.

AMERICA SHALL BE JUDGED AS SODOM AND GOMORRAH

Again, the Lord compares the total destruction of Sodom to what will befall America. *"As God overthrew Sodom and Gomorrah and the neighbor cities thereof, saith the Lord; so shall no man abide there, neither shall any son of man dwell therein."*[24] Ancient Babylon was not destroyed as Sodom and Gomorrah, but was overthrown by the Medes. America however, will burn like Sodom. If you don't have the Lord as your shield on that day, you will be destroyed. And if God is speaking to you about leaving, you better obey Him!

We are told the whole earth will be shaken, and the nations will mourn, when they see America destroyed. *"At the noise of the taking of Babylon the earth is moved, and the cry is heard among the nations."* [25]

116

The destruction of America will throw the entire world into a crisis. The world's economy will collapse as the dollar becomes worthless. The largest import market in the world will be destroyed in one hour. Fear and panic will cover the nations of earth on that day. If the great Babylon, America, can fall in one hour, who can stand?

THE LORD WILL NOT FORSAKE HIS REMNANT

The Lord promises that he will not forsake his true remnant, which have repented and returned unto him. Though we have also sinned against the Lord, He is merciful to forgive us even at this late hour. Our God is a God of great mercy and His loving kindness extends forever to His chosen bride.

> *For Israel hath not been forsaken, nor Judah of his GOD, of the Lord of hosts; though their land was filled with sin against the Holy One of Israel. Flee out of the midst of Babylon, and deliver every man his soul: be not cut off in her iniquity; for this is the time of the Lord's vengeance; he will render unto her a recompense.* [26]

The Lord patiently repeats His instructions to His remnant to flee Babylon America. They are to leave, and deliver everyone their soul, from the hour of God's judgment of America.

AMERICA WILL BE FILLED WITH FOREIGN SOLDIERS

Jeremiah tells us that God will fill America with men who will lift up a shout against her. *"The Lord of hosts hath sworn by himself, saying, Surely I will fill thee with men, as with caterpillars; and they shall lift up a shout against thee."* [21] Today, over one million foreign soldiers are now on our soil as part of the plan for a UN occupation of America, which is called Operation Cable Splicer. This prophecy is being fulfilled literally as the Lord fills America with foreign soldiers who will soon raise a shout against us.

THE PEOPLE SHALL LABOR FOR FIRE

God tells us the people of America will labor in the last days in vain. *"Thus saith the Lord of hosts; The broad walls of Babylon shall be utterly broken, and her high gates shall be burned with fire; and the people shall labor in vain, and the folk in the fire, and they shall be weary."* [28] They shall be weary from their long hours serving the gods of wood and stone which their hands have made. Today, we find Americans working harder than ever to fill up their 401(k) accounts, and pay for their luxurious lifestyles. It will all be in vain, as the nation is destroyed in one hour!

Revelation 18 speaks of the judgment upon America: *"And a mighty angel took up a stone like a great millstone, and cast it into the sea, saying, Thus with violence shall that great city Babylon be thrown down, and shall be found no more at all."* Modern Babylon will never rise again! *"And Jeremiah said to Seraiah, When thou comest to Babylon, and shalt see, and shalt read all these words; Then shalt thou say, O Lord, thou hast spoken against this place, to cut it off, that none shall remain in it, neither man nor beast, but that it shall be desolate for ever. And it shall be, when thou hast made an end of reading this book, that thou shalt bind a stone to it, and cast it into the midst of Euphrates: And thou shalt say, Thus shall Babylon sink, and shall not rise from the evil that I will bring upon her: and they shall be weary. Thus far are the words of Jeremiah."*[29] These prophecies will be fulfilled in America very soon.

THE LORD COMMANDS HIS PEOPLE TO LEAVE THE COUNTRY

The Lord tells the leaders of His people, *"Remove out of the midst of Babylon, and go forth out of the land of the Chaldeans, and be as the he goats before the flocks."*[30] In simple terms, leave the country! Jeremiah 50 reveals America as the end time Babylon, and in verse four we are told the majority of the people will leave only after the fall of our nation, and they shall go weeping and they will be seeking the way to Zion.

Today, so many who have heard the sound of the trumpet are praying and asking God what to do. Read the word! I asked the Lord the same question. He told me, *"Search the Scriptures for the detailed instructions for this hour are in the word of God."* I don't intend to get into a debate on Bible translations, but many of these modern versions completely mistranslate the key instructional prophecies for this hour while the King James Version has a true message for the remnant. A coincidence? I think not. These new Bibles also omit many of the references to prayer and fasting, deleting the word fasting. So what do you think you should be doing in this hour? Fasting and praying, and asking God for mercy for your family and your loved ones. In the prophecy of Joel, the Lord instructs us, *"Sanctify ye a fast, call a solemn assembly, gather the elders and all the inhabitants of the land into the house of the Lord your GOD, and cry unto the Lord, Alas for the day! for the day of the Lord is at hand, and as a destruction from the Almighty shall it come."*[31]

All of us should be fasting and praying as the hour draws near. Many within the remnant are fasting each Thursday to pray for the deliverance of God's remnant. Dear friend, you might also consider reading a Bible that wasn't published by a company owned by the Illuminati. Remember, Jesus warned us the deception in the last days would be great. It is everywhere around you. Turn off your television, and get into the word of God.

The voice of them that flee and escape out of the land of Babylon, to declare in Zion the vengeance of the Lord our God, the vengeance of his temple. [32] Babylon is suddenly fallen and destroyed: howl for her; take balm for her pain, if so be she may be healed. [33]

We are told that Babylon is a nation abundant in wealth and great treasures. *"O thou that dwellest upon many waters, abundant in treasures, thine end is come, and the measure of thy covetousness."* [34] The Scripture tells us America won't get a shot off in her defense; her destruction will be so sudden and complete she won't even defend herself. In one day dear reader, all you see around you in America will be gone. *"The mighty men of Babylon have forborn to fight, they have remained in their holds: their might hath failed; they became as women: they have burned her dwelling places; her bars are broken."* [35]

A TIME OF HARVEST WILL COME AFTER HER JUDGMENT

Here we have the first indication that after the time of judgment, the time of threshing, there will be a harvest in her as well. *"For thus saith the Lord of hosts, the God of Israel; The daughter of Babylon is like a threshing floor, it is time to thresh her yet in a little while, and the time of her harvest shall come."* [36]

The survivors in America will witness a great turning to the Lord, of those left alive after the destruction of the nation. *"How is Sheshach taken! And how is the praise of the whole earth surprised! How is Babylon become an astonishment among the nations!"* [37] Again, the reference is to a sudden and surprising destruction of the greatest nation on earth, and how astonished the other nations will be at the judgment of America.

THE LORD REPEATS HIS WARNING STAND NOT STILL

Again, the Lord instructs His people to leave the country and deliver themselves. *"My people, go ye out of the midst of her, and deliver ye every man his soul from the fierce anger of the Lord. And lest your heart faint, and ye fear for the rumor that shall be heard in the land; a rumor shall both come one year, and after that in another year shall come a rumor, and violence in the land, ruler against ruler."* [38]

The final warning signs before the judgment are rumors, first in one year and then another, followed by violence in the land, and ruler against ruler. The present hour fits this perfectly; the growing violence in American cities, from Antifa to right wing extremists, alongside the political battles between the radicalized progressives and President Trump present a literal fulfillment of this verse.

Many groups will raise opposition to the planned takeover of the US, but they will not succeed, for all of the nation's fall under the dominion of the prince, save Edom and Moab.

The LORD again reminds His people to leave, go away, do not stand still! *"As Babylon hath caused the slain of Israel to fall, so at Babylon shall fall the slain of all the earth. Ye that have escaped the sword, go away, stand not still: remember the Lord afar off, and let Jerusalem come into your mind."*[39] And where are they to go? God says let Jerusalem come to mind, think about Jerusalem and the land of Israel. Think of the strong city of the Psalms – Petra or Selah!

THE MERCHANTS OF THE EARTH
SHALL WEEP AND MOURN

We are told that after the fall of America Babylon, the world's economic powers will weep, for they have lost their principal export market, and no one buys their goods anymore. *"And the merchants of the earth shall weep and mourn over her; for no man buys their merchandise any more"*[40]

Only America could fit this prophecy. If you are unclear about the status of America as the world's principal export market, think about which nation runs the world's largest trade deficit. It is not Europe or Japan. It is not China or South America. It is certainly not Iraq!

The merchants of the earth all sell to America. And when she burns, they will all weep, and no one will buy their merchandise anymore. The worldwide economic collapse which will follow the fall of America will be devastating. The US dollar will be worthless, and US Treasury Bonds will be thrown in the streets. Most of the nations of the earth have substantial investments in the United States. In one hour, these will all be vaporized, and the rest of the world will collapse in a global depression of unprecedented scale. The nations of the earth will all weep, and no man will buy their goods anymore!

> *And saying, Alas, alas, that great city, that was clothed in fine linen, and purple, and scarlet, and decked with gold, and precious stones, and pearls! For in one hour so great riches is come to nought. And every shipmaster, and all the company in ships, and sailors, and as many as trade by sea, stood afar off, And cried when they saw the smoke of her burning, saying, What city is like unto this great city!* [41]

Our trading partners will stand afar off, afraid to come near the US, for fear of her plagues, the biological weapons, the radiation, the riots and the civil war that will fall on our land at the same time!

THE REMNANT WILL RETURN TO ZION

When America is finally destroyed, the remnant which will be spared will then all leave the country and they shall seek to find the way to Zion. They will recognize the only place of safety now is in the land of Israel, and in the sanctuary of Edom and Moab, which is in the wilderness of Jordan, and is part of the land of greater Israel. Notice though, they will weep as they seek the way to Zion, for they will seek to find their way in a most difficult time.

> *In those days, and in that time, saith the Lord, the children of Israel shall come, they and the children of Judah together, going and weeping: they shall go, and seek the Lord their God. They shall ask the way to Zion with their faces thitherward, saying, Come, and let us join ourselves to the Lord in a perpetual covenant that shall not be forgotten.* [42]

The Lord gives those who are spared and included in His remnant, the ones who the Lord reserves, the assurance that He will forgive their sins in that hour.

> *In those days, and in that time, saith the Lord, the iniquity of Israel shall be sought for, and there shall be none; and the sins of Judah, and they shall not be found: for I will pardon them whom I reserve.* [43]

Dear reader, the time is indeed short. I encourage you, repent of all of your sins, and turn back to the God of Israel, who alone is the King of the Universe. Call upon his name. Pray and ask him if Yeshua whom the gentiles call Jesus is indeed his son, the Messiah, who was promised to come.

Seek the Lord your God with all of your heart. For great is the God of Israel, and mighty is His arm to save all those who humble themselves and call upon his name, and who will walk with Him in holiness and obedience. I encourage every American believer to also pray and ask him when you should leave the land of America. Remember the warnings of our God. "They shall all depart. No man shall dwell there anymore. Babylon the Great is fallen, fallen, and she will never rise again!"

The night is coming upon you soon America, and when it comes, it will bring your end with it. Behold, it is even now at the door.

For more information on the 70 year reign of America Babylon look for the documentary America Babylon by Benjamin Baruch on you tube or visit the following webpage for more information on the Last Days of America Babylon: https://prophecyinvestigators.org/the-last-days-of-babylon/

THE DAY OF THE LORD IS AT HAND

CHAPTER

6

THE REMNANT SHALL RETURN
Isaiah 10:21

Throughout the word of God, the Lord declares in the last days He will again gather His Holy remnant back to the land of Israel. The prophet Isaiah was used by the Lord to speak the word of God to Ancient Israel about the coming of the Messiah Jesus Christ. Contained in this book of the Bible are prophecies of both the first coming and the second coming of the Lord. Isaiah's prophecies describe the return of the Lord at the end of the age, and the judgments which shall come at that time. He also unveils the deliverance plan for the remnant which shall be saved in the last days.

THE REMNANT SHALL BE FEW AND VERY SMALL

The promises of our Lord speak of a great deliverance in this hour of testing, the day of vengeance of our God. The word makes it clear that the remnant are few and very small in number. *"Except the Lord of hosts had left unto us a very small remnant, we should have been as Sodom, and we should have been like unto Gomorrah."* [1] Let us fear the Lord for the greatness of His judgments and the mercy He has shown unto us whom He has quickened in this hour. The Lord speaks of the time of judgment when children will oppress the people, and women will act as rulers among the people. *"As for my people, children are their oppressors, and women rule over them. Oh my people, they which lead thee cause thee to err, and destroy the way of thy paths."* [2]

SEAL THE LAW AMONG MY DISCIPLES

We are instructed not to walk as the nation's walk, nor to fear what they fear, but to fear only the Lord. The law, which is the word of God, is to be sealed among the disciples of the Lord. To seal the law is to preserve and protect it. The true disciples will have the law sealed in their hearts, and if anyone speaks not according to the law, and the testimony of the prophets, then we know there is no light in them.

> *The Lord spoke to me ...and instructed me that I should not walk in the way of this people... neither fear ye their fear, nor be afraid. Sanctify the Lord of hosts himself; and let him be your fear, and let him be your dread. And he shall be for a sanctuary; but for a stone of stumbling and for a rock*

123

of offence... And many among them shall stumble, and fall, and be broken, and be snared, and be taken. Bind up the testimony, and seal the law among my disciples. I will wait upon the Lord, that hideth his face from the house of Jacob, and I will look for him. Behold, I and the children whom the Lord hath given me are for signs and for wonders in Israel from the Lord of hosts, which dwelleth in mount Zion... To the law and to the testimony: if they speak not according to this word, it is because there is no light in them. And they shall pass through it, hardly bestead and hungry: and it shall come to pass, that when they shall be hungry, they shall fret themselves, and curse their king and their God, and look upward. And they shall look unto the earth; and behold trouble and darkness, dimness of anguish; and they shall be driven to darkness. [3]

The remnant are described as those that *"escape"*[4] and we are told that *"The remnant shall return, even the remnant of Jacob, unto the mighty God. For though thy people Israel be as the sand of the sea, yet a remnant of them shall return: the consumption decreed shall overflow with righteousness."* [5] A great consumption has been decreed by the Lord, and only a remnant shall return. We should greatly fear the Lord, for we are sinners, even as those that are going to the sword.

THE SECOND RECOVERY OF THE LAND OF ISRAEL

The second recovery of the nation of Israel, back to their land, began in the late 19th century. The remnant are "the outcasts of Israel". The Lord promises *"He shall set up an ensign for the nations, and shall assemble the outcasts of Israel, and gather together the dispersed of Judah from the four corners of the earth."*[6] They are the true spiritual nation, comprising both Jews and Gentiles who are found written in the Book of Life. They are worthy to be able to stand, and endure the hour of testing.

And it shall come to pass in that day, that the remnant of Israel, and such as are escaped of the house of Jacob, shall no more again stay upon him that smote them; but shall stay upon the Lord, the Holy One of Israel, in truth. The remnant shall return, even the remnant of Jacob, unto the mighty God. For though thy people Israel be as the sand of the sea, yet a remnant of them shall return: the consumption decreed shall overflow with righteousness. Isaiah 10:20-22

The Lord also reveals that His remnant will be gathered from the four corners of the earth, and they will lay their hands upon Edom and Moab and the children of Ammon shall obey them. They shall possess the land of Edom and Moab. This area of southern Jordan is actually part of greater Israel, and part of the Promised Land given to the descendants of Abraham. If we are of true Israel, it is also our land.

And it shall come to pass in that day, that the Lord shall set his hand again the second time to recover the remnant of his people... he shall set up an ensign for the nations, and shall assemble the outcasts of Israel and gather together the dispersed of Judah from the four corners of the earth. The envy also of Ephraim shall depart, and the adversaries of Judah shall be cut off. Ephraim shall not envy Judah, and Judah shall not vex Ephraim. But they shall fly upon the shoulders of the Philistines toward the west; they shall spoil them of the east together: they shall lay their hand upon Edom and Moab: and the children of Ammon shall obey them. Isaiah 11:11-14

EVERYONE THAT IS FOUND
SHALL BE THRUST THROUGH

The Lord commands us to hide ourselves, for this is the hour of His indignation. He also tells us that everyone will turn to his own people, and flee back to his own land. When the Lord comes in final judgment of the earth, everyone that is found will be *"thrust through"*, and their children will be *"dashed to pieces"* and their wives *"ravished."* He also declares the beautiful cities of America Babylon will be judged like Sodom, torched! *"And Babylon, the glory of kingdoms, the beauty of the Chaldees' excellence, shall be as when God overthrew Sodom and Gomorrah."*[8] This is a reference to the coastal areas of California, Florida and New York. These are the beauty of Babylon's excellence, and the pride of America Babylon. They will all burn in one hour! I saw this at the end of my 911 dream; southern California was covered in mushroom clouds, and then the ashes began to fall from the sky.

And it shall be as the chased roe, and as a sheep that no man taketh up: they shall every man turn to his own people, and flee every one into his own land. Every one that is found shall be thrust through and every one that is joined unto them shall fall by the sword. Their children also shall be dashed to pieces before their eyes: their houses shall be spoiled, and their wives ravished. Behold, I will stir up the Medes against them, which shall not regard silver; and as for gold, they shall not delight in it. Their bows also shall dash the young men to pieces; and they shall have no pity on the fruit of the womb; their eye shall not spare children. And Babylon, the glory of kingdoms, the beauty of the Chaldees' excellency, shall be as when God overthrew Sodom and Gomorrah. Isaiah 13:14-19

THE REMNANT SHALL TAKE
CAPTIVE THE ENEMIES OF ISRAEL

The Lord will once again set Israel in their own land; the Scripture declares everyone flees to their own land. The strangers that cleave unto Israel will be their servants, and Israel shall take captive those who once held them captive. This is Edom and Moab, who at one time captured Israel as they fled.

> For the Lord will have mercy on Jacob, and will yet choose Israel, and set
> them in their own land: and the strangers shall be joined with them, and
> they shall cleave to the house of Jacob. And the people shall take them, and
> bring them to their place: and the house of Israel shall possess them in the
> land of the Lord for servants and handmaids: and they shall take them
> captives, whose captives they were; and they shall rule over their
> oppressors. [9]

Those who hold the false doctrines of replacement theology will dispute that these scriptures apply to the Gentile believers, yet God only has one people true Israel.

The Word shows that the "*lamb*" is to be sent "*to the ruler of the land from Sela*" which is Petra, to the wilderness unto the mount of the daughter of Zion. Petra is next to mount Hor where Moses and Aaron went up to meet the Lord, while the children of Israel waited in the valley below. This is the same wilderness area which the Lord is preparing right now for His remnant to possess, even Edom and Moab.

The lamb is the remnant that is to be protected during the Great Tribulation and Moab will provide a covering to the outcasts of Israel from the face of the spoiler. The spoiler is the antichrist. The sinners and the evil men are the extortionist who are at their end, for the oppressors are about to be consumed out of the land.

> Send ye the lamb to the ruler of the land from Sela to the wilderness, unto
> the mount of the daughter of Zion. For it shall be, that, as a wandering
> bird cast out of the nest, so the daughters of Moab shall be at the fords of
> Arnon. Take counsel, execute judgment; make thy shadow as the night in
> the midst of the noonday; hide the outcasts; bewray not him that
> wandereth. Let mine outcasts dwell with thee Moab: be thou a covert to
> them from the face of the spoiler; for the extortioner is at an end, the
> spoiler ceaseth, the oppressors are consumed out of the land. Isaiah 16:1-4

THE REMNANT SHALL BE AS A
GLEANING IN THE LAND

The Lord describes His remnant as a gleaning in the land. This is from the harvest law of the gleaning. The harvest was to be performed only once. Whatever crop was missed was to be left for the poor in the land. This is a picture of the remnant which will be left. The few that are left will have respect for God, and not the work of their hands, their money or idols.

Behold, Damascus is taken away from being a city, and it shall be a ruinous heap... And in that day, it shall come to pass, that the glory of Jacob shall be made thin, and the fatness of his flesh shall wax lean. And it shall be as when the harvestman gathereth the corn, and reapeth the ears with his arm; and it shall be as he that gathereth ears in the valley of Rephaim. Yet gleaning grapes shall be left in it, as the shaking of an olive tree, two or three berries in the top of the uppermost bough, four or five in the outmost fruitful branches thereof, saith the Lord God of Israel. At that day shall a man look to his Maker, and his eyes shall have respect to the Holy One of Israel. And he shall not look to the altars, the work of his hands, neither shall respect that which his fingers have made. Isaiah 17:1-8

The Lord speaks of the mountain in the wilderness where He will prepare a feast for His people. There He will take away the veil that is blinding the eyes of the people. The veil is sin and unbelief in the word of God. It is the veil which blinds the heart of man to the truth of God. The Lord also states again that this mountain is where His hand will rest; He is taking it for His people, and as a result Moab shall be trodden down. Praise God for his plan!

For thou hast been a strength to the poor, a strength to the needy in his distress, a refuge from the storm, a shadow from the heat, when the blast of the terrible ones is as a storm against the wall. Thou shalt bring down the noise of strangers, as the heat in a dry place; even the heat with the shadow of a cloud: the branch of the terrible ones shall be brought low. And in this mountain shall the Lord of hosts make unto all people a feast of fat things, a feast of wines on the lees, of fat things full of marrow, of wines on the lees well refined. And he will destroy in this mountain the face of the covering cast over all people, and the vail that is spread over all nations. He will swallow up death in victory; and the Lord God will wipe away tears from off all faces; and the rebuke of his people shall he take away from off all the earth: for the Lord hath spoken it. And it shall be said in that day, Lo, this is our God; we have waited for him, and he will save us: this is the Lord; we have waited for him, we will be glad and rejoice in his salvation. For in this mountain shall the hand of the Lord rest, and Moab shall be trodden down under him, even as straw is trodden down for the dunghill. Isaiah 25:4-10

COME MY PEOPLE, AND HIDE FOR A LITTLE MOMENT

The Lord commands us to hide ourselves in our chambers, and to shut the door, much like He hid Noah in the ark. It was the Lord who shut the door behind Noah. The Lord will also be our rear guard and our defense, if we obey Him. *"Come, my people, enter thou into thy chambers, and shut thy doors about thee: hide thyself as it were for a little moment, until the indignation be overpast. For, behold, the Lord cometh out of his place to punish the inhabitants of the earth for their iniquity: the earth also shall disclose her blood, and shall no more cover her slain.*"[10] The Scripture here is speaking about the time of the end, when the Lord comes to punish the inhabitants of the earth. We do well to obey His commands, for everyone that is found will be killed with the sword.

THE LORD WILL RISE AND STAND IN JUDGMENT

The Lord tells us He will rise to stand in judgment. This is the same word He spoke to me declaring, *"The Lord God Almighty is standing now, ready to judge the entire earth!"* The Lord always stands to judge the people. The Lord is about to perform *"His strange act, His strange work."* He describes His judgment as a strange work; for it is a work the people don't expect or understand. It is also a strange act, for the Lord takes no delight in the judgment of man. Our God delights in mercy, justice and loving kindness. But God is also a God of righteousness and judgment and for this reason, He has decreed that one day He will judge the entire earth.

The Lord has appointed the sword for judgment. This sword will bring His people to true repentance, and destroy the wicked. Our God is a consuming fire; let us fear Him and Him alone.

> *For the Lord shall rise up as in mount Perazim, he shall be wroth as in the valley of Gibeon, that he may do his work, his strange work; and bring to pass his act, his strange act. Now therefore be ye not mockers, lest your bands be made strong: for I have heard from the Lord God of hosts a consumption, even determined upon the whole earth. Isaiah 28:21-22*

THE LEADERS OF THE PEOPLE
ARE UNABLE TO UNDERSTAND

The Lord tells us the leaders among the people cannot read His word for they are unable to understand it, because they are not seeking Him with their hearts, only with their lips, Again, the Lord reiterates the marvelous solution he has planned; He will destroy the wisdom of those wise in their own eyes!

> *For the Lord hath poured out upon you the spirit of deep sleep, and hath closed your eyes: the prophets and your rulers, the seers hath he covered. And the vision of all is become unto you as the words of a book that is sealed, which men deliver to one that is learned, saying, Read this, I pray thee: and he saith, I cannot; for it is sealed: And the book is delivered to him that is not learned, saying, Read this, I pray thee: and he saith, I am not learned. Wherefore the Lord said, Forasmuch as this people draw near me with their mouth, and with their lips do honor me, but have removed their heart far from me, and their fear toward me is taught by the precept of men: Therefore, behold, I will proceed to do a marvelous work among*

this people, even a marvelous work and a wonder: for the wisdom of their wise men shall perish, and the understanding of their prudent men shall be hid. Isaiah 29:10-14

WOE TO THOSE WHO GO DOWN UNTO EGYPT

Isaiah warns us against turning to the world for help or deliverance for the world cannot help us; and it will only bring us shame and confusion.

Woe to the rebellious children, saith the Lord, that take counsel, but not of me; and that cover with a covering, but not of my spirit, that they may add sin to sin: That walk to go down into Egypt, and have not asked at my mouth; to strengthen themselves in the strength of Pharaoh, and to trust in the shadow of Egypt! Therefore shall the strength of Pharaoh be your shame, and the trust in the shadow of Egypt your confusion. Isaiah 30:1-3

THE PEOPLE SHALL BE AS THORNS
CUT UP AND BURNED IN THE FIRE

The Lord speaks of standing in judgment, and describes the people as *"thorns cut up"* and *"they shall be burned in the fire."* The people are described as *"thorns"* for they are unfruitful, having failed to abide in Him. These are the branches which have withered, having failed to produce true fruit in the spirit. These are the persecuted believers of America.

The Lord spoke of this judgment on the believers who would not abide in Him saying: *"I am the true vine, and my Father is the husbandman. Every branch in me that beareth not fruit he taketh away: and every branch that beareth fruit, he purgeth it, that it may bring forth more fruit ...If a man abide not in me, he is cast forth as a branch, and is withered; and men gather them, and cast them into the fire, and they are burned."* [11]

Those who will not abide and walk in His spirit will be literally gathered up by men, and cast into the fire! These are the martyrs who will be "as thorns cut up" and their bodies will be burned in the fire. After they are killed, the martyrs will be cremated in the death camps of the prince. And who will be found among the remnant? Only those who walk righteously and their place of safety will be the munitions or rocks. The word for munitions is מִצָּד, *mets-ad* [12] and it is found only in this verse. It means a covering from an ambush, a castle, or a stronghold.

The Hebrew word for rocks is סֶלַע, *seh'-lah* [13] which is Petra in the Greek and it means a fortress or stronghold of rocks. The Lord spells out the place where the remnant will be defended: the place of safety is the mountain of Petra, in the land of Edom and Moab. This is the place spoken of in Revelation 12, where the woman, true Israel flees. This place is prepared by God himself. It is beautiful. I have seen it with my own eyes. There are seven springs of pure water there, the air is pure, and there is a highway there, called the King's Highway. May the Lord grant us the faith to hear and believe, and to submit to His plan, and not to rely on our own understanding, nor go and hide in the shadow of Pharaoh. The ambush will soon snare the people of the earth, and where will you be found dear reader?

> *Now will I rise, saith the Lord; now will I be exalted; now will I lift up myself. Ye shall conceive chaff, ye shall bring forth stubble: your breath, as fire, shall devour you. And the people shall be as the burnings of lime: as thorns cut up shall they be burned in the fire. Hear, ye that are far off, what I have done; and, ye that are near, acknowledge my might. The sinners in Zion are afraid; fearfulness hath surprised the hypocrites. Who among us shall dwell with the devouring fire? who among us shall dwell with ever-lasting burnings? He that walketh righteously, and speaketh uprightly; he that despiseth the gain of oppressions, that shaketh his hands from holding of bribes, that stoppeth his ears from hearing of blood, and shutteth his eyes from seeing evil; He shall dwell on high: his place of defense shall be the munitions of rocks: bread shall be given him; his waters shall be sure. Thine eyes shall see the king in his beauty: they shall behold the land that is very far off. Isaiah 33:10-17*

THE WILDERNESS SHALL BE GLAD FOR THEM

The Lord speaks of the wilderness being glad for His people and describes it as a solitary place. One place has been provided by God to the remnant as a shelter from the storm. Believers were never promised safety in America, for we are all aliens here, but the Lord has made a promise to Judah and to all of the remnant of Israel. This promise is a place of safety, where we can rest without fear, beyond the reach of the destroyer, who will conquer many nations. This place of safety is Petra!

> *The wilderness and the solitary place shall be glad for them; and the desert shall rejoice, and blossom as the rose. It shall blossom abundantly, and rejoice even with joy and singing: the glory of Lebanon shall be given unto it, the excellency of Carmel and Sharon, they shall see the glory of the LORD, and the excellency of our GOD. Isaiah 35:1-2*

The Lord describes the highway that will be found in this wilderness, for it is the way of holiness. The highway which runs through Petra is named "The King's Highway." This is the way He would have us walk, in holiness and truth. All who are found on this highway will walk as He walked.

And a highway shall be there, and a way, and it shall be called The way of holiness; the unclean shall not pass over it; but it shall be for those: the wayfaring men, though fools, shall not err therein. No lion shall be there, nor any ravenous beast shall go up thereon, it shall not be found there; but the redeemed shall walk there: And the ransomed of the Lord shall return, and come to Zion with songs and everlasting joy upon their heads: they shall obtain joy and gladness, and sorrow and sighing shall flee away. Isaiah 35:8-10

The Lord speaks again about the wilderness, and the highway the redeemed of the Lord will walk upon, for it is a straight road called the way of holiness. We had better straighten our hearts, for he will dwell among his remnant in holiness even as he dwelt among the children of Israel after they left Egypt. The Exodus foreshadowed this very hour and we are going to the very same place, and there we will wait for him, even as they waited to enter the land. How awesome is our God, how marvelous are his ways, and his wonders to perform. Who is wise that can discern these things of the Spirit? Let him declare it! Who hears from God? Let him speak.

Comfort ye, comfort ye my people, saith your God. Speak ye comfortably to Jerusalem, and cry unto her, that her warfare is accomplished, that her iniquity is pardoned: for she hath received of the Lord's hand double for all her sins. The voice of him that cries in the wilderness, Prepare ye the way of the Lord, make straight in the desert a highway for our God. Isaiah 40:1-3

THE GOD OF ISRAEL WILL NOT FORSAKE THEM

The Lord describes the changes He will make in the wilderness, providing both water and plantings for His people, to provide for their needs. Little flock, don't be fearful, for your Father knows your needs, and He has promised to provide for you. You must do your part; obey and fear only Him.

When the poor and needy seek water, and there is none, and their tongue faileth for thirst, I the Lord will hear them, I the God of Israel will not forsake them. I will open rivers in high places, and fountains in the midst of the valleys: I will make the wilderness a pool of water, and the dry land springs of water. I will plant in the wilderness the cedar, the shittah tree, and the myrtle, and the oil tree; I will set in the desert the fir tree, and the pine, and the box tree together: Isaiah 41:17-19

The Lord is doing a new thing now. He has held His peace a long time, but now He will destroy the wicked, and bring His people in paths they have not known. Behold, you who are reading these words, will you be found among those waiting for Him on that day? Repent, and turn with your whole heart, and you may find grace and mercy from Him. Our God is a God of great mercy, desiring mercy and obedience before sacrifice.

Behold, the former things are come to pass, and new things do I declare: before they spring forth I tell you of them. Sing unto the Lord a new song and his praise from the end of the earth, ye that go down to the sea, and all that is therein; the isles, and the inhabitants thereof. Let the wilderness and the cities thereof lift up their voice, the villages that Kedar doth inhabit: let the inhabitants of the rock sing, let them shout from the top of the mountains. Let them give glory unto the Lord, and declare his praise in the islands. The Lord shall go forth as a mighty man, he shall stir up jealousy like a man of war: he shall cry, yea, roar; he shall prevail against his enemies. I have long time held my peace; I have been still, and refrained myself now will I cry like a travailing woman; I will destroy and devour at once. I will make waste mountains and hills, and dry up all their herbs; and I will make the rivers islands, and I will dry up the pools. And I will bring the blind by a way that they knew not; I will lead them in paths that they have not known: I will make darkness light before them, and crooked things straight. These things will I do unto them, and not forsake them. Isaiah 42:9-16

FEAR NOT, I WILL BRING MY SONS FROM FAR

The Lord tells us, all of the people will be brought back, *"even every one that is called by my name."* To state the obvious, when the Lord speaks of *"everyone"* He means everyone! Again he says, *"Let the people be assembled"* and to those *that escape, come near together, and assemble yourselves to come. Assemble yourselves and come; draw near together, ye that are escaped of the nations: they have no knowledge that set up the wood of their graven image, and pray unto a God that cannot save."*[14] Let us come, for the time is at hand.

Fear not: for I am with thee: I will bring thy seed from the east, and gather thee from the west; I will say to the north, Give up; and to the south, Keep not back: bring my sons from far, and my daughters from the ends of the earth; Even every one that is called by my name: for I have created him for my glory, I have formed him; yea, I have made him. Bring forth the blind people that have eyes, and the deaf that have ears. Let all the nations be gathered together, and let the people be assembled: who among them can declare this and show us former things? Let them bring forth their witnesses, that they may be justified: or let them hear and say It is truth. Isaiah 43:5-9

Remember the former things of old: for I am God, and there is none else; I am God, and there is none like me, declaring the end from the beginning, and from ancient times the things that are not yet done, saying, My counsel shall stand, and I will do all my pleasure: Calling a ravenous bird from the east, the man that executes my counsel from a far country: yea, I have spoken it, I will also bring it to pass; I have purposed it, I will also do it. Isaiah 46:9-11

GO FORTH FROM BABYLON, FLEE THE LAND OF THE CHALDEANS

The Lord tells His people to flee from the land of Babylon and the Babylonian system of religion. He sends this message to the end of the earth. *"Go ye forth of Babylon, flee from the Chaldeans, with a voice of singing declare ye, tell this, utter it even to the end of the earth; say ye, The Lord hath redeemed his servant Jacob."* [15] This prophecy could not have been fulfilled in the time before the fall of ancient Babylon as the Jews were in slavery and unable to leave. Following the Great War, the people will all know they must leave the kingdom of the prince and go to the fortress of rocks, to Petra. The Lord then compares this redemption to the deliverance from Egypt, when He led His people through the deserts. *"And they thirsted not when he led them through the deserts: he caused the waters to flow out of the rock for them: he clave the rock also, and the waters gushed out."* [16] We will go out even as they went out, for great is the Lord who saves us. The above verse also speaks of the way in the wilderness prepared for God's people.

HE THAT HAS MERCY ON THEM SHALL LEAD THEM

The Lord promises to have mercy upon His remnant, and to lead them home. They will neither hunger nor thirst, for the Lord will meet their needs. Truly the Lord will comfort His people who trust in Him and walk before Him in obedience and holiness.

> *They shall not hunger nor thirst; neither shall the heat nor sun smite them: for he that hath mercy on them shall lead them, even by the springs of water shall he guide them. And I will make all my mountains a way, and my highways shall be exalted. Behold, these shall come from far: and, lo, these from the north and from the west. Sing, O heavens; and be joyful, O earth; and break forth into singing, O mountains: for the Lord hath comforted his people, and will have mercy upon his afflicted. Isaiah 49:10-13*

Praise the Lord for His goodness unto us who He is delivering. The Lord will lift up His hand to the Gentiles, *"and they shall bring my sons in their arms, and thy daughters shall be carried upon their shoulders. And kings shall be thy nursing fathers... they shall bow down to thee with their face toward the earth."* Isaiah 49:22 God promises to protect the children of His remnant and the kings of the gentiles will provide for His people. Is there anything too hard for the Lord? I think not! In the midst of the great tribulation, the LORD says He will make the wilderness like Eden, and joy and gladness shall be found there.

> For the Lord shall comfort Zion: he will comfort all her waste places; and he will make her wilderness like Eden, and her desert like the garden of the Lord; joy and gladness shall be found therein, thanksgiving, and the voice of melody. Isaiah 51:3

DEPART, DEPART AND GO OUT
AND TOUCH NO UNCLEAN THING

The Lord again tells the people it is time to leave; the time to depart has come, and the remnant shall touch no unclean thing. You must cleanse your hearts, and your hands, if you want to stand on the day that the Son of man is revealed. I would encourage you to read *"Matters of the Heart"*, which is the essential part of the cleansing your soul, and also the first part of *Search the Scriptures, Vol. 1: Out of the Darkness*. If you don't have access to the book, look for the audio message on the internet and then diligently begin to search out the matters of your heart.

> Depart ye, depart ye, go ye out from thence, touch no unclean thing; go ye out of the midst of her; be ye clean, that bear the vessels of the Lord. For ye shall not go out with haste, nor go by flight: for the Lord will go before you; and the God of Israel will be your reward. Isaiah 52:11-12

The Lord declares that Gentiles who join Israel to serve the Lord, and who love the name of the Lord, will also be brought to the holy mountain which is the wilderness of Petra. And every one of them who is spared, will honor and keep the word of the Lord written by the spirit of God in their hearts.

> Also the sons of the stranger, that join themselves to the Lord, to serve him, and to love the name of the Lord, to be his servants, every one that keeps the Sabbath from polluting it and taketh hold of my covenant; Even them will I bring to my holy mountain, and make them joyful in my house of prayer: their burnt offerings and their sacrifices shall be accepted upon mine altar: for mine house shall be called an house of prayer for all people. The Lord God which gathereth the outcasts of Israel saith, yet will I gather others to him, beside those that are gathered unto him. Isaiah 56:6-8

THEY SHALL BUILD THE OLD WASTE CITIES

The Lord speaks about His Second Coming and that His people shall rebuild the desolate places. This speaks of the ships of Tarshish, which will evacuate people out of the US from the coastal areas of Texas, and the islands of

Central America where the remnant will rest on their way home. Even now, these refuge stations are being prepared for the people.

> *Surely the isles shall wait for me, and the ships of Tarshish first, to bring thy sons from far, their silver and their gold with them, unto the name of the Lord thy God, and to the Holy One of Israel, because he hath glorified thee. And the sons of strangers shall build up thy walls, and their kings shall minister unto thee: for in my wrath I smote thee, but in my favor have I had mercy on thee. Isaiah 60:9-10*

The prophecy of the Messiah in Isaiah 61 also declares the remnant shall build the old waste places, and raise up the former desolations:

> *The Spirit of the Lord God is upon me; because the Lord hath anointed me to preach good tidings unto the meek; he hath sent me to bind up the brokenhearted, to proclaim liberty to the captives, and the opening of the prison to them that are bound; To proclaim the acceptable year of the Lord, and the day of vengeance of our God; to comfort all that mourn... And they shall build the old wastes, they shall raise up the former desolations, and they shall repair the waste cities, the desolations of many generations. And strangers shall stand and feed your flocks, and the sons of the alien shall be your plowmen and your vinedressers. Isaiah 61:1-5*

WHO IS THIS THAT COMES FROM EDOM?

The Lord asks *"Who is this that cometh from Edom?"* This is the second coming of the LORD. He first returns to Edom, to recover His remnant that are waiting for Him there, and His angels will gather the rest of His elect from the four corners of the earth. These are His army who were sent to fight the dragon, and to witness of the Lord, in the kingdom of darkness.

> *Who is this that cometh from Edom, with dyed garments from Bozrah? this that is glorious in his apparel, travelling in the greatness of his strength? I that speak in righteousness, mighty to save. Therefore art thou red in thine apparel, and thy garments like him that treadeth in the winefat? I have trodden the winepress alone; and of the people there was none with me: for I will tread them in mine anger, and trample them in my fury; and their blood shall be sprinkled upon my garments, and I will stain all my raiment. For the day of vengeance is in mine heart, and the year of my redeemed is come. Isaiah 63:1-4*

The Lord again declares His remnant shall be found in a cluster, in a group, and He goes on to declare that they shall inherit His mountains, and His servants shall dwell there. *"Thus saith the Lord, as the new wine is found in the cluster, and one saith, Destroy it not; for a blessing is in it: so will I do for my servants' sakes, that I may not destroy them all. And I will bring forth a seed out of Jacob, and out of Judah an inheritor of my mountains: and mine elect shall inherit it, and my servants shall dwell there."* [17]

The deliverance plan of the remnant returning to Israel, and to the land of Edom and Moab is not exclusive to the book of Isaiah. In the book of Daniel, chapter 11 the Lord declares Edom and Moab will not fall under the control of the prince. *"He shall enter also into the glorious land, and many countries shall be overthrown: but these shall escape out of his hand, even Edom, and Moab, and the chief of the children of Ammon."* [18] The chief of the children of Ammon refers to the royal family of Jordan who will also escape.

In the book of Habakkuk, the prophet declares that his vision is for an appointed time, which is the time of the end. The prophet is also told the people would be unable to hear the truth: *"Behold ye among the heathen, and regard, and wonder marvelously: for I will work a work in your days, which ye will not believe, though it be told you."*[19] The prophet is instructed to make his vision plain, so that all who read it could clearly understand the message: *Run!*

> *I will stand upon my watch, and set me upon the tower, and will watch to see what he will say unto me, and what I shall answer when I am reproved. And the Lord answered me, and said, write the vision, and make it plain upon tables, that he may run that reads it. For the vision is yet for an appointed time, but at the end it shall speak, and not lie: though it tarry, wait for it; because it will surely come.* [20]

THEY THAT ESCAPE SHALL ESCAPE

Ezekiel also tells us that those who escape *"shall escape."* They will have to *"run"* as Habakkuk declares, and they will *"hide themselves."* They will be found *"on the mountains"*, each mourning for his own sins. As the remnant witnesses the judgments falling upon the earth, and upon the Church, they will weep for their iniquities, for only by the mercy of Jesus Christ and His lovingkindness, have they been spared.

> *But they that escape of them shall escape and shall be on the mountains like doves of the valleys, all of them mourning, every one for his iniquity. All hands shall be feeble, and all knees shall be weak as water. They shall also gird themselves with sackcloth, and horror shall cover them; and shame shall be upon all faces, and baldness upon all their heads. Ezekiel 7:16-18*

Revelation 12 contains a specific prophecy of the place of safety prepared by God where the Lord will fulfill his promise to Judah, and to the remnant of

Israel. The dragon will be enraged that he cannot reach the people in Edom, so he will turn and go to make war with those who dwell in the other parts of the earth. If you plan on continuing to live in the other areas of the world, such as the US, you can be certain that this nation will be conquered by the prince, and you will have to make war with the dragon personally. If you are called to this ministry, may God bless and protect your life.

> *And to the woman were given two wings of a great eagle, that she might fly into the wilderness, into her place, where she is nourished for a time, and times, and half a time, from the face of the serpent. And the dragon was wroth with the woman, and went to make war with the remnant of her seed, which keep the commandments of God, and have the testimony of Jesus Christ. Revelation 12:14,17*

Again in Amos, the Lord provides a last days' prophecy of his people possessing the remnant of Edom. "*That they may possess the remnant of Edom ...saith the Lord that doeth this. Behold, the days come, saith the Lord, that the plowman shall overtake the reaper, and the treader of grapes him that soweth seed; and the mountains shall drop sweet wine, and all the hills shall melt. And I will bring again the captivity of my people of Israel, and they shall build the waste cities, and inhabit them. And I will plant them upon their land, and they shall no more be pulled up out of their land which I have given them, saith the Lord thy God.*" [21]

I WILL SURELY GATHER THE REMNANT OF ISRAEL

In Micah the Lord declares that He will again assemble all of Jacob, and that He will gather the remnant of Israel together. He will put them together as the sheep of Bozrah in the land of Edom! And they shall make a great noise because there is such a large multitude that has all been gathered. Praise the Lord that He has prepared a place of safety for us to hide in, while His men of war fight the dragon in the cities which have been conquered by the prince. "*I will surely assemble, O Jacob, all of thee; I will surely gather the remnant of Israel; I will put them together as the sheep of Bozrah, as the flock in the midst of their fold: they shall make great noise by reason of the multitude of men. The breaker is come up before them: they have broken up, and have passed through the gate, and are gone out by it: and their king shall pass before them and the Lord on the head of them.*" [22]

Again, the Lord declares His remnant will spoil Moab, and the remnant of My people shall possess the land of Moab. This hasn't been fulfilled yet, but the day is at hand. "*And the coast shall be for the remnant of the house of Judah... the Lord their God shall visit them, and turn away their captivity. I have heard the reproach of Moab, and the revilings of the children of Ammon, whereby they have reproached my people, and magnified themselves against their border. Therefore as I live, saith the LORD of hosts, the God of Israel, Surely Moab shall be as Sodom, and the children of Ammon as Gomorrah... the residue of my people shall spoil them, and the remnant of my people shall possess them."* [23]

The Lord says the people of the nations will cling to the Jews for they will know the Lord is with them. The Lord humbled the Jews by sending the Gentiles to preach the word of the Lord to them. Now He will humble the Gentiles, by sending an anointed army of Jews to deliver them from the beast. And they will take hold of the coat of a Jew; saying let us go with you, for we know God is with you. *"Thus saith the Lord of hosts; Behold, I will save my people from the east country, and from the west country; And I will bring them, and they shall dwell in the midst of Jerusalem: and they shall be my people, and I will be their God, in truth and in righteousness... And it shall come to pass, that as ye were a curse among the heathen, O house of Judah, and house of Israel; so will I save you, and ye shall be a blessing: fear not, but let your hands be strong... Thus saith the LORD of hosts; In those days it shall come to pass, that ten men shall take hold out of all languages of the nations, even shall take hold of the skirt of him that is a Jew, saying, We will go with you: for we have heard that God is with you."*[24]

Again in the book of Numbers the Lord repeats this prophecy of the possession of Edom.

> *He hath said, which heard the words of God, and knew the knowledge of the most High, which saw the vision of the Almighty, falling into a trance, but having his eyes open: I shall see him, but not now: I shall behold him, but not nigh: there shall come a Star out of Jacob, and a Sceptre shall rise out of Israel, and shall smite the corners of Moab, and destroy all the children of Sheth. And Edom shall be a possession, Seir also shall be a possession for his enemies; and Israel shall do valiantly.* [25]

OVER EDOM HAVE I CAST MY SHOE

The Lord has cast His shoe as the kinsman redeemer over the land of Edom which had been given unto the curse. The Scripture then reveals prophetically the question: *"Moab is my washpot; over Edom will I cast out my shoe... Who will bring me into the strong city? who will lead me into Edom?"*[26] The prophet Amos speaks of the Day of the Lord as the time when the tabernacle of David is raised up, and the Lord speaks again of the remnant possessing Edom: *"In that day will I raise up the tabernacle of David that is fallen, and close up the breaches thereof; and I will raise up his ruins, and I will build it as in the days of old: That they may possess the remnant of Edom, and of all the heathen, which are called by my name, saith the Lord that doeth this."*[27]

The Lord declares His judgment upon Edom again in the prophecies of Obadiah and declares that the remnant shall possess the possessions of Edom. *"Shall I not in that day, saith the Lord, even destroy the wise men out of Edom, and understanding out of the mount of Esau? ...For thy violence against thy brother Jacob shame shall cover thee, and thou shalt be cut off for ever ...For the day of the Lord is near upon all the heathen: as thou hast done, it shall be done unto thee ...But upon mount Zion shall be deliverance, and there shall be holiness; and the house of Jacob shall possess their possessions."*[28]

Many of the words established by God are repeated and fulfilled twice. The Lord repeats the prophecy of the redemption of Edom again in Psalm 108. *"Moab is my washpot; over Edom will I cast out my shoe; over Philistia will I triumph. Who will bring me into the strong city? who will lead me into Edom?"*[29]

The Lord speaks through Micah telling His little flock, *"Arise ye, and depart; for this is not your rest: because it is polluted, it shall destroy you, even with a sore destruction."*[30]

The Lord is saying move on children, for this land is no longer a place of rest. The land wherein you dwell has now become defiled before me, and I stand now ready to judge this wicked nation. You must move on, to the place which I have prepared for your rest. Follow me, and do not fear, for I the Lord will go before you, and I shall be your rear guard.

> *"I will surely assemble, O Jacob, all of thee; I will surely gather the remnant of Israel; I will put them together as the sheep of Bozrah, as the flock in the midst of their fold: they shall make great noise by reason of the multitude of men."* [31] Oh the manifold wisdom of God. Who can hear His voice? Who can discern what the Spirit is saying to the bride? I am full of power by the Spirit of the Lord, and of judgment, and of might, to declare unto Jacob his transgression, and to Israel his sin. For the Spirit of the Holy Lord says now to His true bride "Come and enter your chambers, my people and I will close the door behind you. Rest in me for a little while, and wait for me while I judge my enemies. For the desolation which is coming shall shortly pass."

> *I said, Hear, I pray you, O heads of Jacob, and ye princes of the house of Israel; Is it not for you to know judgment? Who hate the good, and love the evil ... Then shall they cry unto the Lord, but he will not hear them: he will even hide his face from them at that time, as they have behaved themselves ill in their doings. Thus saith the Lord concerning the prophets that make my people err, ...and cry, Peace; and he that putteth not into their mouths, ...Therefore night shall be unto you, that ye shall not have a vision; and it shall be dark unto you, that ye shall not divine; and the sun shall go down over the prophets, and the day shall be dark over them. Then shall the seers be ashamed, and the diviners confounded: yea, they shall all cover their lips; for there is no answer of God. But truly I am full of power by the spirit of the Lord, and of judgment, and of might, to declare unto Jacob his transgression, and to Israel his sin. Micah 3:1,4-8*

THERE IS A REMNANT ACCORDING TO
THE ELECTION OF GRACE

Esaias also crieth concerning Israel, Though the number of the children of Israel be as the sand of the sea, a remnant shall be saved: For he will finish the work, and cut it short in righteousness: because a short work will the Lord make upon the earth. And as Esaias said before, Except the Lord of Sabbath had left us a seed, we had been as Sodom, and been made like unto Gomorrah. Romans 9:27-29

Even so then at this present time also there is a remnant according to the election of grace. Romans 11:5

May the God of Israel, even our Father in heaven open our eyes to see that everyone who is the bride of Christ is the true seed of Abraham. They are grafted into the true vine, which is Yeshua, the Messiah of Israel. They share these precious promises of a great deliverance. May we have eyes of faith to trust God and obey His word and to no longer rely on the world, or the arm of the flesh for safety for the Lord alone is our salvation. Let us submit to His will in faith and humility, and follow His plan.

CHAPTER

7

HERE IS THE MIND WHICH HAS WISDOM

Revelation 17:9

The apostle John in the book of Revelation, Chapter 17, is shown a picture of the woman, Mystery Babylon, seated upon many waters and who is also riding the beast. This vision is one of the tests of the men of wisdom. Those who have the true understanding of God can both identify, and reveal the mystery of the woman, and the beast on which she rides.

I WILL TELL YOU THE MYSTERY OF THE WOMAN

And there came one of the seven angels which had the seven vials, and talked with me saying unto me, Come hither; I will shew unto thee the judgment of the great whore that sitteth upon many waters: With whom the kings of the earth have committed fornication, and the inhabitants of the earth have been made drunk with the wine of her fornication. So he carried me away in the spirit into the wilderness: and I saw a woman sit upon a scarlet colored beast, full of names of blasphemy, having seven heads and ten horns. Revelation 17:1-3

The woman, Mystery Babylon, is clothed with royal clothing signifying her honor and authority over all of mankind. In the eyes of the world, she is rich and wealthy, covered with gold and precious stones. To those who dwell in darkness, Mystery Babylon is admired and worshipped. She is the pride of the whole earth. People from all the nations of the world come unto her, seeking pleasures in the life of this present age from the wealth which is in her hand. Her great riches are the splendor of her glory.

Mystery Babylon is also the false religious system of man and the mother of apostate Christianity. The nations of the earth have been deceived by her spiritual immorality. She is worshipped by those who are perishing, who have been deceived by her false doctrines and damnable heresies.

In the eyes of God, she is full of abominations, and the filth of her fornication and wickedness. She is the mother of all the harlots and abominations of the earth! Not only is she full of wickedness and sin, but she leads the nations into the same abominations, and the whole earth has been deceived by her vain glory! She spreads her wickedness among the whole world, thereby corrupting the nations, and seducing them in her immorality. She has promised the nations freedom and happiness, all the while leading them into the slavery of sin! She claims to have the light of the gospel, and to be the bride of Christ, but in reality, she is the bride of Satan, the great deceiver of the nations.

> *And the woman was arrayed in purple and scarlet colour and decked with gold and precious stones and pearls, having a golden cup in her hand full of abominations and filthiness of her fornication: And upon her forehead was a name written, MYSTERY, BABYLON THE GREAT, THE MOTHER OF HARLOTS AND ABOMINATIONS OF THE EARTH.* [1]

John witnesses the woman is drunk, intoxicated, having lost her right mind, she is delirious, not from wine, but from blood; the blood of the saints of the Most High God. Mystery Babylon has persecuted and martyred the saints of God throughout the ages. Believers have questioned how has America shed the blood of God's people?

The truth would shock you. First, over fifty million innocent babies have been murdered in America; and that is only a small part of the story, for the death count worldwide from American abortion practices is estimated at over five hundred million. Second, think of the slaves, who were kidnapped, and then they and their families were murdered and abused, and many of them were believers. Third, think of the bloodshed in all of the wars started on false pretenses by this country. Think of the American corporations owned by the rich men of the earth, and all the damage they have done to the earth and to humanity. And the list goes on endlessly.

Though her true nature is revealed to John, he too, in his mortal mind wonders with great admiration at her beauty and her wealth. The angel then admonishes John, *"Why are you marveling? I will tell you the mystery of the woman and the beast that carries her."* The woman has no power of her own, for she is being carried, and lifted up by the beast himself. She is his testament to the peoples of the world, who follow her in her carnality and are seduced by her immorality.

> *And I saw the woman drunken with the blood of the saints, and with the blood of the martyrs of Jesus: and when I saw her, I wondered with great admiration. And the angel said unto me, Wherefore didst thou marvel? I will tell thee the mystery of the woman, and of the beast that carrieth her, which hath the seven heads and ten horns. Revelation 17:6-7*

142

THE BEAST WAS, AND IS NOT, AND SHALL ASCEND AGAIN

The angel then begins to reveal the mystery of the beast, *"who was, and is not."* At the time of this writing, the beast is no longer in power, but he shall come again, ascending out of the bottomless pit, only to go into perdition for eternity. *"The beast that thou sawest was, and is not; and shall ascend out of the bottomless pit, and go into perdition: and they that dwell on the earth shall wonder, whose names were not written in the book of life from the foundation of the world. And here is the mind which hath wisdom. The seven heads are seven mountains, on which the woman sitteth And there are seven kings: five are fallen, and one is, and the other is not yet come; and when he cometh, he must continue a short space. And the beast that was, and is not, even he is the eighth, and is of the seven, and goeth into perdition. And the ten horns which thou sawest are ten kings, which have received no kingdom ...but receive power as kings one hour with the beast."* [2]

This is the riddle of Revelation 17 which the men of wisdom can discern the meaning of:

1. The seven heads of the beast.
2. The seven mountains on which the woman sits
3. The identity of the seven kings, five of which have fallen.
4. The identity of the beast itself, the 8th king, and of the seven.
5. The ten horns, which rule as kings for one hour with the beast.
6. The identity of the woman Mystery Babylon.

THE GOD OF HEAVEN GIVES WISDOM UNTO THE WISE

This mystery has been revealed by the Lord Himself, for the mind of man has not revealed this matter. The seven heads of the beast are both governments and institutions used by the beast, to exercise authority and dominion over the earth. In its manifest forms, the beast appears as both kings and mountains. These heads signify authority, one who is over, or above, in the seat of power. At the time of the writing of this prophecy, the sixth king ruled in Rome, represented by the two legs of iron of Daniel's prophecy. The legs of iron are also symbolic, for under the rule of Rome, the beast now transforms itself, and divides into two diverse institutions of power. The beast is the great deceiver, and it is always seeking to hide its true nature from mankind.

From the time of the Roman Empire, the beast began operating through two diverse institutions, which are seen in the vision as kings and mountains. From these two bases of power, the beast will seek to subdue the people of the earth under its tyranny and depravity.

143

THE BEAST IN ITS VISIBLE FORM
KINGDOMS OF GOVERNMENT

The beast first appears as seven kings. They are the visible form of the beast appearing as human governments. The word for king in the original Greek is *basileus*, which means a foundation of power, a sovereign or a ruler. The seven kings represent seven diverse empires or governments which will rule over the entire earth. Through the thrones of these kings, the beast himself, who is the eighth king, exercises his authority as the supreme ruler over the political realm of mankind. The seven kings who conquer the earth under the authority of the beast are:

1. Egypt
2. Assyria
3. Babylon of the Chaldeans
4. The Medes and Persians
5. Greece under Alexander
6. Rome
7. The New World Order of United Nations

The first five kingdoms had fallen by the writing of this prophecy. Rome, the sixth was still in power. And the other, which is not yet come, is the New World Order. This final kingdom shall only abide for a little while - 42 months. Each of the kingdoms of the beast conquered the known world at that time. The first two had risen and fallen from power when Daniel was shown the prophetic revelation of what was yet to come. They were excluded from his vision, having already passed from the scene, yet these were also the beast exercising his dominion in the political history of man. Though appearing as independent sovereigns, these kings are puppets of the beast. The seven kings sit upon the throne of the beast, and rule in his authority, over the political realm of mankind.

THE BEAST HIMSELF IS THE EIGHTH KING

We are told *"The beast himself is the eighth king, and he is of the seven."* This tells us the true nature of the seven, for the beast himself has been king in these empires all along. The beast does not rule in his own right, or in his own name, but rather rules through these horns which he has lifted up his seven kings. The identity of the beast that *"was, and is not, but shall ascend out of the bottomless pit"* is Satan, the great dragon. We are told *"he was, and is not"* for he *"was"* in authority over all the earth at one time, until Jesus Christ took the sins of the world upon Himself. In shedding His Precious Blood as a perfect sacrifice to God in His death on the cross, Jesus stripped the devil of his power, having canceled the accusations against us. Then the beast was cast down, and now *"he is not"* in authority. All power and authority is now in the hands of Jesus Christ, and the Holy Spirit who restrains the beast, will allow him a little time to rule the kingdom of the earth once again, in the last half of the 70th week of Daniel.

Scripture testifies of this judgment on the prince of the world, the beast, *"Of judgment, because the prince of this world is judged."*[3] He was judged at the cross, and then he was cast out of heaven into the bottomless pit. *"Now is the judgment of this world: now shall the prince of this world be cast out."*[4] The chosen of the Lord now have the authority, because the beast is no longer the ruler of the earth. *"I beheld Satan as lightning fall from heaven. Behold, I give unto you power to tread on serpents and scorpions, and over all the power of the enemy: and nothing shall by any means hurt you."*[5] Oh what praise and thanksgiving should this truth generate in our hearts. Lord Jesus, thank you for suffering and dying for our sins. Thank you for the power of your Blood as the Lamb of God, and for your Word, which is our testimony, whereby we can overcome the dragon. We praise your name Lord Jesus, for your amazing grace and the riches of your mercy. Open our eyes to see the incredible price you paid to redeem our lives. Help us Lord, to live holy and pure lives in this present hour that we may give glory and honor to you. Lord give us ears to hear, and hearts to obey you, that we might glorify and lift up your Holy Name. Amen.

In the present hour, the beast is not in authority! Praise God! Jesus Christ is the Lord and the keys of death and Hades are in His hand, yet the beast continues to work, and wait for the day which is coming soon, when he will be released for a short time. *"For the mystery of iniquity doth already work: only he who now letteth will let, until he be taken out of the way. And then shall that Wicked be revealed, whom the Lord shall consume with the spirit of his mouth, and shall destroy with the brightness of his coming."*[6]

The Scripture testifies the little prince will come after the working of Satan: *"Even him, whose coming is after the working of Satan with all power and signs and lying wonders, And with all deceivableness of unrighteousness in them that perish; because they received not the love of the truth, that they might be saved. And for this cause God shall send them strong delusion, that they should believe a lie: That they all might be damned who believed not the truth, but had pleasure in unrighteousness."*[7]

The little prince is the seventh king of the beast. He will lead the seventh and final kingdom. The beast is himself the eighth king who works in his people. The sons of darkness abide in the beast, even as the true believers, the chosen elect of God, abide in Christ.

THE DAY OF THE LORD IS AT HAND

THE SEVEN TRUE SHEPHERDS OF ISRAEL

The seven kings of the beast are also a counterfeit of seven shepherds whom the Lord will raise up in the last days, as prophesied in the book of Micah, chapter 5. This prophecy contains details of both the first and second coming of our Lord. Most people can identify the prophecies of the first coming. We are told that the Messiah who is to be ruler in all of Israel is He whose *"going forth is from everlasting."* The prophet declares that the Messiah is the Lord, for He comes forth from "everlasting!"

Micah also prophesied that Jesus would come from Bethlehem. *"They shall smite the judge of Israel with a rod upon the cheek. But thou, Bethlehem Ephratah, though thou be little among the thousands of Judah, yet out of thee shall he come forth unto me that is to be ruler in Israel; whose goings forth have been from of old, from everlasting."*[8] The above prophesy was fulfilled literally by Jesus Christ in His first coming.

The prophet then tells us from that time, which is the first coming of Jesus; the Lord will give up His nation Israel until the time that she who is travailing has brought forth. The meaning of the travailing of Israel, and the last days of the kingdom, will be discussed in chapter eight: *"The Lord will be the Hope of His people."*

This is the time for Israel to give birth again, and for the remnant to return to the land of Israel *"and they shall abide"* for *"he (Jesus) shall (now) be great unto the ends of the earth."* The power of Jesus Christ as the LION OF JUDAH will be made manifest on this planet in greatness unseen in the history of man, and it will extend to the very end of the earth! Oh people of God, wait until you see what our Lord has planned! Do not fear, chosen ones, your God is coming, just as He promised, and He will walk with you right through the fire! Micah then tells us *"This man (Jesus) shall be the peace"* when the Assyrian shall invade the land, which is in the final battle of Ezekiel 38. Then *"we (Israel) shall raise against him seven shepherds, and eight principal men."* Micah 5:5

These seven shepherds are the seven overseers appointed by the Lord as apostles to His remnant, during the tribulation. They are His seven kings, and He Himself is the eighth principal man. The seven kings of the beast, and the beast himself who is also the eighth, are just one more counterfeit of the true work of God.

> *Therefore will he give them up, until the time that she which travaileth hath brought forth: then the remnant of his brethren shall return unto the children of Israel. And he shall stand and feed in the strength of the Lord, in the majesty of the name of the Lord his God; and they shall abide: for*

now shall he be great unto the ends of the earth. And this man shall be the peace, when the Assyrian shall come into our land: and when he shall tread in our palaces, then shall we raise against him seven shepherds, and eight principal men. Micah 5:3-5

And having raised up seven shepherds, the Lord uses them to waste the land of Assyria with the sword. *"And they shall waste the land of Assyria with the sword, and the land of Nimrod in the entrances thereof thus shall he deliver us from the Assyrian, when he cometh into our land, and when he treadeth within our borders."*[9] These seven men shall lift their hands and pray. Then the sword will fall on the enemies of Israel. These are but some of the prophecies of the second 3 ½ year ministry of Jesus Christ as the Lion of Judah. Read on in Micah Chapter five, for the prophet reveals more about the mighty remnant who will walk as lions in the anointing of the Lord Jesus during the last days.

The seven kings are an exact counterfeit of the true government God has established for His people in the last days of the tribulation, which are the seven shepherds.

THE SEVEN MOUNTAINS OF THE BEAST

The seven mountains are a counterfeit of another type. The Greek word for mountain is *or'-os* which means to rise, or to be lifted up, above the plain. This counterfeit lifts itself up in another realm, outside of and separate from the world of government. Again, the objective of the beast is the same. These mountains are the beast kingdom in another form, manifesting his deception upon the souls of mankind. We are told that the mountains are the seven hills on which the woman sits. The city of seven hills is Rome and at the time of the prophecy, Mystery Babylon had her seat of authority in Rome and the legs of iron were ruling the nations. And at that time, the beast divided his religious system from his political government. In all the prior kingdoms of Babylon, the religious institution and the king were united, for the emperor was viewed as a god. This is the first instance of the separation of the religion of Babylon from the state.

Now, during the rule of Rome, the secular institutions of church and state are separated for the first time. These secular institutions are created by the beast to deceive mankind. With the beginning of the collapse of Rome, the emperor formally organized the political power of the state under a separate religious institution, which he called the Holy Roman Church.

In Revelation 17 we are told Mystery Babylon has blasphemous names written on her. Blasphemy is to call that which is unholy, holy. Thus, the very name of this religious branch of the Roman government is blasphemy.

THE DAY OF THE LORD IS AT HAND

Kings bear but a short life span, and then their kingdoms are given to another, whereas mountains endure throughout the millennium. They change not; regardless of which king sits upon the throne of man, these mountains endure and are unchanging through the ages. They are not affected by the death of the monarch, for the mountains are an institution which is greater than the men who rule them. The word oros, which means to be lifted up above the plains is a symbol of the professional priesthood that would rule the false churches. The seven mountains represent the false religions of man including apostate Christianity which began in Rome. The seven mountains are the false religions of the seven empires of the beast.

The mountains represent the high places of the earth, to which the people have always turned, in fashioning for themselves a place to worship God in ways which seem right in their eyes. It is here, on the high places, that the *"rulers of the darkness of this world,"* who are *"spirits of wickedness in high places"* unveil revelation brought through angels of light, who bear doctrines of demons, to deceive the many who only do that which seems right in their eyes, but not in the eyes of the Lord. These mountains appear as citadels of truth to the men who look up to them, but the Lord has already condemned them, saying *"I will destroy your high places"* for these are the high places of Ba'al, and they are full of all of the abominations of the earth. These high places are the religious institutions of men, and the vain religious worship of the people who remain lost in the darkness, having never turned from their sins.

They are the resemblance of the curse which was to be poured out as prophesied by Zechariah, for they are the institutions of men which were built in *"the land of Shinar"* which are the plains of Babylon, where men exalt themselves in the place of authority over the people and the *"many"* who worship there are called the *"congregation of the dead."* Unto them is the *"ministry of death"* given, as the only portion provided a people who, having never received the love of the truth, are left to perish in their sins.

Thus, the beast continues his rule over the people of the earth, now as the great deceiver, corrupting their souls. These institutions have also martyred millions of true believers who refused to deny the truth of Jesus Christ and His Holy Word. Thus, we know that Mystery Babylon, the harlot, is both the governments of this world, which are opposed to God, and the false religious systems of the earth. She is indeed a mystery, for who could have known such deception would come.

148

THE MYSTERY OF THE TEN KINGS

The ten kings are descendants of the ten toes which survive the collapse of the Roman Empire. These kings will come to power from within the political and religious institutions of the beast which have ruled over the centuries.

The Order of the Illuminati, according to the story which they told to the world, was founded by a Jesuit priest named Adam Weishaupt. The Order of the Illuminati was actually founded by Satan, as alliance between the occultists and sorcerers who would rise in power as members of the royal families of Europe and as the leaders of the false churches. The ten kings, who come to power with the beast for one hour, are literal descendants of this small group of people who call themselves the Elite, or Olympians, for they are the holders of the light, which was cast down from heaven.

They are the political rulers in the last days that seize the kingdom by intrigue. At the end of the age, the ten kings of the Order of the Illuminati, will bring the New World Order of the beast to power. Their only purpose is to create a One World Government, and to then give their power to the beast. We are told the ten kings hate the woman; and so their first act will be to destroy America Babylon as a precursor to the rise of their New World Order. "*These have one mind, and shall give their power and strength unto the beast. These shall make war with the Lamb, and the Lamb shall overcome them: for he is Lord of lords, and King of kings: and they that are with him are called, and chosen, and faithful.*"[10]

In destroying the daughter of Babylon, the United States of America, which rules the earth at the time of the end, they create a world crisis, which allows them to seize the throne. They are responsible for World War III, after which the nations will surrender their sovereignty to the beast. When the ten kings seize the kingdom at the time of the end, Rome is no longer the ruling empire. Mystery Babylon has risen again, on a distant shore, far away over the great sea, in the new world which they called America. The angel now tells John that Modern Babylon is seated upon many nations, and peoples and tongues. This is America in the last days, before the rule of the antichrist. The rulers of the Illuminati hate America; and they are even now planning to destroy her, to make her desolate, and naked, and to burn her cities with fire.

> *The waters which thou saw, where the whore sits, are peoples, and multitudes, and nations, and tongues. And the ten horns which thou saw upon the beast, these shall hate the whore, and shall make her desolate and naked, and shall eat her flesh, and burn her with fire. For God bath put in their hearts to fulfil his will, and to agree, and give their kingdom unto the beast, until the words of God shall be fulfilled.* [11]

149

We are told, Mystery Babylon is the great nation which rules the earth at the time of the end, immediately before the prince comes to power. *"And the woman which thou saw is that great city, which reigns over the kings of the earth."*[12]

This is America, who is also call the daughter of Babylon, for she is a descendent of the final King of Babylon, who will rule the final one world government from the throne of England.

LET HIM WITH WISDOM CALCULATE
THE NUMBER OF THE BEAST

The apostle John is shown the beast rising up out of the sea of humanity in Revelation 13. As the beast rises from the sea and comes to power, it has the head of a lion, the body of a leopard and the feet of a bear. *"And I stood upon the sand of the sea, and saw a beast rise up out of the sea, having seven heads and ten horns, and upon his horns ten crowns, and upon his heads the name of blasphemy. And the beast which I saw was like unto a leopard, and his feet were as the feet of a bear, and his mouth as the mouth of a lion: and the dragon gave him his power, and his seat, and great authority."* [13] *"And he causes all, small and great, rich and poor, free and bond, to receive a mark in their right hand, or in their foreheads: And that no man might buy or sell, save he that had the mark, or the name of the beast, or the number of his name. Here is wisdom. Let him that hath understanding count the number of the beast: for it is the number of a man; and his number is 666."*[14]

The beast will require all the citizens of the earth who dwell within his kingdom to take a mark on their hand or forehead. This is the mark of the beast, and it is the number of his name, 666. The technology to imprint the mark was first developed in 1959. The technology for the mark has been available for years. The Order introduced the first credit cards in the same year to begin the conditioning of the public. Only now, has the psychology of the people been made ready.

In 1979 I had a series of five interviews with a company known as IBM. My last interview was with one of their senior executives. At the end of the interview he asked me the standard final question, "Do you have any questions for me?" "I only have one: I have learned from five independent sources within your company that IBM has developed an infrared laser tattoo device to imprint a laser tattoo on the hand or the forehead of every person, to identify them for the electronic money system which is coming. And that your company is presently storing these devices in warehouses in Europe and America. And that the identification mark is three sets of six digits. Is this true?" "That is old news" was his only reply. Everyone in the kingdom of the beast will bear the mark.

That is why the remnant must flee to the wilderness prepared by God. You will neither be able to buy or sell anything in the beast cities. They will hunt you, and seek to kill you, but if you have been chosen in His remnant, He will hide you, but you must soon leave the kingdom of the beast.

THE MYSTERY OF THE BEAST
AND THE NUMBER OF HIS NAME 666

Prophecy often has both a literal and a symbolic application. The symbols used to describe the beast tell us about the nature of his actions and identify his throne of power. First, it has the head of a lion. This tells us the seat of authority of the beast will come out of England, which is symbolized by the lion.

Second, it has the body of the leopard. The leopard comes from the Nazi empire pictured in Daniel's vision. The body of the beast symbolizes how the beast will operate. It moves with its body. The beast empire shall be organized with a governmental system similar to the Nazi party, with its political identity one of socialism, and it will subdue the whole earth with the same lightening war tactics of Nazi Germany.

Even now, the tactics and laws being implemented in the USA are a carbon copy of those used in Nazi Germany. The recent gun control bill passed in the USA is an exact duplicate of the one the Nazis passed following the Reichstag fire. The feet of the beast are from the bear. It will trample its subjects with the same brutal oppression of the Soviet empire. The beast will have its seat of power in the Royal family of Windsor, while its tactics will be borrowed from the Nazi era and its brutality will be like unto the Soviet bloodshed of Stalin and Lenin. Lastly, the union of these three beasts is symbolic of the United Nations of the New World Order which this beast will head. And America, she has been judged by the time the beast rises out of the sea of humanity.

THE HERALDIC BEAST OF THE HOUSE OF WINDSOR

There is also a literal fulfillment of this Scripture. Let us examine the symbol of the Royal Family of Windsor carefully. It is called the Heraldic Beast. It has the head of a lion, the body of a leopard and the feet of a bear. This is the exact picture of the beast of Revelation 13. The Royal family of Windsor has been flying this flag for 500 years, and no one even noticed!

THE DAY OF THE LORD IS AT HAND

The antichrist comes as a prince out of the house of Windsor. When we are told to calculate the number of the beast, the true answer will be derived using the Hebrew gematria system; which is the numerical values of the twenty-two letters of the Hebrew alphabet. Let me present it as follows:

A 1	J 10	S 100
B 2	K 20	T 200
C 3	L 30	U 300
D 4	M 40	V 400
E 5	N 50	W 0
F 6	0 60	X 0
G 7	P 70	Y 0
H 8	Q 80	Z 0
I 9	R 90	

The antichrist is the most widely known politician in the world today. His face has been put in front of every nation on the globe, every two weeks, for the last thirty years. You have seen him often. Daniel tells us he is "the prince who shall come" in his own name representing his father the Devil. He is the son of perdition and he makes his appearance before the world as a prince.

PRINCE	CHARLES	OF	WALES
(70+90+9+50+3+5)	(3+8+1+90+30+5+100)	(60+6)	(0+1+30+5+100)

666

The name Charles means "man". It is the number of a man; it is the number of a "Charles." I translated the prince's name into Hebrew while studying at the Hebrew University in Jerusalem, Israel with the help of my Israeli friends. In Hebrew, his name totals 666. Others have run the calculation in Greek. Again, the answer is the same, 666. English is the language of the Babylon in the modern world. Greek is the language of the ancient world, and the language of the New Testament writings. Hebrew is the language of the prophets themselves. In these three languages, the identity of the prince is unveiled and confirmed. In the mouth of two or three witnesses, all truth shall be confirmed.

Here Is The Mind Which Has Wisdom

When Jesus hung on the cross, a sign was nailed above his head testifying to the world that he was "The King of the Jews." It was written in three languages, representing three witnesses of His true identity; in these last days, three witnesses, in three languages, also unveil the identity of the antichrist.

The symbol of Wales is the red dragon. At the prince's coronation, the Queen pointed to the banners of the red dragon which were flying over the assembly and said *"This dragon has given you his power, his throne and his great authority."*[15] She quoted the verse in Revelation which would be spoken of the beast. He responded by saying "This day I have become your Lord man and am worthy of your earthly worship". His mother the Queen has been quoted speaking of Charles saying "He is the chosen one".[16]

The Prince of Wales is also known as the Black Prince, and this title is presented on his coat of arms in symbolic form as three ostrich feathers. The coat of arms also contains a picture of the red dragon, which he serves. The caption in Latin below these symbols reads "I the Black Prince do serve the Red Dragon." The coat of arms for Prince Charles also contains all the symbols of the antichrist revealed in Scripture. He has ten Heraldic beasts in this coat of arms. He is the first monarch ever to have ten. He is the head of the Order of the Illuminati and the head of worldwide Freemasonry. The family tree of Prince Charles shows him to be a descendant of King David of Israel. "According to Anglo-Israelites, the queen descends from King David. The queen's lineage, published in 1977 as `The Illustrious Lineage of The Royal House of Britain' depicts her household as `The House of David - The Royal Line.'" [17]

The prince is the most popular international figure in Israel today. In late 1996, Israeli television ran a special on the prince. At the end of the show, they disclosed his lineage chart showing him to be the "son of David" and the rabbis left the viewers with the question - could he be the Messiah? No. He is the false messiah; he is the antichrist. Let him who has wisdom count the number of the beast, for it is the number of a man. It is the number of a Charles. "There is more evidence to prove that he (Prince Charles) is the anti-messiah than most people have to prove their own identity. He has been involved in the occult. He wants to be king of Europe. Is he the anti-messiah? I'll let the Lord reveal him at the abomination of desolation. Is he involved with the Middle East peace accord? His personal attorney arranged the first meetings which took place in Norway. Was he at Rabin's funeral to witness the confirming of the covenant with the grave? He sat in the first row in the seventh seat." [18]

THE DAY OF THE LORD IS AT HAND

CHAPTER
8
THE LORD WILL BE
THE HOPE OF HIS PEOPLE
Joel 3:16

The prophecies of the bible are foundational to the faith of the people of God. Over one third of Scripture is devoted to prophecy, much of which deals with the last days and the coming Great Day of the Lord. If the vision of prophecy is lost, the foundation is destroyed and the people soon fall into ruin. *"If the foundations be destroyed, what can the righteous do?"*[1] Scripture testifies to the importance of prophecy and its proper understanding. *"For through him we both have access by one Spirit unto the Father. Now therefore ye are no more strangers and foreigners, but fellow citizens with the saints and of the household of GOD; And are built upon the foundation of the apostles and prophets, JESUS CHRIST himself being the chief corner stone."* [2]

THE TESTIMONY OF JESUS
IS THE SPIRIT OF PROPHECY

The message of all of the prophets is the revelation of Jesus Christ. They are His witness and the testimony that Jesus is the Messiah of Israel. He is our kinsman redeemer. He is both our peace and our salvation. The testimony of Jesus is the Spirit of all prophecy:

> *I am thy fellow servant, and of thy brethren that have the testimony of Jesus: worship God: for the testimony of Jesus is the spirit of prophecy.* [3]

Those who ignore or dismiss prophecy do so to their own harm, for the prophecies have been given as our instructions, and as a warning to us that we might take heed.

Solomon writes in Proverbs 22:3 that the prudent, those with insight, who can see beyond the surface into what lies ahead, will hide themselves from the evil: *"A prudent man foresees the evil, and hides himself but the simple pass on, and are punished."*

THE DAY OF THE LORD IS AT HAND

NO PROPHECY IS OF PRIVATE INTERPRETATION

Many dismiss the study of prophecy based on an incomplete knowledge of Scripture. They have been taught no man can know the day or the hour, so they assume there is no value in watching as the Lord commands. They also assume that prophecy is subject to various interpretations. It is not, there is one true interpretation, which is revealed by the Spirit. Many false teachers have come, just as Jesus warned, but those who have the Holy Spirit can discern the true from the false.

> We have also a more sure word of prophecy; whereunto ye do well that ye take heed, as unto a light that shines in a dark place, until the day dawn, and the day star arise in your hearts: Knowing this first that no prophecy of the scripture is of any private interpretation. For the prophecy came not in old time by the will of man: but holy men of God spake as they were moved by the Holy Ghost. 4

THOSE THINGS WHICH MUST SHORTLY COME TO PASS

The revelation of St. John was given to show the bondservants of Jesus those things which must shortly come to pass. The message of the book was a specific prophecy to the remnant who are alive in the last days, and was meant for their specific instruction.

> The Revelation of Jesus Christ, which God gave unto him, to show unto his servants things which must shortly come to pass: and he sent and signified it by his angel unto his servant John. Revelation 1:1

THE PRUDENT SHALL KEEP SILENT IN THAT TIME

Prophecy is not only important, it is critical to the people to whom it was sent. Through prophecy, the Lord provides guidance and direction, which in times such as these is critical. The prophet Amos speaks also of the time of judgment as a time when "the prudent shall keep silence." Why? Because the days are evil and they are hiding themselves. They know from the prophecy it is a dangerous time, where one doesn't draw any unnecessary attention to oneself. Indeed, wisdom today is to do only what the Lord commands.

We should be praying about every decision, taking nothing for granted, for these days are full of great evil, and the time is very short. Think not that the prudent will stop everyone they meet to warn them of the approaching lion, for they know better. The citizens of Babylon want nothing to do with this message. The Babylonians wish to continue sleeping, and simply enjoy the final days of their cruise on the great ship Titanic. Nor will they hear, for their hearts are hardened, so it is better to keep silent, and only speak when the Lord commands:

> *Therefore the prudent shall keep silence in that time; for it is an evil time. Amos 5:13*

> *Redeeming the time, because the days are evil. Wherefore be ye not unwise, but understanding what the will of the Lord is. Ephesians 5:16-17*

Those who are prudent can foresee the day of evil and they will take note. Indeed, when you finally wake from your sleep, and recognize this is really happening, you will diligently seek the Lord, and ask Him what He calls you to do. In Jeremiah 4:7 we are told *"the lion has come out of the thicket."* The lion is no longer in hiding, but is clearly visible for the prudent to see. The verse continues, *"And the destroyer of the gentiles is on his way."* This is the antichrist, who is the destroyer of the Gentiles. He is the mouth of the Lion, the head of the beast.

THE WISE SHALL UNDERSTAND

The angel who answered Daniel at the end of his prophecy speaks of those who are prudent in the last days, those who can understand that the prophecies are being fulfilled saying *"none of the wicked shall understand, but the wise shall understand."* [5] We are also told that at that time many shall run to and fro, and the knowledge of mankind shall be greatly increased.

> *But thou, O Daniel, shut up the words, and seal the book, even to the time of the end: many shall run to and fro, and knowledge shall be increased. Daniel 12:4*

> *And he said, Go thy way, Daniel: for the words are closed up and sealed till the time of the end. Many shall be purified, and made white, and tried; but the wicked shall do wickedly: and none of the wicked shall understand; but the wise shall understand. Daniel 12:9-10*

MEN'S HEARTS SHALL FAIL THEM FOR FEAR

This chapter is written to the remnant, and those who are prudent, to encourage you to look to the Lord, for He is our hope and our peace. They are the wise who shall understand. The Lord knew these days would come, and told us in advance, *"In the world you will have tribulation, but be of good cheer, for I have overcome the world!"* [6] We are supposed to be of good cheer.

THE DAY OF THE LORD IS AT HAND

It is God's plan that we would rejoice as we see these things which will terrify the nations of the earth. We are to be a haven of rest and peace, as a witness to the people of the earth, that their hearts could find peace. Yet the events of the end of the age and the soon coming of the Lord are fearful if seen only through the eyes of the natural man. Great and terrible judgments will soon fall upon our land, and then upon the entire earth. Jesus spoke of the things saying:

> And there shall be signs in the sun, and in the moon, and in the stars; and upon the earth distress of nations, with perplexity; the sea and the waves roaring; Men's hearts failing them for fear and for looking after those things which are coming on the earth: for the powers of heaven shall be shaken. And then shall they see the Son of man coming in a cloud with power and great glory. And when these things begin to come to pass, then look up, and lift up your heads; for your redemption draws nigh. Luke 21:25-28

In the Lord's own words, we know during the last days there will be signs in the sun, the moon and the stars, and great distress of nations, with perplexity. The heathen, who don't know the Lord, will have no idea what is happening as these signs begin to herald the soon coming King! The sea in Scripture is symbolic of the people of the earth, and its waves will be roaring. They will be crying out, gripped with fear such as they have never known. The hearts of the people will literally fail, and panic will seize the nations of the earth, as they see these things coming to pass. There shall be a great shaking upon the earth, and the very powers of heaven shall be shaken!

HIS THUNDER ANNOUNCES THE COMING STORM

A great storm is approaching our world and when a storm approaches, the first evidence is the sound of distant thunder. The storm is almost upon us, and the thunder now being heard is the true word of our God being spoken to the remnant. *"His thunder announces the coming storm; even the cattle make known its approach."*[7] The cattle in this scripture are a picture of the people of the Lord who can hear the prophetic word, and know the storm will soon be revealed. The prophetic word of the Lord announces the word of God as thunder. *"The voice of thy thunder was in the heaven: the lightning's lightened the world: the earth trembled and shook "*[8]

The Lord uses His voice of thunder to announce the hour of judgment. *"Hast thou an arm like God? or canst thou thunder with a voice like him?"*[9] Today, all over America, the Lord is announcing the coming storm. David Wilkerson wrote a newsletter aptly entitled: *The only Hope in the Coming Storm.*

The LORD Shall Be The Hope Of His People

The storm is about to begin, and when it does, it will come forth with all of its fury, but first it begins with the rain which is now falling, for a gentle rain of the true word of God precedes the violence of the storm. *"My doctrine shall drop as the rain; my speech shall distil as the dew, as the small rain upon the tender herb, and as the showers upon the grass."*[10]

The word of God is pictured as falling upon the earth as a gentle rain, but only those who can discern in the Spirit can receive this latter-day rain. The Lord has been speaking His word of warning to America for many years, but the people are all deaf, dumb and blind. Our nation has come to the point of no return, while only a few recognize the final hour is now upon us. *"The days of visitation are come, the days of recompense are come; Israel shall know it: the prophet is a fool, the spiritual man is mad, for the multitude of thine iniquity, and the great hatred."* [11] The proper meaning of this verse is the prophet is thought to be a fool, and the spiritual ones are seen as crazy! Why? Because the people are so backslidden and blinded by their sin, they cannot discern the word of God. Woe unto you America, and those who stand among you to mock my word, saith the Lord! Is not my word fire, declares the Lord! It shall burn all who have betrayed my holiness, and despised my grace.

THEY SHALL SEE THE SON OF MAN COMING

At the end of the tribulation period, Luke 21:27 declares *"then shall they see the Son of man coming in a cloud with power and great glory"* This is a picture of the days immediately preceding the Second Coming. Jesus tells his own, when you see these things come to pass, and the men of the earth who don't know the Lord are literally dying from fear, *"you lift up your heads for your redemption is drawing near!"*

Jesus tells His faithful remnant to lift your heads, don't be downcast and filled with fear like the heathen, for your redemption is coming. How will the bride of Christ be able to lift their heads in the midst of the most terrible time the world has even known? By looking to the Lord, and keeping our eyes and our faith fixed upon him and by trusting in his word.

Dear reader, the last days are described by the prophets as The Day of the Lord. It is His day, and none other! Jesus Christ will be in complete control of everything! We who know the Lord can rejoice, but we must learn to walk in faith, not trusting our own understanding, nor looking on the outward circumstances, but looking to His word and His precious promises to His faithful ones.

THE DAY OF THE LORD IS AT HAND

I WILL PROTECT THAT WHICH IS MINE

The Lord is coming to bring the final judgment and if you are not right with God, you have every reason to fear! Dear saint, if you know Him, and have opened the door of your heart to Him as Lord, you have no reason to fear anything but the Lord!

> *And hereby we do know that we know him, if we keep his commandments. He that says, I know him, and keeps not his commandments, is a liar, and the truth is not in him. But who so ever keeps his word, in him verily is the love of God perfected: hereby know we that we are in him. He that says he abides in him ought himself also so to walk, even as he walked.* [12]

Understand this, to find Him you must first seek Him with all of your heart, and turn from all your secret sins. The righteous remnant, who will endure these final hours, walk in holiness and faithful obedience. If you have bowed your heart in humble submission to the Lord, you have no reason to fear anything. Fear only the Lord, for this is the beginning of wisdom.

I was shown the Day of the Lord in the fall of 1996 and for seven days, it burned within my soul, with a fire I cannot even begin to describe. I spent hours every day weeping, and crying out to the Lord. Every time I would begin to pray, I would fall to the ground on my face before my God. The Lord had shown me the terrible judgment which would come upon the apostate church in America. I witnessed the severe judgment, which must first come upon the church.

I had been translated into the future, where I found myself standing in one of the detention camps, with my wife and children. As the soldiers tore my wife and children from my arms, I experienced a level of heartbreak I would never have imagined could even exist on this earth. After I was returned to my living room, I immediately fell to the ground on my face screaming and weeping as I cried out, "Lord, what must we do to be saved from these judgments?" Jesus answered me in a clear, audible voice saying:

"I WILL PROTECT THAT WHICH IS MINE AND EVERYTHING ELSE WILL BE DESTROYED!"

This then is the test dear friend; does your life belong to the Lord? Do you belong to the Him? Does He own your life? Is your body sanctified unto Him? Have you died to yourself, surrendering all to Him and His will? If you have, and you are His, you have nothing to fear. Only fear the Lord, for that is the beginning of wisdom. This is the very word Jesus spoke himself in the gospel. How we failed to discern His true meaning: *"For whosoever will save his life shall lose it; but whosoever shall lose his life for my sake and the gospel's, the same shall save it."*[13]

IN THE FEAR OF THE LORD IS STRONG CONFIDENCE

Then I cried out to the Lord, "I need to know what to do and I can't trust man in this hour, I must hear from you." The Lord answered me saying *"Search the scriptures, for the detailed instructions for this hour are in the word of God."* I remember feeling a sigh of relief thinking "that's good; we can trust everything we find in the word of God." The scripture declares the starting point on the road to wisdom and understanding is the fear of the Lord.

"The fear of the Lord is the beginning of knowledge: but fools despise wisdom and instruction."[14] *"The fear of the Lord is the beginning of wisdom: and the knowledge of the holy is understanding."*[15] *"In the fear of the Lord is strong confidence: and his children shall have a place of refuge. The fear of the Lord is a fountain of life, to depart from the snares of death."*[16] The Lord Jesus himself had *"quick understanding in the fear of the Lord."* He is our example, and our King, and if He feared God, so should we. For if a man truly fears the Lord, he will fear nothing else, for our God is a sovereign King. He is the very King of the Universe and nothing can harm us without His consent.

> *And there shall come forth a rod out of the stem of Jesse, and a Branch shall grow out of his roots: And the spirit of the Lord shall rest upon him, the spirit of wisdom and understanding, the spirit of counsel and might, the spirit of knowledge and of the fear of the Lord;_And shall make him of quick understanding in the fear of the Lord: and he shall not judge after the sight of his eyes, neither reprove after the hearing of his ears: But with righteousness shall he judge the poor, and reprove with equity for the meek of the earth: and he shall smite the earth with the rod of his mouth, and with the breath of his lips shall he slay the wicked.* [17]

SEEK HOLINESS WITHOUT WHICH
NO MAN SHALL SEE GOD

The elect of God are distinguished by their holiness unto the Lord. *"Follow peace with all men, and holiness, without which no man shall see the Lord."*[18] Holiness means to be separated and set apart unto God. The holiness of the Lord is to be manifest in every area of our lives. Learning to submit to the Lord in obedience is the first step in our sanctification. The chosen have a choice. Will you allow Jesus to be Lord in your life? The remnant who are delivered by the Lord all walk before Him in holiness.

THE DAY OF THE LORD IS AT HAND

Isaiah speaks of the path walked by the remnant, *"And an highway shall be there, and a way, and it shall be called The way of holiness; the unclean shall not pass over it; but it shall be for those: the wayfaring men, though fools, shall not err therein."*[19]

The holiness of the righteous is received by faith in Jesus Christ, but it must be received and appropriated into our lives. The perfect will of the Father is that we walk before Him in obedience and holiness, being sanctified from all dead works of the flesh, submitting all to His will, that His glory would be manifest in our lives. This is the heart of the Lord for His holy ones, who He calls His remnant.

> *Upon mount Zion shall be deliverance, and there shall be holiness; and the house of Jacob shall possess their possessions. And the house of Jacob shall be a fire, and the house of Joseph a flame, and the house of Esau for stubble, and they shall kindle in them, and devour them.* [20]

Mount Zion is the city of God, and the place where the Lord will dwell within His people. It is the spiritual temple built by the Lord himself in the hearts of His chosen ones. All who are found in Zion in the last days will walk in holiness. Their hearts have been purged of the idolatry of the present age, and the lusts of the flesh which have defiled the many who think themselves saved.

> *Having therefore these promises, dearly beloved, let us cleanse ourselves from all filthiness of the flesh and spirit, perfecting holiness in the fear of God.* [21]

The night is far spent, and the new day is dawning. It is time to focus on our total redemption, and to lay aside the works of the flesh which so easily entangle us. *"Be ye holy; for I am holy."*[22]

The Lord is about to anoint again His holy people, those who honor Him with all of their hearts, and not just their lips. If we wish to be found among the remnant, then we must cleanse our hearts, and touch not the unclean thing, and return to the Lord. Repent, fast and pray, for the Lord is merciful, and He has promised to hear us. The day you seek Him with your whole heart, then you shall find Him.

The Lord declares the way to life is straight and narrow, and very few find it. *"Strait is the gate, and narrow is the way, which leadeth unto life, and few there be that find it."*[24] The word for narrow is *thlee'-bo* [25] which means to afflict, trouble, suffer tribulation and narrow. It is through much tribulation that we enter the kingdom.

The LORD Shall Be The Hope Of His People

The chosen ones are "few." The word means little in number. The chosen ones, who separate themselves from the company of the many who are called, are those who follow on to know the Lord at all costs. They are the remnant, His little flock. Jesus warned us to watch and pray that we may numbered among the remnant who are accounted worthy to stand and endure the tribulation.

> *Watch ye therefore, and pray always, that ye may be accounted worthy to escape all these things that shall come to pass, and to stand before the Son of man. Luke 21:36*

The word "to stand" is *histay-mee*[26] which means to literally abide, or be appointed, to continue and to stand in the presence of the Lord. The word "before" is *em'-pros-then*[27] which means in front of, in the presence of, or literally in the place of. The word for the phrase "that ye may be accounted worthy" is *kat-is-khoo'-o*[28] which means to overpower and to prevail against. The word "to escape" is *ek-fyoo'-go*[29] which means to flee out and escape. The remnant are those who have been appointed to stand in His place during the last half of the 70th week. They are the overcomers to whom the seven promises of the book of Revelation apply:

> *To him that overcomes will I give to eat of the tree of life, which is in the midst of the paradise of God... He that overcomes shall not be hurt of the second death. To him that overcomes will I give to eat of the hidden manna, and will give him a white stone, and in the stone a new name written, which no man knows saving he that receives it... And he that overcomes, and keeps my works unto the end, to him will I give power over the nations. Revelation 2:7-26*

And he shall rule them with a rod of iron; as the vessels of a potter shall they be broken to shivers: even as I received of my Father. And I will give him the morning star.

> *He that overcomes, the same shall be clothed in white raiment; and I will not blot out his name out of the book of life, but I will confess his name before my Father, and before his angels... Him that overcomes will I make a pillar in the temple of my God, and he shall go no more out. and I will write upon him the name of my God, and the name of the city of my God, which is new Jerusalem, which cometh down out of heaven from my God: and I will write upon him my new name... To him that overcomes will I grant to sit with me in my throne, even as I also overcame, and am set down with my Father in his throne. He that hath an ear, let him hear what the Spirit saith unto the churches. [30]*

163

And I heard a great voice out of heaven saying, Behold, the tabernacle of God is with men, and he will dwell with them, and they shall be his people, and God himself shall be with them, and be their God. And God shall wipe away all tears from their eyes; and there shall be no more death, neither sorrow, nor crying, neither shall there be any more pain: for the former things are passed away. And he that sat upon the throne said, Behold, I make all things new. And he said unto me, Write: for these words are true and faithful. And he said unto me, It is done. I am Alpha and Omega, the beginning and the end. I will give unto him that is athirst of the fountain of the water of life freely. He that overcometh shall inherit all things; and I will be his God, and he shall be my son. Revelation 21:3-7

HE HAS CHOSEN US IN HIM BEFORE
THE FOUNDATION OF THE WORLD

The covenant of faith, which was the promise to our father Abraham, was established by God before the foundations of the world; it is an eternal covenant, for it spans both eternity past and future. *"Blessed be the God and Father of our Lord Jesus Christ, who hath blessed us with all spiritual blessings in heavenly places in Christ: According as he hath chosen us in him before the foundation of the world, that we should be holy and without blame before him in love."*[31]

The true children of Abraham, who are the remnant of Israel, were predestined by God to participate in the holy covenant. From the beginning of eternity past, the Father chose us for adoption into His family through this covenant of faith. And having accepted us in the beloved, God provided redemption through His own blood in the eternal covenant.

Having predestinated us unto the adoption of children by JESUS CHRIST to himself, according to the good pleasure of his will, To the praise of the glory of his grace, wherein he hath made us accepted in the beloved. In whom we have redemption through his blood, the forgiveness of sins, according to the riches of his grace; Wherein he hath abounded toward us in all wisdom and prudence. [32]

This was His promise to Abraham from the beginning. *"The Lord will provide himself a lamb."* This is the mystery of our great salvation, and it was revealed in Jesus Christ. *"Having made known unto us the mystery of his will, according to his good pleasure which he hath purposed in himself That in the dispensation of the fulness of times he might gather together in one all things in Christ, both which are in heaven, and which are on earth; even in him."* [33]

The LORD Shall Be The Hope Of His People

The promise of God to His elect was of an inheritance, and He has done this according to His own will. The evidence of the covenant in our lives is the promise of the Holy Spirit, which is the seal that we are God's own possession.

> *In whom also we have obtained an inheritance, being predestinated according to the purpose of him who worketh all things after the counsel of his own will: That we should be to the praise of his glory, who first trusted in Christ. In whom ye also trusted, after that ye heard the word of truth, the gospel of your salvation: in whom also after that ye believed, ye were sealed with that holy Spirit of promise, Which is the earnest of our inheritance until the redemption of the purchased possession, unto the praise of his glory.*[34]

THE LORD SHALL ROAR FROM ZION

In the prophecies of Joel, we are given a picture of the multitudes which will gather in the valley of decision - the valley of Jezreel, where the final battle of Armageddon will be fought. And the Lord will roar out of Zion, shaking the heavens and the earth with the sound of His voice! When the earth begins to shake, and the nations are gripped with fear, the Lord will be the only hope of His people. He will become the strength of the children of Israel. Our only hope is in the Lord. We who are His faithful remnant will stand on His word, and we will stand in His strength and not in our own.

> *Multitudes, multitudes in the valley of decision: for the day of the Lord is near in the valley of decision. The sun and the moon shall be darkened, and the stars shall withdraw their shining. The Lord also shall roar out of Zion, and utter his voice from Jerusalem; and the heavens and the earth shall shake: but the Lord will be the hope of his people, and the strength of the children of Israel.*[35]

FEAR NOT SAYS THE LORD
FOR I WILL COME TO PROVE YOU

The promises of God are contained in the Holy Scriptures and the Word of the Lord commands us to fear not what man can do unto us. Even in the midst of the fiery trial that faces us, fear the Lord and him alone. *"Is anything too hard for the Lord?"*[36] Our God is a strong tower and the righteous run into Him and they are safe! *"Behold, the Lord thy God hath set the land before thee: go up and possess it, as the Lord God of thy fathers hath said unto thee; fear not, neither be discouraged." Deuteronomy 1:21*

THE DAY OF THE LORD IS AT HAND

THE COVENANT OF FAITH WHICH
WAS MADE BY THE LORD OUR GOD

If we are to survive the great tribulation, then we must understand our rights under the blood covenant of God. The word covenant[37] is בְּרִית, *ber-eeth* which means to cut a compact made by passing between pieces of flesh. The first covenant of Scripture was with Noah.

> *With thee will I establish my covenant; and thou shall come into the ark, thou, and thy sons, and thy wife, and thy sons' wives with thee... And God said, This is the token of the covenant which I make between me and you and every living creature that is with you, for perpetual generations: I do set my bow in the cloud, and it shall be for a token of a covenant between me and the earth. And it shall come to pass, when I bring a cloud over the earth, that the bow shall be seen in the cloud and I shall establish my covenant with you, and your seed after you.* [38]

God's covenant is His word, and it stands eternal. *"God's covenants are established more firmly than the pillars of heaven or the foundations of the earth, and cannot be disannulled."* [39] It is the will of the Lord to keep and perform His holy covenants with His people. Do you doubt His strength to keep His covenant? Believe in Him. Trust Him. He has promised, if you call on His name in truth, He will hear you from His Holy Temple.

FEAR NOT MY CHOSEN ONES
I AM THY SHIELD

The Lord entered into covenant with Abram when *"the word of the Lord came unto Abram in a vision, saying, Fear not, Abram: I am thy shield, and thy exceeding great reward."* [40] The Lord took Abram and said unto him *"Look now toward heaven, and tell the stars, if thou be able to number them: and he said unto him, So shall thy seed be. And he believed in the Lord; and he counted it to him for righteousness."* [41] This covenant was by faith, for through believing what God said, it was counted to him for righteousness. This is the everlasting covenant and it was first revealed unto Abraham, *"I will establish my covenant between me and thee and thy seed after thee in their generations for an everlasting covenant, to be a God unto thee, and to thy seed after thee."* [42]

David who also inherited this covenant said, *"he hath made with me an everlasting covenant, ordered in all things, and sure: for this is all my salvation, and all my desire"* [43] The Lord declares *"I have made a covenant with my chosen, I have sworn unto David my servant, Thy seed will I establish forever, and build up thy throne to all generations."* [44]

The LORD Shall Be The Hope Of His People

Praise the Lord all you His chosen ones, for He has already done great things for you! *"O Lord God of Israel, there is no God like thee in the heaven, nor in the earth; which keepest covenant, and shewest mercy unto thy servants, that walk before thee with all their hearts."* [45]

THE COVENANT THROUGH JESUS CHRIST

The covenant of faith which Abraham received was through Jesus Christ, and the many who have been grafted into Israel, are the seeds of the promise, *"that the blessing of Abraham might come on the Gentiles through Jesus Christ; that we might receive the promise of the Spirit through faith."*[45]

The covenant was given to Abraham and his seed. To them alone was the promise of God by faith made, and this promise was hidden in Christ from the beginning of time. *"Now to Abraham and his seed were the promises made. He saith not, and to seeds, as of many; but as of one, and to thy seed, which is Christ."* [46] The covenant of faith was also confirmed by God the Father through Jesus Christ, before the law was given to the children of Israel in the wilderness. Therefore, the law could not disannul the covenant, for if the covenant was by the law, then it was not a promise by faith.

> *And this I say, that the covenant, that was confirmed before of God in Christ, the law, which was four hundred and thirty years after, cannot disannul, that it should make the promise of none effect. For if the inheritance be of the law, it is no more of promise: but God gave it to Abraham by promise.* [47]

> *And he said unto him, I am the Lord that brought thee out of Ur of the Chaldees, to give thee this land to inherit it. And he said, Lord God, whereby shall I know that I shall inherit it? And he said unto him, Take me an heifer of three years old, and a she goat of three years old, and a ram of three years old, and a turtledove, and a young pigeon.* [48]

This was the sacrifice which evidenced the covenant of God with Abram our father and the certainty of God's promise to perform the covenant. *"And he said unto him, Take me an heifer of three years old, and a she goat of three years old, and a ram of three years old, and a turtledove, and a young pigeon. And he took unto him all these, and divided them in the midst, and laid each piece one against another: but the birds divided he not."* [49] The cutting of the three-year-old heifer was symbolic of the death of our Lord. Under the temple worship, the altar must be first cleansed with the sacrifice of a three-year old heifer, thus this represented the altar which the Lord himself would prepare on Calvary where the price of the covenant by faith was paid in His own blood.

A SMOKING FURNACE
AND A BURNING LAMP PASSED BETWEEN

As night fell on the sacrifice Abram had made before God, the Lord began to perform the covenant He was making with Abram and all of His seed, the children of the promise. And it came to pass, that, when the sun went down, and it was dark, behold a smoking furnace, and a burning lamp that passed between those pieces. In the same day the Lord made a covenant with Abram, saying, unto thy seed have I given this land, from the river of Egypt unto the great river, the river Euphrates. [50]

Commentators teach that the fiery furnace signified the affliction of Abram's seed in Egypt, and the lamp symbolized their salvation.[51] The smoking furnace is a picture of God our Father, and the burning lamp is His Son Jesus who is the light of the world and the Word of God. When the sun went down, and the darkness fell, a smoking furnace and a burning lamp appeared literally before Abraham as the Eternal Covenant was forged in flesh which was cut, and consecrated in the blood which was poured out. Abram watched as God the Father and the Son walked in the Holy Covenant together. These symbols which Abram saw portrayed the covenant which was performed by God in the heavens above that very day. This is the covenant of the promise Abraham received from God, which he would inherit by faith. Jesus Christ entered into the blood covenant with the Father alone. Jesus stood in Abraham's place and for his seed to the last generation. The Father and Jesus walked in a figure eight between the blood sacrifice. This signified the eternal nature of this covenant.

For Zion's sake will I not hold my peace, and for Jerusalem's sake I will not rest, until the righteousness thereof go forth as brightness, and the salvation thereof as a lamp that burneth [52]

The Lord said, Shall I hide from Abraham that thing which I do; Seeing that Abraham shall surely become a great and mighty nation, and all the nations of the earth shall be blessed in him? For I know him, that he will command his children and his household after him, and they shall keep the way of the LORD, to do justice and judgment; that the Lord may bring upon Abraham that which he hath spoken of him.[53]

The Lord had literally become Abraham's shield. The Hebrew language does not contain the word covenant. The proper meaning is an alliance cut in blood. Under the terms of a blood covenant, if you fight with one of the members, you must fight with both of them unto all generations. All who would fight Abram, must first fight the Lord.

The LORD Shall Be The Hope Of His People

And all who would oppose the Lord became the enemies of Abraham. Under the terms of a blood covenant, both parties swear to protect the other to the death. Through this covenant God literally said, "I will die for you, and no weapon formed against you shall prosper. I shall protect you. Your enemies are now my enemies. You fight no one. I will defend you myself. Your enemies may come against you one way, but I will raise my hand against them, and they will flee seven ways before you." The Lord promises that He will provide for us, and protect us Himself! He will guide us, if we will just be obedient in thought, word and deed. The King of the Universe, the Ancient of Days himself stands behind His promises and He will honor and do them! We have his promise, if we will just honor him and obey him!

And I prayed unto the Lord my God, and made my confession, and said, O Lord, the great and dreadful God, keeping the covenant and mercy to them that love him, and to them that keep his commandments. [54]

THE LORD CALLS YOU HIS DEARLY BELOVED

God called Abram his friend and the word is אֹהֵב, *awhab* [55] which means to have strong affection for someone, and to love them dearly. This word for friend is only used in four places in the scripture, all of which refer to the Lord's great love for Abram and his seed. In Proverbs, the Lord speaks of His love for us saying, *"there is a friend that sticks closer than a brother."*[56] Truly the Lord is a closer friend than any brother, for these may betray and forsake, but the Lord will never forget His covenant with his beloved ones! *"But thou, Israel, art my servant, Jacob whom I have chosen, the seed of Abraham my friend."*[57] The Lord also speaks of His faithfulness in wounding us to turn us from our transgression: *"Faithful are the wounds of a friend; but the kisses of an enemy are deceitful."*[58] In all other places in Scripture, the word used for *"friend"* is different. The most common is רֵיעַ *ray'-ah*[59] which can be used for brother, companion, fellow, friend, husband, or neighbor. When speaking of His elect, the Lord speaks with strong affection declaring them to be *"my dearly beloved."* In ancient times, friends who were dearly beloved would enter into blood covenant with each other promising their faithful help to each other for their lives and their children's lives. This is our covenant with the Lord Jesus Christ.

THE ETERNAL COVENANT
BETWEEN FATHER GOD AND HIS SON

A blood covenant must be tested and confirmed to prove it is true. This is the work of the Messiah. He comes to confirm the covenant and prove it is true. This is the New Covenant, which our Father made with Jesus as our head, and it was confirmed in the blood of His Son. The New Covenant is between the Father and the Son alone. You are only the prize, little flock. You are the present given to him as his reward. His faithful obedience to the Father earned him the right to save you! You had nothing to do with the confirmation of this covenant. Enter into your rest. Our great and awesome Lord did this all by Himself! The blood of the father is passed to his children, not the blood of the mother. The blood which Jesus shed on the cross was from our Father in heaven. When Jesus Christ died, the God of the universe died. We stand totally dependent upon the Lord for this covenant and for its saving power. And we shall overcome, by the Blood of the Lamb and the word of our testimony.

Jesus Christ fulfilled the Old Covenant of the law for us; everything Jesus did was done under the Old Covenant. Now Jesus Christ is preparing to fulfill the promise of the New Covenant which is the salvation of those who are standing under it. In order to stand in this covenant, we must appropriate the blood of the lamb on our lives through faith and repentance unto obedience. The Feast in which we celebrate this covenant is the Passover. The obedient Israelites put the blood on their doors, and the angel of death had to pass over their homes. The Lord also commanded them to remove all leaven from their dwellings. They were to search even the corners of their rooms, so that no leaven would remain. Leaven is a symbol of sin. We too must search our hearts, and remove all the leaven through repentance, which is turning from our disobedience and surrendering to the Lord.

THERE APPEARED A GREAT WONDER IN HEAVEN

And there appeared a great wonder in heaven; a woman clothed with the sun, and the moon under her feet, and upon her head a crown of twelve stars: And she being with child cried, travailing in birth, and pained to be delivered. And there appeared another wonder in heaven; and behold a great red dragon, having seven heads and ten horns, and seven crowns upon his heads. And his tail drew the third part of the stars of heaven, and did cast them to the earth: and the dragon stood before the woman which was ready to be delivered, for to devour her child as soon as it was born. And she brought forth a man child, who was to rule all nations with a rod of iron: and her child was caught up unto God, and to his throne. And the woman fled into the wilderness, where she hath a place prepared of God, that they should feed her there a thousand two hundred and threescore days.[60]

The word used for "wonder" is *say-mi'-on*[61] which means a sign which is ceremonial or supernatural, or a miracle. The woman in travail is a sign of a great wonder which will be revealed at the end of the age. The woman who stands upon the moon is Israel, who will give birth to the Messiah; the man child, who is to rule the nations with a rod of iron. She is clothed with the sun, which represents the righteousness of Christ received by her through faith. Israel stands upon the moon, for it marks the times of the sacred calendar of the nation. All of the pagan nations mark their calendar by the sun, while the times and seasons of Israel are only marked by the moon. The moon only reflects the light of another greater body. Israel in all her greatness is only reflecting the glory of the Lord. She is wearing a crown of twelve stars, representing the twelve tribes of the nation and the twelve apostles of the New Covenant.

The woman is seen in travail, crying out and ready to give birth. Some assume this speaks only of the literal birth of the Messiah. John was told in chapter four, "I will show you things which must be hereafter" for the revelation in its entirety, is of events which shall come in the future. The birth of the man-child is symbolic of the birth of the kingdom of God in the life of the sanctified believer in the last days prior to the tribulation. The travail is the anguish which comes upon these saints as their old nature is finally crucified with Christ. As their old life is laid to rest, the new creation is brought forth into this world. Matthew Henry's commentary speaks to this passage clearly, "She was safely delivered of a man-child, by which some understand Christ... but others, with greater propriety, a race of true believers, strong and united, resembling Christ, and designed, under him, to rule the nations with a rod of iron; that is, to judge the world by their doctrine and lives now, and as assessors with Christ at the great day." [62]

These believers who give birth to the kingdom do not just resemble Christ, for we shall see from the Scripture, these sanctified one's will walk with the Lord, and follow him wherever he goes. These are the lions which are coming from Judah. And they come to make war for their King! They are the weapons of his indignation who were prophesied to come. "I have commanded my sanctified ones; I have also called my mighty ones for mine anger. They come from a far country, from the end of heaven, even the LORD, and they are the weapons of his indignation, to destroy the whole land. Howl ye; for the day of the LORD is at hand." Isaiah 13:3-6

"Christ came the first time with a birth, and He will come the second time with a birth. The difference between these two births is that the first birth was a physical birth, coming through physical Israel, while the second birth will be a spiritual birth coming through spiritual Israel." [63] Jesus tells us, "For whosoever shall do the will of my Father which is in heaven, the same is my brother, and sister, and mother." [64] He is speaking of those who would surrender to Him fully and thus they will give birth to the kingdom of God in this world once again.

YOU SHALL WEEP ...
UNTIL A MAN IS BORN INTO THE WORLD

Jesus spoke of this mystery through a parable which He taught to the disciples: *"Do ye inquire among yourselves of that I said, A little while, and ye shall not see me: and again, a little while, and ye shall see me? Verily, verily, I say unto you, That ye shall weep and lament, but the world shall rejoice: and ye shall be sorrowful, but your sorrow shall be turned into joy. A woman when she is in travail hath sorrow, because her hour is come: but as soon as she is delivered of the child, she remembers no more the anguish, for joy that a man is born into the world... And in that day ye shall ask me nothing."*[65]

The Lord is speaking of His Second Coming, which will also begin with a birth. This is the mystery of the revelation of Jesus Christ, for He is about to be born in the lives of His chosen remnant. They shall walk in His power and authority, and not as a lamb anymore, but as the Lion from Judah!

HE THAT DWELLS IN THE
SECRET PLACE OF THE MOST HIGH

Jesus Christ opened up the way to enter the Holy of Holies. In His first coming, Jesus tore the veil in two by His death on the cross. At the second coming, His remnant will be those who are found inside, dwelling in the secret place of the Most High. The temple is a picture of the Church. The outer court is the Church assembly, where the mixed multitudes gather to hear the word of God proclaimed to the nations. The inner sanctuary is the place of the anointing of His Holy Spirit. Those who are chosen can enter in, and receive the baptism of His Spirit. Some mistake this for salvation, having never received the anointing. They also teach the Lord no longer speaks to His people, for they have never heard him either. The Holy of Holies is the sacred place in the presence of God. If you enter therein, you can hear the Lord with your ears in an audible voice.

The outer court, where the mixed multitude gathers, is filled with sin and compromise, brought into the house of God by people who have not yet turned fully from their sins. It will be destroyed during the tribulation, trodden under by the gentile nations, and burned to the ground. No one who continues to dwell there will survive what is coming. Do you want to be safe? Then follow Jesus into the most Holy Place!

> *And there was given me a reed like unto a rod: and the angel stood, saying, Rise, and measure the temple of God, and the altar, and them that worship therein. But the court which is without the temple leave out, and*

measure it not, for it is given unto the Gentiles: and the holy city shall they tread under foot forty and two months. Revelation 11:1-2

He that dwelleth in the secret place of the most High shall abide under the shadow of the Almighty. I will say of the LORD, He is my refuge and my fortress: my God; in him will I trust. Surely he shall deliver thee from the snare of the fowler, and from the noisome pestilence. He shall cover thee with his feathers, and under his wings shalt thou trust: his truth shall be thy shield and buckler. Thou shalt not be afraid for the terror by night; nor for the arrow that flieth by day; Nor for the pestilence that walketh in darkness; nor for the destruction that wasteth at noonday. A thousand shall fall at thy side, and ten thousand at thy right hand; but it shall not come nigh thee. Only with thine eyes shalt thou behold and see the reward of the wicked. Because thou hast made the LORD, which is my refuge, even the most High, thy habitation; There shall no evil befall thee, neither shall any plague come nigh thy dwelling. For he shall give his angels charge over thee, to keep thee in all thy ways. Psalm 91:1-11

If you have never heard the voice of the Lord, it is because you have stayed in the outer court, and have never gone into His Holy Temple. You cannot speak with the Lord from outside of His house. In the outer court are the many which have been called. The Lord sends His teachers and prophets to speak to the people in the outer court, bidding them to come into His sanctuary. But you must repent or you will not be allowed in. The Lord declares, *"And in that day there shall be no more the Canaanite in the house of the LORD of hosts."* [66]

The word for Canaanite [67] כנעני, *ken-ah-an-ee* means a merchant, or a trafficker. The false prophets who have come in his name are spiritual Canaanites, for they traffic in the word of the Lord. They shall soon be cast out, and will not even be allowed to approach his house. Peter warned us that false prophets would come. *"There were false prophets among the people, even as there shall be false teachers among you, who privily shall bring in damnable heresies, even denying the Lord that bought them, and bring upon themselves swift destruction. And many shall follow their pernicious ways; by reason of whom the way of truth shall be evil spoken of And through covetousness shall they with feigned words make merchandise of you."* [68] They shall make merchandise of the people of God. Much of the false church is run as a business, by spiritual Canaanites, who do not know the Lord. And they have brought in damnable heresies, and lied to God's people.

In the Holiest place, the Lord himself dwells with His people. He is our shield. He is our defense. By His power, His mighty army shall make war. The anointed remnant will soon appear before the nations, bursting upon the scene full of the power of the Lord. And the children of men, the apostates and the tares, shall cry out in fear before the anointed ones of the Lord. The Lions from Judah are coming, and these anointed ones will hold the lightning sword of the Lord in their hands and out of their mouth, the nations will hear the thunder of God's voice. They shall become terrified when the Lion of Judah is revealed in their midst, and they shall cry out, "Who are you? Who are you?"

The anointed remnant will declare, "I am the bow in His hand; His weapon prepared and fashioned for war! I have come to destroy the mountains. I shall break the nations in pieces, and cast down all the kings of the earth from their thrones. I am full of the power of His Spirit, and I shall teach the people His truth as I bring healing to His land." The prophets reveal the true ministry of anointed ones at the end of the age:

> *Thou art my battle axe and weapons of war: for with thee will I break in pieces the nations, and with thee will I destroy kingdoms; And with thee will I break in pieces the horse and his rider; and with thee will I break in pieces the chariot and his rider; With thee also will I break in pieces man and woman; and with thee will I break in pieces old and young... And I will render unto Babylon and to all the inhabitants of Chaldea all their evil that they have done in Zion in your sight, saith the Lord.* [69]

THE REMNANT SHALL RETURN
UNTO THE CHILDREN OF ISRAEL

Micah also prophesied of this sign: *"But thou, Bethlehem Ephratah, though thou be little among the thousands of Judah, yet out of thee shall he come forth unto me that is to be ruler in Israel; whose goings forth have been from of old, from everlasting. Therefore will he give them up, until the time that she which travaileth hath brought forth: then the remnant of his brethren shall return unto the children of Israel. And he shall stand and feed in the strength of the Lord, in the majesty of the name of the Lord his God; and they shall abide: for now shall he be great unto the ends of the earth. And this man shall be the peace, when the Assyrian shall come into our land: and when he shall tread in our palaces, then shall we raise against him seven shepherds, and eight principal men."* [70]

The Lord will give up Israel, His people, until the time that the woman is ready to give birth. *"Then the remnant of his brethren shall return unto the children of Israel."* [71] The remnant are those who are worthy to stand and endure the hour of testing which will come upon the whole earth as a snare. The time of this prophecy is the Great Tribulation, and the prophecy is literal.

The LORD Shall Be The Hope Of His People

The remnant will physically return to the land of Israel from all over the earth during the last days. They will flee the kingdom of darkness to the place of safety prepared by God in the wilderness. This prophecy is also symbolic. The remnant will also return to the true vine, the New Covenant of Israel, which they were grafted into, by putting off the pagan teachings, which have deceived apostate Christianity.

Jeremiah also presents the travail of the woman Israel, as a question, in his prophecy of the time of Jacob's trouble: *"Ask ye now, and see whether a man doth travail with child? wherefore do I see every man with his hands on his loins, as a woman in travail, and all faces are turned into paleness? Alas! For that day is great, so that none is like it: it is even the time of Jacob's trouble; but he shall be saved out of it." Jeremiah 30:6-7*

This prophecy has dual fulfillment; the unbelievers and the apostates will travail in fear, and will become like women. They will no longer have the strength of a man. The remnant will also be in travail, not in fear, but in the anguish of death, for they will finally put off their old nature completely and in so doing, give birth to the Kingdom of God.

THE DAY WHEN THE SON OF MAN IS REVEALED

This mystery of the last days birth of the Messiah within the remnant of Israel was prophesied by the Lord himself. In Luke, Jesus teaches us about the events of the Great Tribulation and his Second Coming which is preceded by him being revealed among the people:

> *Even thus shall it be in the day when the Son of man is revealed. In that day, he which shall be upon the housetop, and his stuff in the house, let him not come down to take it away: and he that is in the field, let him likewise not return back. Remember Lot's wife. Whosoever shall seek to save his life shall lose it.* [72]

In Matthew's account, Jesus speaks of the same day saying, *"When you see the abomination set up"* which refers to the antichrist being revealed. Now Jesus is referring to the day when the Son of man is revealed. This is the birth of the woman in travail. The day she gives birth, the Son of man will be revealed upon the earth once again, only this time in His children, and then, on the same day, the Great Tribulation shall begin.

"And she brought forth a man child, who was to rule all nations with a rod of iron: and her child was caught up unto God, and to his throne." [73] His children will rule with a rod of iron. The iron represents the absolute authority and the rule of God which will be made manifest in the life of these sanctified ones. They are

175

pictured as caught up unto God and to His throne. The life they now live is hid in Christ, and it is He who lives through them. Jesus is seated upon the throne of God, and His remnant warriors will walk in His power. These are the lions that will come forth from the remnant of Jacob, to make war during the Great Tribulation. It is these men whom the Lord is referring to, when He speaks of *"the day when the Son of man is revealed."*

THE REMNANT OF JACOB SHALL BE
AS LIONS AMONG THE SHEEP

And the remnant of Jacob shall be in the midst of many people as a dew from the Lord, as the showers upon the grass, that tarrieth not for man, nor waiteth for the sons of men. And the remnant of Jacob shall be among the Gentiles in the midst of many people as a lion among the beasts of the forest, as a young lion among the flocks of sheep: who, if he go through, both treadeth down, and teareth in pieces, and none can deliver. Thine hand shall be lifted up upon thine adversaries, and all thine enemies shall be cut off. Micah 5:7-9

These are the Lions of Judah. The prophet speaks of Israel as Jacob, referring to the people of God who walk in the flesh. The remnant shall be distinguished, for they shall be full of the Holy Spirit. They are pictured as lions among the beasts of the forest. They will be more powerful than anything they face and they will walk among the people of this earth as a lion would walk through a flock of sheep or goats. The word for sheep is צֹאן, *tsone* [74] which means a flock of sheep or goats and is figurative of men. They will come to protect the sheep, and they will come to overthrow the goats. These lions from Judah will pass through unhindered and unstoppable! Those who do oppose them will be run over or be torn into pieces! And if anyone comes against them, they have but to lift their hand and God will cut off all of their enemies.

I HAVE CALLED MY MIGHTY ONES FOR MY ANGER

Lift ye up a banner upon the high mountain, exalt the voice unto them, shake the hand, that they may go into the gates of the nobles. I have commanded my sanctified ones; I have also called my mighty ones for mine anger, even them that rejoice in my highness. The noise of a multitude in the mountains, like as of a great people; a tumultuous noise of the kingdoms of nations gathered together: the Lord of hosts musters the host of the battle. They come from a far country, from the end of heaven, even the Lord, and the weapons of his indignation, to destroy the whole land. [75]

These are the sanctified army of God which will be sent into the world during the Great Tribulation. They are the host of the Lord and He musters them for battle.

The Lord hath opened his armory, and hath brought forth the weapons of his indignation: for this is the work of the Lord GOD of hosts in the land of the Chaldeans. [76]

These men are His weapons to be used in the hour of His indignation, and they will come to destroy the whole land. We are told they come from a far country, for the remnant will be among all the nations when they give birth to the kingdom. We are also told they come from the end of heaven, even the Lord. It is the Lord himself in these sanctified ones who is doing this work. These men are merely servants executing the King's orders and they come to battle the dragon. These men are the holy army of God, and they shall walk as young lions among the flocks of sheep and goats.

THE LAMB WILL STAND WITH 144,000
OF HIS ANOINTED ONES

The beginning of the Great Tribulation opens with the Lamb standing on mount Zion and with him are 144,000 of his sanctified ones. These sons of Abraham, from the twelve tribes of Israel, are the first fruits of the Revelation of JESUS CHRIST!

It may be hard for some to comprehend that the Lord will actually come within his people to make war with the beast, and to tread out the winepress of his wrath, but this is precisely the ministry of the anointed ones described in Isaiah 13, verses 1 to 6:

The burden of Babylon, which Isaiah the son of Amoz did see. Lift ye up a banner upon the high mountain, exalt the voice unto them, shake the hand, that they may go into the gates of the nobles. I have commanded my sanctified ones, I have also called my mighty ones for mine anger, even them that rejoice in my highness. The noise of a multitude in the mountains, like as of a great people; a tumultuous noise of the kingdoms of nations gathered together: the Lord of hosts mustereth the host of the battle. They come from a far country, from the end of heaven, even the Lord, and he weapons of his indignation, to destroy the whole land. Howl ye; for the day of the Lord is at hand; it shall come as a destruction from the Almighty.

He calls these sanctified ones, "His Mighty Ones" and they have been called for his anger, for they are the weapons of His indignation and they come to execute the judgment written. In Psalm 149 we read *"Let the saints be joyful in glory: let them sing aloud upon their beds. Let the high praises of God be in their mouth, and a two-edged sword in their hand; To execute vengeance upon the heathen, and punishments upon the people; To bind their kings with chains, and their nobles with fetters of iron; To execute upon them the judgment written: this honors have all his saints."*

In Psalm 118, we read: *"All nations compassed me about: but in the name of the Lord will I destroy them. They compassed me about; yea, they compassed me about: but in the name of the Lord I will destroy them. They compassed me about like bees; they are quenched as the fire of thorns: for in the name of the Lord I will destroy them."*

> *And I looked, and, lo, a Lamb stood on the mount Zion, and with him an hundred forty and four thousand, having his Father's name written in their foreheads.... And they sung as it were a new song before the throne... and no man could learn that song but the hundred and forty and four thousand, which were redeemed from the earth. These are they which were not defiled with women: for they are virgins. These are they which follow the Lamb whithersoever he goeth. These were redeemed from among men, being the first fruits unto God and to the Lamb. And in their mouth was found no guile: for they are without fault before the throne of God.*
> Revelation 14:1-5

Children, the LION FROM THE TRIBE OF JUDAH will come for you! You, who are His chosen remnant, the delight of His heart, He will surely not forsake you, nor will He turn His ear from your cries. Though the enemy of your soul plots to take your very life, both you and your family, do not fear! The Lord will remember His covenant with Israel.

"The secret of the Lord is with them that fear him; and he will show them his covenant."[86] The covenant is by faith and is evidenced by the obedience of those covered therein. *"The mercy of the Lord is from everlasting to everlasting upon them that fear him, and his righteousness unto their children's children; to all those who keep his covenant, and to those that remember his commandments to do them."*[87] Oh let us give Praise to His name, for His mercy endures forever!

"Listen to me, everyone who has a fearful heart; Be strong, fear not: behold, your God is coming with vengeance, even God with a recompense for His enemies. It is He who will come and save you."[88] Behold, the Lord God will come with His strong hand, and his arm shall rule for him: and his reward is with him, and his work before him.[89] For the Lord will come with fire, and with his chariots like a whirl-wind, to render his anger with fury, and his rebuke with flames of fire. For by fire and by his

sword will the Lord plead with all flesh: and the slain of the Lord shall be many in that day.[90]

This is the army of God. They are 144,000 strong from the twelve tribes of Israel, and they are coming! They come from a far country but they will be gathered together in Zion. They come from the end of heaven, even the Lord. This is the mystery of the revelation of JESUS CHRIST. These are the LIONS FROM JUDAH! These are the chosen ones of whom the Lord says, *"I have commanded my sanctified ones; I have also called my mighty ones for my anger."*[91]

Some people in the faith have struggled with the thought that our God still makes war, and calls forth from among the people, men of war. Children, sit down and be silent before the Lord, for this is His hour. Do not raise your voice against the word of the Lord, or the messengers of His covenant. Let all flesh be silent before him, for the Lord is restoring his order to all things. *"Delight is not seemly for a fool; much less for a servant to rule over princes."* [92]

IN RIGHTEOUSNESS HE DOES JUDGE AND MAKE WAR

The war which is about to be fought is the final battle in 6,000 years of conflict. This battle is the Lord's. *"The Lord your God who goes before you, he shall fight for you, according to all that he did for you in Egypt before your eyes."*[93]

> *And I saw heaven opened, and behold a white horse; and he that sat upon him was called Faithful and True, and in righteousness he doth judge and make war.* [94]

David says of the Lord, *"He teaches my hands to war; so that a bow of steel is broken by mine arms."*[95] The prophet Zechariah speaks of the mighty men of God who are coming to fight this war saying, *"And they shall be as mighty men, which tread down their enemies in the mire of the streets in the battle: and they shall fight, because the Lord is with them."*[96] Each of the men who are called and sanctified for this purpose will say, *"Blessed be the LORD my strength, who teaches my hands to war"*[97]

I remember when I was young; the Lord spoke to me many times saying, *"When you turn forty, I am going to use you and I am making you into a weapon, and we will level the mountains!"* I would wonder, what will happen when I turn forty? And what did God mean that one day I would become a weapon? And what are these mountains which would one day fall? If a word be from God, then let the day declare it!

THE DAY OF THE LORD IS AT HAND

PROCLAIM AMONG THE GENTILES - PREPARE FOR WAR

Proclaim ye this among the Gentiles; Prepare war, wake up the mighty men, let all the men of war draw near; let them come up: Beat your plowshares into swords, and your pruning hooks into spears: let the weak say, I am strong. Assemble yourselves, and come, all ye heathen, and gather yourselves together round about: there <u>cause thy mighty ones to come down</u>, O Lord. Let the heathen be wakened, and come up to the valley of Jehoshaphat: for there will I sit to judge all the heathen round about. Put ye in the sickle, for the harvest is ripe: come, get you down; for the press is full, the fats overflow; for their wickedness is great. Multitudes, multitudes in the valley of decision: for the day of the Lord is near in the valley of decision. The sun and the moon shall be darkened, and the stars shall withdraw their shining. [98]

That day will soon be here. The words of the prophet Joel will now be fulfilled. The nations are all preparing for war, and the Lord is about to cause His mighty ones to come down! Intelligence reports in the fall of 2018 confirm the enemies of America have begun preparations for the coming war. Their troops are being assembled, their equipment readied, and their armies are moving into position for actual war with the west. Such mobilizations are expensive, and are not undertaken lightly.

THE LORD OUR GOD WILL BOW
THE HEAVENS AND COME DOWN

When the waves of death encompass me, and the floods of the un-godly men make me afraid; and the sorrows of hell surround me, in my distress I will call upon the Lord, and I will cry to my God: and he will hear my voice out of his temple, and my cry will enter into his ears. Then the earth will shake and tremble; the foundations of heaven will move and shake, because he will be wroth. There will go up a smoke out of his nostrils, and fire out of his mouth will devour; coals will be kindled by it. He will bow the heavens also, and come down; with darkness under his feet. And he will ride upon a cherub, and will fly: and he will be seen upon the wings of the wind. And he will make darkness pavilions round about him, dark waters, and thick clouds of the skies.

Through the brightness before him the coals of fire are kindled. The Lord will thunder from heaven, and the most High will utter his voice. And he will send out arrows, and scatter them; and His lightning will trouble them. And the channels of the sea will appear, the foundations of the world will be discovered, at the rebuking of the Lord, at the blast of the breath of his nostrils. He will send from above, he will take me; and he will draw me out of many waters; He will deliver me from my strong enemy, and from them that hate me: for they are too strong for me. They prepared the day of my calamity: but the Lord will be my stay. He will bring me forth also into a large place: he will deliver me, because he delights in me. I am His beloved. The Lord will reward me according to my righteousness: according to the cleanness of my hands he will recompense me. For I have kept the ways of the Lord, and have not wickedly departed from my God.[99]

MY MESSENGER SHALL COME,
AND WHO CAN ABIDE IN THAT DAY?

Behold, I will send my messenger, and he shall prepare the way before me: and the Lord, whom ye seek, shall suddenly come to his temple, even the messenger of the covenant, whom ye delight in: behold, he shall come, saith the Lord of hosts. But who may abide the day of his coming? and who shall stand when he appears? for he is like a refiner's fire, and like fullers' soap: And he shall sit as a refiner and purifier of silver: and he shall purify the sons of Levi, and purge them as gold and silver, that they may offer unto the Lord an offering in righteousness. Then shall the offering of Judah and Jerusalem be pleasant unto the Lord, as in the days of old, and as in former years. And I will come near to you to judgment; and I will be a swift witness. [100]

The messengers of the Lord who come in the office and anointing of Elijah are the weapons of the Lord; I refer to them as the anointed ones, for they are His mighty ones, the Lions from Judah, and they come forth from the Lord himself.

And when ye see this, your heart shall rejoice, and your bones shall flourish like an herb: and the hand of the Lord shall be known toward his servants, and his indignation toward his enemies. For, behold, the Lord will come with fire, and with his chariots like a whirlwind, to render his anger with fury, and his rebuke with flames of fire. For by fire and by his sword will the Lord plead with all flesh: and the slain of the Lord shall be many. [101]

The word for fire is אֵשׁ *esh* [102] which means burning, fiery, and flaming hot. The Lord is describing the messengers of his covenant whom He is sending before he appears and they will come forth with the fire of God in the words of their mouth. As they utter the declarations of divined judgment, their words will bring forth whirlwind of God's judgment and this word is סוּפָה, *soo-faw* [103] which means a hurricane, a tempest, and a whirlwind.

THE DAY OF THE LORD IS AT HAND

These are the anointed messengers of the Lord and they come full of the wrath of God. The word for "wrath" is חֵמָא, *khay-maw*[104] which means anger, furious rage and indignation. And his rage will soon be poured out upon this ruination. The 144,000 are the ones whom the Lord has called for His anger.

The word used for sword is חֶרֶב, *kheh'-reb*[105], which means to gleam, a flash, a sharply polished blade or point of a weapon. The Lord has determined to judge the apostate people with fire, and who can abide in the day of His coming unto us in His mighty ones?

> *Therefore shall the Lord, the Lord of hosts, send among his fat ones leanness; and under his glory he shall kindle a burning like the burning of a fire. And the light of Israel shall be for a fire, and his Holy One for a flame: and it shall burn and devour his thorns and his briers in one day; And shall consume the glory of his forest, and of his fruitful field, both soul and body: and they shall be as when a standard bearer fainteth. And the rest of the trees of his forest shall be few, that a child may write them. And it shall come to pass in that day, that the remnant of Israel, and such as are escaped of the house of Jacob, shall no more again stay upon him that smote them; but shall stay upon the Lord, the Holy One of Israel, in truth. The remnant shall return, even the remnant of Jacob, unto the mighty God.* [106]

THE LORD YOUR GOD IS HE THAT GOES WITH YOU, FEAR NOT!

> *And I say unto you my friends, Be not afraid of them that kill the body, and after that have no more that they can do. But I will forewarn you whom ye shall fear: Fear him, which after he hath killed hath power to cast into hell; yea, I say unto you, Fear him. Are not five sparrows sold for two farthings, and not one of them is forgotten before God? But even the very hairs o f your head are all numbered. Fear not therefore: ye are of more value than many sparrows.* [107]

> *And shall say unto them, Hear, O Israel, ye approach this day unto battle against your enemies: let not your hearts faint, fear not, and do not tremble, neither be ye terrified because of them; For the Lord your God is he that goeth with you, to fight for you against your enemies, to save you.*[108] *Be strong and of a good courage, fear not, nor be afraid of them: for the Lord thy God, He it is that doth go with thee; he will not fail thee, nor forsake thee.*[109] *And the Lord, he it is that doth go before thee; he will be with thee, he will not fail thee, neither forsake thee: fear not, neither be dismayed.* [110]

182

And Joshua said unto them, Fear not, nor be dismayed, be strong and of good courage: for thus shall the Lord do to all your enemies against whom ye fight. [111] *And I said unto you, I am the Lord your God; fear not the gods of the Amorites, in whose land ye dwell.* [112] *The Lord said unto him, Peace be unto thee; fear not, thou shalt not die.* [113]

And Samuel said unto the people, Fear not: ye have done all this wickedness: yet turn not aside from following the Lord, but serve the Lord with all your heart; And turn ye not aside: for then should ye go after vain things, which cannot profit nor deliver; for they are vain. For the Lord will not forsake his people for his great name's sake: because it hath pleased the Lord to make you his people. Moreover as for me, God forbid that I should sin against the Lord in ceasing to pray for you: but I will teach you the good and the right way: Only fear the Lord, and serve him in truth with all your heart: for consider how great things he hath done for you. But if ye shall still do wickedly, ye shall be consumed, both ye and your king. [114]

AND ELISHA PRAYED OPEN HIS EYES THAT HE MAY SEE

And he answered, Fear not: for they that be with us are more than they that be with them. And Elisha prayed, and said, Lord, I pray thee, open his eyes, that he may see. And the Lord opened the eyes of the young man; and he saw: and, behold, the mountain was full of horses and chariots of fire round about Elisha. [115] *Say to them that are of a fearful heart, Be strong, fear not: behold, your God will come with vengeance, even God with a recompense; he will come and save you.* [116] *For I the Lord thy God will hold thy right hand, saying unto thee, Fear not, I will help thee.* [117] *Fear not, O land; be glad and rejoice: for the Lord will do great things."*[118]

But now thus saith the Lord that created thee, O Jacob, and he that formed thee, O Israel, Fear not. for I have redeemed thee, I have called thee by thy name; thou art mine. When thou passest through the waters, I will be with thee; and through the rivers, they shall not overflow thee: when thou walkest through the fire, thou shalt not be burned; neither shall the flame kindle upon thee. For I am the Lord thy God, the Holy One of Israel, thy Saviour: I gave Egypt for thy ransom, Ethiopia and Seba for thee. Since thou wast precious in my sight, thou hast been honourable, and I have loved thee: therefore will I give men for thee, and people for thy life. Fear not. for I am with thee: I will bring thy seed from the east, and gather thee from the west; I will say to the north, Give up; and to the south, Keep not back: bring my sons from far, and my daughters from the ends of the earth; Even every one that is called by my name: for I have created him for my glory, I have formed him; yea, I have made him. [119]

THE DAY OF THE LORD IS AT HAND

ONLY A FEW HAVE BEEN CHOSEN

There are many who have been called, but only a *"few"* have been chosen, and the chosen ones must submit to the final burning and purging of the flesh, which is the carnal Adamic nature that resides in all of us from the fall.

Only those who are willing to be separated unto God will become the first fruits of His resurrection, and the Lord will keep them, for they are vessels he has prepared and they will become the weapons of His indignation, in the hour of His wrath, for they are the mighty ones He has called.

> *Seven days thou shalt make an atonement for the altar, and sanctify it; and it shall be an altar most holy: whatsoever touches the altar shall be holy.* [120]

The remnant placed their lives upon the altar of God as a living sacrifice; they have given everything to the Lord, and they held nothing back. They have no other gods, no silver wedge hidden in their tent, and no hidden sins still lodged within. The man-child company, which shall come forth from among them, will be born again totally in the Spirit; they are the true sons of God, who will come to maturity first, and they will walk in the full measure of the stature of Jesus Christ, bearing His rod of iron in the Spirit.

The woman, who is spiritual Israel, is in travail even now. The Lord recently spoke to me saying *"heaven is expecting."* The Spirit of God now whispers in the wind, while the remnant is in travail, each of them pained to be delivered of the child. In heaven above, the Father awaits the birth of another son, for heaven is about to bring to birth the man-child of the book of Revelation, who shall become the grandsons of God. They are *"redeemed"* from among men, and they are about to be born again upon the earth. These chosen ones have been redeemed from out of this last generation, and they will be given the authority and the power to rule the nations with His rod of iron. Before their birth, these sons of the King have been hidden from the church and the world.

The woman, who is true Israel, is about to be persecuted in an unprecedented onslaught from the dragon, but she will be protected by God through the Son of His right hand; they are the 144,000 who will come forth as the Lions from Judah. They were willing to be separated unto God, and have placed their all on his altar that burns in the heavens, for they are the first fruits of the Revelation of Jesus Christ.

> *Seven days thou shalt make an atonement for the altar, and sanctify it; and it shall be an altar most holy: whatsoever touches the altar shall be holy.* [120]

184

The LORD Shall Be The Hope Of His People

The 144,000 are no longer defiled with women, for they have come out of the Babylonian system of religion, and are no longer defiled with the apostasy which is known as modern American Christianity. The woman Babylon is both the antichrist government of the nations, and the false Church which claims His name, but does not obey His voice. They are the mixed multitude, who are lost in their sins, though they believe they are saved, yet they are drunk, having become intoxicated with the wine of iniquity and are now deceived by the woman Jezebel, who represents the spirit of rebellion and pride now so prevalent in the apostate churches.

The remnant has come out from among them as God commanded. The first fruits of the Lord are waiting for the anointing which will come from on high, the latter day rain, which shall come in the time of the former rains, in the month of Nissan, when the corn becomes *Aviv*.

They have died to the flesh, and many have walked through the ashes of the fires of God, which consumed their entire lives. Some of them were utterly burned in the fires, and it was with love and grace that the Lord brought them to the end of themselves, and to the place appointed for their death. It was love that killed me, and now love has come to set me free. The pain some of them have walked through was almost without measure, and the price they paid was everything. They suffered the loss of their entire lives, for everything they loved, and all of their carnal self, was utterly burned in the flames.

> *In the day when the keepers of the house shall tremble, and the strong men shall bow themselves, and the grinders cease because they are few, and those that look out of the windows be darkened, And the doors shall be shut in the streets, when the sound of the grinding is low, and he shall rise up at the voice of the bird, and all the daughters of musick shall be brought low; Also when they shall be afraid of that which is high, and fears shall be in the way, and the almond tree shall flourish, and the grasshopper shall be a burden, and desire shall fail: because man goeth to his long home, and the mourners go about the streets.* [121]

The almond tree symbolizes the prophetic word of God, for it is the first ripening tree in Israel; its name means the awakener, and it is the word שָׁקֵד, *shâqêd* which means the *earliest* or the first tree to bloom. And as the judgment falls, the almond trees shall awaken and flourish once again, while the desire of all flesh shall fail.

> *In flaming fire taking vengeance on them that know not God, and that obey not the gospel of our Lord Jesus Christ: Who shall be punished with everlasting destruction from the presence of the Lord, and from the glory*

of his power; When he shall come to be glorified in his saints, and to be admired in all them that believe. II Thessalonians 1:8-10

FEAR NOT, LITTLE FLOCK

Fear not, little flock; for it is your Father's good pleasure to give you the kingdom. Sell that ye have, and give alms; provide yourselves bags which wax not old, a treasure in the heavens that faileth not, where no thief approacheth, neither moth corrupteth. For where your treasure is, there will your heart be also. Let your loins be girded about, and your lights burning; And ye yourselves like unto men that wait for their Lord, when he will return from the wedding; that when he cometh and knocketh, they may open unto him immediately. [122]

Blessed are those servants, whom the Lord when he cometh shall find watching: verily I say unto you, that he shall gird himself, and make them to sit down to meat, and will come forth and serve them. [124]

FEAR NOT, I AM THE FIRST AND THE LAST

And when I saw him, I fell at his feet as dead. And he laid his right hand upon me, saying unto me, Fear not, I am the first and the last.[125] *But fear not thou, O my servant Jacob, and be not dismayed, O Israel: for, behold, I will save thee from afar off, and thy seed from the land of their captivity; and Jacob shall return, and be in rest and at ease, and none shall make him afraid.* [126] *Thou drewest near in the day that I called upon thee: thou saidst, Fear not. O Lord, thou hast pleaded the causes of my soul; thou hast redeemed my life. O Lord, thou hast seen my wrong: judge thou my cause. Thou hast seen all their vengeance and all their imaginations against me. Thou hast heard their reproach, O Lord, and all their imaginations* [127]

CHAPTER
9
WE HAVE HEARD OF THE PRIDE OF MOAB
Isaiah 16:6

The Lord declares in His word the curses which would come if His nation Israel refused to obey His voice, and followed their own ways into rebellion. America and her false religious system have also refused to obey the Lord and have chosen their own way. The people of America are hardened in their rebellion. They shall witness these same curses poured out upon them.

> *I am the Lord your God, which brought you forth out of the land of Egypt, that ye should not be their bondmen; and I have broken the bands of your yoke, and made you go upright. But if ye will not hearken unto me ... And if ye shall despise my statutes, or if your soul abhor my judgments, so that ye will not do all my commandments, but that ye break my covenant: I also will do this unto you, I will even appoint over you terror ... and ye shall sow your seed in vain, for your enemies shall eat it and ye shall be slain before your enemies: they that hate you shall reign over you; and ye shall flee when none pursueth you And I will break the pride of your power. And your strength shall be spent in vain... I will also send wild beasts among you.. And I will bring a sword upon you that shall avenge the quarrel of my covenant. I will send the pestilence among you; and ye shall be delivered into the hand of the enemy. And I will make your cities waste, and bring your sanctuaries unto desolation... And I will scatter you among the heathen, and will draw out a sword after you: and your land shall be desolate, and your cities waste. Leviticus 26:13-33*

THE SIN OF PRIDE GOES BEFORE THE FALL

The sin of pride is an abomination to the Lord. Everyone that is proud and exalted in their own eyes shall be brought down! "*The lofty looks of man shall be humbled, and the haughtiness of men shall be bowed down, and the Lord alone shall be exalted in that day. For the day of the Lord of hosts shall be upon every one that is proud and lofty, and upon every one that is lifted up; and he shall be brought low.*"[1]

THE DAY OF THE LORD IS AT HAND

The exaltation of man in his arrogance receives a harsh rebuke from the Lord. The attitude and the speech of the proud men are detestable before our God. Throughout Scripture, the Lord repeats his admonition against pride, for pride and its related sins of arrogance and all forms of boasting are despised by God. He declares He hates them, *"The fear of the Lord is to hate evil: pride, and arrogancy, and the evil way, and the froward mouth, do I hate."*[2] *"Pride goeth before destruction and a haughty spirit before a fall."*[3]

The Lord spoke about the end of the world to Ezekiel describing this as the time when pride has budded!

> *Moreover the word of the Lord came unto me, saying.. .An end, the end is come upon the four corners of the land. Now is the end come upon thee, and I will send mine anger upon thee, and will judge thee according to thy ways, and will recompense upon thee all thine abominations. And mine eye shall not spare thee, neither will I have pity: but I will recompense thy ways upon thee, and thine abominations shall be in the midst of thee: and ye shall know that I am the Lord. Thus saith the Lord God; An evil, an only evil, behold, is come. An end is come, the end is come: it watches for thee; behold, it is come. The morning is come unto thee, O thou that dwells in the land: the time is come, the day of trouble is near, and not the sounding again of the mountains. Now will I shortly pour out my fury upon thee, and accomplish mine anger upon thee: and I will judge thee according to thy ways, and will recompense thee for all thine abominations. And mine eye shall not spare, neither will I have pity: I will recompense thee according to thy ways and thine abominations that are in the midst of thee; and ye shall know that I am the Lord that smiteth. Behold the day, behold, it is come: the morning is God forth; the rod hath blossomed, pride hath budded.*[4]

The Lord speaks in the book of Obadiah to the nation of Moab. *"The arrogance of your heart has deceived you, you who live in the clefts of the rock, in the loftiness of your dwelling place, who say in your heart, `Who will bring me down to earth?' Though you build high like the eagle, though you set your nest among the stars, from there I will bring you down, declares the Lord."*[5]

America has committed the same sins as Moab. She also has set her throne on high as an eagle, and she will face the same judgment. The Lord declares even if you built your nest among the stars, from there I will bring you down. America and her space program may have reached to the stars, but from this great height she will be brought down.

THE LORD WILL PUNISH THOSE
WHO ARE STAGNANT IN SPIRIT

Zephaniah declares, in the Day of Judgment, the Lord will go through the land and will search for those things hidden in the darkness.

> *And it will come about at that time that I will search Jerusalem with lamps, and I will punish the men who are stagnant in spirit, who say in their hearts, `The Lord will not do good or evil!' Moreover, their wealth will become plunder, and their houses desolate; yes, they will build houses but not inhabit them and plant vineyards but not drink their wine.*[6]

The Lord will punish all those who are stagnant in their spirit. These men are neither hot nor cold, but are lukewarm. These men, stagnant in spirit, refuse to hear the prophetic message, and they say to themselves in their hearts, "the Lord will do neither good nor evil". These men walk as unbelievers, for they refuse to believe the Lord will intervene in the world. They reject the word of God's prophets, and even mock it within themselves. God says their wealth will become plunder, and their houses will be deserted. They will lose everything in the Day of Judgment which they derided.

The prophet declares that the Lord will punish these stagnant ones at the time of the end of the age, for his words speak of The Day of The Lord:

> *Near is the great day of the Lord, near and coming very quickly; listen, the day of the Lord! In it the warrior cries out bitterly. A day of wrath is that day, a day of trouble and distress, a day of destruction and desolation, a day of darkness and gloom, a day of clouds and thick darkness, A day of trumpet and battle cry, against the fortified cities and the high corner towers. And I will bring distress on men, so that they will walk like the blind, because they have sinned against the Lord; and their blood will be poured out like dust, and their flesh like dung. Neither their silver nor their gold will be able to deliver them on the day of the Lord's wrath; and all the earth will be devoured in the fire of His jealousy, for He will make a complete end, indeed a terrifying one, of all the inhabitants of the earth.'* [7]

AMERICA HAS COMMITTED
THE SIN OF MOAB GREAT PRIDE

"We have heard of the pride of Moab; he is very proud: even of his haughtiness, and his pride, and his wrath: but his lies shall not be so."[8]

Moab was very proud and full of arrogance. America has committed the same sins before God. Our nation is like Moab, and the prophecies against her also speak against America.

> *Therefore shall Moab howl for Moab, every one shall howl... surely they are stricken. For the fields of Heshbon languish, and the vine of Sibmah: the Lords of the heathen have broken down the principal plants thereof, they are come even unto Jazer, they wandered through the wilderness: her branches are stretched out, they are gone over the sea.* [9]

Who is wise in spirit that he may discern the hidden things in the word?

THE SUMMER HARVEST
SHALL FAIL BEFORE THE JUDGMENT

The judgment on Moab began with the failing of a summer harvest. So too, in America, the judgment of God will begin in the time of a future summer harvest season. The nation will be struck with heat and drought, and her summer harvest will fail. This is the sign to the remnant, that the judgment is about to begin, and it is time to flee.

> *Therefore I will bewail with the weeping of Jazer the vine of Sibmah: I will water thee with my tears ... for the shouting for thy summer fruits and for thy harvest is fallen. And gladness is taken away, and joy out of the plentiful field; and in the vineyards there shall be no singing, neither shall there be shouting: the treaders shall tread out no wine in their presses; I have made their vintage shouting to cease.* [10]

When the judgment begins to fall, Moab shall come into his sanctuary to pray, but he will not prevail. *"And it shall come to pass, when it is seen that Moab is weary on the high place, that he shall come to his sanctuary to pray; but he shall not prevail. This is the word that the Lord hath spoken concerning Moab since that time."* [11] America too, once her judgment commences will seek to pray for relief but it will not be granted her. This word has been spoken concerning Moab and the sins of Moab, which are the sins of national pride since that time. Every nation which exalted itself as Moab, will be judged in the same fashion. The Lord changes not. Every word he speaks shall come to pass. *"But now the Lord hath spoken, saying, Within three years, as the years of an hireling, and the glory of Moab shall be contemned, with all that great multitude; and the remnant shall be very small and feeble."* [12] The word also tells us the remnant of America, those who survive her judgment will be very small and feeble. Only a small number of people will escape what is about to come to pass in America.

We Have Heard Of The Pride Of Moab

Lest we be doubters that these words have no bearing on the events of the end of the age, Isaiah immediately speaks of the destruction of Damascus which will occur at the end of the age. *"Behold, Damascus is taken away from being a city, and it shall be a ruinous heap."*[13] This is the destruction which will fall on Damascus following the next war in Israel and Damascus will be no more!

Moab is warned to flee into the wilderness for the spoiler will come upon every city. America has also been at ease from her youth.

> *Flee, save your lives, and be like the heath in the wilderness. For because thou hast trusted in thy works and in thy treasures, thou shalt also be taken ...And the spoiler shall come upon every city, and no city shall escape. Give wings unto Moab, that it may flee and get away: for the cities thereof shall be desolate, without any to dwell therein. Cursed be he that doeth the work of the Lord deceitfully, and cursed be he that keeps back his sword from blood. Moab hath been at ease from his youth, and he hath settled on his lees, and hath not been emptied from vessel to vessel, neither hath he God into captivity: therefore his taste remained in him, and his scent is not changed. Therefore, behold, the days come, saith the Lord, that I will send unto him wanderers, that shall cause him to wander, and shall empty his vessels, and break their bottles.*[14]

A generation of Americans has never known the judgment of the Lord, so they have settled on their lees, and they have not been poured out and cleaned, but rather, they have the residue of sin hardened within their hearts. Rather than cleaning these vessels, the Lord is going to shatter them. America will be spoiled and everyone will flee out of her cities. Her young men are going to go down to the slaughter.

> *Moab is spoiled, and God up out of her cities, and his chosen young men are God down to the slaughter, saith the King, whose name is the Lord of hosts. The calamity of Moab is near to come, and his affliction hasteth fast. All ye that are about him, bemoan him; and all ye that know his name, say, How is the strong staff broken, and the beautiful rod!* [15]

The calamity is near to come, and this great affliction hastens quickly upon our land. How is the strong staff broken? How the power of America is thrown down to the ground! Again the people are warned to leave the cities. Go up into the mountains and live among the rocks.

> *O ye that dwell in Moab, leave the cities, and dwell in the rock, and be like the dove that maketh her nest in the sides of the hole's mouth. We have heard the pride of Moab (he is exceeding proud), his loftiness, and his*

arrogancy, and his pride, and the haughtiness of his heart. I know his wrath, saith the Lord; but it shall not be so; his lies shall not so effect it.[16]

We have heard of the pride of America, she is very proud and haughty in her heart. And she has great wrath, but she will not stand, says the Lord. Again we are reminded of the timing of the judgment, for it will begin when her summer fruit fails and the spoiler comes upon her summer harvest.

O vine of Sibmah, I will weep for thee with the weeping of Jazer: thy plants are gone over the sea, they reach even to the sea of Jazer: the spoiler is fallen upon thy summer fruits and upon thy vintage.[17]

America will be judged shortly after the failure of her harvest in the season of fall. Her destruction will be final, and complete, and the fulfillment of these words will be incomprehensible to the mind of man.

Behold you who dwell among the heathen, and regard, and wonder marvelously: for I will do a work in your days, which you will not believe, though it be told to you. Habakkuk 1:5

CHAPTER

10

BABYLON THE GREAT IS FALLEN, FALLEN

Revelation 18:2

The book of Revelation contains a series of visions of the events during the Great Tribulation. They are revealed one after another, yet they do not occur chronologically in time. These are a series of revelations, presented as visions, of what is to come upon the earth during the time of God's judgment of the world. Many scholars make the error of assuming the events are in sequential order, they are not.

THE LAMB STOOD ON MOUNT ZION
WITH HIS ANOINTED ONES

The beginning of the Judgment by God is contained within Chapter 14, which opens with the vision of the Lamb, Jesus Christ on mount Zion, and with him, 144,000 of his sanctified ones.

> And I looked, and, lo, _a Lamb stood on the mount Sion, and with him an_
> _hundred forty and four thousand, having his Father's name written in_
> _their foreheads._ And I heard a voice from heaven, as the voice of many
> waters, and as the voice of a great thunder: and I heard the voice of
> harpers harping with their harps: And they sung as it were a new song
> before the throne, and before the four beasts, and the elders: and no man
> could learn that song but the hundred and forty and four thousand, which
> were redeemed from the earth. _These are they which were not defiled with_
> _women: for they are virgins._ These are they which follow the Lamb
> whithersoever he goeth. _These were redeemed from among men, being the_
> _first fruits unto God and to the Lamb._ And in their mouth was found no
> guile: for they are without fault before the throne of God. Rev. 14:1-5

These are the army of God, spoken of by Isaiah in chapter 13 which is entitled, _"The burden of Babylon which Isaiah did see."_ The 144,000 are seen gathered into the mountains of Zion, standing with the Lamb. These are the chosen men of whom the Lord says: _"I have called my sanctified ones; I have also called my mighty ones for my anger, even them who rejoice in my highness."_[1]

THE DAY OF THE LORD IS AT HAND

THE HOUR OF GOD'S JUDGMENT HAS COME

Immediately after the Lamb gathers his army, a voice thunders from heaven with the sound of many waters declaring *"FEAR GOD, AND GIVE GLORY UNTO HIM; FOR THE HOUR OF HIS JUDGMENT HAS COME!"* Rev. 14:7

This is the heavenly declaration of the commencement of the judgment of God; this scene takes place at the very start of God's judgment upon the earth. Immediately, a second angel declares *"Babylon is fallen, is fallen, that great city!"* The fall of Babylon is the first event following the announcement of the hour of judgment by God. America Babylon is destroyed immediately prior to the tribulation period, but she is not the final kingdom of Babylon - America is the daughter of Babylon and what will follow is the seventh kingdom of Babylon, in which Lucifer will rule the One World Government of the New World Order in possession of the antichrist. And He is the eighth king, and the final kingdom of the beast empire will manifest the full and uncensored evil of Lucifer himself. It too will fall, in one hour, which lasts 42 months.

> *And I saw another angel fly in the midst of heaven, having the everlasting gospel to preach unto them that dwell on the earth, and to every nation, and kindred, and tongue, and people, Saying with a loud voice, <u>Fear GOD, and give glory to him; for the hour of his judgment is come:</u> and worship him that made heaven, and earth, and the sea, and the fountains of waters. And there followed another angel, saying, <u>Babylon is fallen, fallen, that, great harlot</u> because she made all nations drink of the wine of the wrath of her fornication. Revelation 14:6-8*

What is the hour of God's judgment? When the Lord speaks of timing, we know a day in His watch is a thousand years in our sight. If we divide 1,000 years by 24 hours, we get approximately 42 years, which is also the number of months of the great tribulation. The hour God's final judgment of the earth is 42 months long. This hour is symbolic of the time the Lord has appointed to judge the earth. This is the judgment of the heathen nations, for the judgment the Church has already begun in the persecution which precedes the tribulation.

When the Lord turns to judge the nations, He starts with the most proud, America Babylon, the reigning super power at the time of the end. The next event is a third angel pronouncing the wrath of God upon all those who worship the beast, for this is God's final warning the people lest they take the mark, which will follow shortly thereafter, in the early part of the tribulation.

Babylon The Great Is Fallen, Fallen

And the third angel followed them, saying with a loud voice, If any man worship the beast and his image, and receive his mark in his forehead, or in his hand, The same shall drink of the wine of the wrath of God, which is poured out without mixture into the cup of his indignation; and he shall be tormented with fire and brimstone in the presence of the holy angels, and in the presence of the Lamb: And the smoke of their torment ascends up for ever and ever: and they have no rest day nor night, who worship the beast and his image, and whosoever receives the mark of his name. Revelation 14:9-11

The patience of the saints is this knowledge: first that those who worship the beast shall be judged by God with righteousness and severity, and second, that those who are faithful to the Lord, even in death, may rest from their labors and their faithful works follow after them. Then we are presented another picture of the judgment, which is a harvest in which the earth will be reaped. The wheat will be gathered into the Father's barn and the tares, they will be gathered into bundles and burned with unquenchable fire, and their torment will ascend up forever!

<u>Here is the patience of the saints: here are they that keep the commandments of God. and the faith of Jesus</u>. And I heard a voice from heaven saying unto me, Write, Blessed are the dead which die in the Lord from henceforth: Yea, saith the Spirit, that they may rest from their labours; and their works do follow them. And I looked, and behold a white cloud, and upon the cloud one sat like unto the Son of man, having on his head a golden crown, and in his hand a sharp sickle. And another angel came out of the temple, crying with a loud voice to him that sat on the cloud, Thrust in thy sickle, and reap: for the time is come for thee to reap; for the harvest of the earth is ripe And he that sat on the cloud thrust in his sickle on the earth; and the earth was reaped. Revelation 14:12-16

Last, another angel with a sharp sickle thrusts his instrument into the winepress of the wrath of God, and the blood flow from the battle of Armageddon will be 1,600 furlongs which is approximately 200 miles. From the valley of Jezreel, 200 miles to the southeast lies the Arnon river, which is the outer edge of the sanctuary prepared for the remnant who at that time will have been fully gathered and safely hid in the mountains of Petra.

And another angel came out of the temple which is in heaven, he also having a sharp sickle. And another angel came out from the altar, which had power over fire; and cried with a loud cry to him that had the sharp sickle, saying, thrust in thy sharp sickle, and gather the clusters of the vine of the earth; for her grapes are fully ripe. And the angel thrust in his sickle into the earth, and gathered the vine of the earth, and cast it into the great winepress of the wrath of God. Revelation 14:17-20

THE DAY OF THE LORD IS AT HAND

From the Scriptures, we know that the judgment on America Babylon occurs at the start of the judgment by God upon the entire earth. And this judgment will be sudden, for in a moment in time, she will fall; but how can this be? America is the greatest nation in the earth at the moment, and who can resist her military might? Like the Titanic that sailed with the envy of the world over 100 years ago, she too is unsinkable, at least in the minds of her passengers sleeping quietly below her decks. Standing above, in the shadows of darkness which have descended upon her as night falls, the watchmen of the Lord announce an iceberg larger in size than any could imagine, waiting in her immediate path. And as the watchmen sound the alarm, only a few will listen to their warning cry, "A Lion has emerged from the thicket and the destroyer of the nations is on his way!" And he will destroy the "mighty" nation first and then turn to "make war" on the saints.

THE PATTERN OF GOD'S JUDGMENT

The history of God's judgments contains a similar pattern each time; those who do not remember history are destined to repeat it. From the Lord's own words, we know the judgment at the time of the end of the age will be similar to the time of Noah: while the people of the earth were full of wickedness, Noah found favor with the Lord. God sent his warnings for one hundred and twenty years, then He sent a final warning as Noah entered the ark. In Sodom, the Lord removed the righteous before destroying the city. In the fall of Jerusalem in 70 AD, the Roman army pulled back for several days to allow the believers time to escape, and everyone else who stayed thinking the city's walls would protect them were destroyed or taken into slavery.

AMERICA WILL NOT BE ABLE
TO STOP THE BLEEDING

The Lord has never allowed a society to promote homosexuality or abortion without bringing His judgment - ours is no different. America is even now under the judgment of the Lord. America will not be able to stop the bleeding; foreign armies will occupy this land. Behold, they are already among you, and you see them not. America has refused the Lord's grace, now she must accept His judgment:

1. Innocent blood has been spilled on the land and it is now defiled.
2. The blood of over 50 million babies has been shed in this land.
3. The sin of America has reached unto the throne of the Holy One.
4. Judgment is now upon the land; it will tarry no longer.
5. The blood of the offender has to be appeased.
6. America rejected the Lord's grace; she will now have to accept His judgment. [2]

IT IS MIDNIGHT AND MANKIND DOES NOT KNOW IT

As the hour of judgment draws near, and it will surely come, we must hide ourselves in the mercy of the Lord, for only those who abide in the Lord and are covered by the blood of Jesus will be spared.

1. The angel of death is coming to America.
2. Pride comes before the fall. America says she sits as a queen, now her judgment is upon her and she will fall in one hour.
3. To the degree she lived luxuriously, she will receive double for her sins.
4. It is midnight, and mankind does not know it. [3]

America is in trouble because America forgot who she was. Our forefathers were men of prayer. The United States was built on the foundation of the Word of God. The Lord does not do anything without first prophesying the word. God will use us in mighty ways if we let him. History is about to be repeated. The Lord is always able to take care of the problem, but he will not do it, if we are in the way. The Lord declares *"Behold, to obey is better than sacrifice."*[4] And in Isaiah we are told *"If ye be willing and obedient, ye shall eat the good of the land."*[5]

The word says that whoever sees his brother in need and does not meet the need, he does not have the love of God in his heart. We are going to have to watch out for each other. The Lord tells us to buy a sword in this hour. Jesus spoke prophetically of this hour saying, *"But now, he that hath a purse let him take it, and likewise his scrip: and he that hath no sword let him sell his garment, and buy one. For I say unto you, that this that is written must yet be accomplished in me, And he was reckoned among the transgressors: for the things concerning me have an end. And they said, Lord, behold, here are two swords. And he said unto them, It is enough."*[6] The sword will not save us, but we must be obedient and follow His word in every detail. The Lord saved Hananiah, Mishael, and Azariah, when they were thrown down bound into the midst of the burning fiery furnace. Then the King of Babylon answered and said, *"I see four men loose, walking in the midst of the fire, and they have no hurt; and the form of the fourth is like the Son of God."* Daniel 3:25

THE FALL OF JERUSALEM

The siege of Jerusalem in 70 AD is symbolic of the judgment that will fall on America; the judgment came because the nation was in sin just like America. The reasons given in Scripture include the oppression of the poor, the land full of violence, false prophets crying peace and safety, and people relying on religion and not on God. The people refused to hear the truth, and they were rejecting God's laws, and were hard-hearted and full of sin.

The same is true of America today. It is interesting that the people in Jerusalem thought God would never destroy the nation of Israel. The people in America today are trusting in their great wealth, which is actually great debt, and their strong military, while we are totally vulnerable to terrorism, and believe she is also invincible. In one hour she will burn! Jesus prophesied the destruction of Jerusalem himself. *"O Jerusalem, Jerusalem, which kills the prophets, and stones them that are sent unto thee; how often would I have gathered thy children together, as a hen doth gather her brood under her wings, and ye would not! Behold, your house is left unto you desolate: and verily I say unto you, You shall not see me, until the time come when ye shall say, Blessed is he that cometh in the name of the Lord."*[8] When the siege of Jerusalem started, the Roman army surrounded the city and then pulled back for several days to give those who would choose to escape an opportunity to leave and those who fled were saved. Several men have spoken that the Lord will give a similar warning to the believers in America through a major sign, and then the remnant will have to flee.

GOD ALWAYS GIVES A FINAL WARNING

The judgments of the past all contained the following pattern:

1. The judgment is prophesied to the people as a warning.
2. The Lord always gives a final warning.
3. God's faithful and obedient people are always given time to flee.
4. Those who disobey and do not heed the warnings are destroyed.
5. The judgment includes plagues, famine and the sword.
6. God remembers his covenant and an obedient remnant is saved.
7. The Lord always gets the glory for saving His remnant.

The Word of God speaks of the fall of America Babylon. *"And after these things I saw another angel come down from heaven, having great power; and the earth was lightened with his glory. And he cried mightily with a strong voice, saying, Babylon the great is fallen, is fallen ... And I heard another voice from heaven, saying, Come out of her, my people, that ye be not partakers of her sins, and that ye receive not of her plagues.* [9]

THE LORD IS PREPARING HIS REMNANT

The Lord is now preparing a remnant people and is teaching them how to prepare for the great hour of testing that is quickly coming upon the entire earth. *"Because thou hast kept the word of my patience, I also will keep thee from the hour of temptation, which shall come upon all the world, to try them that dwell upon the earth."* [10]

In 1 Thessalonians 5:2-4, the word declares we should not be in the dark about the sudden coming of the Day of Judgment. *"For yourselves know perfectly that the day of the Lord so cometh as a thief in the night. For when they shall say, Peace and safety; then sudden destruction cometh upon them, as travail upon a woman with child; and they shall not escape. But ye, brethren, are not in darkness, that that day should overtake you as a thief."* We should be able to see the signs and be preparing for the imminent judgment upon the entire earth.

THE SOON AND CERTAIN JUDGMENT UPON AMERICA

The Scripture gives us insight into the timing of the coming judgment upon America. Daniel's seventy weeks prophecy reveals the Great Tribulation will begin following seven weeks from the commandment to restore the Holy City, an event fulfilled by an act of the Knesset in April of 1949. The seven weeks is completed by a Jubilee cycle which is together a period of 50 years, and this points to the birth of the man-child after the fall of 2021.

1. We will witness the judgment of America Babylon after the end of her 70-year reign over the nations, which ends in March of 2021.
2. Civil war will come to America before her final judgment.
3. Financial collapse and martial law will precede the civil war.
4. In one day, America will burn and suffer massive losses.
5. The east and west coasts will be destroyed by nuclear fire.
6. Biological weapons will be used in the other U.S. cities.
7. The U.S. will suffer a staggering loss of life.

America as we know it will soon be over; the nation we all know will not survive the judgments that are coming upon her. The judgment is certain to happen, and we are responsible to prepare and take action. There are things you must do to prepare for the tough times immediately ahead. Before the holocaust in Germany, the Lord sent people to warn the Jews to leave the country because a terrible thing was about to happen. Those who listened sold their possessions and converted them to diamonds and fled. They were obedient and saved both their lives and property. Others left at the last minute, and only saved their lives. The majority refused to hear and obey the message, and lost everything including their lives.

Another greater holocaust is coming; we had better prepare, for we stand at the door. The land will conflict within the government before the final judgment of fire! *"And lest your heart faint, and ye fear for the rumour that shall be heard in the land; a rumour shall both come one year, and after that in another year shall come a rumour, and violence in the land, ruler against ruler."*[11]

199

THE DAY OF THE LORD IS AT HAND

THE ONLY WAY OUT IS TO LEAVE EARLY

God always gives us a final warning; we live under the rule of a sovereign King who loves us. Will you be ready for what is coming? You must take care of the spiritual needs first. You must be able to hear His voice, or you will be one of the frightened ones. What will you do when the panic hits your city? The only way out of the cities is to leave early! Everyone will flee the cities of America Babylon! *"Her cities are a desolation, a dry land, and a wilderness, a land wherein no man dwelleth, neither doth any son of man pass thereby."* [12]

The day will come when you must hear His still small voice, and when it's time to go, you must obey, or it will cost you everything. Remember, there never has been a time when the Lord didn't deliver a remnant. You must learn the power of the name of Jesus Christ and the word of authority of divine command: the power to enforce the authority of the kingdom of God in our lives, our homes and our families.

1. We must learn to stand in his authority.
2. To do this, you must be grounded in the word of God.
3. Clean out your house, and deal with any area of sin in your life.
4. You must plead the Blood of Jesus over your life, your loved ones and your property.

This is done verbally by faith. You have the right to claim the covering of the Blood of Jesus, so be obedient and pray! The prophecies of many of the men of God, David Wilkerson, Dumitru Duduman, and others proclaim the sudden destruction of the United States. The Lord told Duduman that "the Church has left me." We need to stop sinning and return to the Lord. If you don't, if you stay in your sin and rebellion, you will be destroyed.

THE LORD IS SENDING HIS PROPHETS WITH HIS FINAL WARNING

The Lord is again sending his prophets with the final warning call, pleading with the people to turn from their sin and repent before the hour of destruction comes upon the land. The pattern is the same, for the people who are hardened in their sins are choosing to listen to the false prophets, who promise peace and safety through the pre-tribulation rapture, yet a remnant is hearing the word of the Lord. They are preparing their hearts to meet the Lord and they are preparing an ark for safety.

Babylon The Great Is Fallen, Fallen

Even thus shall it be in the day when the Son of man is revealed. In that day, he which shall be upon the housetop, and his stuff in the house, let him not come down to take it away: and he that is in the field, let him likewise not return back. Remember Lot's wife. Whosoever shall seek to save his life shall lose it; and whosoever shall lose his life shall preserve it. I tell you, in that night there shall be two men in one bed; the one shall be taken, and the other shall be left. Two women shall be grinding together; the one shall be taken, and the other left. And they answered and said unto him, Where, Lord? And he said unto them, Where so ever the body is, thither will the eagles be gathered together. Luke 17:30-37

The Lord tells us that the day the Son of man is revealed, we are to flee, and do not even go back into your house to get your things, but flee immediately. The reference to the day *"when the Son of man is revealed"* speaks of the 144,000 who will be sealed and when the Lord himself begins to walk through the world in the footsteps of His mighty ones for 3 ½ years as THE LION FROM THE TRIBE OF JUDAH. This occurs at the same time that the abomination occurs, for both princes now come forth and are revealed to mankind, to fulfill the last half of the covenant of their fathers.

Notice this is not a reference to the Second Coming. We don't have to flee at that time. The Lord is referring to the revelation of his two witnesses, and the army of the 144,000, who will be anointed and revealed at the same time that *"the one who makes desolate is revealed"* and then the judgment will begin. The reference to the ones taken speaks of those who will die in the judgment and the ones that are left are the remnant, for the apostles question him, "where Lord?" asking where will they be taken to? His answer, where the vultures will gather, and it speaks of the death of the ones taken.

Remember in Daniel, we are told the prince will make war with the saints. *"I beheld, and the same horn made war with the saints, and prevailed against them;"*[13] Again, we are told the prince has power for only 3 ½ years: *"Thus he said, The fourth beast shall be the fourth kingdom upon earth, which shall be diverse from all kingdoms, and shall devour the whole earth, and shall tread it down, and break it in pieces. And the ten horns out of this kingdom are ten kings that shall arise: and another shall rise after them; and he shall be diverse from the first, and he shall subdue three kings. And he shall speak great words against the most High, and shall wear out the saints of the most High, and think to change times and laws: and they shall be given into his hand until a time and times and the dividing of time."*[14] The reference to wearing out the saints speaks of the slave labor camps which the outer court believers will be held in until their death as martyrs.

In Revelation 14:7-8 we read: *"Fear God, and give glory to him; for the hour of his judgment is come: and worship him that made heaven, and earth, and the sea, and the fountains of waters. And there followed another angel, saying, Babylon is fallen,*

201

is fallen, that great city, because she made all nations drink of the wine of the wrath of her fornication." In Revelation 12:6 we are told this same 3 1/2-year period is the time of the flight of the woman, *"And the woman fled into the wilderness, where she hath a place prepared of God, that they should feed her there a thousand two hundred and threescore days."*

The worldwide dominance of the prince is made clear in Revelation 13:7, *"And it was given unto him to make war with the saints, and to overcome them: and power was given him over all kindreds, and tongues, and nations."* One of the first acts of the prince is to destroy the mighty people. In Daniel 8:24 we read, *"And his power shall be mighty, but not by his own power: and he shall destroy wonderfully, and shall prosper, and practice, and shall destroy the mighty and the holy people."*

This reference is to the destruction of the world's last super power, the mighty nation, which is destroyed before his war on the holy people. This mighty nation of course is the rider on the white horse, whose king, lives in the White House, the U.S.A., which will fall immediately prior to the setting up of the one world Government.

In Revelation 17:15-18, Apostle John wrote: *"And he saith unto me, The waters which thou saw, where the whore sits, are peoples, and multitudes, and nations, and tongues. And the ten horns which thou saw upon the beast, these shall hate the whore, and shall make her desolate and naked, and shall eat her flesh, and burn her with fire. For God hath put in their hearts to fulfil his will, and to agree, and give their kingdom unto the beast, until the words of God shall be fulfilled. And the woman which thou saw is that great city, which reigns over the kings of the earth."*

The city is a reference to the nation state at the time of the end, which is reigning over the nations of the earth, the one remaining super power, the U.S.A.

In Isaiah 47:5, the Lord describes the daughter of Babylon as the lady of kingdoms *"Sit thou silent, and get thee into darkness, O daughter of the Chaldeans: for thou shalt no more be called, The lady of kingdoms."* And again, the Scripture reiterates in Isaiah 47:8-9 that the people of Babylon dwell "carelessly." *"Therefore hear now this, thou that art given to pleasures, that dwellest carelessly, that sayest in thine heart, I am, and none else beside me; I shall not sit as a widow, neither shall I know the loss of children: But these two things shall come to thee in a moment in one day, the loss of children and widowhood: they shall come upon thee in their perfection for the multitude of thy sorceries, and for the great abundance of thine enchantments."*

In Isaiah 13:19 the LORD states the beautiful parts of the Babylonian kingdom (the coastlands) will be overthrown and destroyed as Sodom: *"And*

Babylon The Great Is Fallen, Fallen

Babylon, the glory of kingdoms, the beauty of the Chaldees' excellency, shall be as when God overthrew Sodom and Gomorrah."

What evidence is there confirming these things? More than you could ever review in 50 years, which is about how long I have been watching diligently. Here is a short summary - highlights of the news you probably didn't hear about, or notice the significance of, while it occurred.

THE REPORT FROM IRON MOUNTAIN

The first public information revealed about the plans of the Illuminati for America began to surface in the public view in the 1960's. One of the most significant leaks was the "Top Secret Report from Iron Mountain" published by Dial Press in 1967.

"In 1961 the Kennedy Administration ordered a Top-Secret study to determine the problems facing the United States if the world moved from an era of war to a Golden Age of Peace. Their first and last meetings were held at a nuclear survival retreat called Iron Mountain. The study was concluded in 1966 and President Johnson gave the order that the report was never to be released. Due to the nature of the conclusions reached, one of the men involved in this study elected to release it to the public at great risk to himself under the name of John Doe. The Report from Iron Mountain was published in 1967 by Dial Press. The establishment promptly renounced it as a hoax. It was no hoax. Iron Mountain is now hard to obtain, but many large libraries still have copies of it. This report looks deep into the soul of the New World Order. Iron Mountain is the covert agenda to bring the world and America under the control of the United Nations. The conclusions reached are now being implemented upon the American people without their knowledge or consent. It is real and no person in America is safe, because in spite of all the denials of authorities, it is real, and these plans are now coming to pass. Iron Mountain explains how the 'rich men' of the earth are operating and why. Iron Mountain is a look into the soul of Lucifer, the Antichrist, long foretold by Jesus Christ, who warned us 2000 years ago, this was coming ... IT IS NOW HERE." [15]

U.S. STATE DEPARTMENT PUBLICATION 7277

In the same year, the United States Department of State issued Publication number 7277, Freedom from War: The United States Program for General Disarmament in a Peaceful World. The introduction states "the United States has introduced at the Sixteenth General Assembly of the United Nations a Program for General and Complete Disarmament in a Peaceful World. It is based on three principles deemed essential to the achievement of practical progress in the disarmament field: First, there must be an immediate disarmament action. Second, all disarmament actions must be subject to effective international controls. Third, adequate peace-keeping machinery must be established. This can only be achieved through the progressive strengthening of international institutions under the United Nations and by creating a United Nations Peace Force to enforce peace as the disarmament process proceeds." [16]

And through his policy also he shall cause craft to prosper in his hand; and he shall magnify himself in his heart, and by peace shall destroy many Daniel 8:25

Publication number 7277 includes a three-stage disarmament process, which we are now in the last part of stage three; these include:

1. Stage One provided that the nuclear threat would be reduced through weapons testing prohibitions, nuclear weapons would be limited, and the armed forces of the USSR and the USA would be reduced.

2. Stage Two included further reductions in national armed forces, establishment of a permanent international peace force within the UN, and the dismantling or conversion of military bases.

3. Stage Three provided the final steps whereby states would only retain those forces and non-nuclear armaments required for the purposes of maintaining internal order and provide agreed manpower for a UN peace force, manufacture of armaments would be prohibited except for those of agreed types and quantities to be used by the UN Peace Force. All other armaments would be destroyed or converted to peaceful purposes.

Thus the "peacekeeping" capabilities of the United Nations would be sufficiently strong as to assure peace and the just settlement of differences in a disarmed world.[17] Few Americans realized the US Department of State embarked on a mission to disarm America in the early 1960's and surrender her military might to a new central government of the world under the United Nations. This is the New World Order and the citizens of America will be brought under its power without a vote or any awareness of this plan.

And in the latter time of their kingdom, when the transgressors are come to the full, a king of fierce countenance, and understanding dark sentences, shall stand up. And his power shall be mighty, but not by his own power: and he shall destroy wonderfully. Daniel 8:23-24

He shall enter peaceably...And such as do wickedly against the covenant shall he corrupt by flatteries: but the people that do know their God shall be strong, and do exploits. And they that understand among the people shall instruct many. Daniel 11:24, 32-33

THE NEW WORLD ORDER

In other published UN documents, we have learned The New World Order and the One World Government was to be established by the year 2000. "The UN-funded commission of Global Governance has completed its three-year study, and has announced publicly its plans to implement global government by the year 2000. They call for a World Conference on Global Governance by 1998 for the purpose of submitting to the world the necessary treaties and agreements for the ratification and implementation by the year 2000." [18]

The rich men of the earth planned to bring the nations under the control of the New World Order around the time of the New Millennium, but the Lord delayed their plans. In order to accomplish this goal, the insiders must first introduce a crisis in the near future, in order to change the political system of the United States of America. Other leaked intelligence confirms the insiders have been instructed by Lucifer to cleanse the earth before the dawn of the so-called "new age" which began with the end of the Mayan calendar. To do this, they must eliminate all of the believers who will not embrace their pagan worldview, so that the earth might experience the next step in the spiritual evolution of man. Little do they realize they are "cleansing the earth" and readying it for the true Millennium which is coming after Jesus returns.

World leaders from all nations now are publicly acknowledging this reality. Norman Cousins, Under Secretary of State declared "World Government is coming, in fact it is inevitable. No arguments for or against it can change that fact."[19] President George Bush introduced the American people to the plan of a New World Order: "What is at stake is more than one small country, it is a big idea, a New World Order, where diverse nations come together to achieve the universal aspirations of mankind based on shared principles and the rule of law The illumination of a thousand points of light... the winds of change are with us now." [20]

Pope John Paul II wrote, "By the end of this decade (AD 2000) we will live under the first one world government that has ever existed in the society of nations. One world government is inevitable." [21] His last statement is true; it is inevitable, for these events have been prophesied by the Spirit of the Lord. His first remarks are false; the world has lived under world government before, in all the prior kingdoms of Mystery Babylon.

THE FALSE MILLENIUM OF THE BEAST

This New World Order, which is about to come to power, is the false millennium, under the false messiah, which rises to power after the counterfeit battle of Armageddon, which is about to be fought in the Middle East. Lucifer counterfeits everything God does. Here at the end of the age, his false messiah, the little prince, will appear before the world to bring "peace and security" after the destruction of America in World War III, which is the nuclear war which will begin in the Middle East:

1. Top Intelligence agencies all confirm the Middle East is ready to explode. War is now raging across the region, in Yemen, Syria, Iraq, while Iran moves to acquire nuclear weapons.

2. The Arab nations have aligned in preparation for war with Israel.

3. The Israelis understand the inevitability of the next war, and are silently preparing for the eventuality of the war of Ezekiel 38.

4. The war plans include an attack on the U.S.A. in a massive domestic terrorist attack using both biological and nuclear weapons smuggled onto U.S. soil. These teams have been coming in for years, and are now fully in place.

5. The war that is coming is prophesied in Ezekiel 38 & 39, where we know the Israelis will suffer substantial losses, but will emerge victorious. When they retaliate with their nuclear arsenal, the Scripture says in Ezekiel 39:6, *"and I will send fire on Magog, and among them that dwell carelessly in the distant (coastlands)."* This is a direct reference to the fall of America Babylon which will take a massive nuclear strike on the east and west coasts.

6. The financial and political collapse which will follow will be absolute. Out of the ruins of the present world order, after the eagle's wings are plucked, then the New World Order of the beast will be lifted up and given dominion over all the earth. Then the Great Tribulation will begin.

MASS DESTRUCTION TERRORISM
IN THE UNITED STATES

The Intelligence Digest in a special report of Terrorism stated, "The widening availability of the means to manufacture or acquire biological, chemical, and/or nuclear weapons; the proliferation of religiously inspired terrorist groups; and the failure to forge a permanent peace between the Arabs/Iran and Israel ... has led to the increasing fear among western security experts that a terrorist attack using weapons of mass destruction is now a question of when, not if."[22]

In their newsletter dated October 3, 1997 they state "the very point of the KGB's nuclear terror bombs was to explode them in an American city "at the right moment"...The crucial difference now is that the bombs are allegedly no longer under Russian control and therefore the United States cannot threaten retaliation, the revelation that KGB-designed, suitcase sized, nuclear terror bombs have gone missing is an important factor in assessing the likelihood and timing of the next Arab-Israeli war."[22] In one hour Babylon will burn!

THE GROWING RISK OF FAMINE IN AMERICA

"The 2020 drought developed last summer following a dry spring. Since then, conditions have deteriorated and continue to worsen to *"the most severe on record in the Southwest,"* according to the Wall Street Journal. [23]

"There is a new crisis looming that could dwarf all the others. It is a global shortage of food: Perhaps the most disturbing aspect of this un-acknowledged crisis is that our own government has given away our strategic food reserves to Russia and a host of other communist countries at a time when our grain reserves are at a 50 year low" [24]

THE IMPENDING STATE OF MARTIAL LAW IN THE US

The United States has been operating under a state of National Emergency since March 9, 1933 under the war powers act. This status was reinstated by every President since Roosevelt. Under the act, the President is vested with dictatorial Powers should he move to declare a national emergency and evoke the Executive Orders Provisions of the Act. Al Gore writing in, *Earth in the Balance,* says on page 48, "There is a threshold coming, and when it is crossed a flood of dramatic change will occur all at once." No doubt!

PRESIDENTIAL EXECUTIVE ORDERS

The President of the United States has quietly accumulated dictatorial powers under the guise of Presidential Executive Orders including the following:

10995 - Seizure of all communications media in the United States
10098 - Seizure of all food supplies, all farms and farm equipment

11000 - Seizure of the American population for work forces under federal supervision, including dividing as necessary according to government plans
11002 - Empowers the Postmaster General to register all men, women and children
11004 -Seizure of all housing and finance authorities to establish Forced Relocation.

Notice these executive orders include the seizure of civilians including the division of families according to government plans. Where do you think they are planning on sending your divided family?

DETENTION CAMPS IN AMERICA

The United States Government has been quietly building Detention Camps on more than 100 U.S. Military bases for the alleged purposes of fighting the War on Drugs. Thus far most of these facilities have limited or no inmates. Capacity of these camps is in the millions. Obviously, the government is planning on stepping up the war on some group in the near future. This was approved by Senate Bill No. 269, 104th Congress, which passed on January 10, 1995 which included in Sec. 152 "to determine the feasibility of the use of military bases available through the defense base closure and realignment process as detention centers". Dept. of Army Civil Affairs Operations Manual FM 41-10 which includes a Destruction Notice on its cover reading "Destroy by any method that will prevent disclosure of contents or reconstruction of the document." The manual outlines procedures to be used for control of civilian populations within the United States including design and operations guidelines for Detention Camps for U.S. citizens.

All of these measures are ostensibly intended to be used in the war against terrorism; but who are the terrorists? The Headline for the March 5, 1997 issue of USA Today states "FBI turns aggressive on terror." The accompanying table titled "Number of Patriot groups rises" states, "There are 857 active patriot groups in the USA up from 809 last year, the groups are defined as militias, common law courts, churches, radio broadcasters, publishers and others who identify themselves as anti-government or as opposed to the New World Order."[25]

When did churches become terrorist organizations? When did a political opinion in the United States become terrorism? People wake up! They have overrun our free institutions and are ready to dismantle our democratic republic and with it your freedom and you don't even know it!

THE CHURCH OF JESUS CHRIST IS THE ENEMY NOW

An official I shall not name was interviewed on CNN by Larry King, discussing the need to crack down on the terrorist elements including radical cults within American society. When asked by King, who are these radical cultists, they responded "A cultist is one who has a strong belief in the bible and the second coming of Christ; who frequently attends bible study; who has a high level of financial giving to a Christian cause; who home schools his children; who has accumulated survival foods; who has a strong belief in the 2nd amendment and ... a strong distrust of big government."[26]

You may find this unbelievable; I did as I sat and witnessed this interview myself. Although this event has been officially denied in an attempted cover up, this event in fact occurred. Other people have contacted me who witnessed this as well. The church of Jesus Christ is the enemy now. The agents of Lucifer, The Order of the Illuminati, have now gained control of our institutions of power. They seized the kingdom by "intrigue and flatteries" as Daniel said. In other words, they just walked right in while no one was watching, and set up shop for the prince of darkness. Jesus said *"You shall be hated by all nations"* and the time has come.

Some have warned me not to write this book, fearing my life would be in danger. I thank them for their concern for my safety, but I must stand bold as our forefathers did and oppose the tyranny of our time regardless of the cost. "To sin by silence when one should protest makes cowards of men." Abraham Lincoln. "The so-called modern Communism is apparently the same hypocritical and deadly world conspiracy to destroy civilization that was founded by the secret order of the Illuminati in Bavaria on May 1, 1776. The world revolution conspiracy appears to have been well organized as to be ever continuing and ever on the alert to take advantage of every opportunity presenting itself or that the conspiracy could create." [27]

"We are on the verge of global transformation. All we need is the right major crisis and the nation will accept the New World Order." [28]

THE MOVE TOWARDS A ONE WORLD RELIGION

1993 was a bad year for the people of this planet; for the pagans who worship the earth itself, the Gaia worshippers, it was a very good year. 1993 was the year darkness began to slowly fall upon the earth. One of the greatest examples of the growing evil is the UN Treaty titled the "Convention on Biological Diversity". President Clinton signed this UN Treaty and submitted it to Congress on November 20th, 1993. Fortunately, Congress had the good sense to defeat this measure. It will be enacted under the power of Executive Orders during the state of Martial Law which is coming soon. The Convention contains ten objectives listed below; read these ten carefully.

1. To make nature the central organizing principle. This places the creation above the creator. In the minds of these pagans, nature is God and man is subject to it.

2. To establish a legal regime that will utilize international treaties to control all policies, from the international level to the national and local levels. They plan to use this treaty and the ones which will follow to usurp the sovereignty of the regional governments of the world and impose their rule of law from the seat of power in the UN. "The New World Order must unite us all in a global partnership which must recognize the transcending sovereignty of nature, of our only one Earth."[29]

3. To make the use of natural resources a cost.

4. To promote the Precautionary principle that scientific evidence is not necessary to implement radical environmental policies. "Lack of full scientific certainty should not be used as a reason for postponing measures to avoid or minimize threats to biological diversity. "[30]

5. To inventory natural and human resources. You have now been reduced to the equivalent of a resource, of no greater value than the other assets in inventories of the one world masters of the global village.

6. To make man equal to all other species. You have the same level of value in the New World Order as a cockroach, or a rat, or a germ for that matter. Actually, in the mind of these pagans, you are seen as the enemy of the earth, and above all others, you are the one species which they will make war with.

7. To classify people as the enemy. "The astounding success of the human species, its proliferation in numbers and in the scale and intensity of its activities, is threatening the future of the Earth's life systems." This is why the elite talk of reducing the earth's population by up to 95%; you and your family are the enemy of their planet, and they intend to do something about it - and do it soon. A new age is coming at the dawn of the year 2000, and they have already announced their plans to have the One World Government in full power and to have the earth cleansed by that time. In less than 15 months, they will have defeated their enemy, the people of the earth, especially the Christians and the Jews in a series of attacks on our nation and the world.

8. To create areas devoid of human presence. This is referred to as de-wilding, the Nazi's promoted a similar program in forcing civilians out of entire regions of the countryside, this time the application will

be far more lethal. Examples of this doctrine in present form include the Wild lands project, National Wildlife Refuges, Wilderness Corridors and Buffer Zones and of course UN Biosphere's. They all sound harmless enough, but you need to read the fine print.

9. <u>To make nature-worship a state religion.</u> "The transformation of our vision of a sustainable civilization into reality will not occur without a major cultural transformation a reorientation of the ethical, moral and spiritual values which provide the primary motivations for human behavior."[32] They are going all the way with this, not only are you a resource, equal to all other species, but your freedom of religious thought threatens their little world system so they are going to impose their faith on you, and if you don't like worshipping the earth and the beast - they have a solution.

10. <u>To promote the traditional lifestyles, cultures, and beliefs of indigenous peoples.</u> Stamping out the Christian heritage isn't enough, they need to replace it with the ancient paganism practiced by indigenous peoples. [33] Friend, the hour is late indeed.

AMERICA TURNS FROM THE TRUTH TO THE BIG LIE

TWA Flight 800, Oklahoma City, Ruby Ridge, Vincent Foster, Ron Brown these are some of the names from the events which will stand forever in time, as the point where America turned from the truth to the big lie, and began the rapid descent from freedom to tyranny, while the majority of the people looked the other way, or couldn't care less. Examine the facts; if you care to look at the truth the evidence is overwhelming.

"Our information is that TWA 800 was struck by an unarmed missile, fired from a US submarine or other submersible platform... this theory is enhanced by the fact that the missile was seen streaking towards the plane by no fewer than 244 witnesses, including a National Guard helicopter pilot. But the FBI's James Kallstrom dismissed the testimony of the eyewitnesses claiming that `Eyewitness testimony is not evidence' Preposterous! Informed sources tell Strategic Investments that Kallstrom told other investigators soon after TWA 800 went down, that `this ain't going to be a missile.' Kallstrom reportedly explained that the American people would `freak' if they knew the truth."[34]
You have been lied to! Every last one of you will "freak" when you finally learn the truth! Jesus warned you, *"Take heed that no man deceive you"*. One of the attorneys involved in the Oklahoma City independent investigation by the Governor stated, "One day when you know what I know, and what I have learned, and that day will come, you will never again look at the government of the United States in the same way."[35] That day is coming soon for America.

THE GLOBAL ETHIC
TOWARDS A ONE WORLD RELIGION

On September 4, 1993, just nine days prior to the signing of the covenant with death in Israel, the leaders of the World Parliament of Religions met in Chicago. Approximately 150 of the world's best known religious leaders met to sign a document called The Global Ethic, better known as Ecumenicalism. They included Christians, Muslims, Buddhists, Hindus, Zoroastrians (Luciferians), Janis, Jews, Neo-Pagans, Satanists, Wiccas, Baha'I, Brahmans, Taoists, Sikhs, and Unitarians. Within this document you will find the phrase "not authentically human", which refers to anyone who holds the archaic dogmas of the past - that their one God is the only God.

This was the same rationale the Nazis used to legitimize the killing of the Jews - they weren't considered human. It isn't just the Jews this time, now it's all of us who believe in the God of Israel, and this time the biggest massacre will be in America. On these doctrines of unity and the spirit of Ecumenicalism, I bring Jesus as my sole witness against this deception and apostasy:

> *Suppose ye that I am come to give peace on earth? I tell you, Nay; but rather division: For from henceforth there shall be five in one house divided, three against two, and two against three. The father shall be divided against the son, and the son against the father; the mother against the daughter, and the daughter against the mother; the mother in law against her daughter in law, and the daughter in law against her mother in law. And he said also to the people, When ye see a cloud rise out of the west, straightway ye say, There cometh a shower; and so it is. And when ye see the south wind blow, ye say, There will be heat; and it cometh to pass. Ye hypocrites, ye can discern the face of the sky and of the earth; but how is it that ye do not discern this time?* Luke 12:51-56

In spite of the Lord's own words that His truth would bring division, today we find the majority of the leaders in American Christianity embracing unity and tolerance and entering into covenants with all forms of religious darkness. And this false religious covenant was signed just nine days before the political covenant of the beast. The time is indeed late. Please pray, test this word and seek the Lord that you may be hid in this hour of judgment. Where are our leaders coming from? Our own President in his last inauguration speech said, "The wrong kind of faith leads to division and conflict. Prejudice and contempt cloaked in the presence of religion or political conviction are no different. These forces have nearly destroyed our nation in the past. We shall overcome them." [36]

When did the wrong kind of faith almost destroy our nation? When did the government begin expressing an opinion on the kind of faith which is right? Listen to what your leaders are saying and learn to read between the lines in their speeches!

THE GLOBALIST AGENDA
FOR YOU AND YOUR FAMILY

The Globalists themselves are more direct in their disclosures of what they are planning for you and your family. Ted Turner speaking at the Gorbachev Forum in 1995 said "A total world population of 250-300 million people, a 95% decline from present levels would be ideal." Dr. Jacques Cousteau is quoted as saying "In order to stabilize world population, we must eliminate 350,000 people per day."

The Orange County Register reported on August 4, 1996 "In 1971, the United States quietly joined a UN program calling for the establishment of "biosphere reserves" around the world, each surrounded by buffer zones devoid of human activities. Since that time, our federal government has classified 47 national parks as such sanctuaries without needing to consult congress. Today, these cover over 51 million acres." Under these areas, the UN has complete domain. U.S. sovereignty has been completely compromised. Without a shot being fired, our nation is being dissolved and no one seems to care.

On June 29, 1993 the President by Executive Order #12852 established the Council on Sustainable Development to advise the President on matters pertaining to "economic growth that will benefit present and future generations without detrimentally affecting the resources or biological systems of the planet." [37] Where did this concept of sustainable economic growth come from? It was lifted right out of the Constitution of the Union of Soviet Socialist Republics (1977), Chapter 2, Article 18. The Elite have been working towards a world government for years, using a myriad of organizations including: The World Federalist Association, World Constitution and Parliament Association, The World Constituent Assembly, Gorbachev Foundation USA, Lucis Trust (Formerly named The Lucifer Trust before 1923), The Trilateral Commission, The Council on Foreign Relations, to name just a few.

THE LUCIFER TRUST

The Lucis Trust (formerly the Lucifer Trust) is one of the first organizations to publicly disclose the satanic nature of this vast conspiracy. Part of this strategy is to move mankind towards worship of the beast itself. In a 1995 memo to friends of the Trust, they write, "Since it was released in 1945 promotion of the Great Invocation has been a constant and central feature of the service activities of the Lucis Trust. It expresses a vision of the oneness of life; it affirms the promise of the reappearance of the christ... we will evoke the recognition by people of goodwill everywhere that all formulations of truth and belief are only partial, formed to suit the psychology and conditions of a particular time and people." This is the spiritual core of tolerance and it is significant that the United Nations has designated 1995 the Year for Tolerance.

In this year of Emergence and Impact on Public Consciousness, we begin a three-year cycle... an understanding of public consciousness is the essence of true citizenship and it is urgently needed by humanity, for humanity is at a turning point." [38]

> *And they worshipped the dragon which gave power unto the beast: and they worshipped the beast, saying, Who is like unto the beast? who is able to make war with him? And there was given unto him a mouth speaking great things and blasphemies; and power was given unto him to continue forty and two months, and it was given unto him to make war with the saints, and to overcome them. Rev. 13:4-7*

The Lord spoke in his law that the penalty for disobedience to his truth would be severe:

> *Thy sons and thy daughters shall be given unto another people, and thine eyes shall look, and fail with longing for them all the day long: and there shall be no might in thine hand. The fruit of thy land, and all thy labours, shall a nation which thou knowest not eat up; and thou shalt be only oppressed and crushed always: So that thou shalt be mad for the sight of thine eyes which thou shalt see. Deuteronomy 28:32-34*

America has thrown out God's laws and with it her freedom. We are now in the last hour of the history of the America we know and love. Wake up America, wake up Church of Jesus Christ, or the next sound you will hear is the prison door slamming shut behind you and your family. I have seen the detention centers with my own eyes; I was translated there from my living room while talking on the telephone. I cried and trembled for seven days. This is real. The judgment is real. Sin is real and the consequences are real. We are not playing a game folks - this is life and death.

TRAGEDY AND HOPE

Dr. Carroll Quigley wrote the treatise on the operations of the Order, Tragedy and Hope, disclosing the secret activities of the Council on Foreign Relations during the early 1960's. This book has all but disappeared from

Babylon The Great Is Fallen, Fallen

American libraries. Most have lost their copy. I reviewed the text in the early 70's. Quigley's title is his message; the tragedy is that we are going to lose our national sovereignty and freedoms under the plans of the New World Order. The hope is that once in place, this super central government will ensure permanent peace. "He says in effect it is now too late for the little people to turn back the tide. In a spirit of kindness, he is therefore urging them not to fight the noose which is already around their necks."[39] The Order uses the Hegelian principle of creating a problem and then proposing as the solution, the goals they wish to achieve. Why do we need this New World Order?

1. To protect the environment
2. To deal with the "world debt" problem
3. To alleviate world hunger
4. To bring about a permanent and lasting peace

The blind guides continue to stumble onward to the pit, while the sheep sleep in line, waiting their turn at the edge of the abyss. "We're on the threshold of the first global civilization. Spiritual unity fits the philosophy of our age: everything is changing, so compromise, cooperate, unify, and adapt" said Episcopal Bishop William A. Swing shortly before leaving on a world tour to build support for his dream: a United Religions, modeled after the UN."[40] Compromise? Why not just throw out the truth altogether and go down in flames; why pretend to be holy when you're headed for hell? You deceive more people when you show up as an angel of light. Another famous American TV preacher, who believes the wide road leads to heaven, says: "I don't think anything has been done in the name of Christ and under the banner of Christianity that has proven more destructive to human personality and hence, counterproductive to the evangelism enterprise than the often crude, uncouth and un-Christian strategy of attempting to make people aware of their lost and sinful condition." [41] Sorry to shatter your dreams, but Jesus said only the straight gate leads to life.

Enter ye in at the strait gate: for wide is the gate, and broad is the way, that leads to destruction, and many there be which go in therein: Because strait is the gate, and narrow is the way. which leads unto life, and few there be that find it. Beware of false prophets, which come to you in sheep's clothing, but inwardly they are ravening wolves. Matthew 7:13-15

Mine eyes shall be upon the faithful of the land, that they may dwell with me: he that walketh in a perfect way, he shall serve me. He that worketh deceit shall not dwell within my house: he that telleth lies shall not tarry in my sight. Psalm 101:6-7

THE DAY OF THE LORD IS AT HAND

Thomas Jefferson: "I tremble for my country when I reflect that God is just and that His justice cannot sleep forever." [42]

WHAT DO WE DO NOW: A GUIDE TO PREPARATIONS

1. Begin with fasting and prayer. We are in a spiritual war and the weapons of our warfare are spiritual.
2. Food - begin to stockpile food, be careful not to be seen as hoarding because looting and seizure will be common place. Hoarding will be illegal, so don't use any ID.
3. Water - This is the most critical need you face.
4. Other Emergency Preparedness Ideas: Americans are the most heavily insured people on the planet, but they are 100% dependent on the system and its infrastructure. It will be turned off in the near future and what are you going to do about it?

THE ENEMY

For we wrestle not against flesh and blood, but against principalities, against powers, against the rulers of the darkness of this world, against spiritual wickedness in high places. Wherefore take unto you the whole armor of God, that ye may be able to withstand in the evil day, and having done all, to stand. Stand therefore, having your loins girt about with truth, and having on the breastplate of righteousness; And your feet shod with the preparation of the gospel of peace; Above all, taking the shield of faith, wherewith ye shall be able to quench all the fiery darts of the wicked. And take the helmet of salvation, and the sword of the Spirit, which is the word of God: Praying always with all prayer and supplication in the Spirit, and watching thereunto with all perseverance and supplication for all saints; And for me, that utterance may be given unto me, that I may open my mouth boldly, to make known the mystery of the gospel. Ephesians 6:12-19

Learn the art of spiritual warfare; taking authority in prayer and speaking aloud the name of Jesus Christ and the power of His Blood.

And they overcame him by the blood of the Lamb and by the word of their testimony; and they loved not their lives unto the death. Revelation 12:11

CHAPTER

11

FIRST THERE SHALL COME AN APOSTASY

II Thessalonians 2:3

Scripture contains many warnings regarding the last days, and the terrible times which would come. *"This know also, that in the last days perilous times shall come. For men shall be lovers of their own selves, covetous, boasters, proud, blasphemers, disobedient to parents, unthankful, unholy, Without natural affection, trucebreakers, false accusers, incontinent, fierce, despisers of those that are good, Traitors, heady, high minded, lovers of pleasures more than lovers of God; Having a form of Godliness, but denying the power thereof: from such turn away."*[1]

Men will be lovers of their own selves, consumed with pleasing and serving their own pleasures. The understanding of many will be darkened, and they will be absorbed in the bondage of the kingdom of self, which is also the kingdom of sin and rebellion. These men will be high minded, and proud to the point of arrogance, lovers of pleasure more than God, and despising that which is good and holy. Thinking it right, they shall live life for the pursuit of their own fleshly happiness. Their minds will be absorbed with what they foolishly call "their self-esteem", which is self-worship. In the last days, the worship of self has become the national religion, and all but the holy remnant have been consumed by this spirit of narcissism.

IN THE LAST DAYS SCOFFERS SHALL COME

The apostle Peter also gave us warning that in the last days scoffers would come, walking after their own lust, mocking the promise of the coming of our Lord. These scoffers are even found within the Church, and they mock the messengers who are telling the people of God, it is time to get ready for the return of the Lord. These scoffers are ignorant, blind as to the signs of the coming judgment, for they do not know the Lord.

Knowing this first, that there shall come in the last days scoffers, walking after their own lusts, and saying, where is the promise of his coming? For since the fathers fell asleep, all things continue as they were from the beginning of the creation. For this they willingly are ignorant of, that by the word of God the heavens were of old, and the earth standing out of the water and in the water. But, beloved, be not ignorant of this one thing,

217

that one day is with the LORD as a thousand years, and a thousand years as one day. 2 Peter 3:3-8

In the last days, the people of God will no longer want to hear sound doctrine, and will turn their ears away from the truth. They will heap to themselves teachers who will teach pleasantries and the people shall be turned to fables: "<u>For the time will come when they will not endure sound doctrine:</u> but after their own lusts shall they heap to themselves teachers, having itching ears; <u>And they shall turn away their ears from the truth, and shall be turned unto fables.</u> 2 Timothy 4:3-4

The modern Church has received these fables with open arms; having refused the true word of God, they have fashioned a gospel unto their own desires. And they have heaped upon themselves teachers who proclaim these same words of error, for this is a very grave and sobering hour, and only a few realize the Great Tribulation and the Day of the Lord is fast upon us. *"Now the Spirit speaks expressly, that in the latter times some shall depart from the faith, giving heed to seducing spirits, and doctrines of devils; Speaking lies in hypocrisy; having their conscience seared with a hot iron"[2]* These wayward churches have fallen from the truth, and cannot hear the warnings of God. Many of the Lord's people in the religious system of man have made kings rule over them just like ancient Israel, having rejected the Lord, they have turned to man. What happened to Israel in the natural is being fulfilled again in the Church in the spiritual. The people have sought falsehoods as a covering and chosen lies for a refuge.

Because ye have said, We have made a covenant with death, and with hell are we at agreement; when the overflowing scourge shall pass through, it shall not come unto us: for we have made lies our refuge, and under falsehood have we hid ourselves. [3]

The false gospel of apostate Christianity and the pre-tribulation rapture deception are false coverings, and they are about to be revealed for what they truly are - covenants from hell. And because of this great evil, the Lord declares, *"Judgment also will I lay to the line, and righteousness to the plummet: and the hail shall sweep away the refuge of lies, and the waters shall overflow the hiding place." [4]*

MY PEOPLE GO INTO CAPTIVITY
FOR LACK OF KNOWLEDGE

It is not going to be very pleasant for the pastors and teachers who have preached these lies. The day of playing church is over, dear reader, and we are about to see the judgment of God fall with such a severity as has never been known from the beginning of time until now.

First There Shall Come An Apostasy

The Lord tells us the honorable men are famished, because they have no knowledge of the truth of the Lord, and who are these honorable men within the Church? They are the pastors, teachers and the false prophets who teach lies. Their congregations are dried up with thirst, for they have not received the living water, rather they have been led to broken cisterns, which cannot hold water.

> *Therefore my people are gone into captivity, because they have no knowledge: and their honourable men are famished, and their multitude dried up with thirst. Therefore hell hath enlarged herself, and opened her mouth without measure: and their glory, and their multitude, and their pomp, and he that rejoiceth, shall descend into it. And mighty man shall be humbled, and the eyes of the lofty shall be humbled: But the LORD of hosts shall be exalted in judgment, and God that is holy shall be sanctified in righteousness.* [5]

> *The Lord's voice crieth unto the city, and the man of wisdom shall see thy name: hear ye the rod, and who hath appointed it. Are there yet the treasures of wickedness in the house of the wicked, and the scant measure that is abominable? Shall I count them pure with the wicked balances, and with the bag of deceitful weights? For the rich men thereof are full of violence, and the inhabitants thereof have spoken lies, and their tongue is deceitful in their mouth.* [6]

The Lord speaks to the wicked city Babylon. The men of wisdom know your true name! Come and sit in the dust, daughter of the Chaldeans! There are two principal errors which have deceived the people of God in America today: The first of these errors is the new gospel of the carnal Christian, which teaches that we no longer have to obey the Lord, but only need to believe in His name. *"Know ye not, that to whom ye yield yourselves servants to obey, his servants ye are to whom ye obey; whether of sin unto death, or of obedience unto righteousness?"* [7] Though we are saved by faith, and faith alone, and our works cannot add to the righteousness which came by JESUS CHRIST through faith, yet our obedience is the evidence of our salvation and is the way of sanctification. *"Many will say to me in that day, Lord, Lord, have we not prophesied in thy name? and in thy name have cast out devils? and in thy name done many wonderful works? And then will I profess unto them, I never knew you: depart from me, ye that work iniquity"* [8] The second error is the pre-tribulation rapture deception, which I will uncover towards the end of this chapter.

STRIVE TO ENTER BY THE NARROW GATE

The word for iniquity in the original Greek is *adikia* (ad-ee-kee'-ah) [9] which is from the word injustice (the act), which means moral wrongfulness (of character, life or act) and is translated as iniquity, unrighteousness, or lawlessness.

> *Then said one unto him. LORD, are there few that be saved? And he said unto them, Strive to enter in at the strait gate: for many, I say unto you, will seek to enter in, and shall not be able. When once the master of the house is risen up, and hath shut to the door, and ye begin to stand without, and to knock at the door, saying, Lord, LORD, open unto us; and he shall answer and say unto you, I know you not whence ye are: Then shall ye begin to say, We have eaten and drunk in thy presence, and thou hast taught in our streets. But he shall say. I tell ,you. I know you not whence ye are: depart from me, all ye workers of iniquity. There shall be weeping and gnashing of teeth, when ye shall see Abraham, and Isaac, and Jacob, and all the prophets, in the kingdom of God, and you yourselves thrust out. And they shall come from the east, and from the west, and from the north, and from the south, and shall sit down in the kingdom of God. And, behold, there are last which shall be first, and there are first which shall be last. Luke 13:23-30*

Matthew Henry's commentary provides a great insight into this promise by the Lord: "(1) All that will be saved must enter in at the strait gate, must undergo a change of the whole man, such as amounts to no less than being born again, and must submit to a strict discipline. (2) those that would enter in at the strait gate must strive to enter. It is a hard matter to get to heaven, and a point that will not be gained without a great deal of care and pains, of difficulty and diligence. We must strive with God in prayer, wrestle as Jacob, strive against sin and Satan. We must strive in every duty of religion; strive with our own hearts, strive as those that run for a prize; excite and exert ourselves to the utmost." [10]

Note this is not outward works of religious observance, but obedience from the heart, and this obedience is to walk in holiness, seeking to deny ourselves and to love our neighbor as ourselves. If this causes you to fear, dear reader, you have heard well, for this is the beginning of the Fear of the Lord. This is why we must be born again, for the old nature cannot please nor obey God.

> *Woe unto you, scribes and Pharisees, hypocrites! for ye are like unto whited sepulchers, which indeed appear beautiful outward, but are within full of dead men's bones, and of all uncleanness. Even so ye also outwardly appear righteous unto men, but within ye are full of hypocrisy and iniquity. Matthew 23:27-28*

A GREAT APOSTASY SHALL
FIRST COME UPON THE CHURCH

Paul warns us specifically that there shall first come a great apostasy or a great falling away, a departure from the truth and from all sound doctrine. The Greek word is *apostasia*[11] which means a defection from truth and a falling away, to forsake the path of holiness.[12]

Matthew Henry's Commentary provides a further insight into this apostasy which would come in the last days, for it is the same spirit of rebellion which inspired the many defections witnessed among the people of God throughout the ages: "A general apostasy, there would come a falling away first from spiritual or religious matters, and from sound doctrine... and a holy life. The apostle speaks of a very great apostasy, not only of some, though it be general, and gradual, it will give occasion to the revelation of the rise of antichrist, that man of sin. And let us observe that no sooner was Christianity planted and rooted in the world than there began to be a defection in the Christian church. It was so in the Old-Testament church ... soon after the promise there was revolting; for example, soon after men began to call upon the name of the Lord all flesh corrupted their way,- soon after the covenant with Noah the Babel-builders bade defiance to heaven, soon after the covenant with Abraham his seed degenerated in Egypt, soon after the Israelites were planted in Canaan... they forsook God and served Ba'al. Soon after God's covenant with David his seed revolted, and served other gods; soon after the return out of captivity there was a general decay of piety... and therefore it was no strange thing that after the planting of Christianity there should come a falling away." [13] Paul writing to the Thessalonians addresses a rumor which had come into the Church that the Day of the Lord and the *"gathering"* of the Church, had already come.

Paul seeks to beseech, to plead with them, that the day of the Lord, and the gathering of the faithful to the Lord, which is the rapture of the Church, will not come until first two things come to pass:

1. A Great Apostasy or falling away from the truth would come
2. The Antichrist will first be revealed

Now we beseech you, brethren, by the coming of our Lord Jesus Christ, and by our gathering together unto him, That ye be not soon shaken in mind, or be troubled that the day of Christ is at hand. Let no man deceive you by any means: for that day shall not come, except there come a falling away first, and that man of sin be revealed, the son of perdition; Who opposeth and exalteth himself above all that is called God, or that is worshipped; so that he as God sitteth in the temple of God, shewing

221

himself that he is God ...And then shall that Wicked be revealed, whom the Lord shall consume with the spirit of his mouth, and shall destroy with the brightness of his coming: Even him, whose coming is after the working of Satan with all power and signs and lying wonders, And with all deceivableness of unrighteousness in them that perish; because they received not the love of the truth, that they might be saved. And for this cause God shall send them strong delusion, that they should believe a lie: That they all might be damned who believed not the truth, but had pleasure in unrighteousness. 2 Thessalonians 2:1-12

AS IT WAS IN THE DAYS OF NOAH

Jesus also warned us that the last days would be *"as it was in the days of Noah, so shall it be also in the days of the Son of man... Likewise also as it was in the days of Lot...But the same day that Lot went out of Sodom it rained fire and brimstone from heaven, and destroyed them all. Even thus shall it be in the day when the Son of man is revealed. In that day, he which shall be upon the housetop, and his stuff in the house, let him not come down to take it away: and he that is in the field, let him likewise not return back. Remember Lot's wife. Whosoever shall seek to save his life shall lose it; and whosoever shall lose his life shall preserve it. I tell you, in that night there shall be two men in one bed; the one shall be taken, and the other shall be left. And they answered and said unto him, Where, Lord? And he said unto them, where so ever the body is, thither will the eagles be gathered together."* [15] This is one of the most misunderstood Scriptures, for those taken are not raptured, rather they are captured, and are taken into captivity!

Jesus tells us it would be like the days of Noah and the days of Lot. In the days of Noah, the earth was full of wickedness and every man did that which was right in his own eyes. *"By faith Noah, being warned of God of things not seen as yet, moved with fear, prepared an ark to the saving of his house; by the which he condemned the world, and became heir of the righteousness which is by faith."* [16] Noah found righteousness with God by faith, and was warned by the Lord of the judgment which would come. Having heard God's warning, Noah believed and was moved with fear to prepare an ark for the saving of his house. Noah believed even though that which God had spoken remained unseen at the time, for it had never rained before on the earth.

Brethren, when you finally understand that these days are coming soon; you too will be moved with fear. Remember, fear only the Lord!

Noah built his ark for one hundred and twenty years, enduring the mocking of scoffers who walked in that hour. Noah stood on the word he had heard from God. This was his only evidence of the judgment that was to come. Noah continued preparing for one hundred and twenty years having just a word from God. Everyone who heard and believed the warning took action, and they were all saved in that hour. All of the scoffers who mocked the message, perished in the judgment, every last one of them. Not one who mocked survived and all who trusted and obeyed were preserved. This is a picture of the remnant, a small group of faithful people, warned by God of judgment to come and given instruction to prepare their house to endure. They all survived the hour. This word is being fulfilled again, and all over the earth, the humble and the poor in spirit are being alerted by the Lord to ready their house. Yet they are a small remnant, even so this too is from the Lord. Lot is also a picture of those who would not prepare their houses.

Before the Day of Judgment, the angels came and removed the righteous, *"and on the same day that Lot went out of Sodom it rained fire and brimstone from heaven, and destroyed them all. Even thus shall it be in the day when the Son of man is revealed."* Luke 17:29-30 Lot and his daughters were homeless the next day, while the Noah company that heard the word and prepared, were able to sleep the next night in their own beds, while Lot's portion was a cave.

THE PRE-TRIBULATION RAPTURE DECEPTION

The majority of modern prophecy teachers embrace a theory which they call the pre-tribulation rapture. This great deception has entered the Church at large and neutralized it. The church has been taught they will not see the final battle, but will be taken out beforehand. As a result, the Church has adopted a position of neutrality, assuming they are not involved in this final battle. This deception has rendered them useless, for they are not preparing spiritually or emotionally for the fight which is ahead. The Scripture is clear. We are staying here through the tribulation. We are not getting raptured out until the last day. We must begin to prepare both our hearts and our homes to endure this hour of testing. There is no chance of a pre-tribulation rapture, none whatsoever! Jesus himself prayed for us saying *"I pray not that thou should take them out of the world, but that thou should keep them from the evil."*[16]

Jesus did not pray that the Father would take us out of the tribulation. Rather He prayed that we would not be taken out of the world. There is not a single biblical text which supports the theory of a rapture of the Church prior to the Great Tribulation. The so-called proof texts are taken totally out of context, and used only as an inference of this great end-time fable. This is a relatively new dogma, and is held primarily in the Church in America. In the nations already witnessing the violent persecution which Jesus warned of, this false doctrine is no longer held. If you tried to teach Christians in China that they would be raptured before the tribulation came, they would perceive you to be insane. The Church in China is already in tribulation.

I HAVE DREAMED A DREAM AND SEEN A VISION

The Pre-tribulation rapture theory was created from a vision of a thirteen-year-old girl, named Margaret MacDonald, of Port Glasgow, Scotland. She had a vision in 1830 where she saw the last days of the earth before the great tribulation. Her vision was misinterpreted and the teaching of a pre-tribulation rapture began to spread until it became embraced by the mainline teachers of the day. There is no biblical basis for this teaching. None whatsoever!

The Scripture warns us that in the last days the people of God, the Church will no longer want to hear sound doctrine but will turn instead to fables, and to make-believe stories from the imaginations of men.

> *"For the time will come when they will not endure sound doctrine; but after their own lusts shall they heap to themselves teachers, having itching ears; And they shall turn away their ears from the truth, and shall be turned unto fables.* [19]

This false teaching is the fable. The Lord refers to it as, "The Great Deception." This false doctrine was created through deception, and then promulgated by the enemy of your soul. The Illuminati invested substantial resources in the promotion and publication of this false doctrine. The purpose was to disarm the Church, so they could slaughter the people of God. And the saints, now seeking to hear pleasant things, and no longer wishing to endure sound doctrine, bought the lie hook, line and sinker. The Church in China and Russia and many other nations were decimated because the people had not prepared themselves for violent persecution. When the missionaries went back into China years after the Communist revolution, the few surviving believers asked "Why did you lie to us?" This false doctrine is primarily held in the apostate nations of the west where real persecution has not yet reared its ugly head.

MARGARET MACDONALD'S
VISION OF THE LAST DAYS

"It was first the awful state of the land that was pressed upon me. I saw the blindness and the infatuation of the people to be very great. I felt the cry of Liberty to be just the hiss of the serpent, to drown them in perdition. The people of God think they are waiting, but they know not what it is they wait for. Suddenly it burst upon the scene with a glorious light... I saw the Lord himself descending from heaven... I saw the error of men who think this will be something seen by the natural eye, but the kingdom of God is liken unto the ten virgins who went forth... the oil the wise took is the light that they may discern, for the kingdom of God cometh not with observation to the natural eye. Only those who have the light of God within them will see the sign of His appearance. Oh the glorious in breaking of God which is now about to burst on this earth... Oh what a holy, holy bride she must be... now shall the glorious mystery of God in our nature be known. The Revelation of Jesus Christ has yet to be opened up. It is not knowledge about God that it contains, it is an entering into God, which only those filled with the Spirit can see, those who have not the Spirit could see nothing. I saw people of God in an awfully dangerous situation, and many about to be deceived and fall. Now will the wicked one be revealed, Oh it will be a fiery trial, and every soul will be shaken. Now shall the awful sight of a false Christ be seen on the earth, for the trial of the church is from the antichrist. It is by being filled with the Spirit that we shall be kept. What had hindered the real life of God from being received by His people was their turning away from Jesus... they were all passing by the cross... I saw on that night, there will be such an outpouring of the Spirit such as has never been - a baptism of fire... the servants of God sealed in their foreheads, and His holy image seen in His people."

This vision reveals the mystery of the second coming in the lives of the holy remnant, and the teachers who created the false doctrine of the pre-tribulation rapture did so out of their own imagination!

WOE UNTO THE PASTORS WHO SCATTER MY FLOCK

The prophet Jeremiah spoke directly to the pastors who would preach a false teaching in the last days which presents a false peace to the people, referring to them as destroying and scattering His sheep. The Lord also says that at that time the people will no longer speak of the deliverance from Egypt, which was the original Exodus. Now the people will speak of this great last days exodus during the time of the Great Tribulation:

Woe be unto the pastors that destroy and scatter the sheep of my pasture! saith the Lord. Therefore thus saith the Lord God of Israel against the pastors that feed my people; Ye have scattered my flock, and driven them away, and have not visited them: behold, I will visit upon you the evil of your doings, saith the Lord. And I will gather the remnant of my flock out of all countries whither I have driven them, and will bring them again to their folds; and they shall be fruitful and increase. And I will set up shepherds over them which shall feed them: and they shall fear no more, nor be dismayed, neither shall they be lacking, saith the Lord. Behold, the days come, saith the Lord, that I will raise unto David a righteous Branch, and a King shall reign and prosper, and shall execute judgment and justice in the earth. In his days Judah shall be saved, and Israel shall dwell safely: and this is his name whereby he shall be called, THE LORD OUR RIGHTEOUSNESS. Therefore, behold, the days come, saith the Lord, that they shall no more say, The Lord liveth, which brought up the children of Israel out of the land of Egypt; But, The Lord liveth, which brought up and which led the seed of the house of Israel out of the north country, and from all countries whither I had driven them; and they shall dwell in their own land. Jeremiah 23:1-8

Jeremiah continues to lament that his heart is broken and that he is like a man who is overcome with wine because of the Lord and the word of His holiness. Jeremiah understands the holiness of the Lord and He knows the people are corrupted and have turned to lies. *"Both the prophet and the priest are profane, in my house I have found their wickedness,"* declares the Lord. These people, though they are in God's house, are full of wickedness, and they shall be driven to darkness.

Mine heart within me is broken because of the prophets; all my bones shake; I am like a drunken man, and like a man whom wine hath overcome, because of the Lord, and because of the words of his holiness. For the land is full of adulterers; for because of swearing the land mourns; the pleasant places of the wilderness are dried up, and their course is evil, and their force is not right. For both prophet and priest are profane; yea, in my house have I found their wickedness, saith the Lord. Wherefore their way shall be unto them as slippery ways in the darkness: they shall be driven on, and fall therein: for I will bring evil upon them, even the year of their visitation, saith the Lord. Jeremiah 23:9-12

I HAVE SEEN THE FOLLY IN THE PROPHETS OF SAMARIA

The Lord continues His rebuke of these false prophets declaring, *"they have prophesied in Baal."* These false prophets are actually under demonic deception, and through this deception they have led the people of God into error. The Lord then warns the people "Do not listen to these false teachers, for they speak a vision of their own imagination." The Lord then tells us, *"They are still teaching this false doctrine to the people who despise me."* This falsehood continues unto the present time. And what is the false teaching? They tell the people, *"You shall have peace, and they teach everyone who walks after the imagination of their own hearts, no evil will come upon you!"*

And I have seen folly in the prophets of Samaria; they prophesied in Baal, and caused my people Israel to err. I have seen also in the prophets of Jerusalem a horrible thing: they commit adultery, and walk in lies, they strengthen also the hands of evildoers, that none doth return from his wickedness: they are all of them unto me as Sodom, and the inhabitants thereof as Gomorrah. Jeremiah 23:13-14

First There Shall Come An Apostasy

Therefore thus saith the Lord of hosts concerning the prophets; Behold, I will feed them with wormwood, and make them drink the water of gall: for from the prophets of Jerusalem is profaneness God forth into all the land. Thus saith the Lord of hosts, Hearken not unto the words of the prophets that prophesy unto you: they make you vain: they speak a vision of their own heart, and not out of the mouth of the Lord. They say still unto them that despise me, The Lord hath said, Ye shall have peace; and they say unto every one that walks after the imagination of his own heart, No evil shall come upon you. Jeremiah 23:13-17

WHO HAS STOOD IN MY COUNSEL AND HEARD MY WORDS?

For who hath stood in the counsel of the Lord, and hath perceived and heard his word? who hath marked his word, and heard it? Behold, a whirlwind of the Lord is God forth in fury, even a grievous whirlwind: it shall fall grievously upon the head of the wicked. The anger of the Lord shall not return, until he have executed, and till he have performed the thoughts of his heart: in the latter days ye shall consider it perfectly. Jeremiah 23: 18-20

The Lord then declares, "Who has stood in my counsel? Who has perceived and heard my words? Who has marked the proper scriptures which speak to the people of this hour, to those in the last days?" The Lord himself declares the truth! *"A whirlwind from the Lord is gone forth in fury! It will fall grievously upon the head of the wicked! And the anger of the Lord shall not return until He has executed those who hold his truth in contempt!"*

I heard the Lord myself, and His voice sounded like the sound of thunder when He said unto me, "Do not tell them this is going to happen. Tell them this word has already gone forth, for it has already been spoken in heaven! The judgment is determined, and it will surely come! WARN THE PEOPLE!!"

Upon hearing this, I trembled with fear. This is precisely the word God spoke to Jeremiah as well, when He said *"A whirlwind is gone forth of the Lord in fury!"* The whirlwind had already gone forth in the heavens, and it will be only be a short time before that word which had already been spoken is performed on the earth! The last statement the Lord makes in this section tells us the timing of this prophecy for He says, *"In the last days you shall understand this perfectly."* In the last days the true meaning of this prophecy would be perfectly understood, for this speaks of the final deception of the saints, the pre-tribulation rapture!

I HAVE NOT SENT THESE PROPHETS YET THEY RAN

The Lord then declares He did not send these false teachers, yet they spoke. The Lord says, "I heard what these false prophets have said, these who teach lies in my name. They say, `I had a dream' yet they are prophets only of the deceit, which is in their own hearts." *"What is the chaff to the wheat,"* declares the Lord! Do you not fear God? Who are you to declare His word? Did He appoint you a prophet or a teacher, or have you appointed yourself? *"Is not my word like fire?"* declares the Lord.

We should greatly fear before we are so presumptuous to suppose we can teach the brethren, for everyone who is called to be a teacher shall receive the greater judgment. Pray for your author, dear reader, for I am compelled by the Spirit to dismiss these false teachings, and to publish the word of truth. I must therefore endure the greater judgment.

> *I have not sent these prophets, yet they ran: I have not spoken to them, yet they prophesied. But if they had stood in my counsel, and had caused my people to hear my words, then they should have turned them from their evil way, and from the evil of their doings. Am I a God at hand, saith the Lord, and not a God afar off? Can any hide himself in secret places that I shall not see him? saith the Lord. Do not I fill heaven and earth? saith the Lord. I have heard what the prophets said, that prophesy lies in my name, saying, I have dreamed, I have dreamed. How long shall this be in the heart of the prophets that prophesy lies? yea, they are prophets of the deceit of their own heart; Which think to cause my people to forget my name by their dreams which they tell every man to his neighbor, as their fathers have forgotten my name for Baal. The prophet that hath a dream, let him tell a dream; and he that hath my word, let him speak my word faithfully. What is the chaff to the wheat? saith the Lord. Is not my word like as a fire? saith the Lord; and like a hammer that breaketh the rock in pieces? Jeremiah 23 21-29*

EACH OF THEM STEALS
MY WORDS FROM HIS NEIGHBOR

The Lord then declares these false teachers have deceived the people causing them to walk in error by their lies and by their lightness. These teachers have made the truth of God a light thing, deceiving the people, for the Lord Himself said *"Strive, agonize, and exert much effort to enter the straight gate."* The truth of God is not a light thing at all! The Lord continues saying, "I did not send these prophets, nor commanded them to speak, and they will be of no profit to my people." And this pre-tribulation deception is of no profit. Rather it has put the people to sleep. Rather than preparing their house and hearts for the hour of testing, they have assumed they will escape it. Both student and teacher of this false doctrine will fall together into the ditch! The Lord also declares that these false teachers *"steal my words from their neighbors."* These false teachers cannot hear from God, so they merely repeat the words spoken by another. Thus many false witnesses are raised mimicking the same false teachings. Woe unto them!

> *Therefore, behold, I am against the prophets, saith the Lord, that steal my words everyone from his neighbor. Behold, I am against the prophets, saith the Lord, that use their tongues, and say, He saith. Behold, I am against them that prophesy false dreams, saith the Lord, and do tell them, and cause my people to err by their lies, and by their lightness; yet I sent them not, nor commanded them: therefore they shall not profit this people at all, saith the Lord. And when this people, or the prophet, or a priest, shall ask thee, saying, What is the burden of the Lord thou shalt then say unto them, What burden? I will even forsake you, saith the Lord. And as for the prophet, and the priest, and the people, that shall say, The burden of the Lord, I will even punish that man and his house. Jeremiah 23:30-34*

JESUS SAID IMMEDIATELY AFTER THE TRIBULATION

Let us examine what the Scripture itself says regarding the timing of the rapture of the church. Jesus, after discussing the events of the Great Tribulation in Matthew chapter 24 says:

> *Immediately after the tribulation of those days shall the sun be darkened, and the moon shall not give her light, and the stars shall fall from heaven, and the powers of the heavens shall be shaken: And then shall appear the sign of the Son of man in heaven: and then shall all the tribes of the earth mourn, and they shall see the Son of man coming in the clouds of heaven with power and great glory. And he shall send his angels with a great sound of a trumpet, and they shall gather together his elect from the four winds, from one end of heaven to the other. Now learn a parable of the fig tree; When his branch is yet tender, and puts forth its leaves, ye know that summer is nigh: So likewise ye, when ye shall see all these things, know that it is near, even at the doors. Matthew 24:29-33*

Notice the timing of these things; immediately after the tribulation. The tribulation has just ended, and then the sign of the Son of man shall appear in the heavens. All of those left standing upon the earth will see the sign of the Son of man, and then all of the people of the earth shall mourn, for they will know that this is Jesus who is coming now to set up His kingdom. And Jesus will then send his angels with the sound of a great trumpet! When this final trumpet sounds after the tribulation, then the angels will gather the elect from the four winds. The four winds refer to the four corners of the earth, where the remnant army of God is stationed. The reference to *"from one end of heaven to the other"* speaks of the saints who have already died and been raised in the first resurrection. Some will dispute that this text speaks of believers being gathered from the earth. The Lord gave the same discourse in Mark's gospel saying, *"And then shall he send his angels, and shall gather together his elect from the four winds, from the uttermost part of the earth to the uttermost part of heaven."*[21] Thus it is clear that this reference speaks of the elect who are taken by the angels. This is the rapture, and it occurs *"immediately after the tribulation"* and on the last day.

AT THE LAST TRUMPET WE SHALL ALL BE CHANGED

Paul also writes about the rapture declaring, *"Behold, I shew you a mystery; we shall not all sleep, but we shall all be changed, In a moment, in the twinkling of an eye, at the last trump: for the trumpet shall sound, and the dead shall be raised incorruptible, and we shall be changed."* [22]

The rapture occurs when the last trumpet sounds. When is the last trumpet? *"And the seventh angel sounded; and there were great voices in heaven, saying, the kingdoms of this world are become the kingdoms of our Lord, and of his Christ; and he shall reign for ever and ever."*[23] Jesus told us in Matthew 24 that after the tribulation of those days, the angels will come with the sound of a great trumpet. This last trumpet is blown after the tribulation! Children, trust the Scriptures and not the teachings of men, who claimed to have dreamed a dream and seen a vision!

Paul writes to dispel rumors that the day of the Lord had already come. Notice he also says, *"and our gathering together unto him."* This gathering is the rapture and it comes at the last trumpet. The rapture is on the final day of the Lord! Notice Paul also says that, *"our gathering to the Lord"* cannot happen until two things occur. First, there must be a great falling away which has already occurred, which is the last days apostasy covered in chapter eleven. Second, the son of perdition must be revealed. This is the antichrist who is revealed at the start of the tribulation. Clearly the saints would be on the earth when the tribulation begins, for the revealing of the prince, to the entire world, must happen first before *"our gathering unto him."*

> *Now we beseech you, brethren, by the coming of our LORD Jesus Christ, and by our gathering together unto him, That ye be not soon shaken in mind, or be troubled, neither by spirit, nor by word, nor by letter as from us, as that the day of Christ is at hand. Let no man deceive you by any means: for that day shall not come, except there come a falling away first, and that man of sin be revealed, the son of perdition; Who opposes and exalts himself above all that is called God, or that is worshipped; so that he as God sitteth in the temple of God, shewing himself that he is God. Remember ye not, that, when I was yet with you, I told you these things? And now*

ye know what withholds that he might be revealed in his time. For the mystery of iniquity doth already work: only he who now letteth will let, until he be taken out of the way. And then shall that Wicked be revealed, whom the Lord shall consume with the spirit of his mouth, and shall destroy with the brightness of his coming. II Thessalonians 2:1-8

THE DAY SHOULD NOT OVERTAKE YOU AS A THIEF

Paul also admonishes that, *"the day of the Lord will come as a thief in the night,"* but we are not of darkness so the day should not overtake us unaware. This day is the beginning of the tribulation and the believer is not to be taken by surprise. Look at the signs the Lord has given us. This is obvious if you are watching. Remember, Jesus commanded us to watch! He didn't suggest that we watch - this was His commandment!

But of the times and the seasons, brethren, ye have no need that I write unto you. For yourselves know perfectly that the day of the Lord so cometh as a thief in the night. For when they shall say, Peace and safety; then sudden destruction cometh upon them, as travail upon a woman with child; and they shall not escape. But ye, brethren, are not in darkness, that that day should overtake you as a thief. I Thessalonians 5:1-4

THESE ARE THEY WHICH CAME OUT OF THE GREAT TRIBULATION

Many scholars argue the Church is not in the book of Revelation and therefore must have been raptured out beforehand. Look at chapter seven. This great multitude is the faithful Church and they came out of the great tribulation.

After this I beheld, and, lo, a great multitude, which no man could number, of all nations, and kindreds, and people, and tongues, stood before the throne, and before the Lamb, clothed with white robes, and palms in their hands; And cried with a loud voice, saying, Salvation to our God which sitteth upon the throne, and unto the Lamb. And all the angels stood round about the throne, and about the elders and the four beasts, and fell before the throne on their faces, and worshipped God, Saying, Amen: Blessing, and glory, and wisdom, and thanksgiving, and honour, and power, and might, be unto our God for ever and ever. Amen. And one of the elders answered, saying unto me, What are these which are arrayed in white robes? and whence came they? And I said unto him, Sir, thou knowest. And he said to me, These are they which came out of great tribulation, and have washed their robes, and made them white in the blood of the Lamb. Revelation 7:9-14

THE DAY OF THE LORD IS AT HAND

The Church is also mentioned in Revelation chapter 17, for by the time of the end, she has become an apostate. This is the Church of Laodicea, and Jesus tells us He is standing at the door outside, knocking and seeking to come in. *"As many as I love, I rebuke and chasten: be zealous therefore, and repent. Behold, I stand at the door, and knock: if any man hear my voice, and open the door, I will come in to him, and will sup with him, and he with me. To him that overcometh will I grant to sit with me in my throne, even as I also overcame, and am set down with my Father in his throne. He that hath an ear, let him hear what the Spirit saith unto the churches."*[24] Daniel was also told about the antichrist *"I beheld, and the same horn made war with the saints, and prevailed against them; Until the Ancient of days came."*[25]

How could the antichrist make war with the saints if they had been taken out before he comes to power? The word is clear! I rest my case on the words of Jesus, Paul and John the apostle. The modern teachers are deceived and continue this deception out of ignorance. These men may be God fearing, but in this critical doctrine, they are themselves deceived and their flocks are headed for destruction!

JUDGMENT IS COMING AND THE CHURCH IS ASLEEP

Judgment is coming and the pre-tribulation rapture message has lulled the church to sleep. There is no precedent for the Lord removing his people before the problem. The Lord prepares his people and preserves them in the midst of the fire. Mankind lives by the pleasure of God's word. Man, whether he likes it or not, lives by the word of God. Mankind, whether we like it or not, is bound by what God says in his word. In the days ahead, the Lord is going to test his people to see what is in their hearts. If it is what the Lord placed there, we are going to receive promises and power beyond what we believe. This is a heart issue and we must be hidden in His hands. We must learn to hear from the Lord ourselves, through the Word, and not to rely on our leaders to teach us His Word.

History always proves the Lord's word comes to pass exactly as He spoke it, every time. God has always protected a remnant in every time of judgment. Jesus told us he did not come to abolish the law, but to fulfill it. We are under both covenants; He fulfilled the old (obedience) and added the new (grace and truth).This is a time when many will become tempted to fear. We must memorize these verses: I John 4:18 *"There is no fear in love; but perfect love casteth out fear."* 2 Timothy 1:7 *"For God hath not given us the spirit of fear; but of power, and of love, and of a sound mind."* We must understand that fear does not come from God; God says DO NOT FEAR!!

First There Shall Come An Apostasy

In Revelation 21:8 He says *"But the fearful, and unbelieving and the abominable, and murderers, and whoremongers, and sorcerers, and idolaters, and all liars, shall have their part in the lake which burneth with fire and brimstone: which is the second death."* We must not fear; this is an issue of obedience. Look at the history of God's judgments. Did he ever rapture his people out before the problem? No, He has never done so in the past and He won't do it now. Jesus prayed not to take us out of the world, but to deliver us in this hour, for this is the greater miracle.

Our deliverance is based on our obedience; if the children of Israel hadn't put the blood of the lamb on their doors, they would not have been delivered. We must get ready physically and spiritually, not fearing but by drawing closer and closer to the Lord. We must learn to pray, listen and then do.

We have the promises of God, the same promises He gave to the children of Israel in the wilderness, if we are obedient, He promises deliverance and safety, if not, we can expect the sword. In Deuteronomy 28:1-22 the Lord gives us the promise of obedience.

> *And it shall come to pass, if thou shalt hearken diligently unto the voice of the Lord thy GOD, to observe and to do all his commandments which I command thee this day, that the Lord thy God will set thee on high above all nations of the earth: And all these blessings shall come on thee, and overtake thee, if thou shalt hearken unto the voice of the Lord thy GOD. Blessed shalt thou be in the city, and blessed shalt thou be in the field. Blessed shall be the fruit of thy body, and the fruit of thy ground, and the fruit of thy cattle, the increase of thy kine, and the flocks of thy sheep. Blessed shall be thy basket and thy store. Blessed shalt thou be when thou comest in, and blessed shalt thou be when thou goest out. The Lord shall cause thine enemies that rise up against thee to be smitten before thy face: they shall come out against thee one way, and flee before thee seven ways. The Lord shall command the blessing upon thee in thy storehouses, and in all that thou settest thine hand unto; and he shall bless thee in the land which the Lord thy God giveth thee. The Lord shall establish thee an holy people unto himself, as he hath sworn unto thee, if thou shalt keep the commandments of the Lord thy GOD, and walk in his ways. And all people of the earth shall see that thou art called by the name of the Lord; and they shall be afraid of thee.*

The promise also contains a curse for disobedience. *"But it shall come to pass, if thou wilt not hearken unto the voice of the Lord thy GOD, to observe to do all his commandments and his statutes which I command thee this day; that all these curses shall come upon thee, and overtake thee: cursed shalt thou be... The Lord shall smite thee with a consumption, and with a fever, and with an inflammation, and with an extreme burning, and with the sword, and with blasting, and with mildew; and they shall pursue thee until thou perish."*

Here we have the words of God, His promise of blessings and protection if we are obedient, or cursing if we chose disobedience and every day we chose the blessing or the curse. If you will obey the Lord, you can be certain of his blessing! The sovereign Lord says, "Know for certain, you are in my hands. Relax in me. If you will be obedient in thought, word and deed, I will certainly deliver you from this hour." "The organized churches of our day have produced congregations of spiritually malnourished people, who are so weak in spirit, that they cannot recognize truth when they see it. Thankfully a small remnant has always been saved in spite of organized religion. In addition to idolatry and apostasy, it was through actual witchcraft entering in, that the secret societies and lodges of the Grand Orient began to take over organized religion. Then came the rock music and the secular entertainment. It was not long until sin was no longer sin. Thus, the very agency that was supposed to fight Satan and all his dark kingdom became a cleverly disguised agency for the Illuminati of the last days to bring about the New World Order. We also have men such as Dr. Robert Schuller, who in his `Institute for Successful Church Leadership' which was held at the Crystal Cathedral, trained over 80 gay and lesbian pastors and lay leaders.[26] Sodom and Gomorrah had come under a Crystal roof." [27]

"We have the current outcry of a coming revival, which will bring the wayward factions of the body of Christ into unity, and will usher in the `great outpouring of the latter rain', which will produce great signs and supernatural wonders within our church services that will cause the unsaved to come flocking in. Could this be why we're experiencing a famine of the word of God in our churches today? Could it be that most cannot, and will not, tolerate the truth when they hear it? *"Wonder; cry ye out, and cry: they are drunken, but not with wine; they stagger, but not with strong drink. For the Lord hath poured out upon you the spirit of deep sleep, and hath closed your eyes: the prophets and your rulers, the seers hath he covered."*[28]

Lest the conservative advocates of the `great escape' deny this... because he is, in his own mind, not prophesying, as he assures his followers of their peace and eternal security, let them also consider *"All the sinners of my people shall die by the sword, which say, The evil shall not overtake nor prevent us."*[29] One form of lie is no different than another in God's eyes, if it is used to deceive His people into apathy and complacency. [31]

"Son of man, the house of Israel is to me become dross: all they are brass, and tin, and iron, and lead, in the midst of the furnace; they are even the

dross of silver. Therefore thus saith the Lord God; because ye are all become dross, behold, therefore I will gather you into the midst of Jerusalem. As they gather silver, and brass, and iron, and lead, and tin, into the midst of the furnace, to blow the fire upon it, to melt it; so will I gather you in mine anger and in my fury, and I will leave you there, and melt you. Yea, I will gather you, and blow upon you in the fire of my wrath, and ye shall be melted in the midst thereof" [32]

The word for *dross* is *seeg* [33] which means refused and scorned. The word is derived from *soog* [34] a primitive root; which means to flinch, to go back, literally to retreat, or figuratively to apostatize, a backslider. The Lord has declared His people, who are called by His name are all backsliders, and they have been refused and scorned.

THE RETURN TO ZION - THE LONG ROAD HOME

The state of Israel was born out of the fires of the holocaust, which the Israelis call the Shoah; so too the gentile believers in Messiah will also be sanctified within the fires of the Great Tribulation which lie immediately ahead of us. And out of this time of Jacob's trouble, the true Zion of the Lord will be cleansed and restored. The return of the Jews to Zion is a picture of the journey the gentiles will now face, for as the scripture declares – to the Jew first, and then to the gentile.

RABBI YEHUDAH ALKALAI

The Lord began to call his people Israel back to himself and to the land, through the teachings of Rabbis whom God touched by his spirit. One of them was named Yehudah Alkalai. He published his first book, *Shema Yisrael* in 1834, in which he called the people to return to the Lord and to the land of ancient Israel. His teachings were based in part on the ancient teachings that the days of the Messiah were to be ushered in by a forerunner of the true miraculous redeemer.

This forerunner of the messiah, whom the Jews called the Son of Joseph, would lead Israel to victory in the war of Gog and Magog, and under him, the land and the people would be restored. Only then would the true Messiah, the Son of David come. In his book, *The Third Redemption* Alkalai wrote, "In the first conquest under Joshua, the Almighty brought the children of Israel into a land that was prepared; its houses were full of useful things, its wells giving water, its vineyards and fields yielding fruit in abundance. This new redemption will – alas, because of our sins, be altogether different: our land is waste and desolate, and we shall have to build houses, dig wells, and plant our own vineyards and fields. We are therefore, commanded not to attempt to go at once and all together to the Holy Land ... the Lord desires that we be redeemed in dignity; we cannot therefore migrate in mass, for we should then have to live as the Bedouins, scattered in tents. Redemption must begin slowly. The land must, by degrees, be built up again and prepared.

"There are two kinds of return: individual and collective. Individual return means that each man should turn away from his evil personal ways and repent and return to obedience to the Lord. Collective return means that all of Israel should return to the land, to receive Divine commandment and to accept the yoke of Heaven. This collective return was foretold by our prophets; even though we are unworthy, Heaven will help us for the sake of our Holy ancestors. I wish to attest to the pain in my soul, of the error of our ancestors, who allowed the Hebrew tongue to be forgotten, and because of this, our people are divided into seventy peoples with seventy languages of the lands of exile. If the Almighty should indeed show us His miraculous favor and gather us into our land, we would not be able to speak to each other. Though it is almost impossible to imagine a revival of the Hebrew language, we must have faith that this too will come, for Joel prophesied that our sons and daughters shall prophesy in the era of Redemption, and that in one language. The Redemption will begin with the efforts of the Jews themselves. So we must organize ourselves, appointing elders, men of piety and wisdom, and from among the elders one shall come who will be revealed as the forerunner of the Messiah, the Son of Joseph, and he will appear from among us in the last days, so that the people will no longer be sheep without a shepherd."

This teaching of the coming of one called the *Son of Joseph* was the Jewish conception of the coming of the forerunner of the Messiah. In Jeremiah we are told the forerunner of the Lord, who is the one who comes before His face, and in the name of the Lord, will also come as a governor out of the midst of the nobles. The verse that Alkalai was preaching from is found in Jeremiah 30:21: *"And their nobles shall be of themselves, and their <u>governor</u> shall proceed from the midst of them; and I will cause him to draw near, and he shall approach unto me: for who is this that <u>engaged </u>his heart to approach unto me? saith the LORD."*

This governor is the one whom Alkalai calls the "Son of Joseph", for he will be lifted up as Joseph, and promoted as a governor by the Lord. The word for governor in Hebrew is מֹשֵׁל *mashawl* and it means one who *rules* and who will be given dominion as a governor; he will be lifted up and caused to rule and given power by the Lord. The word for engaged is ערב *ảrab, aw-rab* which means to *braid*, that is *intermix*; to *give one's heart in a kind of exchange*: to engage, or to give as a pledge, and to give oneself as a surety.

First There Shall Come An Apostasy

Jeremiah speaks of the governor whom the Lord is sending; he is the one who has engaged his heart with the Lord. He gave his heart and his life in an exchange with God, such that his heart will be braided together with the heart of the Lord at the time of his revealing unto the children of Israel.

Jeremiah 50:44 declares: "*Behold, he shall come up like a lion from the swelling of Jordan unto the habitation of the strong: but I will make them suddenly run away from her: and who is this <u>chosen man</u>, that I may appoint over her? For who is like me? And who will appoint me the time? And who is that <u>**shepherd**</u> that will stand <u>**before me**</u>?*" And who is this chosen one? The word *"chosen"* in this text is בחר, *bachar* and it means to *try* and *select* one who is acceptable, and who has been *appointed*, and *chosen*, an *excellent one*, and of him much will be required.

The one chosen by the Lord is also described as a shepherd who stands before the Lord. And who is that shepherd? The word for *"shepherd"* is רעה, *ra'ah*, and it means to *tend* a flock, to *pasture* the flock of the Lord; and he rules over the flock as an associate, or as a companion, to keep company with, and be a friend, or make friendship with the sheep, as a pastor, or a shepherd. Though he comes as their governor, he comes as a friend of the sheep, and not as their ruler.

And who will stand before me asks the Lord? The Hebrew word for *"before me"* is פנים *paniym*, which comes from the root word פנה, *paneh*, which means the *face*; or *before the* face of the Lord, with his favour. The governor whom the Lord shall appoint is one who has been honored to stand in the very presence of the Lord. He was prophesied to come, and he will bear the Shewbread, לחם, which is the word *Lechem* in Hebrew.

This is the bread which comes from Bethlehem, בית לחם, which is *Bet Lechem* in Hebrew, and it means the House of the Shewbread, or the City of the Shewbread. The governor whom the Lord has chosen also comes from Bethlehem, even as the Lord was born in Bethlehem. The full meaning of this text in Hebrew speaks of this coming one, as one who stands up straight and throughout times past, walked with the Lord.

Jeremiah 50 speaks of a shepherd who stands before the face of the Lord, as one who is chosen of the Lord from among the last generation. It has been given unto him to stand in the very presence of the Lord, even before the face of the Most High God. He will be appointed by the Lord over the remnant as a governor. And God says of him: who is like me? And who will appoint me the time? How is he like the Lord? He has a heart after the Lord's owns heart within him; for he comes as a shepherd who cares for the sheep. The religious may be angered at this truth, for it does not fit within their doctrines, but there is a chosen one among us now, and he shall soon be appointed as the governor by the Lord, and he will be revealed soon, and in many ways, he is very much like the Lord.

His genealogy comes from Bethlehem; it was there that his family tree was born, and he too, was a man of sorrows, acquainted with grief. He was despised by the congregation and cast out of their midst. The people esteemed him not, and in his trial of fire, they deemed him stricken of God. He was hidden by God for a season of time in the wilderness, and it was there, in the deserts, where he grew strong in the Spirit till the day of his shewing unto Israel. He will come in the Name of the Lord, and his coming is immediately before the Great and Awesome Day begins, and behold, his coming is nigh at hand.

Jeremiah 50:45-46 states, *"Hear ye the counsel of the LORD that he hath taken against Babylon; and his purposes, that he hath purposed against the land of the Chaldeans: Surely the least of the flock shall draw them out: surely he shall make their habitation desolate with them. At the noise of the taking of Babylon the earth is moved, and the cry is heard among the nations."*

Jeremiah describes the governor who has been appointed in this hour as one who is among *the least of the flock*; in the natural mind, one would assume God would select his chosen one from the among the greatest ones, but alas, the ways of God are not the ways of man. The Lord chooses one of the least of them, one who has already been burned in the fires like unto the life of Job, and one who has suffered as Joseph suffered, at the hands of both his brothers and the Egyptians.

The word used in this text for least is צעיר, *tsaw-ore'* and it means the lowest in value, ignoble: least, or a little one, one of the youngest. He chooses one of the least among them, for the lowest ones among his saints all know they are nothing, whereas the great men, they all think they are something, and therefore they are rejected of the Lord.

The coming of two anointed ones is also prophesied in the writings of Zechariah, in 4:11-14: *"Then answered I, and said unto him, what are these two olive trees upon the right side of the candlestick and upon the left side thereof? And I answered again, and said unto him, what be these two olive branches which through the two golden pipes empty the golden oil out of themselves? And he answered me and said, Knowest thou not what these be? And I said, No, my lord. Then said he, These are the two anointed ones, that stand by the Lord of the whole earth."*

"Thus speaks the LORD of hosts, saying, Behold the man whose name is The BRANCH; and he shall grow up out of his place, and he shall build the temple of the LORD." Zechariah 6:12

First There Shall Come An Apostasy

And he shall build the temple of the Lord with a plumb line of truth in his hand, and the hand of the Lord shall be mighty upon him, and his coming among us has been foretold of old, for he comes in the Name of the Lord, to make straight the way for the people of God. And he shall grow up from out of his place; the word *"his place"* used in this verse is תחת, *takh'-ath* and it means, from the *bottom* or the place of *total depression* and *utter despair*.

He comes from the absolute bottom and from the lowest place of all. Like Job, whose life the Lord had utterly burned in the fire, he is first brought to the end of himself through years of despair and the loss of all things. Before he is lifted up by the Lord, he must first be cast down into the depths of the sea, like unto Jonah, so that the end of all flesh would come within him, for only then can the life of the Spirit set us totally free.

Zechariah 6:13 testifies of the two anointed ones who shall build the temple of the Lord; they shall bear the glory of our God, and they sit and rule upon thrones, and shall be as priests before God, standing in the gap, for the people. And the counsel of peace shall be between them, both the priests and the Lord, for they shall be at peace, one with one another.

> *Even he shall build the temple of the LORD; and he shall bear the glory, and shall sit and rule upon his throne; and he shall be a priest upon his throne: and the counsel of peace shall be between them both.*

The prophet Malachi also spoke of one who would come before the day of the Lord, in chapter four: *"Behold, I will send you Elijah the prophet before the coming of the great and dreadful day of the LORD: And he shall turn the heart of the fathers to the children, and the heart of the children to their fathers, lest I come and smite the earth with a curse."* The one who will be revealed as the Son of Joseph, and who will be promoted as the governor over the household of God, is the coming prophet of Elijah, or one who comes in his office.

THE DAY OF THE LORD IS AT HAND

CHAPTER
12

RETURN OH LORD, HOW LONG?
Psalm 90:13

The coming of the Messiah of Israel has been the hope of God's people from the time of Moses. His first coming as the Holy Lamb of God, to be slain for the sins of the world on the Feast of Passover, was missed by the religious leadership of that day. They had been instructed in the prophecies, and told to watch for one who would come. Yet they could not see, for the nation had fallen into deep apostasy, and thus they rejected the Lord and would not come unto him, that they might be saved. The Lord Himself also commands us to watch, or we will find that He has come upon us as a thief in the night and in an hour we didn't know:

> *Remember therefore how thou hast received and heard, and hold fast, and repent. If therefore thou shalt not watch, I will come on thee as a thief, and thou shalt not know what hour I will come upon thee.* [1]

Jesus, when teaching His disciples about His Second Coming, warned us that the events of the end of the age will come as a snare upon all who dwell on the face of the earth. A snare is an unseen trap, which captures its prey suddenly. Again, in the Gospels He commands us to *"watch ... and pray always, that ye may be accounted worthy to escape all these things that shall come to pass and to stand before the Son of Man."* [2]

WHY CAN'T YOU TELL THE SIGNS OF THE TIMES

Jesus rebuked the Pharisees and Sadducees who came seeking a sign from heaven. His rebuke contains a message; you can tell the signs of the weather, why then can't you tell the signs of the times?

> *The Pharisees also with the Sadducees came, and tempting desired him that he would shew them a sign from heaven. He answered and said unto them, when it is evening, ye say, It will be fair weather: for the sky is red. And in the morning, It will be foul weather today: for the sky is red and lowering. O ye hypocrites, ye can discern the face of the sky; but can ye not discern the signs of the times?* [3]

THE DAY OF THE LORD IS AT HAND

Jesus was referring to the signs in the prophecies which pointed clearly to the time when He would come and the many works He would do to fulfill the Word of God. Yet they in their blindness, could see none of this. Dear reader, can you see? Are your eyes opened, to see the signs in the stars, in the sun, the moon, and even upon the earth?

The Lord laments that even the animal kingdom knows their appointed times, but the people of God, do not know the time which has been appointed for their visitation and judgment. *"Even the stork in the heavens knows her appointed times; and the turtledove, the swift, and the swallow observe the time of their coming. But My people do not know the judgment of the Lord."*[4]

The modern Church in America is about to make the same mistake, with disastrous effects, and this even after they have been commanded to watch and had the warning of Israel's missing the first visitation. *"Who is the wise man who may understand this? And who is he to whom the mouth of the Lord has spoken, that he may declare it? Why does the land perish and burn up like a wilderness, so that no one can pass through? "*[5]

What exactly do the scriptures reveal to us about the return of the Lord? Skeptics will no doubt quote the verse *"No man knows the day or the hour"*, dismissing any attempt to gain insight into the timing of the Lord's coming. But this was not the meaning of the Lord's statement. This phrase is a Hebrew idiom, and it refers to the new moons and feasts of Israel where no man could know the exact day or hour of the feast which began only when the new moon appeared, and therefore had to await the coming of the new moon.

Likewise, in the Second Coming, no one will know the exact day or hour, but we are given many signs of the impending judgment, which will precede His actual return to the earth on the last day. Throughout the scriptures we are commanded to watch, and the Lord expects us to obey him. The word of God contains many passages which provide us insight into the season of the beginning of God's judgment upon the earth. The first prophetic witness is found in the beginning of all things, for in the story of creation, in the beginning, the Lord has told us about the timing of the end of the age.

DECLARING THE END FROM THE BEGINNING

I am God, and there is none like me, Declaring the end from the beginning, and from ancient times the things that are not yet done, saying, My counsel shall stand, and I will do all my pleasure: Calling a ravenous bird from the east, the man that executes my counsel from a far country: yea, I have spoken it, I will also bring it to pass; I have purposed it, I will also do it. Isaiah 46:9-11

Return Oh Lord, How Long?

The Lord tells us that He has declared the end from the beginning and he is referring to the story of creation, where the Word of God gives us a prophetic picture of the seven millenniums of mankind upon the earth. They are presented to us as seven days of creation and each day represents 1,000 years of history, for to the Lord a day is as 1,000 years, and 1,000 years is but a day. The modern Church has lost sight of many biblical truths, this being one of them. The scholars at the time of Jesus knew the meaning of this promise by God, and that is one of the reasons they rejected Jesus as Messiah. They erred as well, for he would come twice, first at the beginning of the fifth day and then again at the start of the seventh day. Jesus referred to the Seventh day of creation as the Third day of His ministry. *"And he said unto them, Go ye, and tell that fox, Behold, I cast out devils, and I do cures today and tomorrow, and on the third day I shall be perfected."* Luke 13:32

This same third day of perfection was prophesied upon Israel, for in the word of God as spoken by the prophet Hosea in 6:2 we read: *"After two days will he revive us: in the third day he will raise us up, and we shall live in his sight."* And it is during the Third day of the ministry of Messiah, which is the Seventh day of creation that Israel shall be raised up, and the remnant of the sons of Israel shall then be perfected. Jesus came at the beginning of the Fifth day as a man, and for two thousand years, during the Fifth and Sixth day, the Spirit of God has ministered the Gospel of Jesus Christ, but now we have entered into the Seventh day, and now the Lord shall become perfected in a remnant of His people.

But when shall these things be? We too must await the sign from heaven, for we do not know the exact day or the precise hour when the New Moon will appear. When the Son of Man is revealed in His people, then shall the New Moon also appear, and the one new man will finally be revealed on a day of clear shining. The Light of Holy One will come upon the moon, and no longer will the moon reflect the light of another, but now the light will come forth from within the vessels which He has chosen as His anointed remnant. The moon represents Israel, and in the anointing of the 144,000 and in their appearing before the people, the New Moon, which is a prophetic picture of the one new man, born again totally in the power of God, shall now appear as the redeemed sons of Israel, and then we shall see him as He is, and we shall know that the coming of the Lord is now at hand.

The Lord told us, you shall not see me again, until you say, *"Blessed is He who comes in the Name of the Lord."* And when you see the blessed ones who come in the Name of the Lord, the anointed messengers, who have been chosen as the Temple He will come within, then you will see Him again, for He will be born again into this earth, only this time He comes as God within the lives of His anointed remnant. *"Behold, I shew you a mystery ... We shall all be changed."*

For the majority within the church, this change will await the coming of the Lord at the sound of the seventh trumpet, but for His anointed ones, who are the First Fruits of His resurrection, it comes upon them before the eyes of the whole earth.

THE MESSAGE OF THE FIRST DAY

In the first day, God created light and darkness, and God separated the light from the darkness. In the first 1,000 years of the history of man, God created Adam, and Adam sinned and was separated from God, and died just before the end of 1,000 years. God told Adam, the day you eat of this fruit, you shall die. Adam died at the age of 930 years near the end of the first day, just as God had said.

THE MESSAGE OF THE SECOND DAY

In the second day, God created the waters, and divided the waters from the heavens. In the second 1,000 years, Noah was saved when God judged the earth by water. The Lord divided the righteous from the wicked though the waters of judgment. "And the Lord said my spirit shall not always strive with man, for that he also is flesh: yet his days shall be an hundred and twenty years. The earth also was corrupt before God, and the earth was filled with violence. And God looked upon the earth, and, behold, it was corrupt; for all flesh had corrupted his way upon the earth. And God said unto Noah, The end of all flesh is come before me; for the earth is filled with violence through them; and, behold, I will destroy them with the earth." 6 The water is also a symbol of the Spirit of God. And at the last day, the Spirit will again divide mankind, and those without His Spirit will be cast out of the kingdom.

THE MESSAGE OF THE THIRD DAY

In the third day, God created the dry land, and the plants yielding fruit and seed after their own kind. At the start of the third 1,000 years, God called Abraham and gave him the promise of the seed which would come. This is the covenant of faith, which God planted into the hearts of the true sons of Israel. Notice, the seed produces after its own kind. This is one of God's laws of creation. That which is sown in the flesh produces after its own kind, whereas that which is sown into the spirit produces fruit unto eternal life.

THE MESSAGE OF THE FOURTH DAY

In the fourth day, God created the lights in the heavens to be signs for seasons and for days and for years. "It is he that builds his stories in the heaven, and hath founded his troop in the earth; he that calls for the waters of the sea, and pours them out upon the face of the earth: The Lord is his name."[7] During the fourth 1,000 year period, God began to send His prophets as lights unto the people to show them the signs of the seasons and to reveal to them those things which God had decreed must be. Isaiah, Jeremiah and the other prophets of Israel all came in the 1,000 years before the Messiah.

THE MESSAGE OF THE FIFTH DAY

In the fifth day, God created the living creatures, and He blessed them and saying "Be fruitful and multiply and fill the waters and the earth." At the beginning of the fifth day, 2,000 years ago, God sent Jesus Christ, the Messiah, to bring the new creation to mankind. Jesus is our redeemer and our deliverer from our sins; through His shed blood, we can be born again as a new creation before God.

THE MESSAGE OF THE SIXTH DAY

In the sixth day, "God created man in our image ... male and female created he them" and God blessed them and told them to be fruitful and multiply, and to fill the earth and have dominion over it. Notice God refers to Himself as "us" speaking of a plurality, for the Lord God Almighty is one, and he is Father, Son and Holy Spirit.

In the last 1,000 years, mankind has multiplied his knowledge and dominion of the earth. Man has even mounted unto the heavens having now walked upon the moon. Man has fulfilled his purpose given to him by God and now mankind stands on the threshold of the seventh day of creation, which is the Day of the Lord.

THE MESSAGE OF THE SEVENTH DAY

The seventh day is The Day of the Lord. In the seventh day God ended his work which He had made, and He rested. God blessed the seventh day, and sanctified it. God declares "I am the Lord of the Sabbath," and the seventh day is the Sabbath Day. The Sabbath Day is a picture of the Messiah and His rule.

In the seventh 1,000 years of the history of man upon the earth, God will bring the rule of his Messiah, and restore His Kingdom upon the earth. This is the millennium which is to come, and it begins with the judgment of God, the Day of Justice.

THE SIX THOUSAND YEARS
OF MANKIND UPON THE EARTH

The ancient scholars taught the 6,000 years doctrine, and it was widely held from the time of the first prophets. The Lord would make a quick work on the earth and all would be fulfilled within 6,000 years. The Lord declares mankind "is flesh: yet his days shall be an hundred and twenty years." The reference to the days of man being 120 years is also prophetic of the 120 Jubilees which the earth shall observe, and then the end of all flesh shall come. Noah spent one hundred and twenty years building the ark, and then the judgment came. Moses lived one hundred and twenty years, and then he died. *"And Moses was an hundred and twenty years old when he died: his eye was not dim, nor his natural force abated."* [8]

One of the reasons why the religious leaders in Jesus' day rejected him was because he did not fulfill the Messianic prophecies as they were expecting. One of these was the 6,000-year doctrine, and only then after the 6,000 years would the Messianic kingdom come. They concluded Jesus could not be the Messiah, for he came at the beginning of the fifth day. But they were ignorant of the truth: He would come twice, first as the Lamb of God, then again at the end of the age, as the Lion from the Tribe of Judah. Thus the oldest biblical prophecy, which is the story of creation, points to the soon coming of our Great King.

Today, the calendars we use are in error. The Jewish calendar lists the present year at the time of this writing as 5774 and it is wrong. Modern scholars believe the year count is off by 240 years, resulting from an error made after the first Babylonian exile. The proper year count following Rosh Hashanah on Sept. 25th 2014 is 6014. We know from the prophecy, the 70th Jubilee ended in 1999. There shall be one hundred and twenty Jubilees in creation, and then the Day of the Lord shall come.

We have already entered into the Day of the Lord but what has been hidden from the people is that before bringing his judgment, the Lord first brought forth a gentle rain of sound doctrine, and began to go and search for his lost sheep who had been scattered on the mountains of Babylon. That time is now ending, and the judgment of Almighty God is about to begin. It is midnight and mankind doesn't know it! While all of humanity is looking for peace and safety, sudden destruction is coming very soon.

THE FEASTS OF ISRAEL

The Seven Feasts of Israel all point to different works of the Messiah. The Feasts are prophetic of the ministry of the Messiah, and the progressive

246

revelation of God's truth to His people Israel. Jesus Christ fulfilled all of the Spring Feasts in His first coming. Many of the famous words and works of Jesus occurred at the various Feast days of Israel. This is one more example of the great falling away from the truth which has occurred here in these last days. Most of the Church is ignorant of the Feasts of the Lord, while they celebrate what are historically pagan holidays, which now are overlaid with a facade of Christianity. But the truth of Jesus has nothing to do with these pagan days, regardless of the facade in which they are now draped. The Truth of the Lord does not change to please the tradition of men. Jesus Christ is the King of the Jews, and He will fulfill the Fall Feasts in His Second Coming.

THE SPRING FEASTS OF ISRAEL
THE FIRST COMING OF THE LORD

In His first coming, Jesus fulfilled all three Spring Feasts literally. The harvest season began with the spring feasts of Israel, and the first crop which was reaped was the barley beginning with the Passover. Jesus was the Passover Lamb who was slain, and He died on Passover. During the seven days which follow Passover, all of Israel was commanded to eat nothing but unleavened bread. This seven-day feast of unleavened bread symbolized the sanctification of the true believer in the Spirit. The word *sanctify* means to be set apart from the world, and to be set apart unto God. This sanctification under the New Covenant is in the Spirit. Jesus warned us to beware of the leaven of the Pharisees. This is the leaven of false religious works, of hypocrisy, iniquity, legalism, and the doctrines of men. Jesus called these "*dead works.*" As believers under the New Covenant, we must empty ourselves of the leaven of religion, and keep the feast of unleavened bread in the spirit. "*Purge out therefore the old leaven, that ye may be a new lump, as ye are unleavened. For even Christ our Passover is sacrificed for us: Therefore let us keep the feast, not with old leaven, neither with the leaven of malice and wickedness; but with the unleavened bread of sincerity and truth.*" [9]

The unleavened bread of the New Covenant is holiness and truth in the inner man. The remnant are purged of the leaven of sin, false religion, and the lust of the world. The chosen ones walk before the Lord in holiness and truth. These are the true worshippers of which Jesus spoke: "*But the hour cometh, and now is, when the true worshippers shall worship the Father in spirit and in truth: for the Father seeketh such to worship him. God is a Spirit: and they that worship him must worship him in spirit and in truth.*"[10]

Those who survive and endure to the end of the seventieth week will be found without leaven, for only the pure will be counted worthy to stand before the Son of man in His coming!

THE DAY OF THE LORD IS AT HAND

THE FIRST FRUITS HARVEST OF THE LORD

Three days after the Passover lamb was slain, on the first day following the Sabbath at the end of the Passover week, the high priest would wave a sheaf of first ripe barley corn before the Lord on the Feast Day of First Fruits to give thanks to the Lord for the harvest which would come. The waving of the sheaf was done in the sign of the cross. After the waving, the corn was threshed and winnowed and all the chaff removed. A measure called the "Omer" was then presented before the Lord, and the high priest would take a handful of the now pure corn out of the Omer, and lift it in his hand before the Lord.

Jesus rose from the dead on the Feast Day of First Fruits and later that same day, the priests waved the sheaf of corn in the Temple and gave thanks before the Lord for the abundant harvest which was to come. Jesus rose as the First Fruits of the resurrection of Israel symbolizing the harvest which would come through His name.

The handful of corn raised up to God in the Temple is a picture of the anointed ones, who are the First Fruits of Jesus Christ in the Book of Revelation. They are the chosen ones, who walk the straight and narrow way that leads to a life of fullness in the Lord. The very nature of Jesus Christ will be born again within these people. These anointed ones are the man-child company of Revelation 12, and they have been chosen from among the remnant, which God shall redeem. They are the barley harvest of the Lord, and upon these sanctified saints will rest the high favor of God. They are the most holy of His little flock. They walk in the light of the Lord, and His face shines upon them. The remnant walk in humility before the Lord, and in them, he delights. Their sole desire is to serve and please the Lord. They have been chosen by the Father as the First Fruits of the harvest of Israel, and they shall be presented to his Son, Jesus as gift for his faithful service to the Father. They are the handful of corn, which is reaped first, before the wheat harvest of Pentecost. "*There shall be a handful of corn in the earth upon the top of the mountains; the fruit thereof shall shake like Lebanon: and they of the city shall flourish like grass of the earth.*" [11]

THE HOLY SEED SHALL BE HIS

The handful of "*corn on top of the mountains*" are pictured as standing with the Lord on Mount Zion in Revelation 14: "*And I looked, and, lo, a Lamb stood on the mount Zion, and with him an hundred forty and four thousand, having his Father's name written in their foreheads.*" They are described as a "*handful*" for they are in the Masters hand, and they are also "*the sons of his right hand.*"

248

Return Oh Lord, How Long?

Twelve thousand sons, from each of the twelve tribes of Israel, selected from among all the elect of God, who are now holy unto the Lord, having been utterly purged in the fire, so that they are no longer *"defiled with women"* for they no longer have any relations with Mystery Babylon or her false prophetess, that woman Jezebel. Now there is found within them, no guile, falsehood or sin. They are altogether holy unto the Lord having been purified in the fires of affliction, such that now *"they which follow the Lamb whithersoever he goes."* They are described as holy unto the Lord, for him only do they serve; they are now clean, and they are described as *"virgins"* for they have now become born again totally, and the life they now live is altogether holy unto God. They are redeemed from among men, and as such, they are the First Fruits unto God and to the Lamb.

As the holy seed of the Father, they shall come to destroy all of the works of the devil, and it is for them that Zion travails. In sorrow and anguish they will be born, *"a remnant seed of the woman Israel."* [12] Only when the corn is ripe, in the time of spring, will the new year begin, but the corn must be ready first, so that it may line up with the cornerstone, for it is the cornerstone, now within the corn, through which this work of the kingdom shall be done.

The resurrection life of Jesus Christ is foreshadowed in the Feast of First Fruits which followed Passover. After the death of our Savior, at dusk, the priests cut down a sheaf of Barley, the first ripe standing grain. *"Ye shall bring a sheaf of the first fruits of your harvest"*[13] The Sheaf is representative of the first fruits of Jesus Christ, the 144,000, who I refer to as the anointed remnant, for they shall stand before God and follow the Lamb *"whither so ever he goes"* for

> *"these were redeemed from among men, being the first fruits unto God and to the Lamb. And in their mouth was found no guile: for they are without fault before the throne of God."* [14]

Malachi speaks of the whole company of the remnant whom the Lord God shall spare during the tribulation:

> *"Then they that feared the Lord spoke often one to another: and the Lord hearkened, and heard it, and a book of remembrance was written before him for them that feared the Lord, and that thought upon his name. And they shall be mine, saith the Lord of hosts, in that day when I make up my jewels; and I will spare them, as a man spares his own son that serves him. Then shall ye return, and discern between the righteous and the wicked, between him that serves God and him that serves him not."* [16]

These lowly saints fear the Lord. They tremble before Him, as they speak often one to another. They have been rejected by the Church, who cannot bear to hear the word of truth which they have received, so they speak only to each other, and share the mysteries which God has hidden within His word. The Lord hearkens as His little ones speak in fear of His name. Among them are found the saints who are in travail, and who are about to give birth to the kingdom. They weep, and cry aloud in anguish, to be delivered from the sin within. They fear the Lord, for they know the fierce judgment which is about to begin.

Like Noah, this little remnant has been shown the time and manner of judgment which will come. The Lord will save each one of them, as a man spares his own son, who labors for him. They are described as the holy seed, for they do the will of the Father. They are all found laboring only for the Lord. Because they fear His name, they have put their trust in no other, and therefore the Lord will have compassion upon them, and the Lord will command his angels to save them, and they will be given charge to deliver them!

> In You, O Lord, I put my trust; let me never be put to shame. Deliver me in Your righteousness, and cause me to escape; incline Your ear to me, and save me. Be my strong refuge, to which I may resort continually; you have given the Commandment to save me, for you are my rock and my fortress. Deliver me, O my God, out of the hand of the wicked, out of the hand of the unrighteous and cruel man. [17]

Oh the praise His little remnant shall bring as an offering before the Lord, for in His mercy, He has commanded His angels to save them in this hour! The word used for save is יָשַׁע, yasha' and it is the root word for the name of the Savior himself, Yeshua. It means to be free, to be safe, to avenge and defend, to deliver, to help, to preserve, to rescue, and to receive the victory. Yeshua is His name, and it will be written upon the foreheads of each one of the holy seeds whom He saves in this hour.

The remnant is likened unto Jeremiah, for they have the very words of God in their mouth. "For you are my hope, O Lord God; you are my trust from my youth. By you I have been upheld from birth; you are he who took me out of my mother's womb. My praise shall be continually of you. I have become as a wonder to many, but you are my strong refuge." [18]

As the prophets of old, the holy seed was chosen from the womb by God, and they will become a wonder to many. The word for *wonder* is מוֹפֵת, mowpheth [19] for they are a miracle, a token and an omen. The deliverance of the remnant in this hour is a miracle, and they are the token of His grace, the first fruits of His resurrection. When you see the armies which have assembled against this nation, and the persecution against the Church, you will understand the miracle of the Lord that any are spared. They are the gleaning which is left behind in the land, for they will be hidden in the secret hiding place of Most High God. And Yeshua will become their salvation. *"The upright shall dwell in the land, and the perfect shall remain. But the wicked shall be cut off from the earth, and the transgressors shall be rooted out of it."*[20]

The word used for *shall dwell* is שָׁכַן *shaw-kan* [21] which means to reside or permanently stay, to abide, and to continue, to remain, and to be at rest. At the time of the end, the remnant will continue to *dwell* in the land, and they will have learned to *abide* in the Sabbath rest of the Lord. They will have continued on and followed the Lord to the cross and will have died to self. They will have ceased from their own works, so that they are now found perfect in Him, are therefore worthy to escape all these things.

The word used for the *perfect* is תָּמִים, *tamiym* [22] which means moral integrity, truth, without blemish, complete, full of sincerity, without spot, undefiled, upright, and perfect. These *perfect* ones shall remain in the land, for they are the righteous ones whom the Lord deems worthy to escape all these things and to stand before Him at the Second Coming.

The word for *shall remain* is יָתַר, *yathar* [23] which means to remain or be left behind; to preserve a remnant. This proverb is a prophecy of the remnant. They walk before the Lord in moral integrity and truth. In the eyes of the Lord they are without blemish, undefiled and upright. This holy remnant abides in Jesus Christ. They have continued on to the cross and have surrendered to Jesus as Lord. They are His precious ones, His dearly beloved ones and He will protect His own! And they shall remain, and they will be left behind while all of the others are taken into captivity.

They are the gleaning left in the land, which was hidden by the Lord during the harvest judgment. He will preserve them as His remnant. The remnant of the Lord, who are the First Fruits of Jesus Christ, are those who remain and who are left behind. *"Watch ye therefore, and pray always, that ye may be accounted worthy to escape all these things that shall come to pass, and to stand before the Son of man."*[24]

THE YEAR OF TRANSITION

A year of transition has been appointed by God. While the nations of the earth make ready for the Great War, which begins the final judgment, in the lives of the remnant God begins equipping them for their long journey ahead. He prepares them, making them ready to overcome in the days in which the Seals of Revelation shall be opened. During the year of transition, the remnant shall be quickened by the Spirit of God during the counting of the Omer, which shall be the final countdown, before the judgment of God is released in the summer which will follow. And the remnant shall know to gather together in solemn assemblies, and in times of fasting and prayer before the Lord.

They shall all be of one accord in the Spirit, far from the religious who accuse them and contend with the word of the Lord, who in their self-righteousness and in the blindness of their own minds, have dismissed the warnings from heaven, and so are unable to hear the truth. In the year of transition, the sickle will be put to the corn once again, and then the count of the Omer will begin. Following the offering of the First Fruits unto the Lord, and after the seven weeks of the Omer, the judgment upon the church will begin, pictured by the cutting down of the wheat during the summer harvest season.

The sickle is put to the corn in the latter rain season of the first month of the sacred calendar. The reaping takes place after the "almond" trees have bloomed. "*And it came to pass, that on the morrow Moses went into the tabernacle of witness; and, behold, the rod of Aaron for the house of Levi was budded, and brought forth buds, and bloomed blossoms, and yielded almonds.*"[26]

The almond tree is the first to bloom in the land, and represents the anointed leadership appointed by the Lord. "*He spake unto Korah and unto all his company, saying, even tomorrow the Lord will shew who are his, and who is holy; and will cause him to come near unto him: even him whom he hath chosen will he cause to come near unto him.*" [27]

During the Great Tribulation which will follow, the Lord will again show who are his, and those who are holy unto Him, for he will anoint and then save his remnant, as the judgment of God begins; while all of those who have raised themselves up, appointing themselves as leaders and teachers in his house, who in truth, were only seeking to exalt themselves, they shall all be cut down as in the rebellion of Korah, who perished in the wilderness.

The First Fruits are represented by the *corn*, and the word used is בר *bar*,[28] which means a winnowing of grain, standing in the field, and the barley which was cut down during the Feast of Unleavened Bread. "*And as soon as the commandment came abroad, the children of Israel brought in abundance the first fruits of corn, wine, and oil, and honey, and of all the increase of the fields; and the tithe of all things brought they in abundantly.*"[29] All of Israel is commanded to count the time from when the sickle is put to the corn, which is the Omer of the Passover. This is the time of the latter day rain, and the remnant will know to gather together during the omer, all of them in one accord. There they will await the fire of the Lord. Count the days, for after seven Sabbath weeks, on the fiftieth day, the fire will fall once again. *"The thing that hath been, it is that which shall be; and that which is done is that which shall be done: and there is no new thing under the sun."*[30]

As in the day the one hundred and twenty gathered in the upper room, so shall it be again. The end of all flesh is at hand, and for the remnant it will begin with the end of the mind of flesh. God's pattern never changes, and to those who see in the Spirit, with the mind of truth, the count of the omer will soon begin. A great cleansing of the presence of the Lord is coming to His chosen ones. We are to pray, *"Ask ye of the Lord rain in the time of the latter rain; so the Lord shall make bright clouds, and give them showers of rain, to every one grass in the field."*[31] The word for *bright clouds* is חזיז, *khaw-zeez*[32] which means a flash of lightning or a bright cloud. The clouds are the anointed messengers who are coming in his power and full of the Shekinah Glory of God.

The end of the present age is the time when all men shall become afraid, and fear shall be in the streets. *"When they shall be afraid of that which is high, and fears shall be in the way, and the almond tree shall flourish, and the grasshopper shall be a burden, and desire shall fail: because man goes to his long home, and the mourners go about the streets"* [33] In that same time, the anointed leadership of the Lord, pictured as an almond tree, shall flourish once again. Jeremiah was shown an almond tree in the spirit to confirm his appointment by the Lord. *"See, I have this day set thee over the nations and over the kingdoms, to root out, and to pull down, and to destroy, and to throw down, to build, and to plant. Moreover the word of the Lord came unto me, saying, Jeremiah, what seest thou? And I said, I see a rod of an almond tree."* [34]

As a Holy prophet, appointed by the Lord, Jeremiah was given authority and power to pull down and destroy nations and it was through Jeremiah's prophetic word, that the Lord decreed the coming judgment. In these last days, the anointed almond trees of the Lord shall fulfill his mission, completing the work which Jeremiah began, and which was written in the scroll for all of time by his servant, Baruch. The anointed ones of Israel shall come forth as these holy prophets once did, and they shall pick up their work, for they shall declare with a loud voice, the prophetic judgments of God, and by their words, they shall bring forth the judgment upon the nations of the earth.

> *"The adversaries of the Lord shall be broken to pieces; out of heaven shall he thunder upon them: the Lord shall judge the ends of the earth; and he shall give strength unto his king, and exalt the horn of his anointed."*[35]

The word for *shall thunder* is רעם, *ra' am*[36] and it means to be violently agitated, as in crashing thunder, to be irritated with anger, and to make to trouble. The anointed messengers of the Lord Jesus Christ will bring forth the prophetic decrees of judgment with "thunder." They will violently oppose all forms of darkness, and will be violently agitated against the enemies of God. They will also irritate their apostate listeners who cannot tolerate the bright light of the true words of God. "*The voice of thy thunder was in the heaven: the lightnings lightened the world: the earth trembled and shook.*"[37] The thunder of God is His prophetic voice, and it will be revealed through these anointed ones. The verse declares that God's prophetic voice "*in the heavens*" comes forth as a whirlwind upon the earth.

The prophetic thunder of God's messengers will be heard in their prophetic declarations of the whirlwind about to come from the Lord! The thunder is contrasted with God's *lightnings*, which will enlighten the world with his truth. The word for *light* is אוֹר, *ore* [39] which means to be luminous, as the break of day, glorious, and to kindle and set on fire, to be enlightened and to shine. The word used for *lightened* the world is בַּרַק, *baraq* [40] which means a flashing sword, or a bright glittering sword, full of lightning. The anointed remnant will bring the whirlwind down, and they will bring the judgment to pass, for they will hold the flashing sword of the word of the Lord in their hands, and with it they shall kindle a fire upon the nations!

These are the Lions from Judah, God's anointed remnant, and they will cause the earth to tremble. The word for *tremble* is רָגַז *ragaz* [41] which means to quiver with violent emotions of anger or fear, and to be sorely afraid, to stand in awe, to be provoked, to be troubled, and to become wroth. The message of God's judgment will initially provoke the heathen and the apostates to anger against the word of the Lord and the messengers of His covenant but as the Lord Himself begins to thunder, and as His word is revealed upon the earth in the fire it kindles, their anger shall turn into sheer terror before the messengers of the Lord. The word of God will come with the force of a whirlwind, and then the apostates and the heathen will be filled with fear as the judgment begins to be poured out. His messengers will become as coals of fire in that hour, burning even the very ground on which they stand along with the ears of the people who surround them.

The voice of God's prophets will be heard as the sound of thunder from the heavens as his word begins to manifest in the whirlwind which will be falling upon the earth. With a flashing sword, "*the lightning*" of the word of the Lord will be revealed to all flesh. The fire of thy lightning will kindle upon the whole world, and all the people of the earth shall tremble and shake. They will stand in awe before thee, and will be overcome with fear of the Lord. They shall all be troubled, and will shake with fear when the prophecies of these messengers begin to be fulfilled. "*Who hath divided a*

watercourse for the overflowing of waters, or a way for the lightning of thunder?" [42]
The word used for *thunder* in this passage is קֹל *kole* [43] meaning to call aloud,
with a voice or a sound, to cry out loud, and proclaim, thundering, and to yell.

THE FEAST OF SHAVUOT

The Israelites were to count from the day of Passover seven Sabbaths, and
then on the following 50th day, they were to observe the Feast of Shavuot,
which the gentiles call Pentecost. The Torah was given unto Moses on the
Feast day of Shavuot, when he first ascended the mountain to appear before
the Lord, and when the mountain burned at the presence of the King. This
feast day foreshadowed the day when the Lord would fulfill His promise to
give a New Covenant to Israel. This is the day the Lord chooses to come
down, and in Moses's time, the mountain burned. *"And the Lord said unto
Moses, Go unto the people, and sanctify them today and tomorrow, and let them
wash their clothes, And be ready against the third day: for the third day the Lord will
come down in the sight of all the people."* [44] The third day is also the time
appointed when the Lord will once again come down, and be revealed in a
remnant of his people, and on that day *"the Son of man shall be revealed"* and it
will occur on the third day, just as Jesus said. *"After two days will he revive us:
in the third day he will raise us up, and we shall live in his sight."* [45]

Following the death of the Passover Lamb of God, the law of the Spirit was
written upon the hearts of men just as the Lord promised through the words
of Jeremiah 500 years earlier. The outpouring of the Spirit under the New
Covenant followed the Passover by fifty days exactly. Shavuot marks the
beginning of the wheat harvest of Israel. The wheat represents the people of
God, and the last days harvest of the earth begins within the Church. *"Now
therefore stand and see this great thing, which the Lord will do before your eyes. Is it
not wheat harvest to day? I will call unto the Lord, and he shall send thunder and
rain; that ye may perceive and see that your wickedness is great, which ye have done
in the sight of the Lord ...and all the people greatly feared the Lord."* [46] The Lord
allowed leaven to be used in the two loaves presented in the temple at
Shavuot. The two loaves foreshadowed the congregation of Jews and
Gentiles who would be part of spiritual Israel. The leaven represents the sin
which would be found within the compromising people. The two loaves are
full of leaven within, so therefore they must be baked.

The compromising Church will be placed within an oven and purified in the
fire at the end of the age, during the Great Tribulation. *"And the people shall be
as the burnings of lime: as thorns cut up shall they be burned in the fire. Hear, ye
that are far off, what I have done; and, ye that are near, acknowledge my might. The
sinners in Zion are afraid; fearfulness hath surprised the hypocrites."* [47]

THE DAY OF THE LORD IS AT HAND

Those who are to cut up like thorns, and burned in the fire of the Great Tribulation are the ones who have hidden the leaven of sin within their hearts; therefore, they are to be cut off and burned, and saved as if through the fire, in order to purify them for the wedding feast. The sinners in His house will all become afraid on that day, and absolute fear and terror will surprise the hypocrites! *"Knowing therefore the terror of the Lord, we persuade men."*[48] May we be accounted worthy to be found among the remnant that the Lord shall choose as His first fruit in a field of corn before the day when the wheat fields shall all burn.

The seven Sabbath weeks which occur between Passover and Shavuot are a picture of the prophecy of seven weeks of years, which Daniel prophesied would occur before the coming of the Messiah as a Prince, in the lives of the anointed ones. *"Seven weeks shall thou number unto thee: begin to number the seven weeks from such time as thou begins to put the sickle to the corn. And thou shalt keep the feast of weeks unto the Lord thy God with a tribute of a freewill offering of thine hand, which thou shalt give unto the Lord thy God, according as the Lord thy God hath blessed thee."* [50]

The Feast of Passover symbolized the first coming of the Lord as the Lamb of God. The Feast of Shavuot is symbolic of the final Jubilee in which Israel will celebrate the deliverance of the people, and it is the Feast of Shavuot which separates the corn harvest from the wheat. The seven weeks prophecy of Daniel will be fulfilled within or shortly after the 50th year following the command to restore Jerusalem in the Spring of 2021 on the day of Nissan 1 .

The remnant will know to make ready during the counting of the Omer, following the Passover of the year. The 50th day from the Passover will open the door in the spirit, as God will again bring his deliverance and restoration in the lives of his remnant, before the beginning of the Great and Terrible Day of the Lord. The feast of Pentecost (which occurs on the 50th day) is symbolic of the Jubilee (the 50th year) and during this final Jubilee, the remnant shall be anointed with power from on high; after the anointing of the remnant, to prepare them, the Day of the Lord will begin in the summer which follows.

> *I saw four angels standing on the four corners of the earth, holding the four winds of the earth, that the wind should not blow on the earth, nor on the sea, nor on any tree. And I saw another angel ascending from the east, having the seal of the living God: and he cried with a loud voice to the four angels, to whom it was given to hurt the earth and the sea, Saying, Hurt not the earth, neither the sea, nor the trees, till we have sealed the servants of our God in their foreheads.* [51]

THE FALL FEASTS OF THE SECOND COMING

Jesus will fulfill the fall feasts of Israel in the second coming. The fall feasts are preceded by the time of Teshuvah, the final ten days of repentance, which follow the month of Elul, and these together being a total of forty days of repentance provided by the Lord before Yom Kippur. These days include the Feast of Trumpets, which is Rosh Hashanah. The Feast of Trumpets calls the people to repent and return to the Lord during the final ten days of Awe before the great day of the Lord on Yom Kippur, the Day of Atonement. Following Yom Kippur is the seventh Feast of Israel, which is known as the Feast of Tabernacles or Sukkot.

The civil new year of Israel begins with the blowing of the Shofar, on the first day of the seventh month of the spiritual calendar. The trumpets announce the beginning of the ten days of Awe which precede the Day of Atonement. The trumpets are a prophetic announcement in the spirit of the coming Day of the Lord. Solomon's temple was completed in the seventh month, which is a picture of the completed spiritual temple of God in the last days, for it too, shall be completed during the fall feasts of Israel.

Yom Kippur represents the Day of the Lord and is a picture of how we are to approach the judgment day of our God. It is a day of fasting and mourning, and of weeping and lamenting, for God takes no joy in the judgment of the wicked, or in the purging fire with which he must purify the people who are all hardened in sin, being bound up in their pride, and thus full of only compromise within. Therefore, we his people are to be silent and abstain from all pleasure on this day as a reminder to us, of the great price required to provide atonement for our sins. Yom Kippur also marks the day of proclaiming the Year of Jubilee. Only after the atonement, could the forgiveness and redemption begin. Lastly, after the tribulation of those days, Yeshua will fulfill The Feast of Tabernacles which is the seventh feast; it will be fulfilled on the day of his Second Coming, which shall be the last day of this present age, and the day when the resurrection of the dead and then the rapture of the remnant will occur. Will we know the day or hour? No. Even during the final Feast of Tabernacles, we will wait as Israel once did, to enter the Promised Land. So too, we among God's remnant who are counted worthy to stand on the final Feast of Tabernacles will wait, while the sign of the Son of Man appears in the heavens, for no man knows the day or the hour, not even the Son of man. And this word will be true, even during the last seven days of the history of this world, for we won't know which day of the seven-day feast, he will actually come again, but every eye shall see him, and all the families of the earth will mourn because of him.

THE DAY OF THE LORD IS AT HAND

The Great Tribulation begins at the Feast of Purim, which is celebrated at the end of winter. Purim represents God's deliverance of Israel from the antichrist. The tribulation will begin around the feast of Purim, on a Sabbath day, and at the end of winter not many years hence. But can we discern any insights into the timing of these events from the Scriptures?

THE PARABLE OF THE FIG TREE

Jesus commanded us to learn the meaning of the parable of the Fig Tree which is Israel. When Israel puts forth her leaves again, you will know that summer is near. The meaning of this parable is that when Israel begins to shoot forth her leaves, then you know the generation which witnesses the restoration of the nation, shall also witness the fulfillment of all things which were written. The Lord said we would know *"summer is near"* and the Lord doesn't waste His words. He chose *"summer"* as a warning. For the judgment upon the Church in the last days begins in the season of summer.

During the writing of this seventh edition, the first frost of winter came upon the northern parts of our nation in the month of November. As the winter cold began to descend upon the land, the Lord shouted loudly in the early morning hours, and his words startled me, awakening me from my sleep, as if a bomb had gone off in my room. I heard him shout loudly and clearly:

Summer is coming soon!
Tell the people to clean their houses!

HIDDEN PROPHECIES IN THE PSALMS

Now learn the parable of the fig tree; When his branch is yet tender, and puts forth leaves, you know that summer is nigh: So likewise ye, when ye shall see all these things, know that it is near, even at the doors. Verily I say unto you, this generation shall not pass, till all these things are fulfilled. Matthew 24:32-34

Hear this, all ye people; give ear, all ye inhabitants of the world: Both low and high, rich and poor, together. My mouth shall speak of wisdom; and the meditation of my heart shall be of understanding. I will incline mine ear to a parable: I will open my dark saying upon the harp. Wherefore should I fear in the days of evil, when the iniquity of my heels shall compass me about? Psalm 49:3-4

Return Oh Lord, How Long?

In Psalm 49, David declares "*I will open my dark saying upon the harp*" [52]. The 'dark saying' to be revealed has been hidden within one of the Psalms. Psalm 49 also speaks of the men of wisdom who would hear the word of the Lord and then gain understanding through meditation or careful study of this matter declaring "*the meditation of my heart shall be of understanding.*" As the Men of Wisdom begin to understand, they would open this dark saying to the many. But which parable is revealed within the Psalms? The hidden secret revealed within the Psalms is the mystery of the parable of the fig tree, the only parable we were commanded by Jesus to study and learn the meaning of.

The mystery of this parable is revealed in Psalm 90, the only Psalm written by Moses, and the dark saying is the number of years which would mark the life and times of the restored nation of Israel in the last days, before the fulfillment of all these things would come. The life of the restored nation of Israel is the length of a generation, as Jesus told us, and the mystery of the parable we were instructed to learn, reveals the length of the generation that would witness both the re-birth of the state of Israel and the fulfillment of all these things - the final judgment of God and the return of the Lord.

In Psalm 90, Moses asks the question regarding the return of the Lord, saying "*Return Oh Lord, How long?*" Bible scholars for the most part have completely missed the significance of this text, yet the Psalm gives us insight into the timing of the Judgment of our God. The Psalm declares that from the beginning of time, and before the mountains were brought forth, or even the creation of the earth itself, from eternity past, the Holy One of Israel was the true King of the Universe. He alone is God and blessed be His Holy Name, whose kingdom is forever and blessed are the ones who come in the name of the Lord to give understanding to the many.

Moses declares the mysteries of these times have been established by God, for a thousand years in his sight, are but one day. And when the days are done, then the Lord will carry them away with a flood. The ones carried away are those who are spiritually dead. In the morning, they grow up like the grass, but soon the sun rises, and in the heat of the day they dry up and are withered and then they are all blown away.

> *Before the mountains were brought forth, or ever thou has formed the earth and the world, even from everlasting to everlasting, thou art God. For a thousand years in thy sight are but as yesterday when it is past, and as a watch in the night. Thou carries them away as with a flood; they are as sleep: in the morning they are like grass which grows up. Psalm 90:2-5*

259

THE DAY OF THE LORD IS AT HAND

TEACH US TO NUMBER OUR DAYS

Moses then asks the Lord, "teach us to count the number of our days, that we might apply our hearts to wisdom; how long will it be until your return Lord?" He continues asking the Lord to repent concerning His servants; that He would not destroy all of them along with all the many who have been appointed to destruction in the judgment of the last days.

> *"So teach us to number our days, that we may apply our hearts unto wisdom. Return, O Lord, how long? and let it repent thee concerning thy servants."*[53]

In verse ten, the Spirit reveals the answer to this prayer of Moses that we might know when would be the time of His coming among us:

> *"The days of our years are threescore years and ten; and if by reason of strength they be fourscore years, yet is their strength labor and sorrow; for it is soon cut off, and we fly away."*[54]

The years appointed to the reborn state of Israel in the last days will be seventy, and only by strength in times of trouble shall they be eighty, for we are soon cut off, and fly away. Shortly at the end of these years, Israel shall be *"cut off"* in the destruction of the Great War which is the war of Ezekiel 38. So how should this be understood? The word of God requires that every word of truth must be confirmed with two or more witnesses in order for us to receive a word of testimony as the truth, or we cannot be lawfully certain of a matter. So, when did Israel put forth her leaves? The prophet Haggai commands us to watch for the date on which the cornerstone of the temple was twice laid, the 24th day of the 9th month. Haggai tells us to consider it. This is the day we are told to watch, for on this same day, the cornerstone for the 2nd restoration of the nation would be also be laid.

On December 19th of 1917, which was the 24th day of the 9th month on the Hebrew calendar, General Allenby conquered Jerusalem for the British Empire. In November of that year, the British government issued the Balfour Declaration, agreeing to support the return of the Jews back to the land of Israel. For the first time in 2,000 years, the mountains of Israel began to put forth their leaves again. And the ruling empire of the earth at that time, had committed itself to support it. Consider it. These events in 1917 opened the door for the people to begin coming home in large numbers. Both Haggai and Ezekiel provide keys to this part of God's great secret which has remained hidden within the Scriptures all these years.

Return Oh Lord, How Long?

> *Consider now from this day and upward, from the four and twentieth day of the ninth month, even from the day that the foundation of the Lord's temple was laid, consider it.*[55] *But ye, O mountains of Israel, ye shall shoot forth your branches, and yield your fruit to my people of Israel; for they are at hand to come.* [57]

The return to the land began with the first Aliyah which occurred from 1882 to 1903. In 1917 the Balfour Declaration was issued by Britain and the return of the people to the land of Israel received the political support of the world's super power at that time. The door to the land was formally opened and the nation itself stood up, some thirty years later, in 1948. But where do we begin to measure the budding of the fig tree and the life of the state of Israel as prophesied in the Psalms? Do we look to 1917 or 1948, the year in which Independence was declared, or perhaps we should begin in 1949, the year in which the first elected government of Israel came to power, and the year in which the United States formally recognized the new nation?

The Scriptures present us with a second riddle regarding the timing of the events at the end of the age, this time asking who will discern the timing of the judgment of the daughter of Babylon as prophesied by Jeremiah in chapters 50 and 51.

WHO WILL APPOINT ME THE TIME?

> *Behold, he shall come up like a lion from the swelling of Jordan unto the habitation of the strong: but I will make them suddenly run away from her: and who is a chosen man, that I may appoint over her? for who is like me? and who will appoint me the time? and who is that shepherd that will stand before me? Jeremiah 50:44*

In Jeremiah's prophecies regarding the judgment of the United States, the Lord asks the question: who will appoint or discern the timing for judgment of America Babylon? Who will declare the time of her fall? Who will give the legal summons to America demanding she appear for her trial by fire? This prophetic riddle is one of the tests required of the men of wisdom hidden within the scriptures.

This is the only verse of bible prophecy where the text reveals that timing of the judgment would be discerned beforehand yet this discernment is not itself a prophecy, as the text does not say, 'who will I reveal the timing to beforehand'. The text uses the word 'appoint' which is the word יָעַד, ya‵ad and it means to *fix* by agreement or appointment; to *summon* to a trial, to appoint or discern a time. Thus, the discernment of the timing of the judgment of America Babylon would not come through a prophetic revelation, but rather would be discerned after careful study and meditation on the parable of the fig tree, and its unveiling within the prophecies hidden within the Psalms; and like the words of God, it too would be purified over time.

The words of the LORD are pure words: as silver tried in a furnace of earth, purified seven times. Psalm 12:6

HIDDEN RIDDLES WITHIN BIBLE PROPHECY

The bible contains a number of prophetic riddles of end time events hidden within Scripture, and the correct answer of these riddles will confirm the men of wisdom who were foretold to come in these last days.

1. The identity of the antichrist described in Revelation 13.
2. The identity of Mystery Babylon and the beast on which she rides described in Revelation 17 and 18.
3. The meaning of the parable of the fig tree which reveals the timing for the fulfillment of all bible prophecy.
4. The timing for the judgment of Babylon in Jeremiah 50:44.
5. The timing for the birth of the man-child of Revelation 12 as prophesied in Daniel's seven weeks prophecy of Daniel 9.

The revealing of the first two of these riddles, the identity of Mystery Babylon at the end of the age and of the antichrist, the prince who is to come, are presented in Chapters 5 and 7. These riddles were relatively easy to solve whereas the final three were anything but. In earlier versions of this book I attempted to reason through the questions presented by the final three riddles; in this final version of the 7th edition I will present the now complete answers.

THE GENERATION THAT SHALL NOT PASS AWAY

I began diligently studying the parable of the fig tree in the fall of 1996, after I was translated into the future and witnessed the beginning of the Day of the Lord. Remember, Jesus commanded us saying, *"now learn the parable of the fig tree"* and of the generation that *"would not pass away until all these things are fulfilled."* Psalm 90 reveals the generation of this parable as 70 years, and if by strength, then the generation would witness 80 years. The Psalm itself reveals the life or the times of the final generation, which would witness both the budding of the fig tree, and the fulfillment of all things, but the Psalm also warns the nation would "soon be cut off" within this time.

Return Oh Lord, How Long?

In discerning the parable, we must first discern the starting date. In earlier editions of this book, I assumed the starting date for this riddle was 1917, but as time passed that date clearly had to be rejected, leaving us with 1948 or 1949 as the only other candidates. The correct answer to the life of the State of Israel at the end of the age is 82.7 year, the actual life expectancy of the average Israeli. This answer is confirmed in Psalm 82 verse 7, "you shall die like men." Men die based upon life expectancy. The year 1949 is also a Jubilee year for Israel, which confirmed by the birth of Jesus in 2 BC, also a Jubilee year.

Birth of the Nation	1949
82.7 Years	2031
WW III Outside Date	2024

Thus, the outside date for World War III would be the fall of 2024 based upon the parable of the fig tree. reasoned by using 82.7 years for the actuarial life for final generation of Israel, and thus is the correct answer for the outside date for the final generation. World war III must take place no later than 2024 or seven years prior, based upon Ezekiel's prophecy that following the war, the people of Israel will burn the weapons for seven years.

And Israel shall go forth, and shall set on fire and burn the weapons…
and they shall burn them with fire for seven years. Ezekiel 39:9

The birth of the nation must be measured from the year 1949, the first year of peace for Israel following the war of Independence, and after Israel was formally recognized by the United States, then the final corrected time line is:

Birth of the Nation	1949
70 Years	2019
WW III Outside Date	2024
82.7 years	2031

The fact that Jesus told us we would need to 'learn' the meaning of this parable implies this would take both time and serious study. The answer to this riddle would only be discerned through much effort and commitment and would not come forth as a prophecy but rather through the hard labor of students of the word who would approach this subject like Bereans. The text in Psalm 90 which reads "*if by reason of strength*" uses the Hebrew word בגבורת, *gheb-oo-rote* which means *force*; or, mighty power, or strength. This word is a derivative of the word *gheb-oo-oeim* which is used to describe the mighty ones, who are the 144,000 and its use in Psalm 90 may imply that after the 70th year, the survival of the nation will rest on the shoulders of the man-child company who are the mighty ones which Daniel prophesied would be born after seven-weeks in the fall of the year 2024 or shortly thereafter. The year 2024 also appears to be confirmed by the sign of Revelation 12 which appeared in the heavens in September of 2107, exactly seven years prior to the date prophesied in Daniel using the spiritual calendar beginning with the month of Nissan in the spirit. Assuming the sign in the heavens in 2017 heralds the birth of the man-child company similar to the star of Bethlehem which heralded the birth of Jesus Christ approximately seven years following its appearance in Matthew, 2024 or shortly thereafter as the date for the birth of the man-child appears confirmed.

THE 70 YEAR CAPTIVITY OF ISRAEL

The Lord restored the nation back to their land in 1948 but he did not restore the people back to himself. Though the nation was regathered in the natural, spiritually the people have been left in captivity to their sin. The judgment of the Lord brought the people of ancient Israel into slavery to Babylon in the natural. In the last days, the prophecy of 70 years of captivity under the rule of Babylon by Jeremiah has been fulfilled a second time with the regathered state of Israel born in slavery under the rule of America Babylon in the spirit. This rule also would last 70 years, expiring in March of 2021. The true king of Babylon is Satan, and his throne over the earth in the last days sits in England, which is the head of the lion that rules over the nations through its power over its descendant empire, America, which are the wings of the eagle of Daniel 7.

The king of Babylon has ruled over the secular state of Israel throughout its history. This is evidenced by the occult symbolism of design of the Knesset, the origin of the state by UN action, the Balfour declaration at the hand of the Lord Rothschild and the British, and lastly the Americans forcing the division of the land under the Oslo accord. The spiritual slavery of the Israeli people is also without debate: 70% of Israelis are atheist, while the religious in Israel themselves are also under deception, following the teachings of men, the Rabbis who rejected the Messiah, perceiving the word of God only through the law of the flesh, the Torah, with almost no understanding of things of the spirit, while only a remnant actually knows the Lord. But the 70 years of slavery will come to an end WW3, and with their end, the 70th week of Daniel will then begin in the year 2024..

In Ezekiel 39:22, God declares that following the Great War, "the house of Israel shall know that I am the Lord their God from that day." And in Ezekiel 39:25 following WW3, "now I will restore the captivity of Jacob, and have mercy upon the whole house of Israel." Thus, the end of the 70 years of spiritual captivity of the re-born state of Israel will occur following the war of Ezekiel 38, a war in which America will be destroyed in one hour.

Return Oh Lord, How Long?

THE 70 YEAR REIGN OF BABYLON

Jeremiah prophesied that Israel would be taken into captivity and serve the King of Babylon for seventy years for their sins against the Lord and when the seventy years were fulfilled, God would judge the king of Babylon and that nation by the hand of Cyrus, king of the Medes and Persians.

> *The nations shall serve the king of Babylon seventy years and when seventy years are accomplished, I will punish the king of Babylon, and that nation, saith the LORD, for their iniquity, and the land of the Chaldeans, and will make it a perpetual desolation. Jeremiah 25:11-12*

If we look closely at the 2nd half of this prophecy, the reference to the "land of the Chaldeans" which would become a perpetual desolation, was not fulfilled in the fall of ancient Babylon, nor was the nation of Babylon reduced to a perpetual desolation at the time of her judgment, as the people continued their lives without much interruption following the conquest of the nation by Cyrus whose first action was to free all of the slaves. Rather than being physically destroyed, the ancient city of Babylon and its people were left unharmed. Yet the text in Jeremiah 25:12 reveals the land of the Chaldeans would become an utter desolation at the time of its judgment. So, what exactly is the meaning of this reference, 'the land of the Chaldeans' and why has this part of the prophecy not yet been fulfilled? The prophecies in Jeremiah 50 and 51 describe the judgment upon America as the daughter of Babylon at the end of age. In this section of scripture, America is referred to as the land of the Chaldeans seven times, and the scripture is emphatically clear, the land of America will become a complete desolation at the time of her judgment. None of the prophecies within Jeremiah 50 and 51 were fulfilled in the fall of ancient Babylon.

> *How is the hammer of the whole earth broken! how is Babylon become a desolation among the nations! And the land shall tremble and sorrow: for every purpose of the LORD shall be performed to make the land of Babylon a desolation without an inhabitant. Jeremiah 50:23, 51:29, 43*

The sword that came upon the King of Babylon in the time of Jeremiah did not come upon the inhabitants of Babylon, the sword only came upon the king and the ruling elite. The inhabitants of Babylon continued to live their lives as if nothing happened. In much of the empire, they didn't know the kingdom had fallen for several months. Yet in Jeremiah 50, we are told the sword will come upon the inhabitants of the daughter of Babylon.

> *A sword is upon the Chaldeans, and upon the inhabitants of Babylon, and upon her princes, and upon her wise men. Jeremiah 50:35*

THE DAY OF THE LORD IS AT HAND

In the judgment of ancient Babylon, the army of the Medes slipped in quietly under the cover of darkness and when the people awoke in the morning it was over, and not a sound was heard. When America is destroyed, the sounds of battle and of great destruction will be heard in the land at the time of her judgment.

> *A sound of battle is in the land, and of great destruction. How is the hammer of the whole earth cut asunder and broken! How is Babylon become a desolation among the nations! Jeremiah 50:22-23*

THE LAND OF THE CHALDEANS

Chaldea is a name commonly assumed as a synonym for the land of Babylon, but the Chaldeans were in fact a separate region to the south which became absorbed into ancient Babylon. The Chaldeans were masters of all forms of incantation, sorcery, witchcraft, and the magical arts. The term Chaldean in Hebrew translates as an astrologer or professional occultist. Chaldeans were counted among the wise men of ancient Babylon as referenced in Daniel 5.

> *There is a man in thy kingdom, in whom is the spirit of the holy gods; and in the days of thy father light and understanding and wisdom, like the wisdom of the gods, was found in him; whom thy father, made master of the magicians, astrologers, Chaldeans and soothsayers Daniel 5:11*

The Chaldeans took the throne of Babylon after the fall of the Assyrian empire in the 7th century BC. Nebuchadnezzar (the second Chaldean king) inherited the throne around 610 BC, and during his reign Babylon was lifted up to became a ruling super power for the first time, and also became the 1st manifestation of Mystery Babylon of Scripture. The city of Babylon's history dates back to the early chapters of the book of Genesis. It was only under the rule of the Chaldeans that ancient Babylon rose from being a nation state to an empire which would dominate its regional part of the world for 70 years.

The history of America has similar parallels. The United States pursued an isolationist foreign policy until the rise of the Modern American empire in the late 1940's. It was during this period, that the satanic shadow government silently assumed control of America and thus Satan began to lift up America as a global empire, and what would become the last days superpower described as the hindermost nation of Jeremiah 50.

> *Behold, the hindermost of the nations shall be a wilderness, a dry land, and a desert. Because of the wrath of the LORD it shall not be inhabited, but it shall be wholly desolate: every one that goes by Babylon shall be astonished, and hiss at all her plagues. Jeremiah 50:12-13*

The word used for hindermost in this text is אַחֲרִית, 'acharîyth which means the *last* and *final* superpower. A similar word is used in Genesis 33:2 where it is translated '*in the west.*'

The shadow government that rules over the end time superpower which rose in the west, are the sorcerers of the same satanic secret societies whose roots trace all the way back to the ancient mystery religion of the Chaldeans, the mystery religion of the beast and the signature of 'Mystery' Babylon.

THE AMERICAN CENTURY

The institutions of power through which America would lead the post-war world were created for most part in 1948; these include the General Agreement on Trade and Tariffs or GATT, NATO, the World Health Organization, the Organization of American States, and the Marshall Plan. The World Council of Churches was also created that year to exercise American leadership over what would become apostate Christianity. All of the leaders of the western world gathered in Washington to witness the signing of the NATO treaty on April 4th, 1949, the official crowning of America as the new leader of the free world.

While the world hoped the new American Century would bring both peace and prosperity, behind the closed doors of the world's secret societies, the Chaldean sorcerers had already seized power in a silent coup d'état. They would consolidate their power through the creation of a shadow government within America's political institutions which would direct America's policies under the rule of the satanic elite who had already acquired ownership control of America's global corporate giants. The establishment would now exercise its rule through control of the media, education, and both political parties.

The other key events of 1949 included the creation of the Council of Europe in August for the purpose of developing a framework to unite Europe while on the same day the Soviet Union tested its first atomic bomb. The Federal Republic of Germany was officially founded in May while in September, America's first mass shooting occurred. On October 1st, Mao Satan declared the creation of the People's Republic of China (PRC) after the end of China's four-year civil war while on December 13th the Knesset voted to move the capital of Israel to Jerusalem. Suddenly all of the end times actors were presented on the world's stage together.

With America now the sole legitimate leader of the free world and firmly under control of the deep state, the Chaldeans began to build an empire. In order to grow quickly, a new enemy was required, so Russia was lifted up as a nuclear power and a new cold war began. As Israel declared Jerusalem their eternal capital, the shadow government forces of the anti-Christ took the first step in moving the nations towards a New World Order with the formation of the Council of Europe.

Ancient Babylon fell on October 12th in the year 539 BC, the same day America celebrates as Columbus Day 2,500 years later. The reign of America Babylon will end with World War III sometime after the 70th year of her rule. Even as ancient Babylon fell in the fall, so too America Babylon will be judged during the harvest season of fall. Jeremiah 50:16 confirms this timing: *"Cut off the sower from Babylon, and him that handles the sickle in the time of harvest."* Thus, the seventy years of America's rule will be measured using the civil calendar which begins with Rosh Ha Shana in the season of fall and the following is the 70-year window of time for America's judgment:

Crowning of America Babylon	April, 1949
The first year of Chaldean Rule	Spring, 1950
Beginning of the 70th year	Spring, 2020
End of the 70th year	Spring, 2021

Jeremiah 25:11 declares that all of the nations would "serve Babylon seventy years" after which her judgement would come. The word used for 'serve' in this text is עָבַד, 'abad; it means to *work*, to *serve*, or causatively to *enslave*, and to become a servant. This word is also a political term, and it means to recognize and accept the rule of another as the Jews did when they became subject to Chaldean power for 70 years. So too in our modern world, the nations rebuilt their economies following WW2 based upon an export model designed to serve the United States. Europe and Japan were severely damaged by the destruction of the 2nd World War and their populations were impoverished. So, the nations all began to 'serve' America, building export industries to harvest their raw materials or produce goods to be sold in America.

In the early years, America paid for this trade in gold, but in 1971, with its gold reserves nearly depleted, Nixon and Kissinger created the petrodollar in a secret agreement with the Saudi regime. In paying for its trade deficit, America would now export only debt, while OPEC would accept only US dollars in payment for oil. These dollars would then be recycled in the US Treasury market, financing the US budget deficit, or they would be used to purchase military weapons from America's arms industry. In exchange, the United States military would ensure the safety of our allies, and especially the Saudi regime.

Return Oh Lord, How Long?

By accepting petrodollars, America's trading partners were knowingly subsidizing the US military budget and the cost could be measured by the level of US currency debasement. In the early years, the cost of this subsidy was quite low; while the perceived value of America's military protection was high. Over its 45-year history, the petrodollar has allowed the United States to export over $10 trillion in debt, an external debt balance of historic proportions, and also a debt which can never be repaid.

The cost of financing America's structural deficits is no longer perceived as low while the value of America's military protection is now quite uncertain. We are one military defeat away from the loss of the petrodollar. The first US warship to be hit by a hyper-sonic missile will mark the end of this era. A global financial collapse will follow almost immediately, leading to the fall of America Babylon in World War III shortly thereafter. Following the next world war, pictured as the Red Horse in the book of Revelation, the Black Horse of famine, plague and death will then devastate the earth. The Black Plague was called the 'Black Death' as it brought misery, death and economic ruin to Europe in the middle of the 14th century. The plague ravaged Europe for seven years, killing an estimated 30% to 60% of the population (30 to 100 million people). It was finally eradicated in the year 1353. In the fall of 2019, the Covid 19 pandemic was unleashed upon the earth on the 666th year anniversary following the eradication of the Black Plague in 1353. On March 22, 2020, the nations of the earth were locked down for the first time on the 3rd day of spring at the beginning of the 70th year of the reign of America Babylon. Following the coming war, the Black Horse will begin to ride again as the world enters the beginning of the time of Jacob's trouble, and the final seven years of human history.

AMERICA IS UNPREPARED

Our nation has never been ready to fight a nuclear war; in fact, we have never prepared for one either. America has no bomb-shelters, no civil defense education, no war preparation drills. Rather America relies upon a single defensive strategy against the threat of nuclear war - the theory of mutually assured destruction, known by its acronym, MAD. Americans were taught to dismiss any threat of war because anyone who would attack us would face certain annihilation. Thus, the risk of America being attacked was reduced to an impossibility. The American people were assured there is no real threat to America – and so the thought of a nuclear war was dismissed out of hand. No one stops to consider that America's only defense against a nuclear war continues to be based upon a relic theory from the Cold War era. When this theory is examined in light of modern military weapons and the changing balance of power in today's world, the MAD theory could be better described as 'insane'.

THE DAY OF THE LORD IS AT HAND

THE COMMUNIST THREAT

North Korea publicly broadcasts their intention to turn America into a heap of "ash and rubble." The same chorus of death is heard throughout Islamic nations. Our enemies talk constantly about our destruction as their people chant "Death to America." There is nobody in the US shouting "Death to Iran" or "Death to the Democratic People's Republic of Korea." Yet America is portrayed as an aggressor within the propaganda of these rogue regimes. Why? In order to justify the coming war against us; and that much should be obvious.

Russia and China are now holding huge civil defense drills, while educating their own people on the protective measures required to survive a nuclear war. Our nation takes no such precautions, we have no such training. The majority of the American people are blissfully ignorant of the true threats we face. The public has been tragically deceived and is now hopelessly misinformed; having chosen to believe lies, they close their eyes to the truth.

HIDING FROM THE TRUTH IN AMERICA

Present day Americans, by and large, value their comfort more than the truth. Jeremiah speaks of such people, whose eyes and ears God has closed. They will not repent and therefore they cannot be healed. Only a remnant survives and our time will be no different. *"I will make them drunk that they may rejoice, and sleep a perpetual sleep, and not wake, saith the LORD. I will bring them down like lambs to the slaughter, like rams with he goats. How is America Babylon taken! And how is the praise of the whole earth surprised."* Jer 51:40, 57

There are many reasons why war is coming soon; I will address just a few. First, the financial position of the US is that of 'a camel waiting for the proverbial straw'. US indebtedness and fiscal imbalances, which can never be repaid, rest upon a foundation of imported capital, and are no longer sustainable. And if they were to continue, the cost of sustaining them would be borne by our trading partners, many of whom we are now discovering to be our enemies.

China has recently completed an alternative international settlement system which will allow nations to settle international payments outside of the US dollar and it is now operational. We are living in the final days of the 'petrodollar' era. When the petrodollar goes, the US will lose its seeming unlimited funding source for its trade deficit, through which we finance our fiscal deficit and our military budget. Without the 'petrodollar' we won't be able to export our debt at near zero interest rates. America will then be confronted with a choice: either surrender its super power status and give up its subsidized standard of living, or go to war to defend it.

THE WORLD IS AT THE TIPPING POINT

The world is at a tipping point by virtually every measure. We are now witnessing a global ecosystem collapse as the oceans, the birds, and the fish die. The so-called economic recovery which began in 2009 was a cruel joke, papered over by trillion-dollar deficits which created our now overextended financial bubbles. The political, moral and social bankruptcy of our country is absolute and it is not just America, but worldwide. Ours has become an empire of lies, where 'truth-tellers' are guilty of treason.

The pseudo-science of climate change is one such example; in the light of truth, it is exposed as a total fraud. Global climate change has nothing to do with carbon emissions; correlation doesn't prove causality. The scientific fact is that the whole solar system is being impacted by cosmic and gamma radiation from a neutron star 1,300 light years away in the vicinity of the Orion constellation. This radiation is heating the core of every planet and is also impacting our sun, which is now increasingly more unstable. This radiation is also heating the core of our planet, thereby weakening the earth's magnetic field which allows greater amounts of solar radiation into our ecosystem, producing a positive feedback loop. The 20 trillion tons of methane gas frozen in the Arctic Circle have begun to melt and the outcome will be cataclysmic. These changes are getting worse by the day and the governments of the world know all of this.

When you examine the history of the war propaganda inside Russia over the last four years, their development of new 5th generation weapons, alongside of their military preparations and current mobilizations, compared with the terrible lack of readiness on the part of US forces, the window of vulnerability is at or near its maximum. During the time of the ABM Treaty, Russia developed dual purpose anti-aircraft missiles which also serve as anti-ballistic missiles (ABM) and Russia has close to 12,000 such missiles. In the US, we have basically none, unless you count 100 or so outdated Nike interceptors from the 1960's.

President Trump's efforts to refurbish our aging nuclear arsenal and strengthen our military forces emasculated by eight years of Obama's social engineering and intentional disarmament, only serves to compel our enemies to attack us before their window of opportunity closes. Most Americans are also unaware our nuclear deterrent is for the most part over 25 years old, and can no longer be assumed reliable given the obsolescence of aging warheads. Coupled with Russia's state of art anti-missile defenses, our enemies can now attack us with impunity.

THE DAY OF THE LORD IS AT HAND

A recent Report by the National Defense Strategy Commission stated, "The U.S. military could suffer unacceptably high casualties and loss of major capital assets in its next conflict. It might struggle to win, or perhaps lose, a war against China or Russia. The United States is particularly at risk of being overwhelmed should its military be forced to fight on two or more fronts simultaneously. In conclusion, we wish to be crystal clear about one thing. The costs of failing to meet America's crisis of national defense and national security will not be measured in abstract concepts like "international stability" and "global order." They will be measured in American lives, American treasure, and American security and prosperity lost. U.S. military superiority is no longer assured and the implications for American interests and American security are severe."

The Center for Security Policy published and article by Mary Fanning and Alan Jones on October 24th, 2018, in which they discussed information obtained from Russian Defense Journals and secret Iranian military documents, stating "Russia and Iran have developed a Pearl Harbor 2.0 plan to sink the entire U.S. Navy fleet as part of coordinated asymmetrical attacks against the United States and U.S. military bases around the world. The plan is to launch Russian Kalibr cruise missiles from submarines, freighter ships, and Trojan Horse Club-K Container Missile System intermodal cargo 'containers' that can be smuggled into U.S. ports and moved into the U.S. interior aboard trains and semi-trucks. In 2015 the Russian journal _'Natsionalnaya Oborona'_ (translation: National Defense) outlined a plan to 'hit them in their ports' with Kalibr cruise missiles that could sink entire US Navy fleets docked in ports across the United States, Europe, and the Middle East." Similar reports by scores of other experts confirm this grim reality; the next world war is indeed truly coming upon us.

THE FINAL PHASE

A number of recent news incidents dismissed as accidents look very much like the final phase of Russia's pre-war preparations, described as the 'overture' by Soviet defector, General Victor Suvorov, in his book, _Spetsnaz: The Inside Story of Russian Special Forces._ Suvorov was the top military official in charge of the special forces The increasing number of 'accidents' alongside our growing scandal filled news fit Suvorov's description of the overture perfectly while the fictitious events he described now seem eerily prophetic. In 2018, a train filled with Republican congressmen just happened to be involved in an accident, and had it derailed, the accident could have killed or injured scores of them. For those who are unaware of the strategy embodied within the overture, Suvorov explains:

"The final months of peace, as in other wars, have an almost palpable air of crisis about them. Incidents, accidents, small disasters add to the tension. Two trains collide on a railway bridge ... a supertanker bursts into flames. In the United States an epidemic of some unidentified disease breaks out and spreads rapidly; at the same time terrible fires begin raging in the west.

"All these operations - because of course none of these events is an accident - and others like them are known officially in the GRU as the 'preparatory period', and unofficially as the 'overture'. The overture is a series of large and small operations the purpose of which is, before actual military operations begin, to weaken the enemy's morale, create an atmosphere of general suspicion, fear and uncertainty, and divert the attention of the enemy's armies and police forces to a huge number of different targets, each of which may be the object of the next attack. The overture is carried by agents of the secret services of the Soviet satellite countries and by mercenaries recruited by intermediaries. The principal method employed at this stage is 'grey terror', that is, a kind of terror which is not conducted in the name of the Soviet Union. The Soviet secret services do not at this stage leave their visiting cards, or leave other people's cards. The terror is carried out in the name of already existing extremist groups not connected in any way with the Soviet Union, or in the name of fictitious organizations."

What we have been witnessing in the news over the last year is a perfect example of the overture. The Russia collusion scandal, the sexual harassment scandals, the spontaneous fires erupting overnight in California, pipeline explosions, numerous train derailments, power outages, and last year's super flu epidemic, these are the exact illustrations Suvorov used to describe what the overture would look like in the eyes of the average American.

THE OCCULT SIGNATURE OF THE AMERICAN GOVERNMENT

The future, for the most part, is unknowable, as mortal men are rarely permitted to peer through its veil. Most people would also prefer not to see into a future as terrible as ours; they would find it too troubling to their souls. Most Americans do not wish to understand how deeply the darkness has infiltrated our country and our institutions of power. They prefer to neither hear nor understand anything about the terrible catastrophe that awaits our nation. The dark forces which now control the shadow government in America are as hideous and evil as they are real. They have led us to the edge of an abyss in which our military was intentionally weakened and our nation left virtually defenseless. The window of vulnerability that exists today was left wide open by their design.

THE DAY OF THE LORD IS AT HAND

These dark forces have ruled over the secret societies of the world from the beginning of time. They are the unseen rulers of this ruined age, and they are under the direct control of Satan. They have dominated the government of our nation for the better part of the last hundred years through their secret societies which are the prophetic link of the United States to 'Mystery' Babylon, for the ruling powers in America are all participants in the same 'mystery religion' practiced in ancient Chaldea.

The book of Revelation reveals the shadow government that rules over America as ten kings who will rule with Beast; they hate the woman 'America Babylon' and so they made our country desolate, and now they plan to burn America with fire. The 2008 financial crisis, the result of a housing crisis which they engineered, was used to loot our nation. And now they plan to use a 3rd world war to literally burn America. There should be no doubt of which nation the prophecy speaks: "And the woman, (Mystery Babylon) which thou saw is that great city (nation state) which reigns over the kings of the earth (at the time of the end)."

The occult signature left behind by these satanic forces can be found in all of the major events of our history; and although this truth can be painful to observe, those who have been called as true watchmen, dare not look away. The assassination of President John F. Kennedy was such an event: the book, KING-KILL/33° Masonic Symbolism in the Assassination of John F. Kennedy, by James Shelby Downard with Michael A. Hoffman II, looks deeply into the occult signature surrounding the murder of JFK. "Masonic betrayal of the 'common man' involves archetypes of fertility and death symbolism seemingly motivated to bring about syncretism in opposing principles in order to 'green' Israel, rebuild the Temple of Solomon and establish a One World government. It is certain that onomatology (and numerology) or the secret science of names (and numbers) forms a very integral part of the mystery school of the higher Masonry.... - *Encyclopedia of Freemasonry"* [57]

Onomatology is the science or study of the origin, forms and mystical meaning of names. Numerology is the science of occult symbolism based upon the mystical meaning of numbers. These are both used as symbols to reveal the presence of the dark arts of sorcery and mystic alchemy which are hidden in plain sight in many of the world's most important events. These symbols are both symbolic clues and numerological keys which the unseen rulers of this fallen world use to unlock pathways to another realm in order to ensure the success of an endeavor. They are employed frequently by the secret societies whenever they attempt to release the power 'as above' in their rituals 'so below'.

When you begin to understand these symbols, you will find them as finger prints at the scene of many crimes, so they ought not to be ignored. "When the ancients saw a scapegoat, they could at least recognize him for what he was: a human sacrifice. When modern man sees one, he does not, or refuses to, recognize him for what he IS; instead he looks for 'scientific' explanations-to explain away the obvious."

America has been chosen as a scapegoat, a blood sacrifice of 300 million souls who will be slain to usher in the rising of the New World Order, and from that destiny she cannot escape. Once this truth is understood, the obvious will be perceived, and truth will never be able to hide in plain sight again. The death of America in World War III was been planned long ago as the opening ceremony for the dawn of a New Age.

APPOINTING THE TIME

The command to restore Jerusalem was issued in April of 1969, and the seven weeks prophecy of Daniel points to the birth of the man-child company, who will fulfill the 2nd half of the seven-year ministry of Jesus as Messiah the Prince, in the year 2024. *"Know therefore and understand, that from the going forth of the commandment to restore and to build Jerusalem unto the Messiah the Prince shall be seven weeks."* [61]

The birth of the man-child may precede the beginning of the judgment of the earth, which is World War III, by some period of time. The parable of the fig tree forecasts the great war no later than the fall of 2024; the 70-year reign of America Babylon is not the same period of time. Jeremiah and his scribe Baruch prophesied for 23 years, and then the judgment came upon ancient Israel. I went on national tour sharing The Day of the LORD is at Hand message in the summer of 1999; and so the year 2022 will represent the 23rd year of my testimony before this nation. I am a direct descendent of Baruch, the scribe of Jeremiah and the 23 years of warning are ending soon. Truly the Day of the LORD is indeed at Hand!

THE SIGNS IN THE SUN, THE MOON AND THE STARS

God told us in the fourth day of creation that he created the lights in the heavens for signs of the seasons and the times of mankind. Jesus also told us that we would also see specific signs in the heavens as evidence that the events of the end of the age were upon us.

> *And there shall be signs in the sun, and in the moon, and in the stars; and upon the earth distress of nations, with perplexity; the sea and the waves roaring. Luke 21:25*

THE DAY OF THE LORD IS AT HAND

In the prophecies of Joel, the Lord declares that he will show signs in the heavens and upon the earth before the coming of the Great and Awesome Day of The Lord.

I will show wonders in the heavens and in the earth, blood, and fire, and pillars of smoke. The sun shall be turned into darkness, and the moon into blood, before the great and the terrible day of the Lord come. Joel 2:30-31

SIGNS IN THE SUN

The scientific community has been observing our sun with great interest in for years. The exploration of space and the use of satellites for communications have required extensive monitoring of the sun. Today, you can access the space weather on the internet, and the activities of the sun are under close scrutiny. Top scientists from within NASA have disclosed confidentially that the governments of the world are all aware the conditions of global warming and global climate change are actually being driven by energy from outside our solar system, from a distant neutron star in the vicinity of the Orion constellation, creating planetary warming throughout the solar system. This energy is also heating the core of the earth, thereby weakening the magnetic fields around the earth creating a positive feedback loop. Lastly, and most importantly, this energy is also heating up the sun.

SIGNS IN THE MOON

At the writing of this Seventh Edition, the heavens are now witnessing a second set of blood moons, only this time, four of them, and they are known as the "*Tetrad*" in which four blood moons appear on the High Holy Days of Israel; these blood moons are a final warning to the nations that the Day of the Lord is coming upon them very soon. The picture on the cover of this book is from the 2nd of these four blood red moons, the eclipse of Tabernacles, on October 8th, 2014. On January 20th, 2019, a final sign will appear in the heavens as a super moon turns blood red over the United States as a final warning.

SIGNS IN THE STARS

The 2014 Winter Olympics were held on the shores of the Black Sea in Sochi, Russia, at the end of winter. I had dedicated 2014 to the Lord as a Sabbath year, and had been fasting and praying over the first sixty days of the New Year; only eating a single meal every few days. Amazing revelations had begun to come forth by the Spirit of God. The teachings entitled, *Job*, and *That Woman Jezebel*, had both been given to me by the Lord in the first two months. They are subjects of my third book, *Search the Scriptures, Volume II: You shall know the Truth.*

In early 2014, the Lord also told me "go and study the meaning of the Black Horse of the Book of Revelation, which will follow immediately after the coming of the Red Horse of War."

BEHOLD A BLACK HORSE

The time of the reign of the White Horse is nearing an end and it will be destroyed by the release of the Red Horse of war, which will take peace from the earth, through the power given unto him with his *"great sword"*. The word for *"great"* in the Greek text is μέγας, or *meg'-as* which means exceedingly big, the greatest, and loudest, and it will cause men to be sore afraid for years to come. The word for *"sword"* in the Greek text is μάχαιρα, or *makh'-ahee-rah* which means a war or judicial punishment by the sword.

The release of this great sword brings the Great War, and an end to the reign of the White Horse. The color red in this verse is the color of burning fire and bloodshed. This time of war also quickly ushers in the coming of the Black Horse, which follows immediately after the Red Horse, for in truth, they come together as a red and black judgment is released upon the earth.

> And when he had opened the third seal, I heard the third beast say, Come and see. And I beheld, and lo a black horse; and he that sat on him had a pair of balances in his hand. And I heard a voice in the midst of the four beasts say, A measure of wheat for a penny, and three measures of barley for a penny; and see thou hurt not the oil and the wine. Revelation 6:5-6

The Black Horse will usher in a time of global economic collapse which will be followed by the 4th horse, the Pale Horse, and the rider sitting upon him is named Death: *"And I looked, and behold a pale horse: and his name that sat on him was Death, and Hell followed with him. And power was given unto them over the fourth part of the earth, to kill with sword, and with hunger, and with death, and with the beasts of the earth." Revelation 6:8*

The reign of the Black Horse heralds the coming of the 4th and final Horseman of Death who will be accompanied by the Dark Ones. Thus, begins the time of the Black Death and the coming of the reign of terror of the Black Prince. The word Black appears in scripture 18 times, representing the absence of light; and that which is enveloped in darkness: as in a black night which is soiled or stained, ushering in a time that is dismal for all. It is a time that is harmful, and evil, for it is the time of the wicked ones, who are the ones with a black heart. Black represents censure and disgrace, disaster and misfortune, and foretells the coming of the Dark Ones whose garments are black as are the garments of the Black Prince, for they are his servants. Their reign first comes in secret and through covert means, as the kingdom of darkness is brought to power through the black op programs of the governments now ruled by the beast, and they operate in the shadows.

> *And it came to pass that the heaven was black with clouds and wind, and there was a great rain. And Ahab rode, and went to Jezreel. 1Kings 18:45*

And the word for *black* in this verse is קדר, *kaw-dar'* and it means to *mourn* in sackcloth, or sordid garments: to be blackish, to be made darkened, and to cause to mourn heavily. As I began my studies of the Black Horse, I was contacted by a close friend with connections inside the intelligence community; he called to advise me that the risk of an incident at the Black Sea during the Sochi Olympics was being taken seriously. The Russian media had been publishing reports by noted Russian astrologers that the signs in the stars in the heavens indicated WWIII would start following an incident which would occur on the shores of the Black Sea. The ruling communists in Russia it turns out are also Chaldeans, and they place great significance on astrology, with the KGB operating large numbers of facilities dedicated to the occult study of the stars. Such reports in the Russian newspapers, would also have been tacitly approved by the Russian government. I told him, "I don't follow astrology, but I have studied carefully the biblical meaning of the stars, and I can take a look at the heavens over the Olympics from the shores of the Black Sea to see if there are any true signs of what might be coming." So, with my computer, I stood upon the shores of the Black Sea, and I rolled the times forward, to look and to discern what the heavens would reveal unto me.

THE BLACK SEA

In the year 1348, 666 years prior to 2014, on the 33rd day of spring, and the 23rd of April, the Servants of Darkness, who are the true rulers of this fallen world, created the Order of the Garter, which would later be known as the Order of the Roundtable from Arthurian legend. They fashioned together five rings as a symbol for their Order and as an image of the five circles of power which bear the hidden structure of their rule. Five rings also represent the five-pointed star of the pentagram, the secret source of their power. Thus, the magic circle used by the Chaldeans was hidden in plain view, represented by five inter-connected rings; rather than display an obvious satanic symbol, they chose five rings to represent the five-pointed star hidden within. And at the round table, sat twenty-four elders, who are the servants of the Black Prince and they call themselves *"Olympians."*

Return Oh Lord, How Long?

The Coat of Arms of the Black Prince, declares him to be the servant of the Red Dragon and his elders, the *"Olympians"* are the holders of the light of darkness which has been cast down upon the earth. Their symbol of five interconnected rings, is recognized around the world. The fire which is the center piece of their ceremony is captured from the very light of the sun. The world cheers their festival of light every four years in the midst of winter, only this year they would cheer from the shores of the Black Sea.

THE BLACK DEATH OF 1348

The Black Death came to the shores of England, in the summer of 1348. The plague had originated in Europe from the shores of the Black Sea, and following the coronation of the elders of the beast on April 23rd, the plague came upon ships which docked in the bosom of Wales, in the city of Dorset, within the month of June.

The Black Death was one of the most devastating pandemics in history, killing an estimated 100 million people, and was preceded by two years of drought, and famine, which brought about an economic collapse, before the plague came. It reached England in the summer of 1348 and peaked in Europe in the years 1348-50. The children would sing, "Ring-a-round the Rosie, A pocket full of posies, Ashes! Ashes! We all fall down." And the ashes were the funeral pyres of the bodies of the dead, which burned day and night for years.

But the posies were mere flowers which provided no protection from the Black Death, any more than the false pretense faith of the last days "posers" will protect them from the Black Death that will accompany the coming of the Black Horse. The Urban Dictionary defines a *"Poser"* as one who pretends to be someone or something which they are not. And the false gospel of Apostate Christianity along with the pretentious faith of the disobedient ones will prove utterly vain in the days ahead.

SIGNS UPON THE EARTH

Jesus told us there would be signs upon the earth including floods, droughts, famines, earthquakes and volcanoes. Joel spoke of signs of blood, fire and pillars of smoke. Over the last few years, El Nino has produced both floods and droughts causing a massive shift in the normal weather patterns of the world. Many of the world's volcanos are also beginning to evidence activity as we race toward the end. The prophecy warns us before the judgment begins, we will witness heat and drought in the land. The US News and World Report cites the recent warming of the earth. "It just keeps getting hotter... There is no sign the trend is easing. The analysis supports, in unprecedented detail, existing conclusions by United Nations-based climate reports that the recent warmth is not only extreme but is rising ever faster. The signs upon the earth and in the stars, and the sun and the moon all confirm the Day of the Lord is at hand!

JESUS IS LORD AND HE IS COMING SOON

The present world order is built upon the leadership and dominance of the United States; after it is destroyed, a New World Order will rise like a phoenix from the ashes. The little prince will have already confirmed the covenant with death (The Treaty with Rabin) for seven years and at some point, during the first 3 ½ years, he will rebuild the world in the vision of his new age. This includes rebuilding the temple, only this time, they will build a Masonic temple on the holy place and at the mid-point of this final seven year period, the little prince will pass through the pillars of the Masonic temple and declare to the world that he is god – thus the world will witness the abomination of desolation spoken of by Daniel the Prophet and whether it includes erecting a graven image to the beast I know not.

HE SHALL COME TO BE GLORIFIED IN HIS SAINTS

It is the mystery of our salvation that Jesus Christ is to be formed within us; each of us conformed into his image, and each of us bearing his glory. The First Fruits of the book of Revelation are merely the first to mature in this process. God's people have been fed so much mixture of truth and error by their pastors, that many of them cannot even understand these mysteries, for the truth is, many of them also wouldn't recognize Jesus if He walked right into their midst. And in the coming days, that is exactly what he is preparing to do!

The day of playing church is over my friends, and we are about to see its end along with destruction in this land the likes of which man has never before beheld with his eyes. The pastors and teachers in most of the churches do not know these things are coming, because they have no true knowledge of God or His ways; nor can they hear from the Lord. How do I know this? Because they have not heard from the Lord; if they could hear him, they would hear him shouting as I did when he said "Prepare for summer!" Rather they are all famished for the true Word, and their people are dried up for thirst. There is no living water within the broken cisterns of the churches of Babylon, for they have all tarried far too long in the sun, and they built their churches as high places, in the land of Shinar, above the plains of Babylon.

There is no true voice of God in their midst, and they have no prophetic word and no vision to restore the people back to the truth of God. The Spirit is telling the remnant to awaken, to see and open our eyes, and to lose ourselves from all that would hinder us from the Lord's purposes for the hour is late! The Father's true sons and daughters have been in the wilderness to humble them and to prove them, so that they would know what was in their hearts and whether they would keep His word or not.

JESUS CHRIST SHALL BE THE HEAD OVER THEM

There is only one head over the remnant, and that is the Lord Jesus Christ. Anyone who claims to be the head over the anointed ones of the Lord, or who tries to assume the authority in the holy camp of God will be found to be a liar, for only Jesus Christ shall lead them, for he alone is the King of Israel. *"Then shall the children of Judah and the children of Israel be gathered together, and appoint themselves one head, and they shall come up out of the land: for great shall be the day of Jezreel."* [66]

The remnant has been hidden away under the shadow of His hand. Soon they will come forth as clean and pure vessels and as the weapons of war to be used for the Lord's indignation. The man-child of Revelation is about to be born; they are the remnant who will come forth in the full image of Christ, possessing His nature, with His name written in their foreheads, and their minds sealed by the Spirit in holiness unto the Lord. They are the final work of the Father, and will manifest His presence among the people.

> *Ask ye of the LORD rain in the time of the latter rain; so the LORD shall make bright clouds, and give them showers of rain, to every one grass in the field.* [68]

And the bright clouds are coming to pour out the living water of His word, onto a very dry ground which today are the hearts of His people.

> *"My doctrine shall drop as the rain, my speech shall distil as the dew, as the small rain upon the tender herb, and as the showers upon the grass "*[69]

There is a holy remnant, but it is made up of only a few; a "handful" of corn on top of the mountains. They are the "Omer" and the tithe from the body. They are the Lord's portion and the first fruits of His resurrection. We are to die to our self and press on to the mark of the high calling of God. That high calling is the full redemption of the spirit, soul and body preserved blameless unto the coming of our Lord.

THE DAY OF THE LORD IS AT HAND

For I reckon that the sufferings of this present time are not worthy to be compared with the glory which shall be revealed in us. For the earnest expectation of the creature waits for the manifestation of the sons of God. [70]

They are the first ripe grain of the field, the first fruits of the harvest and they are pure of any defilements of the flesh, thus they will be hated and rejected by the Church, and will have all manner of evil spoken against them. They also have the favor of the Lord, and therefore the world and the compromised Church will reject them. These are the Joseph Company of the Lord, and the elder leadership of the Church will hate them even as Joseph was hated by his brethren. They are also the weapons of the Lord.

A fire is kindled in mine anger, and it shall burn unto the lowest hell, and shall consume the earth with her increase, and set on fire the foundations of the mountains... I will render vengeance to mine enemies, and will reward them that hate me. I will make mine arrows drunk with blood, and my sword shall devour flesh... Rejoice, O ye nations, with his people: for he will avenge the blood of his servants, and will render vengeance to his adversaries, and will be merciful unto his land, and to his people. [71]

For all people will walk every one in the name of his god, and we will walk in the name of the Lord our God for ever and ever. In that day, saith the Lord, will I assemble her that halteth, and I will gather her that is driven out, and her that I have afflicted; And I will make her that halted a remnant, and her that was cast far off a strong nation: and the Lord shall reign over them in mount Zion from henceforth, even for ever. And thou, O tower of the flock, the strong hold of the daughter of Zion. unto thee shall it come, even the first dominion: the kingdom shall come to the daughter of Jerusalem " [72]

The remnant walks in the name of the Lord only; they have been outcasts from the assembly, and they were rejected by the people. The word for *halted* is צלע *tsala* [73] which means to limp. The remnant has been limping, for they have been wounded in the house of their friends. The word for *outcast* is נדח *nadach* [74], which means literally to expel and strike, to inflict, and to cast down, to drive away, and to be outcast. They are the afflicted of the Lord, the lowly ones whom the Lord has been preparing in the fires of His judgment. The word for *afflicted* is רעע, *raw-ah* [75] which means to break down in pieces, to do evil, do harm, to hurt, and to punish. The remnant has known many afflictions through the hands of their friends.

They are the outcasts of the assembly, who have been mistreated by the people, even as Joseph was betrayed by his brethren. The word for *remnant* is

282

שְׁאֵרִית, *sheh-ay-reeth*[76] which means a remainder or residual, the surviving final portion, those who are left and remain. The remnant shall also be given the first dominion of the kingdom. The word for *dominion* is מִשַׁל, *mashal*[77], which means to rule, or to be given power to rule, to those who possess the sovereign authority.

These are the outcasts of Israel, who have been gathered together by Father God, and redeemed and renewed in the resurrection power of Jesus Christ, and they shall be presented to the Lord Jesus as the present which he has been promised by his Father.

These are the saviors who shall come up on Mount Zion to judge the mountains of Esau. They will possess the land of Edom, and through their hand, the Lord will judge the nations. They are referred to as saviors, for through their hand the Lord will bring His deliverance to His people. They are described as "a fire" for the presence of God shall burn within the remnant.

> *But upon mount Zion shall be deliverance, and there shall be holiness ... And saviors shall come up on mount Zion to judge the mount of Esau: and the kingdom shall be the Lord's.* [78]

> *But thou, Bethlehem Ephrata, though thou be little among the thousands of Judah, yet out of thee shall he come forth unto me that is to be ruler in Israel; whose goings forth have been from of old, from everlasting.* [79]

> *For behold, the LORD is coming forth from His place. He will come down and tread on the high places of the earth. The mountains will melt under Him.* [80] *I saw when the Lamb opened one of the seals, and I heard, as it were the noise of thunder, one of the four beasts saying, come and see. And I saw, and behold a white horse: and he that sat on him had a bow; and a crown was given unto him: and he went forth conquering* [81] *When I have bent Judah for me, filled the bow with Ephraim, and raised up thy sons, O Zion, against thy sons, O Greece, and made thee as the sword of a mighty man.* [82]

THIS IS THE LORD'S DOING
AND IT IS MARVELOUS IN OUR EYES

Psalm 118 declares the work of the Lord within the 144,000 will be *marvelous* in our eyes; the word *marvelous* or פָּלָא, *pala'o* means to separate, or to distinguish and to set apart; in which the Lord will accomplish hidden things which are too high understand, where he will do marvelous things, and where his miracles will be performed, for he will make wonderful things, even that which is too wondrous to behold.

At the first, the work must *chasten them sore* and the word is הדחה , *dachach* and it means to be pushed down and driven away, to be overthrow and to be made an outcast, to be thrust at, as with a weapon, and to be thrown down as in a violent struggle. These are the fires of affliction through which the anointed ones will be born, and these fires were necessary for their coming out of Babylon, to separate them from the mixed multitude who are all content to dwell within the outer court, so that their hearts could be set free from all of those things which bind men to their sins.

The Lord chastened his righteous ones *sorely* for the judgments and the purging fires which these chosen ones have walked through to prepare them for this hour have been very intense indeed. In times past, they were overthrown by their own sin, and then condemned by the many within the church. Afflicted and wounded, they became outcasts and were left to wander alone through the wilderness, and through seasons of emptiness. It was there in the wilderness that the hand of the enemy was used as a weapon to wound them further, and he thrust at them *sore*; and it was within these purging fires, that God did *chasten them all the more.* All of these blows and afflictions were delivered under the direction of the Lord, to humble, and to purge, and to prepare vessels chosen for the greatest hour and for entrance into the House of the Lord. Before a vessel may be used by the God, it first must be utterly emptied out, and the higher the calling, the more intense the fires to endure. Those chosen for the use of the Lord in the ministry of Jesus Christ in this hour, have had a purging process that exceeded even the portion given unto Job. The arrows of the Most High, lodged deep within their souls, and for some of them the arrows were aimed as a death blow to the heart of the flesh. As the Lord said of Job, "*I destroyed him*" so too, the Lord brought his anointed ones to the very end of themselves, and from there, the Lord led them into the Valley of Dry Bones, where they experienced the desolation and the deep despair known only to the people of Israel, who in times past cried out from their hearts, "*our hope is lost, for we have been cut off.*"

The Lord then left them alone in the Valley of Darkness and in a land of desolation for years which seemed to never end. It was there that they learned to worship their God in the midst of the fires of despair and unending grief, while they were being bruised by the power of the horns of death and despair, which came out of hell itself. Alone in this wilderness, through cold and dark nights, they cried out in tears, as Zion long ago once did, *"The Lord has forsaken me, and my God has forgotten me."*

And when they had finally come to the end of themselves, and the time of their wandering had ended, then the Lord brought them unto the threshing floor of Ornan, and then unto the cross of Jesus Christ, to the place which had been appointed for the absolute final breaking of their souls and for the shattering of their human hearts.

Those who have walked through these fires know in their souls the life which Job lived, and what he learned from his season of burning and the loss of all things; but those were all but light afflictions compared with the loss of the ones whom he deeply loved. On top of such unimaginable grief, they were given an overwhelming affliction in the flesh, which was poured out upon them, such that their mind was overcome with burning fire, along with a body wrecked with pain, which never seemed to heal. During his time of affliction, Job would awaken every morning to yet another day of unending misery, only to wish once again, that he'd never even been born as a man. This was the lot and the portion given unto those whom the Lord had chosen as his anointed ones, for at the first, they had to be made sorrowful unto death, so that they could learn to kneel at Heaven's door.

"But the Lord has not given us over unto death." These remnant warriors, having been purified with fires unthinkable, were brought to the place which only martyrs have known. It was there that their souls were totally emptied out, and yet their lives were not lost.

"There is always a merciful limit to the scourging of the children of God. Forty stripes save one were all that an Israelite might receive, and the Lord will never allow that final one, that killing stroke, to fall upon his children. Their pains are for their instruction, and not for their destruction. Blessed be the name of God, for though he may chasten us, and as severe as these chastens may be, he will not condemn us."[86]

The Lord is now Opening the Gates of Righteousness. Now that their trial of fire has ended, the Lord delivers them from the powers of darkness and death, and the Lord comes unto them, to comfort them in the new day. When they call upon the name of the Lord, it is now with rejoicing in their souls and they humbly ask for admission at the Gates of Righteousness, that they might leave the outer court behind, and enter into the House of the Holy One. And there they all faithfully wait, bowed down to the ground, before the door of the Lord's house for the time which he has appointed, and the day of the Lord's own choosing, when they will finally be welcomed within.

THE DAY OF THE LORD IS AT HAND

These Gates of Righteousness are the doors to the Lord's house, and the entrance to the palaces of the King. These Gates are the very life of the Lord Jesus Christ, and before they enter into the resurrection power of our Lord, they must first enter through the final crucifixion of the life of self, which must be laid into the ground, and buried with him. We must die within his death if we are to receive his new nature, so that his righteousness may come forth within us, for if we are to be born again totally by the Spirit of God, we must enter in through his death, and through his cross.

This is the reason for the fires and the purging. This is the reason for the season of pain and for the loss of all things. This is the reason why the chosen remnant was given the same portion appointed unto Job and why they were outcasts like King David hiding in caves, and held in the prisons of Egypt like Joseph, who was forsaken and afflicted by his brothers, so they could finally receive the power of the death of Jesus Christ. For only then can one receive the true power of his righteous resurrection within, for Jesus himself said unto us *"truly I am the door"* and there is no other way to approach Heaven's throne.

THE TESTIMONY OF THE 144,000

And having now entered through the Gate of Righteousness, they sing from the mountains of Zion in the very presence of the King: *"I will praise thee O Lord, and I thank thee for saving me from the power of sin, and for the new life in you which will now begin."* Having entered into the house of the Lord, they now talk directly with the Lord, for being chosen to enter in; they have also been called to abide with him. They can now hear heavens choir worshiping before the Lord as they sing *"Holy, Holy, Holy is the Lord."* The anointed ones shall also lift up their voices with the hosts of Heaven, and begin to sing a new song before the throne of the Lamb and before our God. "And I heard a voice from heaven, as the voice of many waters, and as the voice of a great thunder: and I heard the voice of harpers harping with their harps: And they sung as it were a new song before the throne, and before the four beasts, and the elders: and no man could learn that song but the hundred and forty and four thousand, which were redeemed from the earth."[87] This is the Lord's doing, and it is marvelous in our eyes!

The anointed ones give thanksgiving to the Lord for his salvation and for delivering them from all of their sins, and freeing them of the tyranny of the flesh. For the Lord has redeemed them from among men, and chosen them to be among the living stones which he has selected for the building of His Glorious Third Temple which will be made by God himself, and fashioned without the hands of men. Jesus Christ, being the chief cornerstone was rejected of men and so too, his living stones, have also been rejected, yet they shall make up the portion of the living temple chosen by the Lord for his dwelling place in the last days, and they shall be the house wherein the Lord chooses to reveal himself as the Son of man within.

THIS IS THE DAY WHICH THE LORD HAS MADE

This is the day of which the Lord has made, and it is the day of our salvation. So, we give unending praise to our beloved friend and our King, Jesus Christ, for leading us to the day of Eternal Sabbath Rest. We are bid by the Spirit of Grace, to enter into the resting place of the Lord, which is the life of the Lord Jesus Christ. Our God has become our salvation, and His life has become our true Sabbath rest which remains for all the people of God. Every saint who is born again by the spirit is bid to enter in and to remain with him, worshiping only the Lord, and serving only him in the spirit of truth; having thus entered into the Sabbath rest of the Lord, we are bid by the Lord to abide therein and remain there perpetually. And it is within His Presence that his chosen ones proclaim his blessings to his people, who cry out from their hearts, shouting praise to the Lord, as they announce the coming of the anointed ones.

BLESSED IS HE WHO COMES IN THE NAME OF THE LORD

The anointed ones, now full of the golden oil, pour out of themselves blessings from the House of the Lord, through which the Lord blesses his people. The word for *blessed* in this scripture is בָּרוּך, *Baruch*, which means blessed one; to kneel and bless God and to give thanks in adoration, and in praise and worship before the Lord, for all of his goodness unto men. Those who come in the name of the Lord are blessed, for they come with the power of God in their hands, and with the living word of God in their hearts, which is the life of the Lord Jesus Christ within them. They come not only in his name, but they come within his word, and within his spirit. And it is within his authority that they declare his righteous deeds to the children of men who live upon the earth. They bless the people of God, with blessings spoken by the Lord Jesus Christ himself, through the mouth of his holy servants, who now speak in the unity of the Spirit of God, for they speak for the Lord saying, "We bless you out of the house of the Lord." The holy messengers now dwell in the house of the Lord, and thus they speak for the Lord, and from the very presence of the Holy One of Israel, for they speak from his throne room.

Our God is the Lord, and he has shown us this light, that we might bind our sacrifice with cords unto the horns of the altar. And the word to *bind* is אָסַר, *aw-sar* which means a yoke that is bound, to hold fast, to put in bonds, and to set in array, and to tie. These who are redeemed from among men have yoked their lives to the brazen altar of sacrifice which burns before the throne of God in the heavens, for they have given themselves as a sacrifice unto the Lord, preferring to bless God with their lives, rather than serve themselves. This true wisdom was found within them, and therefore, when the time for the end of all flesh would come, having given up their lives as a living sacrifice, the Lord commands that they be saved in this hour through the power of His name.

In the lives of the holy remnant, the end of all flesh begins with the end of the mind of the flesh within, which shall now be totally consumed as a red heifer offering before the Temple on High. After their carnal mind has been reduced to ashes, their spirits will finally be set free, and then filled with the pure living water of the Holy Spirit, and that without measure, that their souls could become completely born again, and that their lives may become a healing balm for the nation.

The Light of the Righteousness of the Lord Jesus Christ will then begin to shine upon the foreheads of the anointed ones, and as Jesus Christ looks down upon them from heaven, he numbers them 12,000 from each tribe. He will then turn to his Eternal Father and be heard to say:

Look what we have done,
And what they shall soon become.
They will now become one in us,
And they shall be one with us.

FINAL WORDS

IN RETURNING AND
REST YOU SHALL BE SAVED
Isaiah 30:15

Twenty-Five years have now passed since the fall of 1996 when the Lord revealed unto me that The Day of the Lord was at hand; I witnessed the soon and certain judgment which will come upon America. Writing this book has been a great blessing, and this seventh edition offers me the opportunity to share some of the things which the Lord has revealed in the years which have followed. My prayer is that the Lord will be gracious and once again anoint my words to share with you; for the fulfillment of all things is truly now at hand.

I HAVE DREAMED A DREAM

In the summer of 2001, I had a dream. I was driving in my truck along the coast of southern California north of LA. I stopped in front of a house on the beach, and as I got out I heard the roar of a jet above me. The sound was louder than any jet I had ever heard before and it startled me. Looking up, I saw a United Airlines 767 race overhead at low altitude and at a very high rate of speed. The sound of the engines scared me. Its engines were screaming as if on full throttle. The jet crossed the sky in a few moments of time, and was gone. Suddenly, another jet appeared, this time an American 767 roaring across the sky; I wondered if the second plane was chasing the first. It too disappeared over the horizon as I stood and watched.

Suddenly two more jets, another American and another United plane came screaming back from the opposite direction. I hurried inside the house where a group of people were gathered; a brother who was on the Internet looked up and said, "Benjamin, I am so glad you are here. I have a question I need to ask you." I said "Wait, I need to show you something first, come outside." Then I thought to myself, this is *a priori* knowledge, he is going to ask me when the war is going to start, and I am going to show him the answer, for these four jets are the beginning of the war.

We walked outside and the jets were gone. The sky had turned dark gray, and in the distance large white clouds touched the ground. I wondered *why are the clouds on the ground?* Then I looked up, and saw six or seven mushroom clouds which appeared to be hundreds of miles wide. Ashes began to fall from the sky. I held my hands out and began to catch them.

THE DAY OF THE LORD IS AT HAND

They were large, thick and appeared as if they were chips of paint, whitish with yellow and brownish colors mixed in. I awoke in the middle of the night knowing I had just been shown a prophetic dream. I couldn't go back to sleep so I got on the Internet and found a friend online who was a military analyst. I shared with him the dream, and he said to me "have you ever seen fallout before?" "No." "Well, that is exactly what fallout looks like."

I asked him, "Do you think the Russians could disguise their bombers to look like commercial aircraft?" He said, "No, I don't think so." "Well" I told him, "I don't understand it, but we are going to be attacked with planes from United and American Airlines." He responded by telling me "Benjamin, that sounds crazy, how could we be attacked by United Airlines?"

Over the next few weeks, I shared this dream with many of my friends. Then, on September 11th, 2001, my phone rang off the hook all morning. The events of that morning were the beginning of World War III, which will culminate in the battle of Ezekiel 38 and a global thermonuclear exchange.

THE FIRST FOUR JUDGMENTS ARE READY TO BEGIN

In late 1999, I was speaking to a group of believers who had gathered outside a church called Rock Harbor, to hear the message of this book. I began to tell them a summary of the word the Lord had revealed. At first, I fumbled with the message, struggling to make sense of this incredible revelation in a few brief sentences. I mentioned the coming terrorism, the financial collapse, the martyrdom of the church in the death camps of the prince, and the ultimate nuclear war which would come as judgments upon America.

As I spoke, I could discern the group, mostly young people in their early 20s, were filled with disbelief as they smirked at my message and laughed at me under their breath. Suddenly the Holy Spirit fell upon me, and I heard the Lord say unto me, "I will take this conversation from here." I thought to myself, that's good, I really don't know what to say anyway. The topic immediately changed, only now I spoke in a loud voice and with authority as I declared:

"THE FIRST FOUR JUDGMENTS ARE READY TO BEGIN,
AND THEY ARE READY TO BREAK FORTH UPON YOU
EVEN NOW!"

Final Words

Then I walked into the crowd and got right into the face of one of the young men, and grabbing him by the arm, I said:

"AND IT IS GOING TO BE JUST LIKE ON YOUR ARM
BROTHER! THE FIRST FOUR JUDGMENTS ARE COMING
FORTH, JUST LIKE ON YOUR ARM!"

He turned and ran and a friend chased after him. I continued speaking to the crowd and minutes later, the friend came back and interrupted me saying: "How did you know about his arm?" I didn't recall doing this so I answered, "Excuse me, I don't know what you are talking about?" "You said the first four judgments were ready to begin and they would be just like on his arm. How did you know?" At that point I could remember doing this. I responded:

"Oh yes, I did say that, but I don't know anything about his arm." "Well, he is sitting in his car so scared he cannot drive, and he asked me; how did this guy know about my arm? I have never seen this guy before." I answered him: "Look, I don't know anything about his arm." "Well, he has a tattoo of the four horsemen of the book of Revelation on his arm." At that point the smirking faces in the crowd grew long. In the back of the audience, a young man raised his hand and began to speak saying "I am a navy seal, and I have been in the military for eight years." Then he began to break down and weep as he shouted: "And everything this man said is true!" The Torah tells us every word of truth will be confirmed by two or more witnesses; that morning the Lord sent two witnesses, the first by His spirit, and the second, a navy seal.

IT IS TIME FOR THE LIGHT OF THE MORNING TO BREAK THROUGH

The Lord sent two more witnesses to confirm his word, only this time the witnesses came from heaven itself. As I awoke one morning, I heard two angels speaking audibly in my room with voices that sounded like trumpets; in perfect and beautiful harmonic tones. I have never heard anything like these voices before and could never have imagined anything like the sound of these two angels.

The first angel stood on my left side and asked the question which is on many of our hearts: *"Do you know what time it is?"* Then the other angel standing on my right answered in a loud voice: *"It is time for the light of the morning to break through!"* We should all be Bereans and study these words carefully for they have truly come from the Lord.

THE DAY OF THE LORD IS AT HAND

Do you know what time it is? It is time. It is now. The judgment is come and is ready to begin. The night of unbelief is almost over. The bright and shining morning star is about to break out upon the earth. The phrase *"the light of the morning"* appears in scripture in one place, speaking of the authority of God.

> *The God of Israel said, the Rock of Israel spake to me, He that ruleth over men must be just, ruling in the fear of God. And he shall be as the light of the morning, when the sun riseth, even a morning without clouds; as the tender grass springing out of the earth by clear shining after rain. Although my house be not so with God; yet he hath made with me an everlasting covenant, ordered in all things, and sure: for this is all my salvation, and all my desire, although he make it not to grow.* [1]

The Lord Himself is the light of the morning. *"We have also a more sure word of prophecy; whereunto ye do well that ye take heed, as unto a light that shineth in a dark place, until the day dawn, and the day star arise in your hearts."*[2] Now is the time for the Day Star to arise in the hearts of the chosen ones who are called faithful and true. The church today stands at the threshold of a new day, a day which will witness the outpouring of the power of God in ways unimaginable. The night is almost over, and the blessed day is about to dawn.

This is the third day following the resurrection of our Lord and the beginning of the seventh day of creation. The long-awaited Sabbath is about to begin in which no man can work. For the world, a time of great darkness is coming; for the body of true believers, the light of God's glory is about to break forth as the light in the morning. Jesus prophesied of this hour in which darkness will fall upon the planet in which no man can work: *"I must work the works of him that sent me, while it is day: the night cometh, when no man can work."* [3] Yet in this night which is coming, God can and will work, and those who are walking in the Spirit at that time will do the greater works which were prophesied to come.

In the Hebrew calendar, the day begins at sundown. We read in Genesis that the evening and the morning were the measure of the first day. In an earlier chapter of this book, I discussed the Jubilee count, which concluded that the seventh day of creation began on Nissan one, in the year 1999 following the seventieth Jubilee. Many questioned the accuracy of this word when the years passed and nothing seemed to occur in the natural. Yet we know from scripture that a new day begins in a time of darkness or evening.

For the Day of the Lord begins not with thunder, nor with lighting, but with a gentle rain of sound doctrine. God speaks to His people in the time of darkness through the sure word of prophecy, but then when the light of day

Final Words

breaks, He speaks to the nations through His judgments, and now the morning light is about to break through, with judgment falling upon the nations.

We often approach the scripture with so many preconceptions and assumptions that many times the true meaning is missed. The beginning of the Day of the Lord is no exception. The average student of Bible prophecy has been taught and assumes the day begins with a massive event which will change the planet. But nowhere in scripture does it say anything of the sort. Actually, the word declares that the Lord first comes as thief in the night, breaking in while we all sleep.

A night intruder comes silently, not making a sound, in order to avoid waking anyone. The first coming of the Messiah is an example of this. When Jesus was born into the world, scarcely anyone noticed. Yet the understanding of that time was that as soon as the Messiah appeared, he would deliver them from the Romans. Nothing could have been further from the truth. Today in these last days, the end time believers have made many similar errors in their thinking, overlaying their understanding of the scriptures with their own opinions and ideas. Margaret McDonald's vision addressed the secret beginning of the Day of the Lord with the Lord breaking in upon us all as a thief in the night:

"It was first the awful state of the land that was pressed upon me. I saw the blindness and the infatuation of the people to be very great. I felt the cry of Liberty to be just the hiss of the Serpent, to drown them in perdition. The people of God think they are waiting, but they know not what it is they wait for. Suddenly it burst upon the scene with a glorious light... I saw the Lord himself descending from heaven... I saw the error of men who think this will be something seen by the natural eye. Oh the glorious in breaking of God which is now about to burst on this earth... Oh what a holy, holy bride she must be..."

"Now shall the glorious mystery of God in our nature be known. The Revelation of Jesus Christ has yet to be opened up. It is not knowledge about God that it contains, it is an entering into God which only those filled with the Spirit can see, those who have not the Spirit could see nothing... I saw people of God in an awfully dangerous situation, and many about to be deceived and fall. Now will the wicked one be revealed, Oh it will be a fiery trial, and every soul will be shaken. Now shall the awful sight of a false Christ be seen on the earth... the trial of the church is from the antichrist. It is being filled with the Spirit that we shall be kept. What had hindered the real life of God from being received by His people was their turning away from Jesus... they were all passing by the cross... I saw on that night, there will be such an outpouring of the Spirit such as has never been, a baptism of fire... the servants of God sealed in their foreheads, and His holy image seen in His people."

Another misconception is that the Day of the Lord begins with the Great Tribulation. Again, this is based solely upon the opinions of men and not the word of God. No, the Day of the Lord begins in ways unseen by the natural eye. For a new day under God's calendar begins at twilight in the gathering darkness, and only when the morning light comes, can the world begin to see the changes which the new day has wrought.

Please understand, the coming of the Lord begins with the in-breaking of the Lord to complete the second half of His seven-year ministry upon the earth and this is not the literal Second Coming, for that will await the conclusion of the Great Tribulation. Rather, first we will witness the coming of the Messiah in the ministry of the anointed messengers.

In order to alleviate any misunderstanding, let me clarify the timing of these events. Daniel writes:

> Know therefore and understand, that from the going forth of the commandment to restore and to build Jerusalem unto the Messiah the Prince shall be seven weeks, and threescore and two weeks: the street shall be built again, and the wall, even in troublous times. And after threescore and two weeks shall Messiah be cut off. [4]

The coming of Messiah the Prince occurs after the completion of the prophecy of the seven weeks following the restoration of Jerusalem. This is the Messiah coming as a ruling prince, not as a suffering servant, and not as the King of kings. The sixty-two weeks is the compass of time from the commandment to restore Jerusalem in the First Coming. Sir Isaac Newton understood this and accurately tied the sixty-two weeks from the commandment to rebuild Jerusalem to the birth of the Messiah in 2 BC.

The First Coming of the Lord was in the natural and began with a supernatural birth. A virgin was with child. The Second Coming begins in the same mysterious way, with a birth, not in the natural but in the spirit.

The Second Coming of the Lord, when every eye shall see Him, is preceded by a supernatural birth in the spirit in which the Lion of Judah is born again within a holy remnant who will walk in the full power of His holy anointing during the time of tribulation. This is the second half of the ministry of the Messiah, for it is He who confirms and fulfills the covenant, which His Father made with Israel for seven years. Having finished the first half Himself as a man, He now completes the second half of His ministry through the Holy Spirit, through the lives of His anointed remnant as the Lion of

Final Words

Judah. Luke describes this in his account of the Second Coming, only the true meaning of his message was hidden from our eyes all of these years. This is the point of Margaret McDonald's prophecy.

Luke writes of this revelation of the Lord:

> Even thus shall it be in the day when the Son of man is revealed. In that day, he which shall be upon the housetop, and his stuff in the house, let him not come down to take it away: and he that is in the field, let him likewise not return back. [5]

This is the same warning that Jesus mentioned in Matthew 24:

> When ye therefore shall see the abomination of desolation, spoken of by Daniel the prophet, stand in the holy place, (whoso readeth, let him understand:) Then let them which be in Judaea flee into the mountains: Let him which is on the housetop not come down to take anything out of his house: Neither let him which is in the field return back to take his clothes For then shall be great tribulation, such as was not since the beginning of the world to this time, no, nor ever shall be. [6]

The scripture is referring to the same day in both texts. The day that the Son of man is revealed is the same day that the abomination of desolation is revealed. Remember where sin abounds grace abounds more.

The word of God is always true and the final hour of sin upon the earth, when sin will abound as never before, will also be the hour of the greatest outpouring of grace in all of history, for the Lord himself shall first appear in His people. *"Christ in you, the hope of glory."* This is the beginning of the Great Tribulation in which Jesus Christ will fulfill the second half of His seven-year ministry upon the earth, not as a lamb anymore, but as the Lion of the Tribe of Judah.

Dear saints, this is the final day, the last hour of the history of man, and in this hour, the Son of man, Jesus Christ will be revealed. The tribulation doesn't start with the disappearance of the saints in a pre-tribulation rapture, but rather with the revelation of Jesus Christ in the 144,000 witnesses which He himself shall appoint.

Scripture also tells us where the Lord will begin His judgment of the earth: from the river Euphrates, which is in Iraq.

> "When its limbs are dry, they are broken off; women come and make a fire with them. For they are not a people of discernment, therefore their maker

will not have compassion on them. And their Creator will not be gracious to them. And it will come about in that day, that the Lord will start His threshing from the flowing stream of the Euphrates to the brook of Egypt; and you will be gathered up one by one, O sons of Israel. (NAS)" [8]

So now the global stage has been fully set; the Middle East is in flames, as war rages in Iraq and Syria, with ISIS challenging the regional powers. War has also come to Ukraine, and from the scripture we know that from the banks of the Euphrates River, the judgment of the earth shall come. These wars which are now raging will not end but rather, will become the spark which shall ignite the next world war which is the great battle of Ezekiel 38.

THE COLUMBIA IS LOST

The Lord has continued to give his warnings to the people of America time and again over the years. The disaster of the space shuttle Columbia is one such example. The Columbia is named after the capital of the United States The District of Columbia. The crash of the shuttle contains a prophetic message to the people of America. The prophecies of the Book of Obadiah speak of this event.

The pride of thine heart hath deceived thee, thou that dwells in the clefts of the rock, whose habitation is high; that saith in his heart, Who shall bring me down to the ground? Though thou exalt thyself as the eagle, and though thou set thy nest among the stars, thence will I bring thee down, saith the LORD. [9]

America has exalted itself more than any other nation; and with the advent of the international space station, she has literally built a nest among the stars. The Lord continues in Obadiah to explain why he is bringing His judgment upon America.

For thy violence against thy brother Jacob shame shall cover thee, and thou shalt be cut off forever. In the day that thou stood on the other side, in the day that the strangers carried away captive his forces, and foreigners entered into his gates, and cast lots upon Jerusalem, even thou was as one of them. [10]

America has now chosen to stand on the other side of the Arab Israeli conflict; standing shoulder to shoulder with the enemies of God demanding a division of the Holy Land and the creation of a Palestinian state. In the day the foreign nations cast lots for the division of the land of Israel and the Holy City of Jerusalem, America stood among them. The shuttle Columbia was destroyed attempting to reenter the atmosphere over the State of Texas and over the county of Palestine. Could anything be clearer? The Columbia disaster foreshadows God casting down the capital of America, for when you lose your capital, you lose your country. The headlines read "The Columbia is Lost". The message: America is lost and your judgment has begun.

The reason America is now being turned over to judgment? She has sided with the enemies of Israel and cast her lot for the division of the Holy Land and the creation of a Palestinian state. Lest anyone think these prophecies are not relevant to these last days, and that this text is not directly referring to the shuttle disaster, look at the balance of the text in Obadiah 1:17-21. The events prophesied therein when Israel possesses the land of Edom have not yet occurred for the text describes the events at the end of the age.

HAVING LAID STUMBLING BLOCKS
ONE BEFORE ANOTHER

In February of 2003 I was attending a solemn assembly prayer meeting where a group of believers had gathered for a weekend of prayer and fasting. Late Saturday evening I returned to my room when the Lord spoke to me "Turn on your television".

I thought, how odd, normally the Lord would want us to turn off the television. I walked over and turned on the tube. CNN came on and I began to watch the tragedy in Rhode Island where a fire had engulfed a night club killing over 100. The picture on the screen was of a human pile of people collapsed one upon the other in the doorway to the club, struggling with their faces in the outside cold air while their bodies remained trapped within the burning building.

As I watched in amazement, the Lord spoke again saying: "This is a picture of my people, who have laid stumbling blocks, one before another, such that they have all fallen to the ground." I stared in amazement at the pictures on TV not realizing the people in that picture all died that night. Having never been freed from the pile of humanity, they had all exploded in flames. This is a picture of my people. We have all laid stumbling blocks, one before another. The time is nigh for us to remove the stumbling blocks and to seek reconciliation one with another. I encourage you, dear reader, to do so prayerfully while there is still time, lest we too, find ourselves trapped by the stumbling blocks which we have laid one before another.

THE DAY OF THE LORD IS AT HAND

A NEW WORLD OF FEAR AND CONTROL

In the beginning of this century, the nation states in the west declared war on an idea called "*terrorism.*" In late 2001, the US and its allies in NATO began a series of military campaigns to defeat the terrorists and to thereby destroy their ideology of "terrorism". Of course, a war against an idea can never actually be won and therefore can never end; consistent with this thesis is the fact that at the time of this writing, the never ending "wars on terror" are entering their twentieth year.

What has ended however, an unfortunate but necessary sacrifice in the war against such a great enemy as "terrorism", are the freedoms within the United States once guaranteed by the US Constitution. Today, Americans can be detained indefinitely without charges or any due process of law simply by virtue of being identified as a suspected member or supporter of the "terrorists." Once apprehended, they can be imprisoned indefinitely, moved outside the country to be tortured, or simply killed. Or just eliminated by order of the President in one of the infamous drone strikes for which the US is now only too famous. If the "war on terror" was actually fought to defend freedom, then the terrorist have won. If the "war on terror" was designed to allow the corporate state to erect the walls of a fascist police state, then the corporations have won, and the beast has won. In either event, it is difficult to find a reasonable rationale to conclude the people, whom the war on terror is allegedly defending, have won anything.

All the war on terror has achieved in the west is the erection of a growing surveillance state along with the destruction of personal liberties and the institutionalization of fear. "Be afraid" is the mantra of the new era of permanent war. Be afraid of the two men hiding in a cave, they have a cell phone. Be afraid, and don't question the violations of law by the corporate criminals who looted the nation's treasury in the 2008 global bank robbery which they called a "*bailout.*" Now the criminals are more direct and to the point - now we are facing "bail ins" where the savings of the common man are simply stolen to cover the losses of the corporate elite. Naysayers may object; but one fact should be obvious – we have entered a state of permanent war, on a global level, and the wars are growing; the people are losing, and the corporations are winning. Chris Hedges writes: "The corporations that profit from permanent war need us to be afraid. Fear stops us from objecting to government spending on a bloated military. Fear means we will not ask unpleasant questions of those in power. Fear permits the government to operate in secret. Fear means we are willing to give up our rights and liberties for promises of security. The imposition of fear ensures that the corporations that wrecked the country cannot be challenged. Fear keeps us penned in like livestock." [11]

Final Words

INTO A DARK NIGHT

The world has forever changed; while the majority of the people have remained asleep, the world of the 21st century has changed in ways few can even imagine. The Information Age of the 1960's promised to herald the dawning of a new age of enlightenment, and an era of greater knowledge and understanding. What has in fact come upon us is an era of darkness and a growing ignorance on the part of the common man. As the people slept, control of all global media content has been consolidated in the hands of a few global corporations, and they have now also erected a frightening global surveillance system. And in so doing, they have created the infrastructure for the rise of the kingdom of the antichrist, in which the global corporations, which the Dark Ones control, now possess the power of total information dominance which will allow them ultimately to challenge the power of the nation states themselves. The deceiver of the souls of men has constructed a world in which our high definition television screens have become instruments to screen out the truth, and block out the light, for "the screen has returned to its traditional meaning; blocking the view and turning out the lights."[12] Mankind should not have gone so quietly into such a dark night.

THE DARK CORPORATE POWERS

The dark corporate powers which now dominate the global media and through their media monopoly, the western democracies hide their real identity behind many different names. They exist in a world of shadows, they operate primarily through deception, and their agenda largely remains veiled in darkness. Their true name, by which they are known within their inner circles of power, is The Order of the Illuminati and they have existed, yet remained unseen, for centuries.

Numerous books have been written disclosing who the Illuminati are: they are the inner circles of the world's secret societies; they are the ruling elite, the international banking families and members of the leading royal families and they now own, and control the world's media. What is far more important, however, than who they are, is to understand exactly what they are and a picture is worth a thousand words: the most accurate picture of the Illuminati is the mythological creature known as the Nosferatu from which we derive the English word; nefarious. "The name **Nosferatu** has been presented as an archaic Romanian word, synonymous with **vampire**... a probable etymology of the term might be derived from the Romanian Necuratu (unclean spirit, *spiritus immundus*) a term typically used to designate **Satan** or the Devil in Romanian." [13]

THE DAY OF THE LORD IS AT HAND

These corporate puppet masters, who are the Nosferatu, now control the global media and they are about to conquer the world for the beast. The destruction of objective journalism, and in its place, the erection of a global propaganda machine was a critical final step in the consolidation of their power. The total destruction of our free press reporting any semblance of truth took an era, which we call the information age, to accomplish. The fact almost no one recognizes the counterfeit which is daily disseminated as news is a testimony to the power of their propaganda. Recording artists attempt to capture the theme of their times within the lyrics of their songs. The hit song *Good Morning to the Night* speaks perfectly of our time: the time of the Nosferatu, and the reign of the Dark Ones. "I thought I knew; now I know.... turn around and say good morning to the night."[14] The *navi-iem of Israel* also spoke of this same hour of darkness which is now coming upon the world: "The night is coming when no man can work."[15] "Alas! For that day is great, there is none like it: it is even the time of Jacob's trouble; but he shall be delivered out of it."[16]

THE CLOUDS OF WAR

Most people cannot imagine the United States could be attacked and defeated by its enemies. Yet this is exactly what the prophetic writings declare is in fact coming to this nation. But how could such a thing happen, you may ask? JR Nyquist, who co-authored *The New Tactics of Global War* addressed this question in a recent seminar. "The hedonistic shopping mall regime never wanted enmity with Russia or anyone else. The existence of a real enemy would threaten the regime's values. Anyone who wrote of enmity was out of bounds. The very thought of an enemy threatened the very basis of the regime, negating its hedonistic assumptions. This must have been obvious to Kremlin strategists and sociologists who had studied American cultural changes during the 1960s and 70s. In fact, Nikolay Popov's 1989 essay was founded on this point. The West preferred shopping and having fun. Politics and war had become the mean little ministers of `a good time.' This attempted reversal of history's pattern might well prove fatal. According to my own analysis, the only thing holding the West's defensive strata together was anti-communism (i.e., anti-Stalinism). Therefore, as Popov explained, `our main task today, in addition to an honest analysis of our past and an elimination of the remnants of Stalinism ... is to divorce Stalinism from communism in the eyes of the world.' The new Iron Curtain would be a curtain of denial constructed by the West. The `peace dividend' meant more welfare pork in the pork barrel and less defense spending, so the left was satisfied. It also translated into economic exuberance and a climbing stock market. The right was triumphant and self-congratulatory. The deception was perfect. Everyone was bought off, emotionally and materially. The truth did not have one chance in a million." [17]

Final Words

The general public in the West assumes the United States is a lone super power and therefore can act unilaterally without serious consequence. The thought that US forces might be defeated by the communist nations is dismissed as absurd. Unfortunately, this confidence in American military supremacy is no longer based upon reality, and rather now relies upon hubris alone. The belief that the US remains the world's lone superpower is seriously misplaced as the balance of military power has shifted dramatically over the last fifteen years only no one bothered to inform the American people. The US no longer holds a clear upper hand in today's conventional or nuclear battlefield.

Russia and their communist allies are now armed with new 5th generation weapons including advanced hypersonic missiles and Russia has surrounded itself with an impenetrable ABM missile shield. These new weapons have shifted the balance of power decidedly in our enemies' favor. Russian defenses include the S-500, a dual-purpose ABM and anti-aircraft missile system. This is a war winning weapon to which the US has no counter measures and which may place the US in a position of nuclear blackmail, should a conventional war erupt.

To state this bluntly, Russian defensive capabilities can likely stop a US ICBM attack, while the US is defenseless against a similar Russian strike. World War III is coming very soon and the US is likely to suffer catastrophic losses. Deagel.com, a research group which tracks worldwide military equipment procurements, forecasts the US will suffer a population loss of 260 million along with a collapse in US GDP off 95% by 2025.

We are witnessing unprecedented pre-war military moves by Russia and China. Russian military officials have been stating publicly on Russian TV that nuclear war with the US is coming. Anti-American propaganda began to dominate Russian political news in earnest beginning in 2014. Preparing the domestic population for war is the first requirement according to Russian military doctrine. Mass mobilization is the final stage and appears to have started. S-400 and S-500 deployments are now occurring around Moscow.

Russian military officials recently told the Russian population they could plant nuclear warheads near the US coastline and destroy US coastal cities. Statements such as this are designed to calm down the Russian population which has become alarmed after years of consistent war propaganda. At the same time, the US news was filled with daily accusations that US officials are Putin supporters or have had inappropriate contact with Russian officials during the term of the Trump administration.

"China's feigned economic cooperation with the West was simply the first stage of a strategic war against the United States. Conservative estimates believe upwards of 50,000 spies are active within the United States at any one time; in addition, as many as 3,500 Chinese front companies currently operate in our country and they are exclusively devoted to the theft of trade secrets and high technology products that can be reverse engineered in China. Over 80% of all intellectual property theft and 90% of all cyberattacks directed at US businesses and US facilities emanate from China." [18]

"China's unilateral expansion of their naval presence into and through the international waters within the South China Sea — or what Beijing now calls China's Blue Territories over the past six years has altered the strategic balance of power dramatically in the Indo-Pacific region. That strategic balance has shifted in favor of the People's Republic of China (PRC) and against America's security and interests." [19]

China has also begun practicing large scale troop deployments by merchant marine vessels. Most observers fear they are practicing an invasion of Taiwan. The purpose of these troop mobilizations is more likely to join a future conflict in support of North Korea at some point, or to occupy the entire peninsula at the conclusion of the war after both the South and the North have destroyed each other.

Large scale mobilizations are very expensive and not undertaken lightly. Once mobilized over this summer, Russian forces would have to either initiate conflict and invade Europe or stand down. It is not practicable for forces to dig in for a harsh winter in rural terrain. They would either stand down or be used. Standing down makes the mobilization a pointless and costly error. That is why Russian generals have made the statement – mobilization is war.

JR Nyquist continues: "It is important (from the communist point of view) that nobody guess the actual situation, that nobody see how far the subversion has gone, or how powerful the communist side has become. While Obama was US President an identical circumstance played out in Washington as in Moscow. In both capitals the communists were depicted as an inconsiderable and irrelevant minority. In reality, the presidents of both countries were committed communists. The levers of power were in their hands, and the world suspected nothing. While Obama worked to disarm the United States, Putin worked to rearm Russia. While Obama undercut our allies abroad, Putin invaded Crimea and intervened in the Middle East. As the danger grew, as Hillary Clinton was sure to be the next and final president, the collaboration between Washington and Moscow was guaranteed to result in America's defeat.

Final Words

"But then a miracle happened. Donald Trump was elected president; a man of impeccable nationalist instinct, of remarkable courage in the face of the enemy. The communists were aghast at his victory. And so, strange as it seems, they decided on a preposterous fraud. While *they* posed as Russia's enemies, Donald Trump would be depicted as Russia's friend.

"Who now dares say the truth about what has happened in this country? Anyone writing in this vein is committing career suicide. Therefore, only someone without a career would dare to write along these lines at all! Even then it means being assigned to a death list, like Anna Politkovskaya and Alexander Litvinenko. (You want a successful career? You want to live? Sing the tune that is assigned. Play a role out of the communist script. You can be a conservative if you wish, but you will be Moscow's conservative.)

"Of course, you probably think I am crazy. You think communism went away in 1991. You think that communism no longer exists. But then you will have to explain how we got here – with communist thugs using open intimidation on the streets of our cities! If communism lost the Cold War, why does it presently hold such power in government agencies, universities and newspapers? Why do you think US counterintelligence is spying on the President of the United States and his staff? Who wants to bring him down? You need to explain all the variable phenomena of today: from the communist-inspired economic sabotage of global warming "science" to the insistence that our border remain a sieve. It is only our enemies who stand to gain from these policies.

"But you cannot get over this idea; namely, that communism is dead. You saw it die on TV. How can we talk once again about Marxism-Leninism? Or as an Estonian presidential candidate once asked in response to my discourse: "What's Marxism-Leninism?" His pained expression relayed the idea that Marxism-Leninism was something that didn't really exist. Nobody believed in it, so why did it matter? Even the communists don't believe in communism anymore. It's as simple as that! Any idiot who tells you that there are true-believing communists should wear a dunce cap. Russia is a democracy. China is capitalist. Cuba is an open society with superb health care. And that nice little North Korean man is a champion of world peace!"

WHAT SHALL WE DO THEN

For thus saith the Lord GOD, the Holy One of Israel; In returning and rest shall ye be saved; in quietness and in confidence shall be your strength: and ye would not. But ye said, No; for we will flee upon horses; therefore shall ye flee: and, We will ride upon the swift; therefore shall they that pursue you be swift. One thousand shall flee at the rebuke of one, at the rebuke of five shall ye flee: till ye be left as a beacon upon the top of a mountain, and as an ensign on an hill. And therefore will the LORD wait, that he may be gracious unto you, and therefore will he be exalted, that he may have mercy upon you: for the LORD is a God of judgment: blessed are all they that wait for him. For the people shall dwell in Zion at Jerusalem: thou shalt weep no more: he will be very gracious unto thee at the voice of thy cry; when he shall hear it, he will answer thee. And though the Lord give you the bread of adversity, and the water of affliction, yet shall not thy teachers be removed into a corner any more, but thine eyes shall see thy teachers. Isaiah 30:15-20

Many people have asked me in light of what is coming, what shall we do? I will attempt to provide some counsel in this regard in these final pages. First, let me comment on spiritual matters. What shall we do? Return to God. Begin to learn to walk in the Spirit. Begin to learn to rest in the Lord. Begin to learn to walk by faith, no longer trusting our money or our ability to meet our needs, but truly trusting the Lord. In order to walk with the Lord in this hour, God is demanding that we walk with Him in true holiness with a pure heart.

This must be so in order for the completeness of Christ to be found in us, and in order that we will have no doubt within us when the hour of testing begins. We must walk with the Lord in a total commitment so that we will also be able to avoid the snares of the world which lay at our feet. Our spiritual preparation is the most important part of preparing, for if we are not right spiritually, we have no hope to survive what is coming, for only a remnant shall be counted worthy to escape and endure the days ahead and to see the sign of the Son of man in the heavens on the last day.

The scripture itself is our guide. Jesus told us in this hour to *"pray without ceasing"*. That would be a good place to start - with prayer. Our prayer lives should become a critical part of everyday. We should set aside a time and a place to pray each day, and our prayer lives should include regular times of fasting, either from food entirely or with vegetable juices. When in times of prayer, remember to use spiritual authority speaking the scriptures and taking authority in the spirit world over the matters you are praying about. By spiritual authority, I am referring to using the authority of the Name of Jesus to command the spirit world to come into alignment with the will of God. We should also use our prayer times for introspection, repentance and renewal. Each of us has areas in our lives which God desires to sanctify, to bring healing and deliverance. We must have the faith and the courage to deal with these areas in the spirit of love and forgiveness.

In responding to the days ahead, we should first and foremost, become people of prayer. Second, let me speak to you about financial matters. We are currently in the midst of the greatest debt expansion in the history of the

Final Words

world. There are only two possible outcomes to a debt bubble. An inflationary debasement of the currency or a deflationary collapse of the economy where the excess debts ultimately drag down the asset values which have been inflated through the debt expansion.

Understanding who owns the system and how they hold their ownership will give you insight into which outcome will occur in the present credit expansion. The world's central banks and the major money center banks are all owned by a closely held group of wealthy families. Remember Satan tempted Jesus stating that all of the kingdoms of the world were his to give to whomever he chose? That explains how the super-rich acquired their wealth. If we have an inflationary outcome to the debt bubble, the result will be a transfer of wealth from the banks and the super-rich families which own them, to the middle-class debtors. Alternatively, if we have a deflationary collapse, we will witness a wealth transfer from the debtors, through asset foreclosures, to the bankers and their families. Over the last 400 years, virtually every major economic crisis in the western world has been deflationary. The ownership of the banking system explains why.

The powers that be use the periodic crisis, which they help create, to take back the wealth from the people. The outcome this time will be no different: a deflationary collapse awaits us. But this time will also be very, very different, given the gross imbalances that have accumulated in the external debt of the United States and the risk of substantial devaluation in the dollar.

While the inflated asset markets for stocks and housing will be falling, the cost of imports such as petroleum will likely be rising. This will create the conditions for a complete financial collapse in the US. The dollar will be under intense pressure in foreign markets driving the prices of imports such as oil through the roof, and likely causing gold and other precious metals to reach new record highs. At the same time, the higher costs of imported energy, and the deflationary drag of the credit contraction, which will follow the bursting of the debt bubble, will likely drag the economy into a global depression of unprecedented scale. So what exactly should we do? In part, that depends on you, where you live, your financial position, and what God is calling you to do. Generally, you should avoid debt at this time like the plague. At the same time, cash will be king, at least for a while. You should therefore keep your liquidity and conserve your cash. If you have an existing debt on your home, and you cannot pay it off without using up all of your liquid resources, then you should build cash and refinance into a fixed rate mortgage.

Alternatively, you could sell your house and raise cash levels. As to savings, you should consider diversifying into multiple currencies and into Gold,

THE DAY OF THE LORD IS AT HAND

Silver and Platinum. In addition, you may consider setting up an offshore bank account or an offshore trust. Of course, these investments are still subject to US Income Taxation, unless you acquire an offshore annuity, which allows for legal tax deferral. Nevertheless, an offshore account is an excellent way to diversify out of the US Dollar, which will face continued devaluation pressures until its ultimate collapse.

Finally, regarding practical matters, once again, you must hear from the Lord for your direct instructions, so my comments should be viewed as general counsel only. When we look at the things that are coming, the first obvious conclusion is that the cities are the most dangerous place to be. The cities of the US are a future disaster in the making. Lacking the necessary food production and other resources to support their populations, the cities are totally dependent upon the maintenance of the current infrastructure for the transmission of food, water, and power and for the preservation of law and order. In the days ahead of us, each of these will likely breakdown, making the cities of the US the most dangerous places to be.

For those who can accept it, the scripture talks about leaving the country. This is a hard message to hear for many. The Lord sent a similar warning to the Jews living in Germany in the 1930's. Several Rabbis received direct revelation from the Lord that a terrible holocaust was coming in Europe and were told the Jews should leave. When confronted with this warning, most Jews in Europe found it unbelievable and simply ignored the warnings. For many, their end came in the ovens of the Nazi concentration camps. So today, the warning to leave America is too hard for many to hear. Believers have actually told me that they thought the Lord would never move all of his people from one country to another. I responded by saying "Really? Have you ever read the book of Exodus?"

In summary, let me say simply, we should do what we can to get out of debt, to get out of the cities, and ultimately to get out of the country. But first and foremost, we should get into prayer and hear from the Lord directly as to what we are to do personally. This is the hour in which the prudent shall keep silent and in which the prudent man hides himself. Please remember me in your prayers as I have been commanded by the Lord to shout this message from the house tops. May the Lord bless you from Zion which is Jerusalem, and give you ears to hear and eyes to see, for these words are faithful and true.

Benjamin Baruch

Epilogue

I wish to share a few final words with my special friends who were there to witness and pray through the early birth pains of the kingdom of God in my life. The Lord Jesus Christ has blessed me mightily, through His word and His Spirit, and through my friends. I wish to express my love and thanks to each of you, for all you have done. Of all the parables our Lord Jesus Christ taught, the parable of the Field Stone will always remind me of the days when I walked and labored beside you. Permit me to share it in my own words. The kingdom of heaven is like a treasure, a precious jewel of infinite value, which was hidden as a Field Stone. Throughout the years, many great men had passed over that field, yet none of them recognized the Word of God which had been hidden therein. One day a little servant, while working in that field, found the treasure. He immediately ran, and sold everything that he had, and purchased that field. Having bought the great treasure, which is the true word of God, he went out rejoicing and proclaiming the truth to the whole world. All the people of the earth would soon hear the word, which had been hidden as a Field Stone.

> *"Behold, I will send you Elijah the prophet before the coming of the great and dreadful day of the LORD: And he shall turn the heart of the fathers to the children, and the heart of the children to their fathers, lest I come and smite the earth with a curse."* Malachi 4:5-6

Most of all, I wish to thank my Beloved Lord and dearest friend, Jesus Christ. You heard my cry Lord, and you have rescued me. In this final hour, you have remembered your covenant with me. Though I was unfaithful to you Lord, in your great mercy, you have remained faithful to me. I am truly one of the least of your saints, and in myself, I am unworthy to even speak your Name. But you have clothed me with your robe of righteousness, and put your word of truth in my mouth. Forever I will sing your praises on Mount Zion. Amen and Amen!! *Baruch Haba B'Shem Adonai!* Blessed is he who comes in the name of the Lord!

הנני שלח מלאכי ופנה דרך לפני ופתאם יבוא אל היכלו

האדון אשר אתם מבקשים ומלאך הברית אשר אתם חפצים

הנה בא אמר יהוה צבאות

מלאכי ג:א

Into the Sea

All of the years of tears are now gone forever, and the memories too, most of them have also been washed away, drowned as it were, and lost as the sands of time, which simply disappeared, into the sea.

And on the night in which Jesus was to be betrayed, he went out into the garden to pray, and his heart was troubled and exceedingly sorrowful unto death.

It is an exceedingly great thing, for a man's heart to be sorrowful unto death, and it's even a greater thing for a man to actually die from the wounding of his heart.

Now is my soul troubled; and what shall I say? Father, save me from this hour: but for this cause came I unto this hour. Father, glorify thy name. Then came a voice from heaven, saying, "I have both glorified it, and will glorify it again." John 12:27-28

These things I have spoken unto you, that in me you might have peace. In the world you shall have tribulation: but be of good cheer; I have overcome the world. John 16:33

In Greek, the word for "exceedingly sorrowful" is: *per-il'-oo-pos* and it means "*great peril*", *sorely grieved or intensely sad:* exceedingly and greatly sorrowful even unto death.

FOOTNOTES

Chapter One Footnotes

1 Matthew 24:5
2 Strong's Number 4105
3 2 Timothy 3:13
4 Strong's Number 1114
5 Removed
6 Ezekiel 9:1-6 NAS
7 Removed
8 2 Peter 3:3
9 Strong's Number 1703
10 John 15:18-21 NAB
11 Strong's Number 5278
12 Daniel 12:11
13 Daniel 11:31
14 Daniel 11:21
15 Daniel 11:21
16 Daniel 11:23
17 Daniel 11:24
18 Daniel 11:36
19 Strong's Number 2195
20 Daniel 11:27
21 Jeremiah 30:7
22 Daniel 12:3-4
23 Daniel 9:26
24 Isaiah 53:5
25 Removed
26 John 3:16
27 Micah 5:1
28 Isaiah 9:6-7
29 Genesis 22:7-8
30 Psalm 22:1
31 Psalm 22
32 ibid
33 ibid
34 Luke 12:49
35 Jeremiah 30:7
36 Nehemiah 6:15
37 Newton, Issaic, *Observations upon the prophecies of Daniel and the Apocalypse of St. John*, Published in London 1733, p 135
38 ibid p. 133 - 134.
39 Ibid p. 137.
40 Revelation 1:10
41 Isaiah 63:4
42 Isaiah 61:2
43 Removed
44 Daniel 9:26
45 Daniel 9:27
46 Jeremiah 30:7
47 Numbers 23:24
48 Daniel 9:24
49 Strong's Number 3722
50 ibid 2856
51 ibid 2377

52 ibid 5030
53 ibid 4886
54 ibid 6944
55 Leviticus 27:28 (NAS)
56 Exodus 26:34
57 Isaiah 62:12
58 Isaiah 6:11-13
59 Leviticus 2:10
60 Numbers 18:9 (NAS)
61 Zechariah 13:8-9
62 Song of Songs 8:5
63 Deuteronomy 33:12
64 Luke 21:36
65 Daniel 9:26
66 Hebrews 10:8-10
67 Daniel 9:27
68 Daniel 9:26
69 John 5:43
70 Isaiah 28:15
71 2 Thessalonians 2:3
72 Televised News Announcement of the signing of the Peace and Security Agreement
73 Exodus 32:28
74 Acts 2:41
75 Isaiah 28:14-15
76 Leviticus 25:23
77 Rabbi Zalman Baruch Melamed Arutz Sheva Israel National Radio
78 Deuteronomy 12:2-18 NAS
79 Shimon Peres, *The New Middle East*
80 Daniel 5:28
81 Isaiah 28:16-22
82 Monte Judah, *Yavoh He is Coming*, January 1997
83 Isaiah 28:16-22
84 Strongs Number 3617
85 Isaiah 10:22-23
86 Ezekiel 37:11-14
87 Intelligence Digest, Russia Brings the Mideast War Closer, Sept. 19, 1997
88 ibid
89 ibid
90 Intelligence Digest, Cyprus Missile Crisis looms closer, April 17, 1998
91 Terrorism and Security Monitor, April 1998
92 The Secret History of the Iraq War - Yosseff Bondansky, Page 510
93 Amos 8:2
94 Mark 13:28
95 Daniel 2:35
96 Isaiah 28:21-22
97 Isaiah 28:21
98 Zechariah 12
99 Zechariah 12:10

Chapter Two Footnotes
1 Daniel 12:8-9
2 Isaiah 29:11-14
3 1 Samuel 3:1
4 Psalm 74:9 NAS
5 Isaiah 49:2-4
6 Isaiah 4:4
7 Matthew 11:7-14
8 Daniel 2:20-22
9 Isaiah 8:20
10 Revelation 13:1-2, 18
11 Revelation 17:3-9
12 Genesis 41:32
13 James Lloyd, Apocalypse Chronicles, Role Reversals and Prophetic Parallels
14 ibid.
15 ibid.
16 ibid.
17 Daniel, 2:43
18 Los Angeles Times, March 27, 1998 p. A10
19 The Economist, December 1992
20 The Scranton Times, January 29, 1997, AP Article by Alexander G. Higgins, Scranton PA
21 Daniel 7:4
22 Daniel 8:23
23 Daniel 8:24
24 Revelation 13:2
25 Daniel 8:23-25
26 Daniel 8:23-25
27 Daniel 8:23-25
28 Daniel 7:25
29 Daniel 7:25

Chapter Three Footnotes
1 Amos 3:7-8
2 Amos 7:14
3 Jeremiah 9:14
4 Ephesians 4:11
5 Removed
6 Genesis 18:17
7 John 15:15
8 John 10:27
9 Amos 3:8
10 Jeremiah 4:7
11 Removed
12 2 Chronicles 36:15-16 (NAS)
13 Deleted
14 Numbers 12:6-8 (NKJ)
15 Luke 6:22-24
16 I King 17:1
17 Luke 1:80
18 Marvin Byers, *Yasser Arafat - An Apocalyptic Character*, Hebron Press, 1997, p. 21-22

19 Marvin Byers, *The Final Victory: The Year 2000*, Treasure House, 1994, p. 25.
20 Marvin Byers, *Yasser Arafat - An Apocalyptic Character*, Hebron Press, 1997, p. 29
21 Strong's Number 3478
22 John 10:14-16
23 Strong's Number 1577
24 Vine's Expository Dictionary of Biblical Words, Thomas Nelson Publishers, 1985
25 Matthew 15:24
26 Matthew 27:42
27 John 1:49
28 Romans 9:6-7
29 Romans 9:27-28
30 Removed
31 Romans 11:1-5
32 Romans 11:25-29
33 Ephesians 2:11-13
34 Hebrews 8:8
35 Genesis 32:28
36 Galatians 6:16
37 Matthew 5:17-18
38 Romans 11:5
39 Jeremiah 3:23
40 1 Peter 4:12
41 Revelation 3:10-11
42 Proverbs 29:18
43 1 Samuel 3:1
44 Amos 8:12
45 Isaiah 9:16
46 Jeremiah 23:19
47 Strong's Number 5591
48 1 Thessalonians 5:2-4
49 Joel 2:32
50 Proverbs 14:34
51 John 14:15
52 Matthew 7:21
53 Jeremiah 8:20
54 Matthew 7:23
55 Strong's Number 6117
56 Matthew 24:9-10
57 Jeremiah 9:4-7
58 Removed
59 Richard M. Rives, Too Long in the Sun, Partaker Publications, 1996, p. 128.
60 ibid.
61 2 Timothy 4:3-4
62 Jeremiah 15:19
63 Psalm 4:3-5
64 Removed

Chapter Four Footnotes
1 Genesis 15:1
2 Mark 9:7
3 Isaiah 33:10

⁴ Isaiah 28:22
⁵ Joel 1:15
⁶ Joel 2:1-2
⁷ Luke 12:49-51 (NAS)
⁸ Amos 5:18-19
⁹ Obadiah 1:15

Chapter Five Footnotes
¹ Revelation 14:8
² Revelation 17:1-2, 5, 18
³ Matthew Henry Commentary, Revelation 17
⁴ David Wilkerson, *Set the Trumpet to thy Mouth*, 1985 used by permission of the publisher, Whitaker House, 30 Hunt Valley Circle, New Kensington, PA 15068
⁵ Dumitru Dudamen, *Through the Fire without Burning*, Hand of Help Ministries
⁶ Dr. Jeff Bakker, Speaking at the Dallas Prophecy Conference, Dallas, Texas, March 1997
⁷ Mike McQuiddy, *The Promise*, Cornerstone Publishing Co, 1997
⁸ Henry Gruver, Joyful Sound Ministries, 601 Walker, Woodbine, IA 51579
⁹ Jeremiah 50:41-42
¹⁰ Jeremiah 50:9
¹¹ Jeremiah 50:41
¹² Jeremiah 51:6
¹³ Jeremiah 51:13
¹⁴ Revelation 18:7-8
¹⁵ Jeremiah 51:27
¹⁶ Ezekiel 38:11
¹⁷ Ezekiel 39:6
¹⁸ Strong's Number 339
¹⁹ Jeremiah 51:62
²⁰ Jeremiah 50:22-24
²¹ Jeremiah 50:31
²² Jeremiah 50:32
²³ Jeremiah 50:38
²⁴ Jeremiah 50:40
²⁵ Jeremiah 50:46
²⁶ Jeremiah 51:5-6
²⁷ Jeremiah 51:14
²⁸ Jeremiah 51:58
²⁹ Jeremiah 51:61-64
³⁰ Jeremiah 50:8
³¹ Joel 1:14-15
³² Jeremiah 50:28
³³ Jeremiah 51:8
³⁴ Jeremiah 51:13
³⁵ Jeremiah 51:30
³⁶ Jeremiah 51:33
³⁷ Jeremiah 51:41
³⁸ Jeremiah 51:45-46
³⁹ Jeremiah 51:48-50
⁴⁰ Revelation 18:11

⁴¹ Revelation 18:16-18
⁴² Jeremiah 50:4-5
⁴³ Jeremiah 50:20

Chapter Six Footnotes
¹ Isaiah 1:9
² Isaiah 3:12
³ Isaiah 8:11-22
⁴ Isaiah 37:32
⁵ Isaiah 10:21-22
⁶ Isaiah 11:12
⁷ Removed
⁸ Isaiah 13:19
⁹ Isaiah 14:1-2
¹⁰ Isaiah 26:20-21
¹¹ John 15:1-6
¹² Strong's Number 4679
¹³ Strong's Number 5553
¹⁴ Isaiah 45:20
¹⁵ Isaiah 48:20
¹⁶ Isaiah 48:21-22
¹⁷ Isaiah 65:8-9
¹⁸ Daniel 11:41
¹⁹ Habakkuk 1:5
²⁰ Habakkuk 2:1-3
²¹ Amos 9:12-15
²² Micah 2:12-13
²³ Zephaniah 2:7-9
²⁴ Zechariah 8:7-23
²⁵ Numbers 24:16-18
²⁶ Psalm 60:8-9
²⁷ Amos 9:11-12
²⁸ Obadiah 1:8-17
²⁹ Psalm 108:9-10
³⁰ Micah 2:10
³¹ Micah 2:12

Chapter Seven Footnotes
¹ Revelation 17:4-5
² Revelation 17:8-12
³ John 16:11
⁴ John 12:31
⁵ Luke 10:18-19
⁶ II Thessalonians 2:7-8
⁷ II Thessalonians 2:9-12
⁸ Micah 5:1-2
⁹ Micah 5:6
¹⁰ Revelation 17:13-14
¹¹ Revelation 17:15-17
¹² Revelation 17:18
¹³ Revelation 13:16-18
¹⁴ Revelation 13:1-2
¹⁵ Monte Judah, Speaking at Beth Yeshua in Orange County, California, November, 1996
¹⁶ ibid.

[17] Tim Cohen, <u>The Anti-Christ and a Cup of Tea</u>, Prophecy House, 1998.
[18] Monte Judah, *Yahov He is Coming*, January 1997

Chapter Eight Footnotes
[1] Psalm 11:3
[2] Ephesians 2:18-20
[3] Revelation 19:10
[4] Peter 1:19-21
[5] Daniel 12:10
[6] John 16:33
[7] Job 36:33 NIV
[8] Psalm 77:18
[9] Job 40:9
[10] Deuteronomy 32:2
[11] Hosea 9:7
[12] John 2:3-6
[13] Mark 8:35
[14] Proverbs 1:7
[15] Proverbs 9:10
[16] Proverbs 14:26-28
[17] Isaiah 11:1-4
[18] Hebrews 12:14
[19] Isaiah 35:8
[20] Obadiah 1:17-18
[21] 2 Corinthians 7:1
[22] 1 Peter 1:16
[23] Deleted
[24] Matthew 7:14
[25] Strong's Number 2346
[26] Strong's Number 2476
[27] Strong's Number 1715
[28] Strong's Number 2729
[29] Strong's Number 1628
[30] Revelation 3:5-22
[31] Ephesians 1:3-4
[32] Ephesians 1:5-8
[33] Ephesians 1:9-10
[34] Ephesians 1:11-14
[35] Joel 3:14-16
[36] Genesis 18:14
[37] Strong's Number 1285
[38] Genesis 6:18, 9:12-14
[39] Matthew Henry's Commentary, Genesis 9:8-11
[40] Genesis 15:1
[41] Genesis 15:5-6
[42] Genesis 17:7
[43] 2 Samuel 23:5
[44] Psalm 89:3-4
[45] 2 Chronicles 6:14
[46] Galatians 3:16
[47] Galatians 3:17-18
[48] Genesis 15:7-9
[49] Genesis 15:9-10
[50] Genesis 15:17-18
[51] Matthew Henry's Commentary Genesis 15:17-21
[52] Isaiah 62:1
[53] Genesis 18:17-19
[54] Daniel 9:4
[55] Strong's Number 157
[56] Proverbs 18:24
[57] Isaiah 41:8
[58] Proverbs 27:6
[59] Strong's Number 7453
[60] Revelation 12:1-6
[61] Strong's Number 4592
[62] Matthew Henry's Commentary
[63] Marvin Byers, The Final Victory: The Year 2000, Treasure House, 1994., p. 36.
[64] Matthew 12:50
[65] John 16:19-23
[66] Zechariah 14:21
[67] Strong's H3669
[68] 2 Peter 2:1-3
[69] Jeremiah 51:20-24
[70] Micah 5:1-5
[71] Jeremiah 30:6-7
[72] Luke 17:30-33
[73] Revelation 12:5
[74] Strong's Number 6629
[75] Isaiah 13:2-5
[76] Jeremiah 50:25
[77] Webster's American Heritage Dictionary, Houghton Mifflin Company, Boston, 1981, p. 888.
[78] Isaiah 41:15
[79] Jeremiah 51:20
[80] Ezekiel 1:4
[81] Isaiah 29:6
[82] Psalm 104:4
[83] Zechariah 12:6
[84] Isaiah 9:19
[85] Deleted
[86] Psalm 25:14
[87] Psalm 103:17-18
[88] Isaiah 35:4
[89] Isaiah 40:10
[90] Isaiah 66:15-16
[91] Isaiah 13:3
[92] 1 Proverbs 19:10
[93] Deuteronomy 1:30
[94] Revelation 19:11
[95] 2 Samuel 22:35
[96] Zechariah 10:5
[97] Psalm 144:1
[98] Joel 3:9-15
[99] 2 Samuel 22:5-22
[100] Malachi 3:1-5

[101] Isaiah 66:14-16
[102] Strong's Number 784
[103] Strong's Number 5492
[104] Strong's Number 2534
[105] Strong's Number 3851
[106] Isaiah 10:16-21
[107] Luke 12:4-7
[108] Deuteronomy 20:3-4
[109] Deuteronomy 31:6
[110] Deuteronomy 31:8
[111] Judges 10:25
[112] Judges 6:10
[113] Judges 6:23
[114] 1 Samuel 12:20-25
[115] II Kings 6:16-17
[116] Isaiah 35:4
[117] Isaiah 41:13
[118] Joel 2:21
[119] Isaiah 43:1-7
[120] Exodus 29:37
[121] Ecclesiastes 12:3-5
[122] Deleted
[123] Deleted
[124] Luke 12:32-37
[125] Revelation 1:17
[126] Jeremiah 46:27
[127] Lamentations 3:57-61
[128] Deleted

Chapter Nine Footnotes

[1] Isaiah 2:11-12
[2] Proverbs 8:13
[3] Proverbs 16:18
[4] Ezekiel 7:1-10
[5] Obadiah 1:3-4 (NAS)
[6] Zephaniah 1:12-13(NAS)
[7] Zephaniahs 1:14-18 (NAS)
[8] Isaiah 16:6
[9] Isaiah 16:7-8
[10] Isaiah 16:9-10
[11] Isaiah 16:12-13
[12] Isaiah 16:13-14
[13] Isaiah 17:1
[14] Jeremiah 48:6-12
[15] Jeremiah 48:15-17
[16] Jeremiah 48:28-30
[17] Jeremiah 48:32

Chapter Ten Footnotes

[1] Isaiah 13:3
[2] Mike McQuiddy, Kingdom Builders International, Speaking in Los Angeles, Feb. 1997
[3] Mike McQuiddy, Kingdom Builders International, Speaking in Los Angeles, Feb. 1997
[4] Samuel 15:22
[5] Isaiah 1:19
[6] Luke 22:36-38
[7] Mike McQuiddy, Kingdom Builders International, Speaking in Los Angeles, Feb. 1997
[8] Luke 13:34-35
[9] Revelation 18:1-4
[10] Revelation 3:10
[11] Jeremiah 51:46
[12] Jeremiah 51:43
[13] Daniel 7:21
[14] Daniel 7:23-25
[15] Report From Iron Mountain Video, Stuart Best, Best Video Productions
[16] Department of State Publication 7277, Freedom from War, U.S. Government Printing Office
[17] Department of State Publication 7277, Freedom from War, U.S. Government Printing Office
[18] UN Commission on Global Governance
[19] Norman Cousins, 1985 Chairman of the Planetary Citizens of the World We Chose
[20] President George Bush, State of the Union Address, January 29, 1991
[21] Pope John Paul II, *Keys of Blood*, Malachi Martin
[22] Intelligence Digest, Mass Destruction Terrorism: Fact of Fiction, September, 1997
[23] The Wall Street Journal, March 9, 2021, Jim Carlton
[24] San Gabriel Valley Tribune, Michael A. Pacer, August 4, 1996
[25] US Today, March 5, 1997
[26] Larry King Live CNN
[27] Senate Investigating Committee on Education, State of California 1953
[28] David Rockefeller, Sept. 14, 1994
[29] Maurice Strong, Closing Speech, Earth Summit, Rio de Janeiro, June 15, 1992
[30] Biological Diversity Treaty, Preamble
[31] Maurice Strong, Lecture given to the Swedish Royal Academy in Stockholm, April 27, 1994
[32] Maurice Strong, Lecture given to the Swedish Royal Academy in Stockholm, April 27, 1994
[33] Summary of the Biological Diversity Treaty published by Texe Marrs, Living Truth Ministries
[34] Strategic Investment, Free Agents in an Unfree world, December 17, 1997
[35] Steven Jones, Esq. 14th Annual Criminal Law Seminar, Aspen Colorado, January 1996

[36] President Clinton Inaugural Address January 20, 1997
[37] The White House, Office of Press Secretary, Executive Order # 12852
[38] Lucis Trust, Memo to Friends, August 1995
[39] Mark Skousen Newsletter review of Tragedy and Hope, from pages 979 - 980.
[40] Southern California Christian Times, March 1996
[41] Robert Schuller, Time Magazine, March 18, 1985
[42] Thomas Jefferson

Chapter Eleven Footnotes
[1] 2 Timothy 3:1-5
[2] 1 Timothy 4:1-2
[3] Isaiah 28:15
[4] Isaiah 28:17
[5] Isaiah 5:13-16
[6] Micah 6:9-12
[7] Romans 6:16
[8] Matthew 7:22-23
[9] Strong's Number 94
[10] Matthew Henry Commentary, Luke
[11] Deleted
[12] Strong's Number 646
[13] 2 Thessalonians 2:3-4
[14] Matthew Henry Commentary, II Thessalonians, Chapter 2
[15] Luke 17:26-37
[16] Hebrews 11:7
[17] John 17:15
[18] Deleted
[19] 2 Timothy 4:3-4
[20] Dave Mac Pherson, The Incredible Cover Up - Exposing the Origins of Rapture Theories, Omega Publications, Medford Oregon, July 1991
[21] Mark 13:27
[22] 1 Corinthians 15:51-52
[23] Revelation 11:15
[24] Revelation 3:19-22
[25] Daniel 7:21-22
[26] Mike McQuiddy, The Promise, Cornerstone Publishing Company
[27] The Marantha Baptist Watchman, August 1997, p. 4.
[28] The Last Trumpet Newsletter, October 1997
[29] Isaiah 29:9-10
[30] Amos 9:10
[31] Voice in the Wilderness, April 1998
[32] Ezekiel 22:18-21
[33] Strong's Number 5509
[34] Strong's Number 5472

Chapter Twelve Footnotes
[1] Revelations 3:3
[2] Luke 21:36
[3] Matthew 16:1-3
[4] Jeremiah 8:7
[5] Jeremiah 9:12
[6] Genesis 6:3,11-13
[7] Amos 9:6
[8] Deuteronomy 34:7
[9] 1 Corinthians 5:7-8
[10] John 4:23-24
[11] Psalm 72:16
[12] Adapted from the Poem by Alice Tompson, Born Oct. 13, 1897, Died May 9, 1993
[13] Leviticus 23:10
[14] Revelation 14:4-5
[15] Deleted
[16] Malachi 3:16-18
[17] Psalm 71:1-4 (NKJ)
[18] Psalm 71:5-7 (NKJ)
[19] Strong's Number 4159
[20] Proverbs 2:21-22
[21] Strong's Number 3498
[22] Strong's Number 8549
[23] Strong's Number 3498
[24] Luke 21:36
[25] Deleted
[26] Numbers 17:8
[27] Numbers 16:5
[28] Strong's Number 1250
[29] 2 Chronicles 31:5
[30] Ecclesiastes 1:9
[31] Zechariah 10:1
[32] Strong's Number 2385
[33] Ecclesiastes 12:5
[34] Jeremiah 1:10-11
[35] 1 Samuel 2:10
[36] Strong's Number 7481
[37] Psalm 77:18
[38] Strong's Number 1534
[39] ibid 215
[40] ibid 1300
[41] ibid 7264
[42] Job 38:25
[43] Strong's Number 6963
[44] Exod 19:10-11
[45] Hosea 6:2
[46] 1 Samuel 12:16-18
[47] Isaiah 33:12-14
[48] 2 Corinthians 5:11
[49] Deleted
[50] Deuteronomy 16:9-10
[51] Revelation 7:1-3
[52] Psalm 49:1-5
[53] Psalm 90:12-13

54 Psalm 90:10
55 Haggai 2:18-19
56 Ezekiel 36:8-9
57 KING-KILL/33°, Masonic Symbolism in the Assassination of John F. Kennedy by James Shelby Downard with Michael A. Hoffman II. This excerpt Copyright©1998
58 Nelsons Illustrated Bible Dictionary, Nelson Bible Publishers, 1986.
59 Nelsons Illustrated Bible Dictionary, Nelson Bible Publishers, 1986.
60 Isaiah 61:1-2
61 Daniel 9:25
62 Greg Killman, Celestial Events, Nissan 21, 5776
63 US News and World Report, "Just how hot is it going to get?", May 4, 1998
64 Deleted
65 Deleted
66 Hosea 1:11
67 Deleted
68 Zechariah 10:1
69 Deuteronomy 32:2
70 Romans 8:18-19
71 Deuteronomy 32:22, 41-43
72 Micah 4:5-8
73 Strong's Number 6760
74 Strong's Number 5080
75 Strong's Number 7489
76 Strong's Number 7611
77 Strong's Number 4475
78 Obadiah 1:17-21
79 Micah 5:2
80 Micah 1:3-4 (NAS)
81 Revelation 6:1-2
82 Zechariah 9:13
83 Deleted
84 Deleted
85 starchild.gsfc.nasa.gov/.../solar_system_lev el2/haumea.html
86 Spurgeon, *The Crossway Classic Commentaries, McGrath and Packer, 1993.*
87 Revelation 14:2, 3

12 Zohar Kampf, Final Comments in the Graduate Studies Course - Personalizing War: Changing News Coverage of Violent Conflict, taught at the Hebrew University, Jerusalem Israel, spring 2013.
13 Wikipedia definition of Nosferatu
14 Elton John, Good Morning to the Night, March 23rd 2012
15 Jesus Christ, Gospel of John 9:4
16 Jeremiah 30:7
17 Jeffrey Nyquist: Winning the Next World War: Penetration, Surprise & Combination; Peter Vincent Pry - The Strategic Nuclear Balance, Vol. II, Nuclear Wars: Exchanges and Outcomes (New York: Taylor & Francis, 1990) - Chapter 8, "War Outcome." Nikolay Popov - Literaturnaya Gazeta (March 1987) - "We Are All in the Same Boat" [an open confession]
18 China – The Great Illusion that Deceived the World, H Richard Austin
19 NAVAL WAR COLLEGE REVIEW, Asia Rising: China's Global Naval Strategy and Expanding Force Structure, Winter 2019

Final Words Footnotes

1 2 Sam 23:3-5
2 2 Pet 1:19
3 John 9:4
4 Dan 9:25-26
5 Luke 17:30-31
6 Matt 24:15-21
7 Col 1:27
8 Isa 27:11-12
9 Obad 1:3-4
10 Obad 1:10-11
11 Chris Hedges, The Death of the Liberal Class

REGISTER THIS BOOK FOR MORE CONTENT AT:

WWW.BENJAMINBARUCH.NET

(Audio's, Published Articles, etc.)